"The concept of evidence-based practice is continually evolving and needs to be applied more systematically to a Christian context. In this volume, top researcher-clinicians come together to provide the state of the art of evidence-based practices for Christian counseling and psychotherapy. It is both broad and deep, and represents a significant advancement in the field of Christian counseling. I highly recommend it for lay counselors, graduate students and seasoned clinicians alike."
Todd W. Hall, Biola University

Evidence-Based Practices for Christian Counseling and Psychotherapy

Edited by Everett L. Worthington Jr., Eric L. Johnson,
Joshua N. Hook and Jamie D. Aten

IVP Academic

An imprint of InterVarsity Press
Downers Grove, Illinois

InterVarsity Press
P.O. Box 1400, Downers Grove, IL 60515-1426
World Wide Web: www.ivpress.com
Email: email@ivpress.com

InterVarsity Press® is the book-publishing division of InterVarsity Christian Fellowship/USA®, a movement of students and faculty active on campus at hundreds of universities, colleges and schools of nursing in the United States of America, and a member movement of the International Fellowship of Evangelical Students. For information about local and regional activities, write Public Relations Dept., InterVarsity Christian Fellowship/USA, 6400 Schroeder Rd., P.O. Box 7895, Madison, WI 53707-7895, or visit the IVCF website at www.intervarsity.org.

All Scripture quotations, unless otherwise indicated, are taken from THE HOLY BIBLE, NEW INTERNATIONAL VERSION®, NIV® Copyright © 1973, 1978, 1984, 2011 by Biblica, Inc.™ Used by permission. All rights reserved worldwide.

While all stories in this book are true, some names and identifying information in this book have been changed to protect the privacy of the individuals involved.

Cover design: Cindy Kiple
Interior design: Beth Hagenberg

ISBN 978-0-8308-4027-4 (print)
ISBN 978-0-8308-6478-2 (digital)

Printed in the United States of America ∞

Library of Congress Cataloging-in-Publication Data

A catalog record for this book is available from the Library of Congress.

P	21	20	19	18	17	16	15	14	13	12	11	10	9	8	7	6	5	4	3	2	1
Y	31	30	29	28	27	26	25	24	23	22	21	20	19	18	17	16	15	14	13		

Contents

129400

1

Introduction to Evidence-Based Practices in Christian Counseling and Psychotherapy

Everett L. Worthington Jr., Eric L. Johnson,
Joshua N. Hook and Jamie D. Aten

This book is for adult learners who wish to broaden and deepen their counseling repertoire and skills. This isn't just another book on practice written for practitioners. Nor is it just another book on research written for researchers. Rather, this is a book about practice *and* research for practitioners and researchers (and students) alike. Its goal is to help readers learn how to deliver Christian evidence-based practices and psychotherapies while also becoming familiar with the state-of-the-art supporting science. Each chapter brings together the best of practice and clinical know-how with sophisticated science and research.

A PRIMER ON EVIDENCE-BASED TREATMENTS

What constitutes "evidence" that a treatment helps clients? We all want to provide and receive the best help possible for any mental health problem. But how do we know what constitutes the "best help"? Of course, we cannot know for sure. People might respond differently to the same treatment. Counselors might be better at doing some types of counseling than others. Some counselors are so interpersonally skilled and personally wise that it might not matter what they do—counseling will be effective by the sheer force of their personality. But even though we cannot know for certain what is the best approach for a particular person with a particular problem, we can collect some evidence and make the best judgment about which treatments have the highest likelihood of being successful. This is what evidence-based practice is about.

Immediately we must ask: What is evidence? There are many types of evidence, but not all evidence is equally good. Suppose a person advocates a particular approach to mental health treatment. He or she is either in business to sell a particular approach (i.e., has written a book or is providing a continuing education workshop) or has invested years of research time in its success. If this person says that the treatment is "successful," you would be wise to ask: What is your evidence supporting its success? You might take the worth of the barrage of successful clients that the practitioner touts with a grain of salt. They might be selected specifically to illustrate the approach. In addition, there is no way to discern whether the clients got better because of the specific treatment or simply because the book writer or conference presenter was personally dynamic and charismatic. You might insist on better scientific evidence as a basis for accepting the success of the treatment.

Suppose you are handed a brochure that says, "A study has proven that the approach is successful." You will probably say: What kind of study was it? Did the study solicit responses from the scientist's or counselor's ten favorite friends? Were the respondents giving an opinion of the treatment's success? Was some kind of objective test done? Were the people who answered the questions the only four people who succeeded at the treatment (without including the ten who dropped out early because they were disappointed in the treatment)?

What if the advocate offers up one or more case studies as evidence of a treatment's success? Case studies can range widely in thoroughness. They can be haphazard summaries of the high points of treatment or just points that are theoretically interesting. They can be composites from many clients, showing methods combined into what looks like a single case but which actually represents several cases. Case studies can also be elaborate descriptions of actual people that involve pre-treatment, post-treatment and follow-up assessments using many methods of objective assessment (see Worthington, Mazzeo & Canter, 2005). Usually case studies appear early in the development of a treatment or in book chapters to illustrate an established treatment. They are considered low-level scientific support, not definitive support.

Or what if the advocate says that the evidence for the efficacy of the treatment is simply that the treatment is consistent with Scripture? While this might be true, many questions remain. The Bible, for example, was written in everyday, lay-person language, rather than in scientific or professional-counseling discourse. Though inspired by God, it uses concepts and terms in a variety of unsystematic ways that do not yield the kind of precision and clarity that we strive for in science or modern professional counseling protocols. As a result, the appeal to Scripture can lead down many different, and sometimes even contradictory, paths. Moreover, how can counselors be sure that the success of their biblically-based counseling is not due to factors other than Scripture, for example, the personality or interpersonal style of the counselor or the counselee? We need careful research to tease apart the influence of different factors that in everyday life are blended together and interact with one another. Also, the Bible reveals to us general helpful principles that apply to all people for all time. How can we find out which biblically based treatments work with different facets of human beings (e.g., rational, emotional, relational) or with different psychological problems or in different cultures? We cannot answer such questions without careful, empirical investigation.

Scientifically rigorous clinical experiments try to take as much of the ambiguity as possible out of language and observation when interpreting the available evidence. So the gold standard of empirical evidence for treatments is called a randomized clinical trial (RCT), in which clients are randomly assigned to treatments. Counselors follow a thorough manual—not slavishly at the expense of clinical judgment, but wisely and flexibly while adhering to the prescribed treatment. RCTs usually use several different counselors (not just one who is particularly gifted or not gifted) with clients who have different personal characteristics and personality traits. Standard assessments are used to determine clinical success, not simply the judgment of the counselors, who have been shown, on average, to overestimate their success relative to the judgments of clients and results by objective measures and outside-trained evaluators. Then this type of treatment is described in detail in a clinical scientific publication, where it is reviewed by other clinical scientists and clinicians who keep poor studies out of published journals. Thus this kind of evidence can provide some confidence that the *treatment* (as opposed to other factors) is actually a major reason for the findings. The RCT controls for the particular charisma of the counselors and standardizes what is done (with the flexibility of clinicians to deviate from the protocol on occasion based on clinical experience and expertise).

Although the RCT is the gold standard of clinical evidence, it is not the only type of evidence that is important. Some studies can be qualitative, using interviews to find out what people liked and didn't like about treatments. Some can be field trials. Field trials lose some precision because they reflect how people actually apply the treatments in real psychotherapy situations. Field trials, also called effectiveness trials, might compare the treatment of interest to treatment-as-usual, giving psychotherapists directives to use, in random (yet prescribed) order, and not the order that depends on the therapists' judgment, the treatment of interest and the treatment they usually use.

In the work-a-day world of psychotherapy, manuals are not usually used. Or if they are used, psychotherapists do not follow them rigorously. When psychotherapists in normal practice use a manualized, evidence-based treatment, the psychotherapist is often not personally excited about the treatment; the practitioner might just be using it because insurance payment demands it. However, field trials—in contrast to RCTs—do use real clients and real counselors in less highly monitored conditions than the typical RCT. Field trials also—in contrast to work-a-day psychotherapy—use manuals, and sessions are usually audiotaped to ensure reasonable (though not slavish) fidelity to the treatment. So, what comes out of field trials is an idea of how people really might use the treatments in the clinic—at least more so than the highly controlled and monitored RCT.

Sometimes single-case designs are used. Typically clients—often six to ten participants in a study—are reported individually. They are assessed regularly using several questionnaires or behavioral measures. For example, each week, partners might complete reports of couple satisfaction, communication and forgiveness. The couple therapist might use a treatment that assessed and gave feedback in the first two weeks of treatment, trained in communication for weeks three through eight, dealt with forgiveness in weeks nine and ten, and terminated in week eleven. The measures would be expected to reveal a continuing increase in couple satisfaction. However, the increase in quality of communication would be most evident during the weeks that communication was the focus of counseling. Increases in forgiveness might be seen most evident in weeks nine and ten. Importantly, therapists could tailor their treatment to the needs of the clients, but the multiple measures would reflect the causal nature of each separate treatment. There are, of course, weaknesses to the design. Therapist expectations or nonspecific factors could be causing the effects, rather than the treatments. Thus, ideally, several therapists using multiple-baseline, single-case designs would be needed.

No single Christian-accommodated treatment has yet been tested in widespread dissemination trials (McHugh & Barlow, 2010). These trials investigate state or nationwide uses of the treatment in which vast numbers of practitioners follow manuals and assessment regimes to determine how effectively a treatment can be disseminated to the public. Problems typically involve ensuring fidelity of treatment to the manual and getting practitioners to conscientiously follow assessment procedures.

Large RCTs, field effectiveness trials and dissemination trials are all individual studies; as such they inevitably involve idiosyncratic elements that might make it difficult to attribute effectiveness solely to the treatment. Thus the platinum standard for evidence of the quality of a treatment is the review of the literature. Qualitative reviews are important, but meta-analytic reviews (which code outcomes on a single standardized scale and aggregate the results numerically across studies) are the highest level of evidence. Because reviews and meta-analyses take into account all of the existing research, local effects tend to balance out. Reviews and meta-analyses can also identify and test elements that the original studies did not explicitly test. For instance, if two-thirds of the studies used mildly depressed clients and one-third used profoundly depressed clients, a meta-analysis could compare whether the treatment worked equally well for each group.

Now you are equipped. As you explore the research supporting each treatment in this book, you can evaluate the strength of the evidence. Thus you can judge your confidence at applying the treatment with your clients.

Evaluating the directness of the evidence. In addition, the experimental evidence might be more or less direct. Treatments can be supported by different types of evidence. Some evidence is about whether or not a treatment works, and other evidence is about why the treatment is thought to produce changes in clients. To support whether or not a Christian treatment works, evidence would ideally demonstrate that a Christian-oriented treatment works better for Christians than a highly similar secular treatment. This evidence would support the notion that the Christian accommodation was having some real effect. The accommodations should be clearly specified (although they usually are not). Less direct evidence would show that a Christian treatment works better for Christians than does a secular treatment that is not similar (i.e., having a different duration or theoretical basis) or than a control group. In these instances, although we have evidence that the Christian treatment is producing some positive effects, we do not know whether it is due to the Christian accommodation specifically.

To investigate why treatments are producing changes in their clients, evidence might support a theory for why change might be stimulated. Treatments may work, but not for the reasons that the theorist claims. David and Montgomery (2011) provide a classic example. Early treatments for malaria were based on the idea that malaria was caused by bad wind. The prescribed preventive treatment, which was very effective, was to close windows to prevent the bad wind from circulating. But this reduced the number of cases of malaria in reality not because it kept out the bad wind but because it kept out the real cause of malaria, infected mosquitoes. For years, couple therapy trained couples in communication under the assumption that poor communication was the cause of couple problems. Fincham, Hall and Beach (2005) showed that poor communication was more an *effect* of a poor marriage rather than the *cause* of a poor marriage. The cause of the poor marriage was likely a compromised emotional bond between the partners.

In this book, we have invited authors to present the strongest evidentially supported, explicitly Christian treatments. Undoubtedly we have missed some important treatments and we apologize for our omissions. However, the treatments summarized should provide a good state-of-the-clinical-science review for a wide range of adult readers, including practitioners, clinical researchers, students, teachers and educated lay people.

WHO SHOULD READ THIS BOOK?

Practicing psychotherapists. Psychotherapists in full-time clinical practice often find that the demands of clinical work make it hard to stay on top of cutting-edge trends. The average day often brings unexpected opportunities and challenges along with already busy hours of clients and paperwork. Some might also find the financial realities of being in full-time clinical practice difficult. For some, this means that every hour not spent in direct services means another hour not paid. For others, it means the average caseload for salaried therapists makes it hard to engage in fruitful peer dialogue that might otherwise create opportunities for staying on top of emerging trends. If this rat-race seems to fit you, you might enjoy reading this book on your schedule—not at the demand of your schedule.

This book can help you work with a wide range of clients and presenting problems. It also will help you address the increased emphasis by insurance companies for proof of outcomes. Professional and Christian ethics demand that psychotherapists provide the best, most effective treatment for particular disorders, which readers will learn about through the chapters that follow. Many of us who are psychotherapists acknowledge that our training was limited, and (what's more) new research and theory are being produced each year, and we struggle to keep up with them.

We know that many secular theories of psychotherapy have been thoroughly researched. But we also know that many of our clients—if we see committed Christians as our clients—want (or may even demand) a straightforward Christian approach that is recognizably Christian. They might, in some cases, even consider that requirement as important (or *more* important) as the proven efficacy of the treatment.

Evidence is crucial in choice of treatment. For example, imagine you are seeking help for a medical condition and you are presented with two alternatives from which to choose. Would you choose to go to a physician who uses scientifically supported medical treatments but might not be a Christian? Or would you rather go to a Christian who uses methods that he or she says are Bible-based, but have no scientific studies that support their efficacy? Or would you drive several hours because you know of a trusted physician in another city that brings both to patient care? Most of us want to have scientifically studied and supported medical treatments as well as biblically consistent treatments. And we should think that our clients want the same thing in terms of their psychological treatment. The good news is that there are now several psychological treatments that are consistent with a Christian worldview and have scientific evidence supporting their efficacy.

We can learn about such evidence-based treatments in several ways. One could systematically search the PsychINFO database for the latest research on evidence-based practice, read and study the articles as they come out, and put promising treatments into practice. This is, we believe, idealistic. Frankly, even academic psychologists who do psychotherapy research do not search PsychINFO so diligently. A second way to expand your repertoire of evidence-based treatments is to take CE workshops at conferences, local training or webinars. Of course, there is no guarantee that a workshop relevant to your area of study will be offered at a conference or that you will be able to find one that is helpful to you. Webinars can be inconvenient because they are usually scheduled at one particular hour of the day, so their timing might conflict with your schedule. And to be frank, in terms of Christian evidence-based practices, there is just not much information and training available.

The most convenient way to find the information is to simply read the chapters in this book—at least the ones that you find particularly interesting or relevant to your practice. As practitioners we often dream of getting our hands on a chapter which not only helps us understand the theory or psychotherapeutic approach, but also to see all of the evidence for it. We can learn from it, and summarize it and send it to insurance panels. These chapters are designed to meet these purposes.

Clinical researchers. A second target audience is clinical researchers who conduct or plan to conduct research evaluating the efficacy of a treatment. For clinical researchers interested in evidence-based Christian treatments, this book should provide knowledge of existing evidence and description of treatments. It will also provide new directions for future research and describe best practices for conducting research outcome studies on Christian treatments.

Students. A third target audience of this book is students. As a textbook it functions to introduce the latest approaches and research in a way that brings students up to speed. Unlike a text in which a single author summarizes the field of counseling theories, couple counseling theories or family theories, this book presents a variety of approaches, each explained by its own practicing experts.

Teachers. A fourth target audience is teachers. This book provides a rich update on the current status of evidence-based Christian accommodated treatments. It serves as a guide for how to conduct the treatments, illustrating each approach with a case study and summarizing the research evidence for the treatment.

Educated lay people. Finally, a fifth target audience is the educated lay person. Many people have mental health problems and may seek individual psychotherapy, couple therapy or family therapy. Others might not need counseling themselves but have family members or friends who are looking for treatment. This book provides a guide to the types of Christian treatments for specific disorders that have clinical research supporting their efficacy. While not every type of psychotherapy may be available in a given local area, this book at least provides a guide for what to look for to get help, or what to recommend to a friend or loved one.

THE CONTENTS OF THE BOOK

In this introduction, we have considered the concept of evidenced-based psychotherapies for Christian counseling and psychotherapy. Here is what to expect in the remainder of the book. We have organized it into four parts. In part 1, the contributors examine evidence for general psychotherapeutic factors such as the therapeutic alliance and empathy, and whether matching client religious preferences by providing Christian-accommodated treatments will affect the outcomes of counseling. In part 2, we have collected chapters related to individual psychotherapy. Part 3 includes treatments aimed at helping couples and groups. This is the longest section of the book, with six chapters. In part 4, we reflect on evidence-based treatments from the viewpoints of editors who have had the opportunity to consider all the chapters provided by these accomplished reviewers of research and practice. Let's take a closer look at each of the chapters. We hope this little capsule summary will whet your appetite for the material to come.

Chapter 2: Evidence-based relationship and therapist factors in Christian counseling and psychotherapy. Scott Stegman and his colleagues highlight the empirical status of evidence-based relationship and therapist factors in Christian psychotherapies. Several factors contribute to effective therapy. One important aspect of effective therapy is tailoring the therapy to the client's personal characteristics, proclivities and worldviews (Norcross, 2002). In 1999 the APA division of psychotherapy task force was commissioned to determine empirically supported relationship factors in therapy. Several methods of customizing therapy to clients were determined to have "promising" empirical support, including tailoring therapy to religious beliefs and values (Worthington & Sandage, 2002). Norcross (2011) has updated these reviews and convened a new panel of experts to review the experimental evidence. The effect of religious and spiritual matching was considered by Worthington, Hook, Davis and McDaniel (2011). The joint task force from the APA divisions of psychotherapy and of clinical psychology gave religious and spiritual matching the highest rating for adequacy of supporting evidence. Stegman et al. review the research to date on issues pertinent to the characteristics of the therapist and therapeutic relationship in Christian psychotherapy.

Chapter 3: Lay Christian counseling for general psychological problems. Christian church-based lay counseling involves religious counseling offered by paraprofessionals. Lay counselors are trained in counseling skills in the context of time-limited therapy. Siang-Yang Tan reviews research on lay Christian counseling, including clinical trials and descriptions of lay counseling approaches.

Chapter 4: Christian devotional meditation for anxiety. Fernando Garzon summarizes Christian devotional meditation, which has long been valued in the Christian church. It generally involves practices or disciplines of prayer or quiet reflection on Scripture. Garzon describes one controlled study (Carlson, Bacaseta & Simanton, 1988) and demonstrates how he uses devotional meditation in psychotherapy.

Chapter 5: Christian-accommodative cognitive therapy for depression. David (Jeff) Jennings and his colleagues review the empirical status of Christian-accommodative cognitive therapy for depression. Christian-accommodative cognitive therapy generally has retained the main features of the existing secular theory (i.e., Beck or Ellis), yet places the therapy in a Christian context. Techniques such as cognitive restructuring and guided imagery are integrated with biblical teaching and religious imagery. Several studies have found evidence that participants in Christian cognitive therapy showed more improvement in depressive symptoms than did participants in the control conditions. Researchers also found that treatment gains (e.g., maintenance of treatment effects) from Christian CT were maintained at follow-up.

Chapter 6: Christian-accommodative trauma-focused cognitive-behavioral therapy for children and adolescents. Donald F. Walker and his colleagues draw on an empirically supported treatment, as well as on insights from the Christian faith, for working with children and adolescents recovering from abuse. This trauma-focused, manualized treatment allows Christian therapists to help clients explore, assess, process and make meaning of abuse via cognitive-behavioral processes. Clinical trials are currently underway.

Chapter 7: Evidence-based principles from psychodynamic and process-experiential psychotherapies. Keith Edwards and Edward (Ward) Davis provide an overview of theory and research supporting approaches to psychotherapy that are based in psychodynamic theory and practice, particularly exploring emotion and attachment within relationships with significant adults and God. Since people develop their sense of self in relationships, those relationships can become the curative focus in psychotherapy. Although no Christian-accommodative RCTs exist at this point, the general approach is strongly supported by secular research. The chapter is particularly strong in practical advice regarding conducting this type of psychotherapy.

Chapter 8: Preparing couples for marriage: The SYMBIS model. Les and Leslie Parrott have developed a popular approach to preparing couples for marriage. The approach can be used to treat marriages in trouble, but is more widely applied to psychoeducation of couples. The Parrotts have created their approach by drawing from many evidence-based approaches. The "saving your marriage before it starts" (SYMBIS) approach has been widely disseminated and used.

Chapter 9: Christian PREP: The prevention and relationship enhancement program. Gary Barnes and his colleagues have developed, tested and disseminated the PREP approach to marriage preparation and enrichment. Christian PREP, founded by Scott Stanley, is a Christian-accommodated treatment for couples at the levels of preparation for marriage and couple enrichment. Christian PREP has been studied in controlled clinical trials, with the research funded by federal agencies. PREP and Christian PREP can also be applied to couple enrichment. Training is available for both the secular and Christian versions. Thousands of people are trained to conduct PREP throughout the world.

Chapter 10: The hope-focused couples approach to counseling and enrichment. Jennifer Ripley and Vickey Maclin have conducted field trials of the hope-focused approach (HFA) to couple therapy. They team with Joshua Hook and Everett Worthington to describe the hope-focused couples approach (HFCA) to helping couples enrich their relationships. They offer a three-part strategy for helping couples enhance motivation, facilitate change and draw strength from God. The HFCA also calls attention to common marital problems and potential solutions. It has been used for psychoeducation and has been investigated extensively in couple enrichment with both Christian and secular samples. The Christian and secular versions of the therapy were compared at Regent University by Ripley's research team.

Chapter 11: The relational conflict restoration model: Empirical evidence for pain-defense and grace-trust patterns in couple reconciliation. James Sells summarizes his approach to helping troubled couples. He draws from both emotionally focused couple therapy and contextual family therapy to create the relational conflict restoration model. This approach has been tested directly with Christians in one pilot study, but it also draws on substantial secular research with general populations and on writing by the theorists of family therapies.

Chapter 12: Marital couples and forgiveness intervention. Fred DiBlasio is one of the leading researchers in forgiveness interventions with couples in counseling. This chapter outlines a brief couples counseling intervention for helping clients learn to forgive. This approach helps create a safe therapeutic environment for couples to discuss and reflect on hurts, as well as to share emotional reactions, which leads to the decision to forgive. DiBlasio discusses the clinical trial research supporting this approach (DiBlasio & Benda, 2008) and outlines a three-hour step-by-step approach that has been shown to increase martial satisfaction and decrease depression among Christian and secular couples.

Chapter 13: Christian-accommodative group interventions to promote forgiveness for transgressions. Julia Kidwell and Nathaniel Wade describe Christian-accommodative group treatment for unforgiveness based on the REACH model of forgiveness (Worthington, 2003), which involves five steps: recall (R) the hurt; empathize (E) with the one who hurt you; offer the altruistic (A) gift of forgiveness; commit (C) to forgive; and hold (H) onto forgiveness. For the Christian treatment, participants were encouraged to draw on their religious beliefs and other religious sources while working toward forgiveness, as well as using prayer and Scripture to help with the forgiveness process. Studies found that participants in the Christian condition showed more improvement in forgiveness than did participants in the control condition, and equivalent improvement in forgiveness as did participants in the secular condition. Other research has used a process-oriented approach to promote forgiveness during group therapy.

Chapter 14: Promising evidence-based treatments. The editors review the treatments discussed in the book to give you a bird's-eye view of how much support is (or is not) available for each approach. We consider whether each approach has evidence supporting its theory of change. We also consider the degree of empirical support of secular versions of the treatment. Finally, we examine the degree of support for each explicitly Christian accommodation of the approach. A table highlights support for each treatment approach so that readers have all of the facts at their fingertips. This chapter also calls attention to Christian interventions that have promise but no empirical support yet.

Chapter 15: Conducting clinical outcome studies in Christian counseling and psychotherapy. The editors of this book review the state-of-the-science recommendations for conducting controlled clinical trials and effectiveness research. Terms such as *efficacy, specificity, effectiveness* and *clinical significance* are defined. Issues such as research design, power, choice of assessment instruments, follow-up data, treatment implementation and data analysis are discussed. This chapter is essential reading for researchers to become equipped to conduct high-quality clinical research. In addition, it is highly recommended for students and clinicians who intend to be informed consumers of clinical research.

Chapter 16: Evidence-based practice in light of the Christian tradition(s):

Reflections and future directions. In this final chapter, the editors identify themes and trends from the previous chapters in light of the Christian tradition. We also address future directions that we believe warrant additional attention. We offer some clinical and training recommendations for advancing evidence-based Christian psychotherapies and provide relevant theological considerations that might guide future work in this area. Finally, the editors outline a brief research prospectus focused on advancing evidence-based practice in Christian counseling and psychotherapy.

JUST THE BEGINNING

We hope we have piqued your interest about what you will learn in the rest of the book, equipped you with the tools and critical attitude you need to evaluate these evidence-based approaches, and given you a helpful overview of what is to come. We have tried to stimulate your appetite. Now it is time to begin the feast with the topic of relationship factors at work in all of the treatments. After that, you'll move on to the main course—the chapters describing specific evidence-based approaches. Finally, you'll finish the meal with our three "dessert" chapters. *Bon appétit!*

ACKNOWLEDGMENTS

We would like to thank David Congdon, our editor at IVP, for all his help throughout the process of getting this to print, along with the entire IVP staff. They are wonderful folks to work with. We also want to thank Whitney Hancock for compiling the two indexes at the end of the book.

REFERENCES

Carlson, C. B., Bacaseta, P. E., & Simanton, D. A. (1988). A controlled evaluation of devotional meditation and progressive relaxation. *Journal of Psychology and Theology, 16,* 362-68.

David, D., & Montgomery, G. H. (2011). The scientific status of psychotherapies: A new evaluative framework for evidence-based psychosocial interventions. *Clinical Psychology: Science and Practice, 18*(2), 89-104.

DiBlasio, F. A., & Benda, B. B. (2008). Forgiveness intervention with married couples: Two empirical analyses. *Journal of Psychology and Christianity, 27,* 150-58.

Fincham, F. D., Hall, J. H., & Beach, S. R. H. (2005). " 'Til lack of forgiveness doth us part": Forgiveness and marriage. In Everett L. Worthington Jr. (Ed.), *Handbook of forgiveness* (pp. 207-25). New York: Brunner-Routledge.

Garzon, F., Tan, S.-Y., Worthington, E. L., Jr., & Worthington, R. K. (2009). Lay counseling approaches and the integration of psychology and Christianity. *Journal of Psychology and Christianity, 28*(2), 113-20.

McHugh, R. K., & Barlow, D. H. (2010). The dissemination and implementation of evidence-based psychological treatments: A review of current efforts. *American Psychologist, 65*(2), 73-84.

Norcross, J. C. (Ed.). (2002). *Psychotherapy relationships that work* (pp. 371-87). New York: Oxford University Press.

Norcross, J. C. (Ed.). (2011). *Psychotherapy relationships that work* (2nd ed.). New York: Oxford University Press.

Worthington, E. L., Jr. (2003). *Forgiving and reconciling: Bridges to wholeness and hope.* Downers Grove, IL: InterVarsity Press.

Worthington, E. L., Jr., Hook, J. N., Davis, D. E., & McDaniel, M. (2011). Religion and spirituality. *Journal of Clinical Psychology: In Session, 67*(2), 204-14.

Worthington, E. L., Jr., Mazzeo, S. E., & Canter, D. E. (2005). Forgiveness-promoting approach: Helping clients REACH forgiveness through using a longer model that teaches reconciliation. In Len Sperry and Edward P. Shafranske (Eds.), *Spiritually-oriented psychotherapy* (pp. 235-57). Washington, DC: American Psychological Association.

Worthington, E. L., Jr., & Sandage, S. J. (2002). Religion and spirituality. In J. C. Norcross (Ed.), *Psychotherapy relationships that work* (pp. 371-87). New York: Oxford University Press.

Part One

EVIDENCE-BASED
GENERAL
PSYCHOTHERAPEUTIC
FACTORS

2

Evidence-Based Relationship and Therapist Factors in Christian Counseling and Psychotherapy

R. Scott Stegman, Sarah L. Kelly
and T. Mark Harwood

The purpose of this chapter is to enhance the effectiveness of psychotherapy by focusing on evidence-based relationship and therapist factors in the context of Christian psychotherapy. According to Norcross (2002b, 2011), relationship and therapist factors take into account who our clients are and who we are as therapists, as well as how we perceive and interact with one another. Relationship and therapist factors have been found to account for a substantial portion of positive client gains. For example, Horvath, Flückiger and Symonds (2011) found that the therapeutic alliance accounts for a large degree of positive therapeutic gain evidenced by clients. They suggested that the relationship may actually account for a greater degree of change than technique. Of particular relevance to our present chapter, initial studies on matching religious clients with religious therapists suggest that religious and spiritual relationship and therapist factors may further strengthen perceived and realized treatment outcomes (Worthington, Hook, Davis & McDaniel, 2011). Though the impact of relationship and therapist factors has received a fair amount of attention over the last decade, uniquely Christian factors have received much less attention.

To help readers learn how to make the most of relationship and therapist factors in their practice, we provide a general overview of client therapeutic religious and spiritual concerns and preferences, and we attempt to parcel out evidence in support of a Christian integrative approach. We then shift our focus by providing a brief summary of the current research available on religion and psychotherapy relationship and therapist factors. Next, we survey evidence-based variables in the psychotherapy relationship that should be monitored and adjusted to each client so as to maximize the effectiveness of the therapeutic relationship. We also suggest some guidelines on how to consider and leverage a client's religious commitment in the therapy relationship. Finally, we will offer several practical tips on how to utilize this information in the psychotherapy room.

WHAT TO KEEP IN MIND ABOUT RELATIONSHIP
AND THERAPIST FACTORS

The therapeutic alliance, or bond between client and therapist, is the quintessential common ground shared by most psychotherapies. How and to what extent this alliance affects the outcome of therapy has been the focus of many studies. Horvath et al. include 190 such studies in their meta-analysis. Likewise, Johansson and Jansson (2010) found that measures of helping alliance taken toward the end of therapy correlated well with psychotherapy outcome. Through meta-analytic studies, Horvath et al. found that the strength of the psychotherapeutic relationship tends to increase positively with time. In an earlier meta-analysis of the therapeutic alliance and psychotherapy outcomes among children and adolescents, Shirk and Karver (2003) found positive correlations between therapeutic alliance and psychotherapy outcomes. The findings mirrored those found among adult populations. Across psychotherapeutic modalities, the strength of the therapeutic alliance builds over time. These findings may also suggest that the psychotherapeutic relationship needs to be monitored (perhaps through questionnaires). This can be done throughout the course of treatment in order to track client progress and help alert the therapist, and client, to any potential relational issues that may need to be addressed to ensure the growth of a strong psychotherapeutic bond and its translation into stronger mental health outcomes.

Several factors appear to influence the therapeutic alliance. Empathy has long been acknowledged as a key element in the development of the therapeutic relationship and has received empirical support over the years. According to meta-analytic findings by Elliott, Bohart, Watson and Greenberg (2011), empathy may account for approximately 4% of variance in clinical outcome studies. The American Psychological Association's joint task force involving Division 29 (psychotherapy) and Division 12 (clinical psychology) also identified several "promising elements" of the therapeutic relationship, including: (a) requesting feedback, (b) repairing alliance ruptures, (c) self-disclosure, (d) management of countertransference, and (e) relational interpretations in psychotherapy (Norcross, 2002a). Other factors that may affect the therapeutic alliance include: (a) severity of client disorder, (b) type of client disorder, (c) client attachment style, (d) therapist use of interpersonal/communication skills, (e) degree of therapist empathy and openness, (f) client-therapist rapport, (g) therapist level of experience, (h) therapist specialized training and preparation, and (i) client-therapist collaboration (Horvath et al., 2011).

In 2011, Norcross convened another joint task force to review meta-analyses of the nine years of subsequent research, which was reported by Norcross and Wampold (2011). Based on the research, the joint task force identified six relationship elements as demonstrably effective: (a) alliance in individual psychotherapy, (b) alliance in youth psychotherapy, (c) alliance in family therapy, (d) cohesion in group therapy, (e) empathy and (f) collecting client feedback. Three relationship elements—consensus, collaboration and positive regard—were evaluated as probably effective. Three relationship elements were evaluated as promising but with insufficient research to judge: congruence and genuineness, repairing alliance ruptures, and managing countertransference.

In 2011, Norcross asked the joint task force also to judge the effectiveness of matching variables—an aspect often of great interest to psychotherapists who see Christian clients. They found that at the highest level of evidential base (that is, judged to be demonstrably effective) were four matching variables. Religion and spirituality—along with culture and reactance-resistance level—were seen as important and demonstrably effective for matching clients' wishes with treatment. Two matching variables were considered to be probably effective: stages of change and coping style. Two were seen as promising but without enough research to judge definitively: expectations and attachment style.

Overall, some of the aforementioned elements, such as repairing alliance ruptures, are often inevitable, and since they may influence other psychotherapy variables, they should be considered significant. For example, the amount of therapist self-disclosure may vary from client to client, but with resistant clients, appropriate self-disclosure can be used as a helpful way to put the client at ease to build and strengthen the therapeutic alliance. Furthermore, inquiring about the client's experience and asking for feedback can foster a therapeutic environment of collaboration. These kinds of practices can strengthen the therapeutic alliance, increase the client's participation and ownership of psychotherapy, and increase the likelihood of positive change.

WHAT'S FAITH GOT TO DO WITH CLIENT-THERAPIST FACTORS?

In this section, we set the stage for a Christian integrative approach to enhancing relationship and psychotherapist factors by providing a brief general review of the research on client religious and spiritual concerns and preferences, as well as introducing the unique needs of Christian clients. We dig further into the literature to bring attention to what research has shown that clients actually want out of psychotherapy regarding issues of faith. We also present a snapshot of research that has examined the impact of matching clients and therapists based on religious factors.

What psychotherapists know. When it comes to working with religious and spiritual clients—especially Christian clients—research suggests that we may not know as much as we might hope. For example, Hage, Hopson, Siegal, Payton and DeFanti (2006) surveyed psychology professionals across numerous settings to determine the amount of training they had received in the area of religion and spirituality. They learned that these professionals generally obtained little training in these matters. Even though Hage et al. did not focus on Christian training programs, in which trainees may receive more training on these topics than in secular programs, this nonetheless remains an important finding. For example, if we take a closer look at the membership rosters of prominent Christian counseling and psychology organizations, we find that a significant number of members are from non-Christian programs like the ones surveyed by Hage and colleagues. Moreover, at a recent symposium at the Christian Association for

Psychological Studies (CAPS), a group of highly regarded Christian educators concluded that a wider range of competencies in Christian counseling and psychology programs is needed to push these fields forward.

We hope, of course, that Christian psychotherapists are sensitive to religious and spiritual issues that might be facing clients. In general, O'Connor and Vandenberg (2005) found that secular psychotherapists tend to pathologize the religious beliefs of their clients. When these beliefs were understood to be part of a religious system, clinicians rated the beliefs as less pathological than those of clients who were not seen against a recognized religious membership backdrop. Furthermore, religious beliefs that varied from the most familiar belief systems of the United States were identified as more pathological than those associated with mainstream religious beliefs. This raises important issues that warrant further study. For example, although Christian therapists are likely to be sensitive to Christian religious and spiritual client issues, are we equally as sensitive to non-Christian clients' religious and spiritual issues? As Christian psychotherapists, we could all benefit from additional training in learning how to better care for Christian as well as non-Christian clients. Moreover, are Christian practitioners, who are necessarily ensconced in a particular religious or spiritual tradition, able to disengage their own stereotypes and prejudices against those who do not share their religious beliefs and values? This simply has not been researched.

What clients want. Researchers have found that engaging clients as active participants in their care, such as collaboratively developing treatment plans and discussing them over the course of treatment, helps to ensure clients' wants and needs are addressed. Studies have shown that such activities help to strengthen the therapeutic alliance and client-therapist bond. Listening and valuing what is important to our clients helps to foster a stronger client-therapist bond by building on relationship and therapist factors (Tryon & Winograd, 2011). So what do clients want from psychotherapy? More specifically, what do Christian clients want from psychotherapy? According to Rose, Westefeld and Ansley (2001), clients find religious and spiritual issues to be relevant for psychotherapy, and many hope to discuss such matters with their therapist. Furthermore, whether a client is religious or not may not be a direct indicator of whether they find religious issues to be relevant to the psychotherapy process. Similarly, Belaire and Young (2002) surveyed religious clients and discovered that Christian clients who were highly conservative had higher expectations that counselors—even secular ones—would utilize their religious beliefs in psychotherapy. A study done with college students at their campus counseling center found that around one out of every five students reported concern around religious or spiritual issues that would be relevant for psychotherapy (Johnson & Hayes, 2003).

It appears that a significant percentage of clients expect religious and spiritual issues to be a part of the therapeutic process and want to make sure that their beliefs are heard and handled with care. Similar studies of highly committed religious clients (Christians in particular) have voiced these themes as well. In fact, a few authors have argued that not addressing the religious and spiritual beliefs of highly committed Christian clients may not only decrease their satisfaction with the therapeutic relationship, but even lead to early termination (e.g., Aten, Mangis & Campbell, 2011). If we remain mindful that many of our clients hope to discuss religious and spiritual issues, new opportunities will likely emerge for exploring our clients' beliefs and values. Researchers have found that if we are able to create an environment where our clients feel safe and understood, they will be more likely to share about their faith. When we do this well, clients become more optimistic about treatment and trust us more, thereby reducing the risk of premature termination (Knox, Catlin, Casper & Schlosser, 2005).

What happens when we match clients and therapists based on beliefs. In general, Herman (1998) has argued that therapist-client matching increases in efficacy as similarity between the client and therapist increases. A fair amount of literature has been devoted specifically to examining this dynamic with regard to the unique needs of matching Christian clients and therapists. For example, Kelly and Strupp (1992) found that client-therapist similarity in belief about the importance of salvation was the only religious variable that significantly influenced outcome. The authors suggested that religious values may be used as a matching variable. At the same time, other clinical studies have found either contradictory evidence (Martinez, 1991) or evidence that nonreligious therapists could deliver religious-oriented treatment (Propst, Ostrom, Watkins, Dean & Mashburn, 1992). Furthermore, in 2002 the APA joint task force found that customizing psychotherapy to a client's religious beliefs and values has promising empirical support (Norcross, 2002b).

However, the clinical utility of client-therapist matching might only be necessary and beneficial for Christian clients under certain circumstances. In a review of the literature, Worthington and Sandage (2002) concluded that highly religious clients prefer religiously similar counselors (and therefore may not seek help from secular sources) and the spiritual language typically embedded in traditional religion. Yet the therapist's level of religious commitment may not be as influential as therapists' willingness to discuss, utilize and affirm the client's religious commitments in psychotherapy. To successfully leverage Christian client-therapist matching variables, therapists need to have a sense of where clients are coming from and find a way to appropriately disclose their own religious values. Christian counselors and psychologists may need to navigate several common complications to this kind of disclosure: (a) Client and clinician may have differing religious values. (b) Clients may filter what they share according to their clinician's stated beliefs rather than revealing their own religious convictions. (c) Clinicians may assume more similarity of values with the client than actually exists. (d) Client and clinician may focus too much on religious issues in a way that overshadows other therapeutic needs.

A flood of research on this subject accumulated subsequent to the review by Worthington and Sandage in 2002. Several treatments (such as Christian cognitive therapy for depression) emerged as empirically supported treatments in a review by Hook and his colleagues (2010). When Worthington, Hook, Davis and McDaniel (2011) meta-analyzed the research studies, they found clear evidence that in pre- to post-treatment assessments, Christian-accommodated (and other religion-accommodated) interventions resulted in improvement. Christian-accommodated treatments were more effective at producing mental health gains in the target symptom than were alternative or control treatments. However, when strictly accommodated Christian treatments were compared with the secular treatments they were modified from, the gains in mental health were no different. However, the gains in spiritual well-being were greater for the Christian-accommodated treatments.

In general, it is beneficial to accommodate to client preferences of psychotherapist and treatment type. For example, Swift, Callahan and Vollmer (2011) meta-analyzed thirty-five studies investigating accommodating to clients' preferences in a variety of issues, and the resulting body of literature was judged by the 2011 task force as demonstrably effective. Worthington, Hook, Davis, Gartner and Jennings (in press) have provided a thorough review of this research and the issues surrounding matching to clients' religious preferences.

PRACTICAL TIPS FOR APPLICATION

In the following, we attempt to equip readers with some practical skills and recommendations for overcoming the obstacles just noted. We build on the literature reviewed thus far, and discuss how Christian psychotherapists might be more intentional in maximizing the usefulness of religious client-therapist factors.

1. *Engage in reflective practices to gain a deeper understanding of one's beliefs as well as to keep potential biases in check.* An attitude of humility and sensitivity is necessary to engage in candid conversations with clients about religion and spirituality. Therefore, it is necessary for Christian counselors and psychotherapists to be aware of and recognize their own religious and spiritual histories, experiences, beliefs and biases. This is important not only for recognizing one's limitations, but also as a first step toward being tolerant and accepting of the client's independent beliefs in order to create a safe space for religious or spiritual dialogue (Richards & Bergin, 2000).

2. *Assess client religious and spiritual beliefs from the onset of treatment.* Christian therapists should include religion and spirituality in routine assessments. An assessment of religiosity should include not only associated groups or denominations, but also values and previous and current spiritual experiences. For example, many patients may identify as Christian and may have chosen a therapist according to their religious values. However, clinicians cannot assume that all their clients universally hold the same values and beliefs. Additionally, therapists should assess whether the client prefers a more implicit or explicit use of religion and spirituality in psychotherapy. As discussed by Worthington, Hook, Davis and McDaniel (2011), clients with stronger religious commitments may benefit more from and prefer more explicitly religious forms of psychotherapy and interven-

tions. Furthermore, therapists should assess the client's preferences regarding religious and spiritual language, as well as spiritual disciplines and practices they hope to utilize in or out of psychotherapy (Doherty, 1999; Rose et al., 2008). If a client prefers a more explicit use of religion or spirituality in psychotherapy, it is recommended that the therapist consult and collaborate with clergy or pastoral professionals when necessary (Gonsiorek et al., 2009).

3. *Use empathy intentionally and "trust the process."* On occasion, Christian therapists might jump the gun a bit when they find out that a client comes from a Christian background. Sometimes this means over-identifying with a client. At other times, the therapist may make untrue or irrelevant assumptions about a client's faith and get caught up in countertransference issues. This might occur, for example, if the therapist grew up in a highly rigid Christian family and had lingering strong feelings, whether positive or negative, about that experience. Another common problem with over-identifying is that therapists are prone to push too quickly for change. Psychotherapy may become too task driven, which might damage the relationship. Because empathy helps build trust, therapists should remember that much empathy may be needed before the client feels comfortable divulging something so personal and life-shaping as his or her spiritual beliefs. When spiritual or religious beliefs are shared and explored in the course of psychotherapy, a good empathic practice may be to affirm and even thank the client for the courage and vulnerability that goes into sharing such beliefs (Young, Dowdle & Flowers, 2009). The practice of basic good listening skills and reflection of the clients' statements (e.g., sometimes using their own language) may indicate to clients that the therapist understands their religious frame of reference (even though he or she may not completely agree with it).

4. *Take a collaborative approach by making clients active players in their own treatment.* Collaboration in psychotherapy is the mutual involvement of both the therapist and the client toward therapeutic tasks and outcome. In general, common measures of collaboration include level of client resistance and cooperation with homework (Tryon & Winograd, 2011). Yet collaboration may look slightly different in Christian counseling and psychotherapy. For example, clients with stronger religious and spiritual belief

systems may desire to have psychotherapy goals and interventions that relate directly to these belief systems. Worthington, Hook, Davis and Mc-Daniels (2011) conducted a meta-analysis revealing that psychotherapy was more effective for both symptom reduction and a sense of spiritual growth among patients who held stronger religious commitments if treatment employed more explicitly religious language and interventions. Because religious commitment and language may be important to Christian clients, the therapist should endeavor to hold a collaborative posture and modify their approach according to the needs of their client.

5. *Pay close attention to how the therapeutic alliance is developing over the course of psychotherapy.* As the studies above indicate, the therapist would do well to monitor the therapeutic alliance throughout the treatment process when working with Christian clients. This can be done through clinical assessments or through "checking in" with the client. Given that the client trusts the therapist enough to be open and honest about how he or she is feeling about the relationship, this practice can be rewarding in a number of ways. First, it demonstrates to the client that the therapist cares for him or her as a person and finds his or her opinion valuable. Second, it demonstrates a collaborative posture that invites the client into the change process even further. Third, it provides valuable information for the therapist on how to adjust the relationship so as to strengthen the therapeutic alliance, which will in turn increase the likelihood of effective psychotherapy. Even if client and counselor both consider themselves Christians, they may differ from one another in many respects. It is important that the therapist monitor his or her reactions to clients who may come across as hyper-religious or rigid in their beliefs. Because these clients in particular may be very sensitive to perceived challenges to their belief system, the risk of damaging the therapeutic alliance is greater.

6. *Know when to adjust the therapeutic alliance.* Beutler, Moleiro and Talebi (2002) have argued that resistance is a common "red flag," which therapists should look for as an indicator that adjustment may be warranted. They focus primarily on resistance as a situational factor rather than as a client trait. In defining resistance as situational, therapists avoid over-pathologizing resistance. Their approach draws a clear distinction between a client who is resistant by character and one who simply is not getting

better and is thus "resistant" to change. Thus clients with less trait resistance respond better to more directive forms of psychotherapy. The opposite is true of clients who are highly resistant; they respond better to a nondirective therapist. Clinicians should also assess for coping style and the client's predisposition to specific psychotherapy interventions. Evidence shows that clients with an internalizing coping style will benefit more from insight-oriented psychotherapy, whereas clients with externalizing coping styles will improve with more behavioral or symptom-focused techniques. Resistance and coping style are two evidence-based ways to adapt psychotherapy according to a client's individual personalities and characteristics.

CONCLUSION

In this chapter, we sought to bring attention to various ways evidence-based relationship factors can be leveraged in Christian counseling and psychotherapy to produce better client outcomes. Chief among these are therapeutic alliance, empathy and collaboration in psychotherapy. Furthermore, adjusting the clinical relationship based on the resistance level and coping styles of a client has also been demonstrated to be advantageous for psychotherapy. Finally, the utilization of religion and spirituality in psychotherapy to particular degrees dependent on the religious commitment level of the client has been found to be beneficial to therapeutic outcome and religious/ spiritual growth, both of which are important to many clients with strong religious convictions. By utilizing these relational variables appropriately in psychotherapy, Christian counselors and psychotherapists bring an added dimension of care shown to bolster already proven techniques and practices.

REFERENCES

Aten, J., Mangis, M., & Campbell, C. (2010). Psychotherapy with rural religious fundamental clients. *Journal of Clinical Psychology: In Session, 66*, 1-11.

Belaire, C., & Young, J. S. (2002). Conservative Christians' expectations of non-Christian counselors. *Counseling and Values, 46*, 175-87.

Bergin, A. E., & Jensen, J. P. (1990). Religiosity of psychotherapists: A national survey. *Psychotherapy: Theory, Research, Practice, Training, 27*(1), 3-7.

Beutler, L. E., Harwood, T. M., Alimohamed, S., & Malik, M. (2002). Functional impairment and coping style. In J. C. Norcross (Ed.), *Psychotherapy relationships that work: Therapists contributions and responsiveness to patients* (pp. 145-70). New York: Oxford University Press.

Beutler, L. E., Harwood, T. M., Bertoni, M., & Thomann, J. (2006) Systematic treatment selection and prescriptive therapy. In G. Stricker & J. Gold (Eds.), *A casebook of psychotherapy integration* (pp. 29-41). Washington, DC: American Psychological Association.

Beutler, L. E., Harwood, T. M., Kimpara, S., Verdirame, D., & Blau, K. (2011). Coping style. *Journal of Clinical Psychology: In Session, 67,* 176-83.

Beutler, L. E., Harwood, T. M., Michelson, A., Xiaoxia, X., & Holiman, J. (2011). Resistance. *Journal of Clinical Psychology: In Session, 67,* 133-42.

Beutler, L. E., Moleiro, C. M., & Talebi, H. (2002). Resistance. In J. C. Norcross (Ed.), *Psychotherapy relationships that work: Therapists contributions and responsiveness to patients* (pp. 129-43). New York: Oxford University Press.

Butcher, J. N., Graham, J. R., Ben-Porath, Y. S., Tellegen, A., Dahlstrom, W. G., & Kaemmer, B. (2001). *MMPI-2: Manual for administration and scoring* (Rev. ed.). Minneapolis: University of Minnesota Press.

Delaney, H. D., Miller, W. R., & Bisonó, A. M. (2007). Religiosity and spirituality among psychologists: A survey of clinician members of the American Psychological Association. *Professional Psychology: Research and Practice, 38*(5), 538-46.

Doherty, W. J. (1999). Morality and spirituality in therapy. In F. Walsh (Ed.), *Spiritual resources in family therapy* (pp. 179-92). New York: Guilford Publications.

Elliott, R., Bohart, A. C., Watson, J. C., & Greenberg, L. S. (2011). In J. C. Norcross (Ed.), *Psychotherapy relationships that work: Evidence-based responsiveness* (2nd ed., pp. 132-52). New York: Oxford University Press.

Gonsiorek, J. C., Richards, P., Pargament, K. I., & McMinn, M. R. (2009). Ethical challenges and opportunities at the edge: Incorporating spirituality and religion into psychotherapy. *Professional Psychology: Research and Practice, 40*(4), 385-95.

Hage, S., Hopson, A., Siegel, M., Payton, G., & DeFanti, E. (2006). Multicultural training in spirituality: An interdisciplinary review. *Counseling and Values, 50,* 217-34.

Harwood, T. M., & Beutler, L. E. (2008). EVTs, EBPs, ESRs, and RIPs: Inspecting the varieties of research based practices. In L. L'Abate (Ed.), *Toward a science of clinical psychology: Laboratory evaluations and interventions* (pp. 161-76). New York: Nova Science Publishers.

Harwood, T. M., & Beutler, L. E. (2009). Assessment of clients in pretreatment planning. In J. N. Butcher (Ed.), *Oxford handbook of personality assessment* (pp. 643-66). New York: Oxford University Press.

Herman, S. M. (1997). Therapist-client similarity on the multimodal structural profile inventory as a predictor of early session impact. *Journal of Psychotherapy Practice and Research, 6*(2), 139-44.

Herman, S. M. (1998). The relationship between therapist-client modality similarity and psychotherapy outcome. *Journal of Psychotherapy Practice and Research, 7*(1), 56-64.

Hook, J. N., Worthington, E. L., Jr., Davis, D. E., Gartner, A. L., Jennings, J., & Hook, J. P. (2010). Empirically supported religious and spiritual therapies. *Journal of Clinical Psychology, 66*(1), 46-72.

Horvath, A. O., Flückiger, C., & Symonds, D. (2011). The alliance. In J. C. Norcross (Ed.), *Psychotherapy relationships that work: Evidence-based responsiveness* (2nd ed., pp. 25-69). New York: Oxford University Press.

Institute of Medicine. (2001). *Crossing the quality chasm: A new health system for the 21st century.* Washington, DC: National Academies Press.

Johansson, H., & Jansson, J. (2010). Therapeutic alliance and outcome in routine psychiatric out-patient treatment: Patient factors and outcome. *Psychology and Psychotherapy: Theory, Research, and Practice, 83,* 193-206.

Johnson, C. V., & Hayes, J. A. (2003). Troubled spirits: Prevalence and predictors of religious and spiritual concerns among university students and counseling center clients. *Journal of Counseling Psychology, 50,* 409-19.

Johnson, C. V., Hayes, J. A., & Wade, N. G. (2007). Psychotherapy with troubled spirits: A qualitative investigation. *Psychotherapy Research, 17,* 450-60.

Kelly, T. A., & Strupp, H. H. (1992). Patient and therapist values in psychotherapy: Perceived changes, assimilation, similarity, and outcome. *Journal of Consulting and Clinical Psychology, 60*(1), 34-40.

Klein, M. H., Kolden, G. G., Michels, J. L., & Chisholm-Stockard, S. (2002). Congruence. In J. C. Norcross (Ed.), *Psychotherapy relationships that work: Therapists contributions and responsiveness to patients* (pp. 217-33). New York: Oxford Univeristy Press.

Knox, S., Catlin, L., Casper, M., & Schlosser, L. Z. (2005). Addressing religion and spirituality in psychotherapy: Clients' perspectives. *Psychotherapy Research, 15,* 287-303.

Martinez, F. I. (1991). Therapist-client convergence and similarity of religious values: Their effect on client improvement. *Journal of Psychology and Christianity, 10,* 137-43.

Norcross, J. C. (2002a). Empirically supported therapy relationships. In J. C. Norcross (Ed.), *Psychotherapy relationships that work: Therapist contributions and responsiveness to patients* (pp. 3-16). New York: Oxford University Press.

Norcross, J. C. (Ed.). (2002b). *Psychotherapy relationships that work: Therapist contributions and responsiveness to patients.* New York: Oxford University Press.

Norcross, J. C. (Ed.). (2011). *Psychotherapy relationships that work: Evidence-based responsiveness* (2nd ed.). New York: Oxford University Press.

Norcross, J. C., & Wampold, B. E. (2011). Evidence-based therapy relationships: Research conclusions and clinical practices. In J. C. Norcross (Ed.), *Psychotherapy relationships that work: Evidence-based responsiveness* (2nd ed., pp. 423-30). New York: Oxford University Press.

O'Connor, S., & Vandenberg, B. (2005). Psychosis or faith? Clinicians' assessment of religious beliefs. *Journal of Consulting and Clinical Psychology, 73,* 610-19.

Paloutzian, R. F. (1996). *Invitation to the psychology of religion* (2nd ed.). Needham Heights, MA: Allyn and Bacon.

Post, B. C., & Wade, N. G. (2009). Religion and spirituality in psychotherapy: A practice-friendly review of research. *Journal of Clinical Psychology, 65*(2), 131-46.

Propst, L. R., Ostrom, R., Watkins, P., Dean, T., & Mashburn, D. (1992). Comparative efficacy of religious and nonreligious cognitive-behavioral therapy for the treatment of clinical depression in religious individuals. *Journal of Consulting and Clinical Psychology, 60,* 94-103.

Richards, P. S., & Bergin, A. E. (Eds.). (2000). *Handbook of psychotherapy and religious diversity.* Washington, DC: American Psychological Association.

Rose, E. M., Westefeld, J. S., & Ansley, T. N. (2001). Spiritual issues in counseling: Clients' beliefs and preferences. *Journal of Counseling Psychology, 48,* 61-71.

Rose, E. M., Westefeld, J. S., & Ansley, T. N. (2008). Spiritual issues in counseling: Clients' beliefs and preferences. *Psychology of Religion and Spirituality, 1,* 18-33.

Shirk, S. R., & Karver, M. (2003). Prediction of treatment outcome from relationship variables in child and adolescent therapy: A meta-analytic review. *Journal of Consulting and Clinical Psychology, 71*(3), 452-64.

Swift, J. K., Callahan, J. L., & Vollmer, B. M. (2011). Preferences. *Journal of Clinical Psychology, 67* (2), 155-65.

Tryon, G. S., & Winograd, G. (2011). Goal consensus and collaboration. In J. C. Norcross (Ed.), *Psychotherapy relationships that work: Evidence-based responsiveness* (2nd ed., pp. 153-67). New York: Oxford University Press.

Worthington, E. L., Jr., Hook, J. N., Davis, D. E., Gartner, A. L., & Jennings, D. J., II. (in press). Conducting empirical research on religiously accommodated treatments. In Kenneth I. Pargament, A. Mahoney, & E. Shafranske (Eds.), *APA handbooks in psychology: APA handbook of psychology, religion, and spirituality* (Vol. 2). Washington, DC: American Psychological Association.

Worthington, E. L., Jr., Hook, J. N., Davis, D. E., & McDaniel, M. A. (2011). Religion and spirituality. *Journal of Clinical Psychology: In Session, 67*(2), 204-14.

Worthington, E. L., Jr., & Sandage, S. J. (2002). Religion and spirituality. In J. C. Norcross (Ed.), *Psychotherapy relationships that work: Therapist contributions and responsiveness to patients* (pp. 383-400). New York: Oxford University Press.

Worthington, E. L., Wade, N. G., Hight, T. L., Ripley, J. S., McCullough, M. E., Berry, J. W., et al. (2003). The Religious Commitment Inventory—10: Development, refinement, and validation of a brief scale for research and counseling. *Journal of Counseling Psychology, 50*(1), 84-96.

Yarhouse, M. A., Butman, R. E., & McRay, B. W. (2005). *Modern psychopathologies.* Downers Grove, IL: InterVarsity Press.

Young, J. S., Dowdle, S., & Flowers, L. (2009). How spirituality can affect the therapeutic alliance. In J. D. Aten & M. M. Leach (Eds.), *Spirituality and the therapeutic process: A comprehensive resource from intake to termination* (pp. 167-92). Washington, DC: American Psychological Association.

3

Lay Christian Counseling for General Psychological Problems

Siang-Yang Tan

The "nonprofessional revolution in mental health" described by Sobey (1970) over 40 years ago has developed even further in recent years. For many reasons—including the sheer need for mental health services, the effort to cut healthcare costs internationally, and reduced benefits of mental health insurance in the United States—the role of paraprofessional or lay counseling in the provision of mental health services has grown tremendously here and abroad (see Garzon & Tilley, 2009; Tan, 1997). Lay counselors or paraprofessional helpers are "those who lack the formal training, experience, or credentials to be professional psychotherapists, but who are nevertheless involved in helping people cope with personal problems" (Tan, 1997, p. 368). They have provided much-needed but increasingly ill-afforded mental health services in various ways, such as through telephone hotlines, suicide-prevention programs, church-based lay counseling services, national caregiving ministries, and peer-helping programs in many schools, colleges, businesses, prisons, religious institutions and other community agencies (Tan, 1992). A major example of paraprofessional or nonprofessional helping is lay Christian counseling for general psychological or emotional problems, usually in a local church context, but also in other parachurch (e.g., Youth for Christ) or Christian ministry (e.g., missionary) contexts (see Tan, 1991, 2002).

Church leaders and Christian counselors often view lay Christian counseling as a legitimate Christian ministry based on biblical teaching. The biblical basis for lay helping, as well as building a deeply connected and loving Christian community, is found in texts such as Romans 15:14, Galatians 6:1-2, John 13:34-35, 1 Thessalonians 5:14 and James 5:16. Furthermore, 1 Peter 2:5-9 emphasizes the priesthood of all believers so that every Christian should be involved in appropriate ministries in the church and beyond, including lay helping and pastoral care, according to the spiritual gifts he or she has been graciously given by the Holy Spirit (see Rom 12; 1 Cor 12; Eph 4; 1 Pet 4:8-11). Besides biblical support for lay Christian counseling ministries, there is also some limited empirical support for the efficacy or effectiveness of lay Christian counseling, although more and better controlled outcome studies are needed before more definitive conclusions can be made (see Garzon & Tilley, 2009; Tan, 1991, 2002).

EMPIRICAL SUPPORT FOR LAY COUNSELING

The empirical support for the effectiveness of lay counseling or nonprofessional or paraprofessional helping in general is quite extensive. Earlier reviews of the research literature with forty-two studies on the comparative effectiveness of paraprofessional and professional helpers (see Durlak, 1979, 1981; Nietzel & Fisher, 1981), as well as subsequent meta-analyses (Berman & Norton, 1985; Hattie, Sharpley & Rogers, 1984; Stein & Lambert, 1995), have similarly concluded that lay counselors are generally as effective as professional therapists for most common problems such as anxiety, stress and depression (see Atkins & Christensen, 2001; Bickman, 1999; Christensen & Jacobson, 1994; Lambert & Bergin, 1994; see also Ali, Rahbar, Naeem & Gul, 2003; Neuner et al., 2008), although there is still some controversy over these findings.

Some research seems to support the greater effectiveness of professional therapists over paraprofessional helpers. For example, professionally trained and experienced therapists have fewer client dropouts than paraprofessionals in outpatient settings (Stein & Lambert, 1995). Professionally trained and experienced therapists were also found to do better than paraprofessionals in a study using manualized treatments with conduct-disordered children (Kendall, Reber, McLeer, Epps & Ronan, 1990), in a study of group cognitive-behavioral therapy for depression at a six-month follow-up

(Bright, Baker & Neimeyer, 1999), and in a study on relaxation training for cancer chemotherapy patients (Carey & Burish, 1987). More recently, Barlow (2004) has concluded that significant clinical expertise and a strong therapeutic relationship are essential for maximizing the efficacy of psychological treatments, particularly for more severely disturbed clients such as those with panic disorder or severe depression (Klein et al., 2003; Norcross, 2002). Therapist variables, such as therapist experience, also contribute significantly to beneficial outcome in such psychological treatments (Huppert et al., 2001). Barlow has therefore strongly advocated the use of highly trained and experienced therapists, especially psychologists, in treating clients with more severe psychopathology (see also Beutler & Kendall, 1995), but the empirical support for his view is still very limited.

These more recent findings, however, do not negate the previously cited empirical evidence supporting the effectiveness of lay counselors when compared with professional therapists. Lay or paraprofessional counselors have therefore generally been found to be effective helpers (see Tan, 2011).

Empirical Support for Lay Christian Counseling

Empirical support for the effectiveness of lay Christian counselor training and lay Christian counseling is limited. Tan (1991) reviewed several studies that evaluated the effectiveness of different lay Christian counselor training programs, including his twelve-session training program, with generally positive results. However, most of the studies did not have a control or comparison group. The only study he mentioned that had a comparison group (comprised of weekly Bible study class students) found that lay Christian counselor trainees improved significantly more on self-ratings of knowledge, competence and confidence about competence in counseling and Christian counseling, and on ratings of genuineness in a videotaped role-play counseling situation by two independent raters, than the comparison group of students (Jernigan, Tan & Gorsuch, 1988; see also Jernigan, 1989). Another study, also with a no-training control group, found that a Christian-based adolescent peer-counseling curriculum (Sturkie & Tan, 1992) used with Christian high school students led to more significant improvements on self-ratings of knowledge and competence in Christian counseling and a stronger preference for an understanding style of response in comparison to the control group. It also led to significantly higher ratings on empathy, genuineness and respect by two independent raters of role-play videotapes (Martin, 1998). There is therefore some evidence from these two evaluations of lay Christian counselor training programs that supports the effectiveness of these training programs in producing significantly better lay Christian counselor responses and self-ratings. However, the crucial evaluation needed is on the effectiveness of the lay Christian counseling provided in terms of client therapeutic outcomes or changes.

Earlier, Tan (1991) also reviewed several studies evaluating the effectiveness of different lay Christian counseling services in terms of client outcomes. The outcome studies covered did not include a control or comparison group, or use random assignment of clients or subjects, or appropriate pre-post counseling assessments (e.g., see Boan & Owens, 1985; Harris, 1985; Walters, 1987). A more recent outcome study included pre-post assessments, with several good outcome measures, revealing significant positive results in client change with adults receiving counseling at a local church lay counseling service, but there was no comparison or control group (Toh, Tan, Osburn & Faber, 1994). A subsequent controlled outcome study (Toh & Tan, 1997), using a no-treatment control group, with random assignment of subjects either to the lay Christian counseling treatment group ($n = 22$) or the no-treatment control group ($n = 24$) found that the treatment group reported significantly more improvement than the control group on all the four outcome measures (target complaints, brief symptom checklist, spiritual well-being scale and global ratings of client's psychological adjustment) and maintained these therapeutic gains at one-month follow-up. This is the only controlled outcome study that has been conducted on lay Christian counseling involving adult clients in a local church context (see Garzon & Tilley, 2009). A recent review of empirically supported religious and spiritual therapies in general (Hook et al., 2010) included Christian lay counseling for general psychological problems as one of several possibly efficacious treatments based on this one controlled outcome study.

Garzon and Tilley (2009) recently reviewed the empirical evidence for the effectiveness of lay Christian counseling subdivided into active listening approaches (e.g., Kenneth Haugk's Stephen Ministry), cognitive and solution-focused approaches (e.g., early Crabb, Backus and Tan), inner healing prayer models (e.g., Francis MacNutt's Christian Healing Ministries; Ed Smith's Theophostic Prayer Ministry) and mixed lay Christian models (e.g., eclectic with an integrated cognitive-behavioral component; Neil Anderson's Freedom in Christ Ministries). While they noted some preliminary evidence for the effectiveness of Freedom in Christ Ministries and Theophostic Prayer Ministry, the lack of controlled outcome studies preclude definitive conclusions. The only randomized waiting list control group study available to date remains Toh and Tan (1997) discussed above. Garzon and Tilley therefore concluded that much more and better controlled outcome research is needed before the effectiveness of lay Christian counseling can be properly evaluated.

While lay counseling in general can be said to be effective—often as effective as professional therapy—lay Christian counseling can only be said to be a possibly efficacious treatment at this time.

THERAPY DESCRIPTION

Lay Christian counseling is not a unitary or uniform approach to helping people with general psychological or emotional problems. As Garzon and Tilley (2009) have noted, there are at least four major categories of lay Christian counseling approaches, mainly from a more conservative, evangelical perspective: active listening, cognitive and solution-focused, inner healing and mixed (see also Garzon et al., 2009). A brief treatment description of each of these four major categories will now be provided, following Garzon and Tilley (2009).

Active-listening approaches. Active-listening approaches to lay Christian counseling include empathy, positive regard and basic listening skills, combined with the use of spiritual resources such as prayer and the Scriptures. A major example of this approach is Stephen Ministry, a Christian caregiving program developed by Kenneth Haugk (see Haugk, 1984) beginning in 1975. It has experienced tremendous growth so that more than 10,000 congregations from over 150 denominations and 21 countries are now using Stephen Ministry in their lay caregiving. Churches first enroll in the Stephen Series program of training, provision of resources and continuing support from the main organization, Stephen Ministries, in St. Louis, Missouri.

They then send their pastor(s) or selected lay leaders to attend a week-long leadership course that trains them in the Stephen Ministry model of lay caregiving and how to implement it in a local church context. The leader(s) of this ministry will subsequently select lay members of the congregation to become Stephen ministers by providing them with fifty hours of lay care training on topics such as active listening; feelings; assertiveness; confidentiality; setting boundaries for helping; ministering to people with specific struggles, such as grief, depression, divorce, crisis or childbirth; ministering to the dying, the suicidal, shut-in persons, older persons and inactive members; making referrals to mental health professionals and other resources; and the appropriate use of prayer and Scripture. The trained lay members are then commissioned in church as Stephen ministers who will meet with a "care-receiver," assigned by a Stephen leader, once a week for an hour. These Stephen ministers will also meet with Stephen leaders for peer supervision twice a month. No controlled outcome studies have been conducted on the effectiveness of Stephen Ministry as a lay Christian counseling or caregiving approach.

Cognitive and solution-focused approaches. The cognitive or cognitive-behavioral approaches to lay Christian counseling emphasize the crucial role of dysfunctional or unbiblical automatic thoughts, self-talk, basic assumptions or core beliefs and schemas in the development of emotional distress or psychological problems (e.g., Backus, 1985; Crabb, 1977). They also include the use of prayer and Scripture in cognitively restructuring or changing such distorted and unbiblical thinking into more realistic and biblical thinking (see Tan, 1991, 2007). Solution-focused approaches to lay Christian counseling have recently been used in the context of lay pastoral care (e.g., see Holland, 2007). Such approaches focus on helping clients to use their unique strengths and resources in working toward problem resolution, as they imagine their futures without the problem.

A specific example of a biblically-based, integrated cognitive-behavioral approach to lay Christian counseling has been developed by Tan (1991; see also Tan, 2007). It incorporates an inner healing prayer component with seven steps (see Tan & Ortberg, 2004) and uses biblical cognitive restructuring (e.g., Crabb's biblical counseling and Backus's misbelief therapy), which replaces unbiblical thinking with scriptural truths. His approach can be taught to lay Christian counseling trainees in a twelve-session training program with three-hour sessions, and there is some empirical evidence supporting the effectiveness of the training program (see Tan, 1991). However, no controlled outcome studies have been done on the effectiveness of cognitive and solution-focused lay Christian counseling approaches.

Inner-healing approaches. Another category of lay Christian counseling consists of inner-healing prayer approaches (also known as healing of memories) that focus on helping clients to journey back to their past under the guidance of the Holy Spirit to uncover painful experiences or memories that may be contributing to their troubled present (see Hurding, 1995, p. 297) and to pray for the presence of Christ or God to minister to them in the context of those painful memories (see Garzon & Burkett, 2002, p. 42). Inner-healing approaches include Francis MacNutt's Christian Healing Ministries and Ed Smith's Theophostic Prayer Ministry (see Smith, 2002, 2007). Smith's approach focuses on identifying lies associated with painful memories and praying for the Lord Jesus to reveal the truth to the client about such lies, leading eventually to peace (see Garzon & Tilley, 2009). Also in this category is John and Paula Sandford's Elijah House Ministry (1982; see also J. Sandford & M. Sandford, 1992; for a review, Garzon, E. Worthington, Tan & R. Worthington, 2009).

All of these methods require training the lay Christian counselor in the particular inner-healing prayer approach. For further details on these approaches and their training programs, see Garzon and Tilley (2009) and Garzon et al. (2009). There is some preliminary evidence for the effectiveness of Theophostic Prayer Ministry, but no definitive conclusions can be made because of the lack of well-controlled outcome studies.

Mixed approaches. This final category of lay Christian counseling consists of mixed approaches, which include either several psychological theoretical perspectives, or more focused examination of theological dimensions such as the role of the sinful nature and the demonic in the development of emotional distress, or both. Two examples of mixed approaches are eclectic with an integrated cognitive behavioral component and Neil Anderson's Freedom in Christ Ministries (see Anderson, 2000a, 2000b, 2003, 2004). Anderson's approach focuses on unbiblical lies, which often cause emotional and spiritual distress and the need to take "the steps to freedom" in seven key areas involving confession and renunciation of certain sinful attitudes and behaviors, and forgiveness (see Garzon et al., 2009). There is some preliminary evidence for the effectiveness of Freedom in Christ Ministries, but again no definitive conclusions can be made because well-controlled outcome studies are still lacking (see Garzon & Tilley, 2009).

There is one randomized waiting list control group outcome study on the effectiveness of an eclectic with an integrated cognitive-behavioral component approach to lay Christian counseling (Toh & Tan, 1997). This study evaluated the effectiveness of lay Christian counseling provided in a local church context (First Evangelical Free Church of Fullerton, California, which had over five thousand attendees at the time the study was conducted). Toh and Tan provide the following details of this lay Christian counseling program for the treatment of general psychological or emotional problems:

> The characteristics of this program include: (a) lay counseling services to those within and outside the church; (b) a formal selection process for lay counselors involving the use of clinical instruments and in-depth interviews; (c) a year-long counselor training program conducted by professionals; (d) post-training supervision provided by licensed mental health professionals; (e) screening and referral of counselees to avoid too severe symptomatology (e.g., applicants with a history of suicidal ideation or attempts, psychotropic medication, severe or chronic psychological dysfunction, and suggested diagnosis of character disorders from the MMPI are referred to mental health professionals); (f) a commitment to a brief, solution-focused therapy (limited to ten sessions) designed for counselees with "temporary adjustment disorders"; and (g) provision of services to adults, adolescents, and couples only (i.e., no services to children). (Toh & Tan, 1997, pp. 260-61)

The year-long training curriculum used to train the lay Christian counselors in this study consists of the following three phases:

> The first phase is a 22 two-hour lecture series covering such single-session topics as the nature of persons; integration and the use of Scriptures; personality and counseling theory; developmental psychology of the individual and family; narcissistic and borderline personalities; children and adolescents as well as child and adolescent therapy; marital and family therapy; divorce, step-parenting and blended families; psychopathology; anxiety and phobic

reactions; depression, grief, and loss; incest rape; addictive/compulsive disorders; eating disorders, anorexia and bulimia; suicide ideation and intervention; stress reduction and biofeedback; and psychotropic medications, hospitalizations, and forensic psychiatry. The second phase involves testing of the potential counselors. . . . The third phase over the last four months of training focuses on empathic listening skills, role play, identifying and handling resistances, and termination. These skills are taught in conjunction with Mann and Goldman's (1982) approach to time-limited psychotherapy. (Toh & Tan, 1997, p. 261)

The category of lay Christian counseling used in this study is therefore an eclectic one with some integration of a cognitive-behavioral component. A similar eclectic approach focusing more on active listening skills as well as some biblically-based cognitive-behavioral components and marital and family counseling—based on Egan (1990a, 1990b), Haugk (1984), Satir and Baldwin (1983) and Tan (1991)—has been used in the lay Christian counseling program at another local church, La Canada Presbyterian Church in La Canada, California. The twenty-six-week training program is conducted every year, usually from March to August (see Tan, 1991). There is some preliminary empirical evidence in a pre-post assessment or program evaluation, but with no control groups or random assignment of subjects or clients, for the effectiveness of this particular eclectic with an integrated cognitive-behavioral component approach to lay Christian counseling (Toh et al., 1994). However, more definitive conclusions cannot be made because of the lack of randomization of subjects and control groups. Clients in this study were seen either for 10 ($n = 9$) or 20 sessions ($n = 9$) of lay Christian counseling.

There are many other lay Christian counseling services and training programs available (see Tan, 1991, 2002), but only one eclectic with an integrated cognitive-behavioral component approach has been evaluated with a randomized waiting list control group design. This study had significant positive findings leading to the present conclusion that lay Christian counseling for general psychological problems can be considered a possibly efficacious treatment (Hook et al., 2010). More and better controlled outcome research is definitely needed on the effectiveness of lay Christian counseling (Garzon & Tilley, 2009).

The Role of the Professional Counselor in Lay Christian Counseling

Professional counselors and psychologists can have an important role in lay Christian counseling. They can help in the following ways (Tan, 1997): training and supervising lay counselors; serving on boards of directors of lay counseling ministries or organizations; educating the public, including churches, about the positive contributions of psychological or mental health services; consulting with churches or parachurch organizations interested in setting up lay counseling services; serving as a referral source when professional counseling or therapy is needed (but avoiding any conflict of interest); conducting outcomes research and evaluating the effectiveness of lay counseling; and educating other mental health professionals about the significant role they can have in the development of lay counselors and lay counseling ministries.

Treatment Implementation

Five steps for starting a lay counseling ministry. In order to implement lay Christian counseling, especially in a local church context, the following five steps for starting a lay counseling ministry are recommended (see Tan, 1991, 1995, 2002). First, an appropriate model of lay Christian counseling ministry for a particular church should be chosen. Besides the *spontaneous, informal model* of lay Christian counseling or people-helping that typically occurs in settings such as homes and restaurants or wherever people meet and share their problems with each other, with no formal selection, training or supervision of lay counselors, there are really only two primary models of lay Christian counseling or caregiving. The first is the *informal, organized* model in which lay counselors or helpers are carefully selected, trained and supervised in an organized ministry of lay Christian counseling or caregiving that occurs in informal settings such as restaurants, homes, hospitals and nursing homes. The second is the *formal, organized* model in which lay counselors are also carefully selected, trained and supervised in an organized ministry of lay Christian counseling or caregiving that takes place in more formal settings such as a lay counseling center in a local church, where appointments are made for the lay counselor to meet at a specific time with a client, couple or family. The first step then is to choose which of these two models is best for a particular local church or parachurch ministry. However, some larger churches may actually choose to use both models to provide different levels of help to those in need. For example, a church with several hundred or several thousand people may implement Stephen Ministry, which fits an informal, organized model, as well as having trained lay Christian counselors provide counseling services through a formal lay counseling center at the church.

Second, full support for the lay Christian counseling ministry and model(s) adopted should be obtained from the local church pastors, pastoral staff and church board, so that the church leadership is one hundred percent behind the lay Christian counseling service as a crucial part of the overall church ministries and outreach. Lay Christian counseling is therefore viewed by the church leadership as a biblically based extension of pastoral care and counseling ministry in the church and beyond.

Third, appropriately gifted and qualified lay Christian counselors from the congregation should be screened and carefully selected, using criteria such as spiritual maturity, psychological and emotional stability, love for and interest in people (demonstrated, e.g, by empathy, genuineness, and warmth or respect); appropriate spiritual gifts for helping others (e.g., encouragement); some life experience; previous training or experience in people-helping (helpful but not essential); age, gender, socioeconomic and ethnic/cultural background relevant to the needs of the congregation and the people needing help; availability; teachability; and ability to maintain confidentiality. Usually an interview is conducted with potential lay counselors before selection is made. The selection process can also be open (i.e., anyone can apply to be a lay counselor) or closed (i.e., based on nominations or recommendations by pastors or church leaders). Psychological testing of potential lay counselors should be avoided or only conducted with great caution and with attention to appropriate ethical guidelines (see Tan, 1997).

Fourth, an adequate training program for lay Christian counselors should be provided. Many lay Christian counselor training programs are now available, some of which have been mentioned earlier in this chapter. They vary in length from several hours of basic training in listening and helping skills, to fifty or more hours of training often spread over several weeks, months or a year. Limitations on the number of lay counselors trained at one time varies from just a few to twenty-five or thirty. Training sessions for two to three hours each session are typically held on a weekly or biweekly basis. A training program should include the following (Collins, 1980): basic Bible knowledge relevant to lay helping: counseling or helping skills with opportunities to practice such skills (e.g., through role-playing); understanding common psychological or emotional problems such as depression, anxiety, stress and spiritual dryness; understanding law and ethics as they apply to lay counseling and awareness of the dangers inherent to helping people; and importance and techniques of referral. Lay Christian counselors need to know their limits and limitations and when and how to make good referrals of clients to professionals. Limits to confidentiality should also be discussed with clients and informed consent be obtained from them before starting lay counseling. Such limits usually include situations involving danger to the client or to others, or child or elder abuse.

A good training program for lay Christian counselors will also include the following components: clear and practically oriented lectures; reading assignments; observation of good counseling skills as modeled or demonstrated by the trainer or professional counselor or through watching a videotape; and experiential practice of counseling skills, especially through role-playing.

Finally, programs or ministries in which the trained lay Christian counselors can serve should be developed, organized and implemented. The specific lay Christian counseling programs or ministries that are eventually implemented will depend on the model(s) of lay counseling services chosen for a particular church. Ongoing training and supervision of the active lay Christian counselors should be provided, preferably by a licensed mental health professional, but at least by a pastor or church leader with some experience in people-helping ministries. Weekly or biweekly supervision of the lay counselors, usually in dyads or small groups, should be conducted, with individual supervision available as needed.

Legal advice should be obtained regarding whether malpractice insurance is needed by the lay counselors (see Sandy, 2009) and whether or not they should be called "lay counselors" and the ministry they do "lay counseling," since in some US states licensing laws limit the use of terms such as *counselor* and *counseling* to licensed professional counselors. It may therefore be necessary in such states to use alternative terms such as *lay helping* and *lay helpers* or *lay caregivers*.

Ten guidelines for setting up a lay counseling center. If a formal, organized model for providing lay Christian counseling services is selected for a particular local church, the following ten guidelines for setting up a lay Christian counseling center should prove helpful (adapted from Partridge, 1983):

1. Determine clear objectives for the lay counseling center.

2. Establish the "ethos" or distinctive character of the center by giving it an appropriate name.

3. Carefully select, train and supervise the lay counselors.

4. Arrange for suitable facilities and office space or rooms for the center.

5. Establish the operating hours of the center.

6. Set up a structure within which the center will function, including having a director and a board of reference.

7. Publicize the services of the center.

8. Clarify what services the center will offer, and what it will *not* offer.

9. Carefully consider the financing or funding for the center, and include it in the annual church budget.

10. Determine the affiliation of the center to the church (Tan, 1995, p. 57).

It is usually advisable to start a church lay counseling center modestly. For example, it can initially be open on two or three evenings a week, rather than five days a week. The range of services and times offered can be expanded over time. However, such gradual growth or expansion of a lay counseling center may not be necessary in a large church where staff, finances and facilities are already available and there is great need for lay counseling services. In this case the center might immediately begin functioning on a full-scale basis (Tan, 2002).

TIPS FOR PRACTICAL APPLICATION

The previous section on treatment implementation already offered many practical tips for starting a lay Christian counseling ministry to help people with general psychological problems such as anxiety, depression, and marital and family struggles. Here I will offer a few other suggestions for practical application.

First, some church lay Christian counseling programs limit the number of sessions they offer to clients. For example, First Evangelical Free Church in Fullerton, California, follows a time-limited therapy framework (see Mann & Goldman, 1982) with a ten-session limit. Clients are referred to other professional therapists if they need more than ten sessions. La Canada Presbyterian Church in La Canada, California, also initially offers clients ten sessions of lay Christian counseling in their program, but clients can negotiate with their lay counselors to extend for another ten sessions at a time in appropriate situations. Other church lay counseling programs do not have such limits, although they still often use a relatively short-term counseling model. Flexibility in limits to the number of sessions provided for clients is recommended, because some clients may need more long-term support (including prayer support). Such clients may need to be seen over a year or two, but sessions can be gradually reduced to once a month.

Second, while ethical guidelines are necessary and should be followed for lay Christian counseling to be conducted in an ethical, efficient and effective way, ethical guidelines for professional practice should not be indiscriminately applied to lay counseling (see Tan, 1991, 2002). This is especially true in the case of peer counseling, which is a particular example of lay counseling with peers involving a certain degree of friendship counseling. Hence, professional caution about avoiding dual-role relationships with clients does not fully apply to such peer or lay counseling situations.

Finally, while lay Christian counseling is usually provided through a formal, organized model such as a church lay counseling center, or through an informal, organized model such as Stephen Ministry, it can also be made more widely available through informal and more spontaneous channels. Such channels include small groups and fellowships, men's and women's ministries, and youth ministries, where leaders informally and spontaneously provide lay Christian counseling or caregiving on a regular basis. Their informal people-helping ministries can be strengthened and encouraged by providing these leaders with some basic training in lay Christian counseling skills, even if they do not serve officially as lay counselors in their church lay counseling program.

CONCLUSION

Lay Christian counseling for general psychological and emotional problems is an important ministry in the local church and other parachurch contexts. As needs significantly increase for mental health services worldwide and as cost-cutting measures in healthcare and benefits drastically reduce mental health coverage in insurance plans in the United States, lay counseling services and ministries will continue to mushroom. Lay Christian counseling will be a crucial answer to such needs and therefore warrants further development as well as more and better outcome research to strengthen the empirical base supporting its effectiveness or efficacy. It is presently considered a probably efficacious treatment for general psychological problems (Hook et al., 2010). It is hoped that it will become an empirically supported treatment or an evidence-based intervention in the years to come as more controlled outcome studies on its efficacy are conducted, especially focusing on specific lay Christian counseling approaches.

Professional therapists, including professional Christian therapists, also need to know more about lay Christian counseling approaches. Many of their clients may have been exposed to such lay Christian counseling that can significantly impact clients' expectations for integration of Christian faith in professional therapy. At the very least, professional therapists need to assess their clients' previous lay counseling experiences and their current expectations for integration in professional therapy (Garzon et al., 2009).

REFERENCES

Ali, B. S., Rahbar, M. H., Naeem, S., & Gul, A. (2003). The effectiveness of counseling on anxiety and depression by minimally trained counselors: A randomized controlled trial. *American Journal of Psychotherapy, 57,* 324-36.

Anderson, N. T. (2000a). *Victory over the darkness: Realizing the power of your identity in Christ* (2nd ed.). Ventura, CA: Regal Books.

Anderson, N. T. (2000b). *The bondage breaker* (2nd ed.). Ventura, CA: Regal Books.

Anderson, N. T. (2003). *Discipleship counseling: The complete guide to helping others walk in freedom and grow in Christ.* Ventura, CA: Regal Books.

Anderson, N. T. (2004). *The steps to freedom in Christ.* Ventura, CA: Gospel Light.

Atkins, D. C., & Christensen, A. (2001). Is professional training worth the bother? A review of the impact of psychological training on client outcome. *Australian Psychologist, 36*(2), 1-9.

Barlow, D. H. (2004). Psychological treatments. *American Psychologist, 59*, 869-78.

Backus, W. (1985). *Telling the truth to troubled people.* Minneapolis, MN: Bethany.

Berman, J. S., & Norton, N. C. (1985). Does professional training make a therapist more effective? *Psychological Bulletin, 98*, 4017.

Beutler, L. E., & Kendall, P. C. (1995). Introduction to the special section: The case for training in the provision of psychological therapy. *Journal of Consulting and Clinical Psychology, 63*, 179-81.

Bickman, L. (1999). Practice makes perfect and other myths about mental health services. *American Psychologist, 54*, 965-78.

Boan, D. M., & Owens, T. (1985). Peer ratings of lay counselor skill as related to client satisfaction. *Journal of Psychology and Christianity, 4*(1), 79-81.

Bright, J. I., Baker, K. D., & Neimeyer, R. A. (1999). Professional and paraprofessional group treatments for depression: A comparison of cognitive-behavioral and mutual support interventions. *Journal of Consulting and Clinical Psychology, 67*, 491-501.

Carey, M. P., & Burish, T. G. (1987). Providing relaxation training to cancer chemotherapy patients: A comparison of three delivery techniques. *Journal of Consulting and Clinical Psychology, 55*, 732-37.

Christensen, A., & Jacobson, N. S. (1994). Who (or what) can do psychotherapy: The status and challenge of nonprofessional therapies. *Psychological Science, 5*, 814.

Collins, G. R. (1980). Lay counseling within the local church. *Leadership, 7*(4), 78-86.

Crabb, L. J., Jr. (1977). *Effective biblical counseling.* Grand Rapids, MI: Zondervan.

Durlak, J. A. (1979). Comparative effectiveness of paraprofessional and professional helpers. *Psychological Bulletin, 86*, 8092.

Durlak, J. A. (1981). Evaluating comparative studies of paraprofessional and professional helpers: A reply to Nietzel and Fisher. *Psychological Bulletin, 89*, 56669.

Egan, G. (1990a). *Exercises in helping skills* (4th ed.). Monterey, CA: Brooks/Cole.

Egan, G. (1990b). *The skilled helper* (4th ed.). Monterey, CA: Brooks/Cole.

Garzon, F., & Burkett, L. (2002). Healing of memories: Models, research, future directions. *Journal of Psychology and Christianity, 21*, 42-49.

Garzon, F., & Tilley, K. (2009). Do lay Christian counseling approaches work? What we currently know. *Journal of Psychology and Christianity, 28*, 130-40.

Garzon, F., Worthington, E. L., Jr., Tan, S.-Y., & Worthington, R. K. (2009). Lay Christian counseling and client expectations for integration in therapy. *Journal of Psychology and Christianity, 28*, 113-20.

Harris, J. (1985). Non-professionals as effective helpers for pastoral counselors. *Journal of Pastoral Care, 39,* 165-72.

Hattie, J. A., Sharpley, C. F., & Rogers, H. J. (1984). Comparative effectiveness of professional and paraprofessional helpers. *Psychological Bulletin, 95,* 53441.

Haugk, K. (1984). *Christian caregiving: A way of life.* Minneapolis, MN: Augsburg.

Holland, J. (2007). Solution-focused lay pastoral care. *Journal of Family and Community Ministries, 21,* 22-30.

Hook, J. N., Worthington, E. L., Jr., Davis, D. E., Jennings, D. J., II., Gartner, A. L., & Hook, J. P. (2010). Empirically supported religious and spiritual therapies. *Journal of Clinical Psychology, 66,* 46-72.

Huppert, J. D., Bufka, L. F., Barlow, D. H., Gorman, J. M., Shear, M. K., & Woods, S. W. (2001). Therapists, therapist variables, and cognitive-behavioral therapy outcome in a multicenter trial for panic disorder. *Journal of Consulting and Clinical Psychology, 69,* 747-55.

Hurding, R. F. (1995). Pathways to wholeness: Christian journeying in a postmodern age. *Journal of Psychology and Christianity, 14,* 293-305.

Jernigan, R. C. (1989). *The effectiveness of a local church lay Christian counselor training program: A controlled study.* Unpublished doctoral dissertation, Graduate School of Psychology, Fuller Theological Seminary, Pasadena, California.

Jernigan, R., Tan, S.-Y., & Gorsuch, R. L. (November, 1988). *The effectiveness of a local church lay Christian counselor training program: A controlled study.* Paper presented at the International Congress on Christian Counseling, Atlanta, Georgia.

Kendall, P. C., Reber, M., McLeer, S., Epps, J., & Ronan, K. R. (1990). Cognitive-behavioral treatment of conduct-disordered children. *Cognitive Therapy and Research, 14,* 279-97.

Klein, D. N., Schwartz, J. E., Santiago, N. J., Vivian, D., Vocisano, C., Castonguay, L. G., et al. (2003). Therapeutic alliance in depression treatment: Controlling for prior change and patient characteristics. *Journal of Consulting and Clinical Psychology, 71,* 997-1006.

Lambert, M. J., & Bergin, A. E. (1994). The effectiveness of psychotherapy. In A. E. Bergin & S. L. Garfield (Eds.), *Handbook of psychotherapy and behavior change* (4th ed., pp. 143-89). New York: Wiley.

Mann, J., & Goldman, R. (1982). *A casebook of time-limited psychotherapy.* New York: McGraw-Hill.

Martin, A. A. (1998). *The effectiveness of Christian adolescent peer counselor training:*

A controlled study. Unpublished doctoral dissertation, Graduate School of Psychology, Fuller Theological Seminary, Pasadena, California.

Neuner, F., Onyut, P. L., Ertl, V., Odenwald, M., Schauer, E., & Elbert, T. (2008). Treatment of posttraumatic stress disorder by trained lay counselors in an African refugee settlement: A randomized controlled trial. *Journal of Consulting and Clinical Psychology, 76,* 686-94.

Nietzel, N. T., & Fisher, S. G. (1981). Effectiveness of professional and paraprofessional helpers: A comment on Durlak. *Psychological Bulletin, 89,* 55565.

Norcross, J. C. (Ed.). (2002). *Psychotherapy relationships that work.* New York: Oxford University Press.

Partridge, T. J. (1983). Ten considerations in establishing a Christian counseling centre. *The Christian Counsellor's Journal, 4*(4), 31-33.

Sandford, J. L., & Sandford, M. (1992). *A comprehensive guide to deliverance and inner healing.* Grand Rapids, MI: Chosen Books.

Sandford, J., & Sandford, P. (1982). *The transformation of the inner man.* Tulsa, OK: Victory House.

Sandy, J. L. (2009). *Church lay counseling risk management guidebook.* Fort Wayne, IN: Brotherhood Mutual Insurance Company.

Satir, V. M., & Baldwin, M. (1983). *Satir step by step.* Palo Alto, CA: Science and Behavior Books.

Smith, E. M. (2002). *Healing life's deepest hurts.* Ann Arbor, MI: Vine Books.

Smith, E. M. (2007). *Theophostic prayer ministry: Basic training seminar manual.* Campbellsville, KY: New Creation Publishing.

Sobey, F. (1970). *The nonprofessional revolution in mental health.* New York: Columbia University Press.

Stein, D. M., & Lambert, M. J. (1995). Graduate training in psychotherapy: Are therapy outcomes enhanced? *Journal of Consulting and Clinical Psychology, 63,* 18296.

Sturkie, J., & Tan, S.-Y. (1992). *Peer counseling in youth groups: Equipping your kids to help each other.* Grand Rapids, MI: Youth Specialties/Zondervan.

Tan, S.-Y. (1991). *Lay counseling: Equipping Christians for a helping ministry.* Grand Rapids, MI: Zondervan.

Tan, S.-Y. (1992). Development and supervision of paraprofessional counselors. In L. VandeCreek, S. Knapp, & T. L. Jackson (Eds.), *Innovations in clinical practice: A sourcebook* (Vol. 11, pp. 431-40). Sarasota, FL: Professional Resource Press.

Tan, S.-Y. (1995). Starting a lay counseling ministry. *Christian Counseling Today 3*(1), 56-57.

Tan, S.-Y. (1997). The role of the psychologist in paraprofessional helping. *Professional Psychology: Research and Practice, 28,* 368-72.

Tan, S.-Y. (2002). Lay helping: The whole church in soul care ministry. In T. Clinton & G. Ohlschlager (Eds.), *Competent Christian counseling* (Vol. 1, pp. 424-36, 759-62). Colorado Springs, CO: WaterBrook Press.

Tan, S.-Y. (2007). Use of prayer and Scripture in cognitive-behavioral therapy. *Journal of Psychology and Christianity, 26,* 101-11.

Tan, S.-Y. (2011). *Counseling and psychotherapy: A Christian perspective.* Grand Rapid, MI: Baker Academic.

Tan, S.-Y., & Ortberg, J. (2004). *Coping with depression* (2nd ed.). Grand Rapids, MI: Baker.

Toh, Y. M., & Tan, S.-Y. (1997). The effectiveness of church-based lay counselors: A controlled outcome study. *Journal of Psychology and Christianity, 16,* 260-67.

Toh, Y. M., Tan, S.-Y., Osburn, C. D., & Faber, D. E. (1994). The evaluation of a church-based lay counseling program: Some preliminary data. *Journal of Psychology and Christianity, 13,* 270-75.

Walters, R. P. (1987). A survey of client satisfaction in a lay counseling program. *Journal of Psychology and Christianity, 6*(2), 62-69.

4

Christian Devotional Meditation for Anxiety

Fernando Garzon

Christian clients and psychotherapists alike generally believe in the importance of Bible study, prayer and church attendance for developing a relationship with God and growing spiritually. Many, however, are not aware of the rich Judeo-Christian heritage of devotional meditation that supplements these disciplines through encouraging a quiet receptivity to God's Word and his presence. As early as the third century, the desert fathers and mothers described these practices (see Burton-Christie, 1993). Christian devotional meditation (CDM) therefore remains a valuable yet little known resource for Christian-accommodative counseling and psychotherapy.

Over the last 15 years, the evangelical Christian community has experienced a resurgence of interest in Christian spiritual formation (e.g., Ortberg, 2002) and the spiritual disciplines (e.g., Foster, 1998). Likewise, counselors and psychotherapists have considered the role of spirituality in treatment (e.g., Aten & Leach, 2009) and spiritual direction as a potential component or adjunct to counseling and psychotherapy for appropriately religious clients (e.g., Tan, 2003).

Nevertheless, the amount of empirical and applied literature on how to utilize CDM with clients is very small. Consequently, Christian psychotherapists and counselors may be unaware of this important accommodative resource that may enhance treatment motivation, compliance and outcome when working with appropriately religious Christian clients who suffer from common clinical conditions such as anxiety disorders.

This chapter therefore provides introductory information regarding

CDM in the counseling and psychotherapy context. It examines the empirical literature supporting CDM's application in the counseling and psychotherapy context and describes three specific CDM strategies potentially useful for Christian clients suffering from anxiety conditions. Finally, a case study illustrates these strategies with an anxious client.

DEFINING CHRISTIAN DEVOTIONAL MEDITATION

CDM involves cultivating intimacy with the living God. It can take a variety of forms, sometimes conceptualized as contemplative prayer in addition to meditation. Thus the terms CDM and *contemplative prayer* are sometimes used interchangeably. Since CDM has a rich heritage spanning the two thousand years of church history, it crosses Roman Catholic, Orthodox, Protestant and evangelical Christian lines (Benner, 2010). This expansive history has led to numerous definitions and CDM forms that are well beyond the length constraints of this chapter to explore fully. Thus, for the purposes of this chapter, CDM may be defined as a variety of strategies designed to enhance focused attention on God, Scripture or oneself with the intent of deepening one's relationship with the Lord, cultivating emotional healing, and/or growing in love toward one's neighbor and oneself.

CHRISTIAN DEVOTIONAL MEDITATION RESEARCH

Few experimental studies exist specifically on CDM; however, interest is growing. Carlson, Bacaseta and Simanton (1988) compared the effects of CDM with the effects of progressive muscle relaxation and a waiting list control condition. Thirty-six Christian participants were divided into the three groups. The CDM group utilized a strategy similar to the Bible passage version of scriptural truth meditation described later in this chapter. Their particular focus was Psalm 23. Both treatment groups were asked to practice twenty minutes a day for two weeks. Results indicated the CDM group had significantly lower anxiety, less anger and reduced muscle tension compared to the other two groups.

In 2005, Wachholtz and Pargament randomly assigned eighty-four college students into a spiritual meditation, secular meditation or relaxation training condition. The spiritual meditation strategy was identical to the scriptural truth meditation (character of God version) described later in this chapter. Sixty-eight participants completed the investigation. The researchers asked participants to practice their meditation for twenty minutes a day for two weeks. Participants then returned to the lab, practiced their meditation for twenty minutes and completed a pain tolerance activity. Anxiety, mood and spiritual outcomes were also measured. The spiritual meditation group reported significantly lower anxiety, more positive mood, more positive spiritual outcomes and demonstrated increased pain tolerance compared to the other two groups.

In 2008, Wachholtz and Pargament expanded their research design, comparing the effects of spiritual meditation, concentrative internally focused secular meditation, externally focused secular meditation and progressive muscle relaxation on eighty-three meditation naïve college students who frequently suffered migraine headaches. The spiritual meditation strategy utilized in their study was identical to the scriptural truth meditation (character of God version) described later in this chapter. Measures of anxiety, negative affect, spiritual well-being, pain tolerance, headache-related self-efficacy and frequency of migraine headaches were given pre- and post-treatment. Results indicated the spiritual meditation group significantly decreased anxiety, negative affect, frequency of migraine headaches, and increased pain tolerance, headache-related self-efficacy, and existential well-being compared to the other experimental conditions. Wachholtz and Pargament concluded that "the spiritual component appears to have a unique additive effect that enhances the ability of meditation to decrease negative affect and anxiety. . . . The addition of an explicitly spiritual component enhanced this effect compared to migraineurs using non-spiritual techniques" (pp. 362-63).

Empirical Status

Only a small body of literature explores CDM. Two studies done by the same researchers (Wachholtz & Pargament, 2005, 2008) represent strategies identical to specific CDM methods and one study done by a different researcher (Carlson et al., 1988) explores a different CDM method. None of these studies has been done on clinical populations, and none has included short- or long-term post-treatment follow-ups. All of them, however, suggest an additive effect for incorporating a client's faith into the meditation process. Given these findings, one can cautiously conclude that preliminary evidence supports CDM as a probably efficacious, probably specific Christian counseling strategy. This preliminary finding must be confirmed with randomized control group or comparative group studies on clinical populations and include short- and long-term post-treatment outcome assessment. Current findings, however, do justify the importance of introducing Christian psychotherapists and counselors to specific CDM interventions.

THREE CHRISTIAN DEVOTIONAL MEDITATION STRATEGIES

Three strategies are offered to enhance the work of psychotherapists and counselors with appropriately religious clients: scriptural truth meditation (STM), scriptural drama meditation (SDM) and Christ-centered present moment awareness (CCPMA). All of these may be considered introductory forms of CDM. For more advanced information on CDM, see Benner (2010) and Merton (1958/1999, 1961/2007).

Scriptural truth meditation. Scriptural truth meditation (STM) involves focused attention on an important truth related to the character of God (STM-G) or focused attention on a short passage from the Bible (STM-B). Psychotherapists can train clients in one of these meditations in about ten minutes of session time. Once a client knows one version, the other may be learned in less time.

Scriptural truth meditation—character of God. In STM-G, the Christian counselor orients the client to CDM principles. The client is not studying truth in an analytical manner, though such study is certainly a worthwhile part of Christian growth. Rather, the client is invited to receive the depth of the truth involved in a short phrase. Such focused attention encourages the phrase's meaning to become deeply embedded in the client's heart rather than just the mind. Often, a handout with a variety of phrases is useful to help the client make a selection (for an example, see handout 1 at the end of this chapter). Many of these short phrases are especially pertinent to anxiety-related conditions. For example, the short phrase "God is in control" may encourage a loosening of the client's need to maintain control of situations, or "God is love" may reduce self-condemnation and increase self-acceptance. The selection of the phrase must be a collaborative effort between the client and psychotherapist. The client should also be encouraged to develop her own phrase that was not part of the original list if so desired. Once the phrase is selected, the Christian counselor encourages the client to slow down, quiet himself and let himself prepare to receive the message embedded in the phrase. Prayer often starts the process (led by the client or counselor), asking the Lord to open the client's heart to receive God's truth at a deeper level.

Many aspects influence the contemplative tone of the meditation. The Christian psychotherapist asks the client to sit in a comfortable position, often with legs uncrossed and hands on the lap. The therapist should consider whether the client has a disability or a cultural background that would make the typical posture non-verbally threatening and counter-productive. Both the Christian psychotherapist and the client make sure all communication devices (cell phone, iPod, etc.) are turned off. The counselor informs the client that while this meditation will focus on a short phrase, it is not uncommon for the mind to wander away from the phrase. Indeed, this is expected and normal. The psychotherapist encourages the client to gently bring herself back to the phrase rather than to judge herself harshly. The concept of grace and our dependence on it may be used with a perfectionistic client to help her relax from any self-critical attitudes.

After passage selection and prayer, the counselor encourages the client to take a deep breath in and to breathe out quietly repeating the phrase. This is done several times, each time with the client saying the phrase as he exhales. After a couple of minutes, the client is invited to begin breathing normally, shifting to repeating the phrase mentally each time he breathes out. When it appears the client is relaxed and focused, the counselor suggests the client continue pondering the phrase, repeating it now at his leisure, especially when he finds his mind wandering. The psychotherapist monitors the client for any signs of nonverbal distress, such as position shifting, coughing, scratching, tense facial expressions, and tense body postures. If these occur, the Christian psychotherapist asks the client to share his experience. After a few more minutes, the counselor should gently bring the client's awareness back to the room and debrief with the client.

Frequently, the client will report an increased sense of relaxation, peace and a deeper awareness of how this character trait of God applies to her personal situation. Deeper self-awareness may also occur, such as realizing behaviors, attitudes or psychological defenses that impede receiving this truth about God. Painful memories may sometimes surface. Occasionally, the client will report feeling sleepy. When insomnia is a component of an anxious client's presentation, the counselor may suggest practicing STM at bedtime to take advantage of this effect. Otherwise, the sleepiness may be normalized as indicative of a need to slow down and rest in general. If the STM-G experience was mixed or negative for the client, the psychotherapist should explore carefully any concerns. The case study in this chapter demonstrates this strategy. A handout to facilitate client training is included at the end of this chapter.

Scriptural truth meditation—biblical passage. In scriptural truth meditations focusing on a Bible passage, similar principles and CDM administration procedures apply. The client should select a passage that may be repeated in one exhale (for example, "The Lord is my shepherd," from Psalm 23:1), or the client may choose a small passage that is broken down into two exhaling breaths. For instance, the client may take a breath in and then exhale with the words, "Come to me, all you who are weary and burdened," followed by another breath in and then exhaling with "and I will give you rest" (Mt 11:28). See handout 2 at the end of this chapter for a potential client information sheet.

Scriptural drama meditation. In the sixteenth century, St. Ignatius of Loyola developed a series of spiritual exercises designed to help participants deepen their experience of Christ's love and to empower them to follow the will of God daily (Fleming, 1978). St. Ignatius used meditations that involved the application of the senses and the imagination to immerse oneself into Gospel stories and parables. The person becomes a participant in the biblical drama, transforming Scripture into a multisensory experience (Endean, 1990; Lonsdale, 1990). Many denominations today apply these exercises in the form of thirty-day retreats, eight-day retreats (or shorter) or over the course of several months within the midst of daily life (Cook, 2004). Having a spiritual director is a common component. Scriptural drama meditation (SDM) therefore applies some of the principles of Ignatius's spiritual exercises in a Christian counseling and psychotherapy context.

The counselor and client carefully select a biblical passage (for example, a Gospel story, such as the woman caught in adultery, or a parable, such as the prodigal son). They discuss the story and the psychotherapist invites the client to enter the story as a "fly on the wall" or to take the role of a character in the story using imagination. The client then "relives" the story through "seeing, hearing, smelling, and physically feeling or touching all that is going on in the Scriptural scene" (Cook, 2004, p. 177). After debriefing, the client may take the role of another character in the Gospel story to gain further insight.

Garzon (2005) provides further detail on SDM in the Christian psychotherapy and counseling context. At the beginning of the meditation, the counselor and client pray together to invite the Lord's covering and healing activity in the entire meditation. Sometimes the scene is slightly altered contextually to fit the client's gender or other circumstance. Often when initially teaching the client this form of CDM, the psychotherapist asks the client to close her eyes and take some deep breaths to relax. The counselor's key role is to provide vivid verbal description of the scenes related to the story. Sometimes the therapist asks open-ended questions to the client about how a specific character was feeling, and at other times the counselor may suggest feelings. Near the end of the meditation, the psychotherapist encourages the client to converse silently or out loud with the Lord about anything discovered in the SDM process, and the SDM concludes with debriefing. The Christian counselor connects the SDM to the client's history and goals as they both consider the merits of further SDM activities.

Christ-centered present moment awareness. Christ-centered present moment awareness (CCPMA) may be conceptualized clinically as a Christian accommodation to empirically supported mindfulness meditation strategies. In short, CCPMA places such present moment awareness in the context of a relationship with God. Such a context invites the client to become aware of God's presence, love and purpose in the present moment, in addition to recognizing ongoing self experience. CCPMA may be useful for clients experiencing anxiety because it deepens their sense of God's ongoing presence with them in their daily lives. It also is useful in detecting and processing negative God images.

In introducing CCPMA meditation, cognitive mindfulness principles

(Kabat-Zinn, 1990) will be reviewed briefly. Many Christian counselors and psychotherapists have some familiarity with these principles through the burgeoning literature and training programs on mindfulness and therapeutic approaches that incorporate these strategies. Second, a mindfulness exercise adapted from Roemer and Orsillo (2009) will be described, and then CCPMA will be explained in detail. While CCPMA bears similarities with mindfulness, it is also very distinctive.

Mindfulness principles include (a) increasing awareness of internal experience (thoughts, feelings, images, bodily sensations) and external experience (sights, sounds, smells, etc.), (b) nonjudgmentally observing one's experience, (c) cultivating compassion toward internal experiences that are difficult, (d) developing openness and curiosity toward experience and (e) returning to present moment awareness when drifting into daydreams or fantasies (Kabat-Zinn, 2005).

Roemer and Orsillo (2009, pp. 119-24) apply mindfulness through asking the client to place herself in a comfortable seated position with her eyes closed. The client is asked to notice the sounds in the room, her body posture, and how her body feels in the chair. Areas of body tension might also be observed. The client is then encouraged to focus on her breathing, noting its rhythmic nature and how the air feels going into the nose and then out. This relaxed focus on the breath is maintained for a few minutes, with the psychotherapist reminding the client occasionally to bring her attention gently back to the breath when she notices it wandering. The psychotherapist then slowly brings her awareness and attention back to the room and external stimuli, processing the experience with her.

Unlike Roemer and Orsillo's (2009) mindfulness meditation, CCPMA is relationally triadic, involving the client's experience of God, the counselor, and himself in the present moment. Below is an example CCPMA script. Ellipses indicate pauses.

> I'd like you to sit comfortably with your eyes closed and your feet on the floor. Notice the sounds in the room [name examples]. . . . Begin to turn your awareness to your body. Notice how you're sitting in the chair, that your hands are folded. . . . Feel your feet in your shoes pressing against the floor, your hips against the chair [give other examples as needed]. . . . Just be aware of your experience, what is happening right now in this moment. . . . While

you're observing this experience, I invite you to become aware of God's presence with us in this room today, that he's here with us and wants to be with you in your experience. [Carefully observe the client's nonverbal behavior. Two things may occur: (1) if the client shows signs of increased tension, inquire as to the client's experience. This may lead to valuable insights regarding negative God images, (2) if the client appears to be responding positively continue with the remainder of the script.] I invite you to yield all you are experiencing to God in this moment. . . . Let go in his presence, releasing your tensions, thoughts and worries into his hands. [At times, the counselor may sense a Scripture is appropriate to encourage this release of stress and worry, such as Matthew 11:28-30, "Come unto me, all you who are weak and heavy laden, and I shall give you rest."] Just "be" with God. . . . When you are ready, return your focus to the room.

The Christian psychotherapist then debriefs with the client about his experience. If the experience has been positive, the therapist may give the client a copy of the script and invite him to practice this form of meditation as homework. If the experience was negative, exploration of the discomfort may provide clues about negative God images, uncomfortable affects, defense mechanisms and trauma symptomology.

Other forms of CCPMA may also be useful. For example, an abbreviated version of CCPMA combines deep breathing with a short prayer to be applied during an anxiety-producing experience. The client takes a deep breath in, applies present moment awareness principles, and slowly exhales a prayer, such as "Lord, I give you control."

CHRISTIAN DEVOTIONAL MEDITATION IMPLEMENTATION

Several factors impact the application of CDM strategies in Christian counseling and psychotherapy. These include the counselor's own practice of CDM, detailed attention to the client's nonverbal cues during CDM, the anxious client's diagnostic characteristics, the anxious client's faith characteristics, the ability to handle common client concerns and the ability to provide resource materials such as books, videos or Internet sites for further CDM development.

CDM is caught as much as it is taught. Counselors and psychotherapists who have incorporated these strategies into their own lives often reflect a peace and spiritual depth that the client senses. This in and of itself can attract a client toward these methods and reduces the chance that the client will see CDM as an abstract array of wellness techniques instead of a means of cultivating a vibrant relationship with the living God that is healing.

Given that most clinicians have training in behavioral relaxation techniques, many previously learned skills cross over to CDM. One especially important skill relates to the ability to monitor subtle nonverbal cues during the CDM process. A cough, change in posture, facial tensing, scratching or other behavior may suggest client discomfort. For example, as noted in CCPMA, a client might have a negative reaction to the thought that God is present with him during the present moment. Such negative reactions are critical to explore in order to assess for negative God images or experiences. Nonverbal cues provide important clues as to when such reactions are occurring.

The client's particular anxiety disorder can lead to adjustments. Since much research is needed on CDM in the Christian psychotherapy setting, the following recommendations are based on the author's own clinical experience. Clients with sexual abuse histories or PTSD may experience flashbacks during a CCPMA meditation. When this occurs, the therapist should shift to bringing the client's awareness back into the room to process the memory, flashback or emergent symptoms. For this reason, Christian counselors should utilize scriptural truth meditation rather than the less directive, more unstructured CCPMA form of meditation at the beginning of work with a trauma client. Only in the later stages of work, after significant traumatic material has been processed, should CCPMA be considered with PTSD clients. Scripture drama meditation may be used cautiously with mild to moderate symptom-level trauma clients. Sometimes through SDM these clients experience powerful images of God's presence that are very healing. For generalized anxiety disorder, all the CDM strategies described may be useful. Panic disorder clients likewise may benefit from each strategy. CCPMA principles may facilitate processing panic attack triggers. The client's motivation to go through interoceptive exposure procedures increases. For obsessive compulsive clients, the application of CCPMA principles may increase motivation to go through exposure with response prevention strategies.

The client's particular religious characteristics are important in determining the viability of CDM strategies; therefore, spiritual assessment and accurate treatment planning are critical. Aten and Leach (2009) provide a wide variety of strategies useful for these endeavors starting from intake and proceeding throughout the course of psychotherapy. Based on clinical experience, the author would add the following assessment observations specific to CDM with devout evangelical Christian clients. Those below the age of thirty-five appear to have fewer reservations about CDM than those above this age. Perhaps this is due to their exposure to stress management techniques and yoga as a part of their educational process compared to older age cohorts. Denominational variation also occurs. Clients from fundamentalist or Pentecostal/charismatic denominations may express more concerns than clients from other denominations. When clients do express worries, these questions tend to focus on two issues: the usage of imagery and the danger of demonic influence.

For those with imagery concerns, scriptural drama meditation might cause more hesitation than scriptural truth meditation, which focuses on the verbal content in a biblical passage or a facet of God's character. Foster (1998) provides helpful advice in addressing these concerns:

> Jesus himself taught in this manner, making constant appeal to the imagination. . . . There is good reason for concern [about using the imagination though], for the imagination, like all our faculties, has participated in the Fall. But just as we can believe that God can take our reason (fallen as it is) and sanctify it and use it for his good purposes, so we believe he can sanctify the imagination and use it for his good purposes. (pp. 25-26)

Christian counselors can also point out how the Bible uses imagery in many passages. Christ's parables and the psalms (such as Ps 23) tap into one's imaginative capabilities in order to convey deep truths about God. Finally, the psychotherapist might also appeal to the client's daily experience of using imagery without realizing it. When one thinks of an airplane, for example, a mental image of a plane accompanies the verbal content "airplane." Should the client continue to have concerns after this processing, alternative CDM forms besides scriptural drama meditation should be used.

Sometimes in CCPMA, clients will express fears that they are exposing themselves to demonic influence if they relax and experience uncomfortable emotional content. The counselor may discuss the believer's authority in Christ and assure the client that CCPMA will begin with prayer asking for God's covering and protection over the entire process. This often resolves such issues.

With all CDM forms, some clients fear the psychotherapist is asking them to empty their minds, which they believe might expose them to demonic influence. In CCPMA, the Christian counselor should clarify that, unlike many eastern meditation strategies, the goal is not to empty one's mind of all content, but to become aware of emotional and mental experience while also recognizing Christ's presence in the moment. Scriptural truth meditation versions likewise do not seek to empty the mind.

Numerous resources exist for helping clients (and therapists) learn more about CDM. Often CDM is placed within the Christian spiritual formation literature as one of the spiritual disciplines. For evangelical Christians, the works of Richard Foster (e.g., 1998, 2002) and John Ortberg (e.g., 2002) are often good introductory points for this literature. The organization *Renovare* (www.renovare.org) provides a variety of books (contemporary and classic), media and other training resources about Christian spiritual formation. As noted previously, works by Merton (1958/1999, 1961/2007) and Benner (2010) expand on this chapter's introduction to CDM. Since CDM may be foreign to many counselors, a concrete example will illustrate CDM's application in treatment.

Case Study

Charles, a fifty-four-year-old, married, white man affiliated with the Pentecostal church, was attending an undergraduate nursing program as a change from a longtime career as a cook. He described primary concerns with longstanding generalized anxiety symptoms (e.g., tension, worry, insomnia and concentration difficulties) currently related to the stressors involved in obtaining a BSN degree. He reported no suicidal, homicidal or substance-abuse issues. I saw Charles in a church outpatient counseling center that utilized a short-term treatment model (ten sessions maximum). While I used many strategies in his care, the information below focuses primarily on the application of CDM strategies.

Charles grew up as the second-born child of a large intact farming family in the Midwest. He had five brothers and four sisters. He described his father as a hardworking, "stern" disciplinarian who seldom showed affection. Charles saw his mother as more supportive and caring. Neither parent used alcohol or drugs; however, the economic pressures of farm life generated much stress in the household. Charles dropped out of school in ninth grade to help out. At the time of counseling, his father and mother were still alive and in relatively good health for their age.

Charles met his wife when he was eighteen years old and moved east to be closer to her family. He worked a series of odd jobs while completing his GED and eventually started cooking in restaurants as his main source of income. His wife worked as a janitor and they had two children, now adults. He reported that his marriage was happy overall, with normal problems and conflicts.

Charles described his Pentecostal faith as a major coping resource throughout his life. Scripture reading, prayer and church attendance were common activities. He derived his primary social support from friendships developed in church. Through his faith that "all things are possible" and encouragement from his church, Charles decided to pursue his career change to nursing. He had been interested in the medical field since he was a young man.

Some elements of Charles's faith experience, however, were not so positive. Charles felt like he "never measured up" to God's standards. He felt bad about worrying so much ("I should not worry as a child of God") and he set unrealistically high standards for himself. He was suspicious of psychotherapy, which led to his decision to seek Christian services at a church-related counseling center.

I conceptualized Charles's distress through a meanings-system framework (Park & Slattery, 2009) that applied acceptance and commitment therapy principles (Hayes, Strosahl & Wilson, 1999) into treatment. Briefly, Charles's self-critical evaluations, experiential avoidance of anxiety, and worry prevented effective problem solving, stress management, and living a life focused on his core values. His faith supplied an important meaning framework which encouraged his pursuit of a nursing career and simultaneously created a high mistrust of psychology. He wanted Christian counseling to incorporate his faith as a key component. CDM strategies were a helpful part of reducing his struggle with anxiety, minimizing the impact of negative self-evaluations, decreasing worry and increasing his sleep. These aspects are explored below.

Given Charles's nursing interest, I framed his struggle with worry as a brain-based neurological process, a concept he quickly grasped. This created some emotional distance and allowed him to examine worry as a meta-cognitive process. I invited him to consider whether his attempts to "stand in Christ" by using Scripture to combat his worry-based thoughts were working well. He readily agreed they were not. Reframing "standing in Christ" as the ability to live a life consistent with his core values no matter what his mind was doing (worrying, self-criticizing, etc.) allowed Charles to consider an alternative strategy. He began to see worry and anxiety as automatic, unfolding processes to which his brain automatically defaulted under stress.

During the initial sessions, I also explained CDM principles. I decided to suggest Christ-centered present moment awareness in the third session. While CCPMA normally takes place after practice with other CDM strategies, Charles's grasp of his experience as an unfolding brain process and my sense of an inner prompting from the Lord led me to try this strategy cautiously.

Similar to the script suggested above in the CCPMA section, I asked Charles to make himself comfortable in his chair, close his eyes, and focus on his bodily and mental experience. After a few minimal prompts, Charles appeared noticeably relaxed and attentive to his bodily experience, so I transitioned to the second phase of the meditation, God-awareness. "While you're noticing your experience, I want you to become aware of God's presence in the room with us today. In the midst of all your thoughts, feelings and concerns, God is here with us right in this moment, [right here] with you." Charles's nonverbal behavior suggested peace and calm so I continued. "Perhaps in this moment, you can just rest in his presence, releasing your tension and worries. . . . The Scripture says, 'Come unto me all who are weak and heavy laden, and I will give you rest.

Take my yoke upon you and learn of me, for I am meek and lowly in heart, and you shall find rest for your soul' (Mt 11:28-30). Let's just sit for a moment in his presence and rest." After a minute, I asked Charles what he was experiencing.

"It's strange in a way. I find myself deeply aware of God's presence here. I found myself drifting to how my day normally goes. I get up, have my quiet time with God, and then I get caught up in the swirl of the day's activities. I don't have a sense of God with me throughout the day. I get all caught up in this weight of stuff." As Charles continued sharing, I felt led to introduce some principles from scriptural drama meditation into the exercise.

"Charles, I wonder if you can allow a 'faith picture' to emerge in your experience now, perhaps a mental image related to the Scripture I just quoted, perhaps something else that describes what your relationship with the Lord feels like."

After a pause, Charles stated, "I see myself standing with a yoke on, but Jesus is not in the yoke with me. He's standing in front of me, with his arms outstretched, inviting me to come to him. I want to come to him, but I feel stuck. I feel like my feet can't move on the ground toward him." I encouraged Charles not to condemn himself for this sense of stuckness, but to be open to the Spirit and learn from it. After a few moments, we ended the meditation and processed the potential meaning of this image. Charles verbalized a sense of responsibility and self-blame for not doing enough for God. He felt this contributed to some of the feeling of being stuck, yet he also noted that Jesus' invitation toward him was warm and caring rather than judgmental. He had not anticipated this.

After the meditation, Charles expressed interest in incorporating CCPMA as a part of his morning devotions. The next week when I inquired as to how these meditations had gone, he reported another imagery experience. "I saw myself lying down on the ground, flat and motionless, like I had no life. I saw Jesus walk up to me, kneel down and stroke me on the cheek." Charles interpreted this experience as Christ's encouragement that he was present with him in his struggles. He noted that Christ would move toward him even when he couldn't move toward Christ. The session continued and toward the end I asked Charles if he would like to learn another CDM strategy. He consented and I introduced him to scriptural truth meditation using the handout at the end of this chapter (see handout 1). In choosing a particular characteristic of God to focus on, Charles developed his own: "God is very caring." He took a few slow deep breaths, repeating the phrase as he exhaled. Then I encouraged him to let his breathing become more normal as he continued to quietly ponder and repeat the phrase, eventually repeating it only mentally. After a few minutes, I debriefed with Charles about his experience. He reported that during the meditation the image he had described at the beginning of the session changed. He now saw Christ helping him to sit up.

Charles's experience of vivid imagery in CDM at such an early stage of treatment is not typical. Generally clients start with scriptural truth meditation and then progress to other versions such as scriptural drama meditation and Christ-centered present moment awareness. As treatment progressed, Charles periodically continued to experience vivid imagery in his practice of CDM. For example, one week he returned to counseling and reported to me that he had a startling realization related to the first image he had (of him wearing a yoke and Christ reaching out to him). Specifically, he realized he was wearing the wrong yoke. It was not the yoke of Christ. It was the yoke of his own performance orientation and people-pleasing. As we processed this new awareness, he realized that the origins of these tendencies came more from trying to please his father than from trying to please Christ. The tendencies were not spiritual at all.

Charles also developed other CDM strategies tailored to his situation. For example, when he found himself worrying during the day, he would take a deep breath in, recognize the neurological process taking place, become aware of God's presence with him, and breathe out the short phrase, "Lord, I give you control." He also applied STM strategies at bedtime, which helped him sleep. These strategies, combined with other interventions, led to significant increases in his daily functioning and effective anxiety coping. By the end of psychotherapy (seven sessions), Charles reported an increase in his grades, decreased anxiety, reduced worry and improved sleep.

Conclusion

Empirical research, as well as two thousand years of Christian history, point to the value of CDM as an evidence-based Christian psychotherapy and counseling practice. This chapter has provided an introduction to this rich resource for work with anxious clients. Both counselor and client may grow profoundly through adopting these spiritual practices.

oo9). *Spirituality and the therapeutic process: A com-*
take to termination. Washington, DC: American Psy-

g to God: Lectio Divina and life as prayer.* Downers
s.

ie word of the desert: Scripture and the quest for ho-*
iasticism. Oxford, England: Oxford University Press.
& Simanton, D. A. (1988). A controlled evauation of
progressive relaxation. *Journal of Psychology and*

raditions: Ignatian prayer with a Protestant African
In P. Scott & A. Bergin's (Eds.), *Casebook for a spir-*
and psychotherpy (pp. 173-86). Washington, DC:
;ociation.
i prayer of the senses. *The Heythrop Journal, 31,* 391-

ility exercises of St. Ignatius: A literal translation and*
.ouis, MO: Institute of Jesuit Sources.
of discipline: The path to spiritual growth* (25th an-
cisco: HarperCollins.
iding the heart's true home.* San Francisco: Harper-

is that apply Scripture in psychotherapy. *Journal of*
33(2), 113-21.
., & Wilson, K. G. (1999). *Acceptance and commitment*
'ord Press.
catastrophe living: Using the wisdom of your body and
and illness. New York: Delta.
ing to our senses: Healing ourselves and the world through
Hyperion.
> see, ears to hear: An introduction to Ignatian spirituality.*
Chicago: Loyola University Press.

Merton, T. (1958/1999). *Thoughts in solitude.* New York: Farrar, Straus, and Giroux.

Merton, T. (1961/2007). *New seeds of contemplation.* New York: New Directions Publishing.

Ortberg, J. (2002). *The life you've always wanted: Spiritual disciplines for ordinary people.* Grand Rapids, MI: Zondervan.

Park, C., & Slattery, J. (2009). Including spirituality in case conceptualizations: A meaning-systems approach. In J. Aten & M. Leach (Eds.), *Spirituality and the therapeutic process: A comprehensive resource from intake to termination* (pp. 121-42). Washington, DC: American Psychological Association.

Roemer, L. O., & Orsillo, S. M. (2009). *Mindfulness- & acceptance-based behavioral therapies in practice.* New York: Guilford Press.

Tan, S.-Y. (2003). Integrating spiritual direction into psychotherapy: Ethical issues and guidelines. *Journal of Psychology and Theology, 31,* 14-23.

Wachholtz, A., & Pargament, K. (2005). Is spirituality a critical ingredient of meditation? Comparing the effects of spiritual meditation, secular meditation and relaxation on spiritual, psychological, cardiac, and pain outcomes. *Journal of Behavioral Medicine, 28,* 369-84.

Wachholtz, A., & Pargament, K. (2008). Migraines and meditation: Does spirituality matter? *Journal of Behavioral Medicine, 31,* 351-66.

Handout 1

Scriptural Truth Meditation
(God's Character Version)

The purpose of scriptural truth meditation focused on God's character is to help us slow down and quietly reflect on a significant truth about who God is. You are not studying this truth in an overly analytical manner, but rather receiving the depth of the truth at the heart level. This can be very helpful when we feel anxious, hurried, stressed or frustrated. Turn off the cell phone, computer, TV and radio. Make yourself comfortable. Pray and ask the Lord to open your heart to receive his truth at a deeper level.

1. Choose a characteristic of God that is meaningful and comforting. Below are a few examples. You may add others as well. I will be glad to help you identify additional traits if you would like.

God is love	God forgives me
God is in control	God is faithful
God is good	God is merciful
Jesus loves me	Jesus is Lord

2. Sit in a comfortable position.

3. Close your eyes in order to become more focused and avoid potential distractions.

4. Take a deep breath in and then breathe out repeating the trait of God you chose.

5. Repeat several times.

6. Quietly reflect on this trait and how this characteristic of God is expressed in your life.

7. Your mind will eventually wander. This is normal. No need to beat yourself up.

8. Simply return to the trait regularly when this occurs.

People vary as to how long they meditate in this fashion. Often ten to fifteen minutes is sufficient. When you are done, you may want to jot down any thoughts from your experience. Feel free to share them with me in our next session or to keep them private.

Handout 2

Scriptural Truth Meditation
(Bible Passage Version)

The purpose of scriptural truth meditation (Bible passage version) is to help us slow down and quietly reflect on a significant truth from Scripture. This can be very helpful when we feel anxious, hurried, stressed or frustrated. Turn off the cell phone, computer, TV and radio. Make yourself comfortable. Pray and ask the Lord to open your heart to receive his truth at a deeper level.

1. Choose a Scripture phrase that is meaningful and comforting. Below are a few samples. Add others that are also encouraging. I will be glad to help you find other passages if you like.

Psalm 23:1: "The Lord is my shepherd."	1 John 4:8b: "God is love."
Philippians 4:13: "I can do all things through him who gives me strength."	Romans 8:1: "Therefore, there is now no condemnation for those who are in Christ Jesus."
Proverbs 3:5a: "Trust in the LORD with all your heart."	Psalm 37:7a: "Be still before the LORD and wait patiently for him."
1 John 1:9a: "If we confess our sins, he is faithful and just and will forgive us our sins."	Matthew 11:28: "Come to me, all you who are weary and burdened, and I will give you rest."

2. Sit in a comfortable position.

3. Close your eyes in order to become more focused and avoid potential distractions.

4. Take a deep breath in and then breathe out repeating the scriptural phrase. You may want to do half of the Scripture in one breath and the other half in your second breath.

5. Repeat several times.

6. Quietly reflect on the passage, pondering its meaning and how its message is expressed in your life.

7. Your mind will eventually wander. This is normal. No need to beat yourself up.

8. Simply return to the Scripture phrase regularly when this occurs.

People vary as to how long they pray the Scripture in this fashion. Often ten to fifteen minutes is sufficient. When you are done, you may want to jot down any thoughts about your experience. Feel free to share them with me in our next session or to keep them private.

Part Two

EVIDENCE-BASED APPROACHES TO PSYCHOTHERAPEUTIC TREATMENT OF INDIVIDUALS

5

Christian-Accommodative Cognitive Therapy for Depression

David J. Jennings II, Don E. Davis,
Joshua N. Hook and Everett L. Worthington Jr.

Cognitive-behavioral therapy and cognitive therapy share many characteristics. Throughout this chapter, we will refer to them as cognitive-behavioral therapy (CBT) rather than make subtle distinctions that in practice are rarely observed. CBT has become the treatment of choice for many mental health disorders among both secular and Christian psychotherapists. Since its inception as a major school of psychotherapy over 40 years ago, CBT has amassed perhaps the strongest empirical base among psychological treatments (Chambless & Ollendick, 2001). Recent adaptations to traditional CBT include mindfulness-based CBT, acceptance and commitment therapy (ACT), and dialectical behavior therapy (DBT). In this chapter, we first present an overview of traditional CBT. Next, we discuss Christian-accommodative CBT interventions and review the empirical support for their use. Finally, we provide a description of a Christian-accommodative treatment for depression, practical tips for its implementation and a case example.

TRADITIONAL CBT

CBT emerged in the 1960s building on the work of traditional behavior therapy. Early cognitive-behavioral theorists shared the fundamental assumption that cognition (i.e., mental activity of all sorts, not merely thoughts or self-verbalizations) plays a central role in the development and maintenance of psychological symptoms such as depression and anxiety (Beck, 1976; Ellis, 1962; Mahoney, 1974; Meichenbaum, 1977). Perhaps the central tenet of this model unifying CBT approaches is the oft-quoted saying of the first-century stoic philosopher Epictetus: "Man is not disturbed by events, but by the view he takes of them." In other words, how people perceive and think about their circumstances is what causes emotional disturbance rather than the circumstances alone. The basic premise that one's thoughts influence emotions and behaviors has come to be called the cognitive model (Beck, 1995) or the cognitive paradigm, and it is taught explicitly to clients in CBT. Accordingly, early theorists believed that because cognition influences behaviors, cognition should be a primary target of intervention to effect emotional and behavioral change.

Modern CBT emphasizes the relationship between cognition, emotions and behaviors. Some of its basic principles include (a) conceptualizing the client's presenting problem in terms of dysfunctional or irrational thinking patterns, (b) emphasizing collaboration and active participation, (c) focusing on the present, (d) educating the client to develop awareness of thinking patterns and core beliefs, and (e) using highly structured therapy sessions and a time-limited, goal-oriented therapeutic approach (Beck, 1995).

Within this framework, the psychotherapist first educates the client on the cognitive model and reinforces the model throughout therapy by assisting clients to identify automatic thoughts and core beliefs that are dysfunctional or irrational in nature. CBT initially focuses on developing clients' awareness of (1) their own dysfunctional or irrational thoughts and beliefs in response to situational cues, and (2) how these thinking patterns contribute to emotional disturbance and problematic behaviors. Subsequent sessions target underlying, core beliefs that might predispose the client to future problems. Interventions generally include helping clients learn and apply skills in challenging, disputing or reframing problematic cognition in order that clients might develop more adaptive thoughts, cognitive processes and behavioral acts. The ultimate goal is to teach clients to do cognitive reappraisals on their own, and thus, in a sense, become their own psychotherapists. Many techniques are used, such as Socratic questioning, role-playing, guided discovery, guided imagery, cognitive rehearsal, homework assignments and empirical testing. Typically, CBT psychotherapists highly collaborate with the client to work toward solutions. Emphasis of treatment within a cognitive-behavioral framework is tailored to the client's specific problem, making CBT suitable for many presenting concerns.

Two specific types of CBT have been accommodated to a Christian psychotherapy approach in studies reviewed below: Aaron Beck's (1976) cognitive therapy and Albert Ellis's (1962) rational emotive therapy (RET). We summarize each in general here, but provide a more specific description of Christian-accommodative CBT later in the chapter. Beck, Rush, Shaw and Emery (1979) developed a cognitive therapeutic approach for treating depression. Specifically, that therapy aims to teach participants to (a) monitor negative automatic thoughts; (b) recognize the connection between thoughts, feelings and behaviors; (c) weigh evidence for and against negative thought patterns; (d) dispute negative automatic thoughts with more realistic interpretations; and (e) learn to identify and replace erroneous core beliefs that contribute to distorted thinking and depression. RET is a form of CBT deriving its origin from the writing of Albert Ellis (1962) who identified eleven common irrational beliefs that cause emotional distress. RET like other forms of CBT is primarily concerned with identifying these irrational beliefs and teaching clients to replace them with healthier ways of thinking.

Regardless of the particular approach, both therapies share the same essential features: (a) relationship building and assessment, (b) introducing and presenting a rationale for the cognitive model, (c) raising the clients' self-awareness by teaching them how to identify and monitor the influence of automatic thoughts and irrational beliefs on their mood and behaviors, and (d) cognitive restructuring through continual identification of dysfunctional or irrational thoughts and beliefs and teaching clients how to correct and replace unhealthy, erroneous thoughts and beliefs with more accurate, healthier ones. In all the Christian-accommodative CBT studies reviewed below, the researchers retained the essential features of these secular approaches while integrating biblical teaching, Christian theology and religious imagery into psychotherapy and other components of treatment (e.g., homework assignments, group discussions, bibliotherapy).

CHRISTIAN-ACCOMMODATIVE CBT

Pecheur (1978) was one of the first Christian psychologists to present a Christian rationale for the use of CBT by outlining parallels between CBT and the process of sanctification. Pecheur noted that the four-stage process of spiritual growth for the believer is very similar to the process of change occurring in cognitive therapy:

> (a) the believer recognizes that his covert thoughts reflect the intents of his heart; (b) the believer becomes an observer of his thoughts by means of heightened awareness and the Word of God; (c) the believer puts off the old man and puts on the new man through the renewing of his mind; (d) the believer's growth is reinforced by the resources of Christianity. (pp. 250-51)

Several scholars have suggested that CBT is particularly useful for working with religious clients (Nielsen, Johnson & Ridley, 2000; Propst, 1988; Tan & Johnson, 2005). Parallels that make CBT an attractive treatment modality for religious clients include its emphasis on (a) core and ultimate beliefs about oneself, one's world and one's relationships (which corresponds nicely with an emphasis on the importance of Christian beliefs); (b) teaching and education in helping clients change (which fits well with Christian theologies emphasizing the power of the Holy Spirit); and (c) actively changing or modifying previously held (and often erroneous) views (Neilson et al., 2000; Tan & Johnson, 2005). This emphasis on "right" thinking and action, along with its substantial empirical support, has helped to make CBT particularly attractive to Christian psychotherapists and scholars. A significant number of Christian-accommodative CBT approaches have now been developed by prominent leaders in the field of integration (Backus, 1985; Crabb, 1977; McMinn, 1991; McMinn & Campbell, 2007; Propst, 1988; Tan & Ortberg, 2004; Worthington, 1982). Thus, although not without its criticisms from a biblical worldview (see Jones & Butman, 2011; Tan 1987 for critiques), CBT is a widely used Christian-accommodative therapy.

Tan (1987) offered several guidelines for conducting Christian counseling and psychotherapy within a CBT framework, stating that a biblical approach to CBT will (a) emphasize the primacy of agape love (1 Cor 13) and the need to develop a warm, empathic and genuine relationship with the client; (b) deal with the past; (c) attend to aspects of Christian experience (without over-emphasizing the cognitive and with consideration of the possibility of demonic involvement); (d) not over-attribute the cause of problems to cognition at the risk of ignoring biological or other factors like familial, societal or cultural influences; (e) emphasize the healing ministry of the Holy Spirit; (f) use techniques that are scripturally consistent; and (g) make use of rigorous outcome research on which to base claims of treatment efficacy. Other Christian-accommodative CBT approaches have emphasized the replacement of unbiblical or irrational beliefs with more accurate beliefs based on the truth of God's Word (Backus, 1985; Crabb, 1977; Neilsen et al., 2000), use of religious imagery (Propst, 1988), use of prayer and Scripture to facilitate cognitive restructuring (Tan, 2007), and integration of CBT with relational models and techniques (McMinn & Campbell, 2007).

Although Christian-accommodative CBT may be based on a number of different CBT approaches, what unites them is the primacy of God's revelation both within the Bible and within the person of Jesus Christ as the ultimate source for correcting faulty ways of thinking. Thus, Christian-accommodative CBT might involve several elements: (a) the use of scriptural rationales as the basis for using the CBT model, (b) the use of biblical passages to refute irrational beliefs and distorted thoughts, (c) the use of prayer and Christian imagery to promote experiencing the healing presence of Christ, and (d) the use of Scripture when assigning homework and developing new coping strategies (Johnson, DeVries, Ridley, Pettorini & Peterson, 1994; Johnson & Ridley, 1992; Pecheur & Edwards, 1984; Propst, 1980; Propst, Ostrom, Watkins, Dean & Mashburn, 1992). However, there appears to be no consensus on exactly how these elements are implemented in Christian psychotherapy. In the next section, we review the empirical evidence for Christian-accommodative CBT for depression and afterward provide a brief critique of the current literature on this approach.

EMPIRICAL SUPPORT FOR CHRISTIAN-ACCOMMODATIVE CBT

Several outcome studies in recent years have examined the efficacy of religious- and spiritually tailored therapies (Hodge, 2006; Hook et al., 2010; McCullough, 1999; Smith, Bartz & Richards, 2007; Wade, Worthington & Vogel, 2007; Worthington, Hook, Davis & McDaniel, 2011). Hook et al.

(2010) reviewed five studies that compared Christian-accommodative CBT to secular CBT, an alternative treatment, or a control condition when treating depression. They found that in three of the studies (Pecheur & Edwards, 1984; Propst, 1980; Propst et al., 1992) participants receiving Christian-accommodative CBT had significantly reduced depressive symptoms than did those in the control group. In two of the studies (Johnson et al., 1994; Johnson & Ridley, 1992), participants receiving Christian-accommodative CBT and those receiving an alternative treatment showed equivalent improvement in depressive symptoms. Based on these results, they concluded that Christian-accommodative CBT showed evidence for efficacy, but it did not perform better than the secular CBT in reducing depression. This finding was consistent with a previous meta-analysis of the same five studies (McCullough, 1999).

In a study that was not included in the above review because it did not employ random assignment to condition, Hawkins, Tan and Turk (1999) compared Christian-accommodative and secular CBT with an inpatient group of clinically depressed adults. Participants in both groups showed equivalent reductions of depressive symptoms, and both groups showed gains in spiritual well-being as a result of treatment. However, participants receiving Christian-accommodative CBT showed greater improvement in spiritual well-being than did those receiving secular CBT. Limitations of the study were that participants self-selected which treatment they preferred on entering the program, and there was no control condition. Nevertheless, the study provided initial evidence that it may be beneficial to offer Christian-accommodative CBT for the treatment of depression with clients who identify as Christians and prefer value-congruent therapy.

We have briefly reviewed the empirical support for Christian-accommodative CBT for depression. Based on the criteria discussed by Chambless and Ollendick (2001), for a treatment to be considered efficacious at least two independent research labs must show that it: (1) outperforms a no-treatment control group, placebo or alternative treatment; or (2) performs as well as an already established efficacious treatment. By that standard, Christian-accommodative CBT for depression is indeed efficacious—one of few explicitly Christian treatments that can make such a claim based on direct experimental evidence. There is little evidence, however, for the specificity of Christian-accommodative CBT for depression. In other words, there does not appear to be much empirical evidence that Christian-accommodative CBT for depression works *better* than secular CBT for depression (Hook et al., 2010; McCullough, 1999). Nevertheless, Christian clients may prefer a Christian-accommodated approach to psychotherapy, which may produce differential effects on treatment satisfaction (McCullough, 1999). Given that Christian-accommodative CBT is equally effective as secular approaches at reducing depressive symptoms in the studies reviewed, Christian-accommodative CBT for depression may be the preferred treatment for Christian clients.

Despite the evidence for its efficacy, Christian-accommodative CBT for depression lacks a consistent treatment protocol in the current literature. Researchers in the reviewed studies used different CBT models and accommodated them in different ways. While sharing some similarities previously described, the above Christian-accommodative CBT approaches for treating depression have several shortcomings. First, few details were given about the modifications and how these were implemented in psychotherapy. Second, there was no indication given of what percentage of the secular CBT approach overlapped between groups. Finally, because the different approaches modified different elements of secular CBT, there was no standardization of what was accommodated.

THERAPY DESCRIPTION

In this section, we outline a Christian-accommodative CBT approach for treating depression. Since there is no single standardized method for accommodating secular CBT to Christian clients, we are drawing on the various Christian-accommodated versions of CBT to present a general model of this approach for the Christian psychotherapist.

Phase 1: Establishing rapport and assessment. The first meeting with a client is critical for establishing rapport with the client and developing a collaborative working relationship. Core therapeutic factors such as empathy, development of the therapeutic alliance, collaborative goal-setting, and fostering positive expectancies are just as important in CBT as in other modes of therapy. Additionally, therapists using Christian-accommodative CBT will be careful to exemplify the compassion and grace of Christ to all clients. The primary task here is to create an environment in which clients feel valued and safe to explore their inner thoughts and presenting concerns without fear of judgment. Valuing the client involves (a) treating the client's presenting concerns seriously, (b) avoiding dismissive, judgmental or premature comments, (c) conveying a sense of empathy and warmth, (d) acknowledging and discussing cultural differences, and (e) respecting theological differences. Throughout treatment, the Christian psychotherapist should respect the client's beliefs even when those beliefs may be contributing to a depressive state. Over time, the Christian psychotherapist will work collaboratively with the client to objectively evaluate the validity of beliefs in light of the whole of Scripture and Christian theology. The task of identifying unhelpful or invalid beliefs is shared with the client in order to maintain a strong therapy alliance.

In this phase, the therapist also seeks to assess the nature and potential etiology of the depressive symptoms. A thorough assessment will consider cognitive, emotional, physical, relational and spiritual contributing factors. We encourage Christian psychotherapists to develop their own formulation of how the client's current spiritual beliefs and practice may be related to their depressive symptoms. For example, the psychotherapist might explore the client's view of God and his or her relationship to God. A client who views God as harsh and punishing may be experiencing an inordinate amount of guilt for perceived sins, which contributes to the depressive state. Furthermore, Christian psychotherapists should assess the client's spiritual view of how their faith is related to their presenting problems. For example, the client may view symptoms as spiritual warfare or a "dark night of the soul." We encourage Christian psychotherapists to draw conclusions cautiously, remaining aware of their theological biases and how these may cause tension in the therapy relationship.

Finally, traditional CBT is highly collaborative. The client is expected to actively participate in establishing goals and setting the therapeutic agenda. Christian psychotherapists seek to establish a collaborative relationship in the first session by soliciting the client's interpretations of the problem and by asking for feedback and feelings about the therapy session. It should be communicated that the client's honest feedback is a welcome and valuable part of the therapeutic process. A Christian-accommodative approach should also exemplify the humility of Christ and show the flexibility to adjust some aspects of the therapeutic process to meet the client's needs while maintaining the basic CBT framework. As part of the assessment process, we also suggest exploring the client's preferences regarding the use of Scripture, prayer, and other religious interventions and resources that might be a part of Christian-accommodative psychotherapy.

Phase 2: Introducing the cognitive model and rationale. Early in the therapeutic process (generally the first session), the Christian psychotherapist will introduce the basic cognitive model and provide the client with a rationale for this treatment modality. Typically, this involves briefly educating clients on the connection between thoughts, feelings and behaviors. In particular, the psychotherapist will introduce the idea that it is not an event that causes emotional distress, but the automatic thoughts and beliefs about the event that determine our emotional reactions. Presenting Ellis's ABC model is an excellent way of accomplishing this task, in which A is the activating event (e.g., loss of job), B is the belief about the event (e.g., "I'm never going to find another job" or "I'm such a loser"), and C is the emotional consequence (e.g., hopelessness, depression). A simple way to illustrate the point is to discuss how people can experience the same type of event or circumstance and have very different emotional reactions to it, which in turn influences subsequent behaviors. For example, in the illustration of losing one's job, one individual may view the job loss as an opportunity to explore new employment options and immediately begin researching new potential job interests, whereas another individual may be devastated by the loss and turn to alcohol abuse.

We suggest that Christian-accommodative CBT include a biblical rationale for the cognitive model and treatment approach. The therapist may use different Scripture references such as: "Do not conform to the pattern of this world, but be transformed by the renewing of your mind" (Rom 12:2); "for as [a person] thinks within himself, so he is" (Prov 23:7 NASB); or the apostle Paul's instruction "to be made new in the attitude of your minds" (Eph 4:23). The point the Christian psychotherapist wants to communicate is that Scripture emphasizes the importance our thinking has for virtuous behaviors and character. Additionally, for the Christian man or woman, having an accurate, biblical view of the self, the world and the future is the foundation for our lives, relationships and hope. A biblical case can be made that it is not our circumstances that should govern our emotions and behaviors; rather, we should set our thoughts on the truth of Scripture and the hope we have in God through Christ our Lord: "Therefore, prepare your *minds* for action; be self-controlled; set your hope fully on the grace to be given you when Jesus Christ is revealed" (1 Pet 1:13 NIV 1984). A great many other Scripture passages can be used as well to instill hope in the depressed client (e.g., Ps 42:5; 62:5; 119:74; Jer 29:11; Lam 3:21; Rom 15:4; 1 Tim 4:9-10; Heb 10:23).

Phase 3: Raising the client's level of self-awareness and self-monitoring. A critical element of all forms of CBT is helping clients gain greater awareness of their thought-life and its influence on their mood and behavior. For many clients, self-monitoring of their moment-to-moment thinking is a new skill that will need to be taught and consistently reinforced throughout psychotherapy. Christian psychotherapists, like their secular counterparts, accomplish this task by actively focusing on clients' thoughts and assisting them to connect events, thoughts, feelings and behaviors in specific circumstances. CBT psychotherapists also often give clients a homework assignment to monitor thoughts, feelings and behaviors throughout the week. In addition, Propst (1988) recommends that clients monitor images and fantasies and pay attention to bodily sensations in order to increase awareness of thoughts and feelings.

The second task of this phase is to help clients begin to identify those thoughts and beliefs that are distorted, irrational or false, which may cause or exacerbate depressive symptoms. This may involve educating clients on some common thought patterns—such as Beck's cognitive distortions (e.g., discounting the positive—that is, telling oneself that positive experiences, qualities or behaviors do not really count) or Ellis's irrational beliefs (e.g., the belief that one must be thoroughly competent, adequate or achieving in all aspects of life in order to be considered worthwhile). The Christian psychotherapist assists clients to identify cognitive distortions and underlying beliefs that are particularly significant for thoughts and feelings of depression and will encourage them to self-monitor for situations that elicit such thoughts.

In a Christian-accommodative approach, we recommend helping clients draw on resources of religious authority (e.g., biblical passages; relevant writings of religious authors) to motivate them to carefully examine their inner life. Some Christian clients may believe that it is wrong or sinful to focus too much on the self, but self-examination was seen as an important spiritual discipline for biblical writers and saints throughout the ages (see Propst, 1988). Distrust of self-examination can be gently challenged with passages such as: "Let us examine our ways and test them, and let us return to the LORD" (Lam 3:40); or "Examine yourselves to see whether you are in the faith; test yourselves" (2 Cor 13:5). The Christian psychotherapist might also use a saint or theologian as an example, but should be careful to draw on the client's sources of religious authority. For instance, John Calvin began his *Institutes of the Christian Religion* stating, "Without knowledge of self, there is no knowledge of God" (Calvin, 1559/2001, p. 1). The idea here is to communicate to the client that self-awareness and self-examination are not equivalent to self-preoccupation but rather are important avenues to spiritual and emotional health.

Phase 4: Cognitive restructuring. As clients gain greater awareness of the thoughts and beliefs that are related to depressive symptoms, the psychotherapist will next assist them to evaluate their thoughts and teach them to modify, dispute or replace dysfunctional cognitions with healthier ones. This process typically involves helping clients to change unrealistic interpretations in immediate situations as well as change underlying false beliefs about themselves. The first step in the change process involves assisting clients to evaluate the evidence for and against negative automatic thoughts and irrational beliefs. The psychotherapist often accomplishes this through a Socratic technique by asking the client questions that help them evaluate the validity of their thinking. The second step in the change process involves assisting clients to choose more adaptive and realistic ways of thinking. This might include modifying distorted cognition (e.g., "just because one bad thing happens doesn't mean my life is falling apart"), disputing irrational beliefs (e.g., "nowhere is it written that I have to be perfect in all aspects of life in order to feel worthwhile"), or replacing core, negative beliefs about one's self with a more accurate, realistic view (e.g., "I am a person of value and worth bestowed by God"). These skills are often then reinforced through homework assignments involving reading, writing, imagery and coping strategies to strengthen new ways of thinking.

Christian-accommodative CBT relies heavily on scriptural authority as the basis for disputing distorted thoughts and irrational beliefs. Indeed, in all of the empirical studies we reviewed, Scripture was used as a key intervention to change thoughts. Tan (2007) highlights a fundamental difference between Christian-accommodative CBT and a secular approach: "Cognitive restructuring of dysfunctional or irrational thinking can be more deeply conducted in Christian CBT with the appropriate use of Scripture, and not just rational or empirical analysis and disputation" (p. 108). Additionally, Tan suggests that in assisting clients to restructure dysfunctional thoughts and beliefs, a Christian approach might ask the client: "What does God have to say about this?" "What do you think the Bible has to say about this?" "What does your faith tradition have to say about this?" (p. 108). Religious clients may often experience emotional turmoil as a result of misinterpretations or misunderstandings of biblical texts or Christian theology (Nielsen et al., 2000). Christian-accommodative CBT for depression will teach clients to evaluate their thinking and beliefs against a biblical view of persons, the life and teachings of Christ, and the whole of Scripture. The use of imagery (Propst, 1988) and inner healing prayer (Tan, 2007) may also be necessary techniques to help clients replace deeply held core beliefs. For example, the Christian psychotherapist may ask clients to recall a traumatic or painful experience and then open themselves to a spiritual experience, such as becoming more aware of God's presence or listening for the Holy Spirit in that moment. Although this kind of intervention is experientially based on the work of the Holy Spirit, such experiences can help clients to develop new cognitive schemas about themselves and about God that can be used by the client and psychotherapist to dispute previously held irrational beliefs.

TREATMENT IMPLEMENTATION

Generally, Christian-accommodative CBT for depression will be highly structured. From the beginning, it is important that the psychotherapist actively involve the client by collaboratively establishing the goals for therapy. Goals should be specific and behaviorally measurable. For instance, if a male client states that he "wants to feel better," the therapist might ask him, "What would you be doing differently if you were feeling better?" If the client states that he would be spending more time with God through prayer and meditating on Scripture, the Christian psychotherapist can work with the client to establish a measurable goal toward this end. The client and psychotherapist will need to discuss the specific details of the goal such as how much time per day will be spent with God, how many days per week will this occur, and what the time with God will entail in order to monitor the client's progress toward achieving the goal.

Goal setting may be particularly challenging when working with a severely depressed client. Depressive clients will likely feel powerless to change anything in their lives and think that everything they attempt ends in failure. It is important to actively engage the client in the process and not take over the therapy session. For the client to regain a sense of control, small steps may be important at the start of therapy so the client can experience some success. For instance, at the end of the first session, the Christian psychotherapist might ask clients for ideas on what they think might help them feel better during the following week. The psychotherapist will collaborate with clients to select small, achievable goals based on clients' own ideas or might offer clients suggestions if they cannot think of anything themselves. Depressed clients may have initial difficulty talking during sessions making goal setting more of a challenge. In this circumstance, McMinn (1991) offers the following guidelines: (a) use reflections, (b) allow reasonable silence, (c) assign easy tasks first and (d) assign a daily activity record, which is used to help clients identify exceptions in their daily lives to self-defeating beliefs.

Once measurable goals for therapy have been established, therapy sessions are highly structured around achieving goals within the cognitive-behavioral frame. The psychotherapist is typically more active and directive than in other forms of therapy (e.g., person-centered) in establishing the therapeutic agenda for each session, but this is still done in a collaborative manner. A typical session will involve (a) getting a brief update on the client's mood and symptoms, (b) collaboratively establishing the agenda for the current session, (c) reviewing homework, (d) consistently reinforcing the cognitive model while working through the depressive state by assisting the client to identify and replace distorted thinking and irrational beliefs, and (e) collaboratively establishing new homework. The psychotherapist should continue to solicit the client's feedback throughout the process and maintain an empathic stance. Notwithstanding CBT's educative and directive nature, core counseling skills such as attending, active listening, reflecting and conveying empathy should be maintained at all times.

The course of psychotherapy will vary depending on the severity of the depression. Mild to moderate forms of depression can sometimes be resolved in as few as twelve sessions; severe depression could take twenty sessions or more (McMinn, 1991). Depression involving genetic factors, suicidality or comorbid issues (e.g., anxiety) will likely prolong therapy. Psychotherapists should consider a medical referral for clients with a severe biological component to depression (i.e., recurrent depressive episodes, family history of depression, debilitating physical symptoms such as insomnia or extreme lethargy). We recommend Christian psychotherapists discuss the possibility of a biological component with clients, whether psychotropic medication may be warranted, and explore their reactions to taking it. For some Christian clients this may be a sensitive issue. The Christian psychotherapist needs to respect the client's values and beliefs, while also educating the client on the benefits and risks of anti-depressants.

Extreme care must be taken with depressed clients experiencing suicidal ideation. Christian psychotherapists should exercise professional standards for suicidal risk, monitor risk throughout psychotherapy, and procure agreements about notifying the counselor if the client feels imminently suicidal. Some clients may have religious beliefs that buffer the influence of thoughts of suicide, whereas others may experience spiritually related distress (e.g., believing that God hates them) that intensifies risk. In developing a safety plan to deal with suicidal thoughts, Christian psychotherapists can help clients draw on spiritual sources of authority to increase their sense of hope.

Finally, depression can be accompanied by a range of other issues such as comorbid anxiety or other Axis I diagnoses, personality disorders, grief and loss, and problems with physical health or chronic pain, to name a few. We suggest psychotherapists collaboratively determine the focus of treatment and limit treatment to what is in the client's power to change. Regardless of circumstances, clients can change how they view their circumstances through the lens of Christian hope revealed through Scripture.

CASE EXAMPLE

Anna was a twenty-one-year-old, Caucasian female attending a Christian college. She grew up in a theologically conservative home and church, and she described herself as a "very committed Christian." She came to Christian psychotherapy because three months ago she found out that her father was involved in an extramarital affair. Her mother is currently seeking a divorce. Since finding out about the affair, Anna has had difficulty concentrating, and her grades, which had always been high, had plummeted. She has had trouble sleeping. In addition, she reported not having energy for anything. Previously very active socially, she has increasingly withdrawn from relationships, including from her boyfriend of a year and a half. Anna denied having thoughts of suicide, but said she sometimes thinks she would be better off dead. On further questioning, she denied having an active plan to end her life, stating she would never commit suicide for fear of going to hell.

During the first session, the Christian psychotherapist provided a warm and supportive environment, giving her the opportunity to share her story and many of her unspoken fears about her parents' pending divorce. She reported having perfectionistic tendencies all her life and secretly believing that her parents' divorce could be God's punishment for her past sins. The psychotherapist introduced the cognitive model explaining the ABC's of RET. To bolster the credibility of the approach for Anna, the psychotherapist provided a biblical rationale for examining her thoughts in light of Scripture. At the end of the first session, the psychotherapist gave Anna a self-monitoring form and explained how to complete it. She was asked to record daily her thoughts and feelings, paying particular attention to events and thoughts associated with feeling depressed. In addition, she and the psychotherapist worked together to identify one activity that she might enjoy. She discussed several past spiritual experiences that occurred while, instead of just talking to God during prayer, she learned to go for short walks and (a) release her frantic thoughts to God, (b) listen to God's voice and (c) enjoy just being with God. They agreed that, on at least three days, she would go for a short walk and practice releasing her thoughts and attending to God's loving presence.

Over the next several sessions, the psychotherapist would review Anna's self-monitoring forms and assist her to identify cognitive distortions that contributed to depressive symptoms. When they located unhelpful thoughts, the psychotherapist would gently question their validity in light of Scripture. Through this process, Anna became increasingly aware of how her thoughts were impacting her mood and behaviors. In particular, she recognized that she had prepared herself for the worst regarding her parents' divorce (catastrophizing) in order to gain a greater sense of control. However, this way of thinking led to other problematic thought patterns, including a tendency to ignore positive aspects of herself and her current life (discounting the positive). The psychotherapist helped Anna draw on Christian sources of authority to dispute these cognitive distortions. One of the most recurrent and painful thoughts she struggled with was her fear that her parents' divorce meant that her own dating relationship was doomed and she would never be happily married. During sessions, the psychotherapist helped Anna through Socratic questioning to evaluate this and other thoughts by weighing the evidence for and against them, including evidence from Scripture. In her quiet time and through conversations with religious mentors, Anna was able to locate several Scriptures (e.g., "for I know the plans I have for you . . . plans to give you hope and a future," Jer 29:11) that directly challenged her fears regarding her future. Homework assignments included reading and writing exercises designed to help Anna continue disputing distorted thinking patterns. Additionally, she completed one behavioral assignment each week that the psychotherapist and Anna agreed on (e.g., exercising three times, going out one night with a friend).

As therapy progressed, Anna's depressive symptoms began improving, and the psychotherapist and Anna began to explore the meaning of Anna's parents' divorce for her view of herself. Through this process Anna identified her core belief that she could never be loved by anyone (including God) unless she was absolutely perfect. For years, she said she had been struggling with a negative body image and feelings of insecurity, which propelled her to strive for perfection in all aspects of her life. Therapy continued to focus on seeking to bring this belief into greater alignment with Scripture. In one of the sessions, the psychotherapist used a guided imagery exercise in which Anna imagined Jesus' reaction to her during a situation in which she was denigrating herself for making a mistake. Anna found Jesus to be surprisingly gracious, kind and comforting in this situation. The psychotherapist encouraged Anna to recall this experience any time she realized she was berating herself for not being perfect. As a homework exercise, she was given several note cards and was asked to write down challenges to her distorted core belief based on biblical examples of God's unconditional love. The psychotherapist instructed Anna to keep her positive truth statement cards with her throughout the week and review them three times a day.

After twelve sessions, Anna had experienced a significant decrease in depressive symptoms. She was re-engaging with her social network and spending more time with her boyfriend. Despite still experiencing some sadness and anger regarding her parents' divorce, she no longer believed God was punishing her or that somehow the divorce was her fault. She also was performing well again in school, but she reported not feeling the need to be perfect at everything and feeling more forgiving towards her mistakes.

CONCLUSION

In this chapter, we described Christian-accommodative CBT for depression and reviewed its empirical support. Six studies have shown Christian-accommodative CBT to either be more effective than a control group or as effective as secular CBT at reducing depressive symptoms. In light of these findings, we can conclude that Christian-accommodative CBT is an efficacious treatment for depression, and it should possibly be considered the treatment of choice when working with clients who prefer therapy that is rooted in Christian beliefs and values.

However, it is uncertain which aspects of the Christian versions of CBT are most effective. Most of the studies reviewed employed prayer, religious imagery and various ways of using Scripture and biblical teaching. This treatment approach would benefit from future studies to determine which interventions might work best under different circumstances and with different clients. In the future, outcome research on the Christian CBT approach should note where the approach under consideration differs from the previous adaptations and why. For now, we know that at least two forms of secular CBT (Beck's cognitive therapy and Ellis's RET) can be effectively adapted to accommodate Christian clients, yet we do not know whether differential outcomes would exist if they were compared and we do not know whether differential ways of adapting the protocols to Christian clients would make them more or less efficacious. We have provided a general model for treating depression using a Christian-accommodative CBT approach, practical suggestions and a case example for current and future practitioners who use this approach with Christian clientele.

REFERENCES

Backus, W. (1985). *Telling the truth to troubled people*. Minneapolis, MN: Bethany House.

Beck, A. T. (1976). *Cognitive therapy and the emotional disorders*. New York: International Universities Press.

Beck, A. T., Rush, A. J., Shaw, B. F., & Emery, G. (1979). *Cognitive therapy of depression*. New York: Guilford Press.

Beck, J. S. (1995). *Cognitive therapy: Basics and beyond*. New York: Guilford Press.

Calvin, J. (1559/2001). Institutes of the Christian religion. In D. K. McKim (Ed.), *Calvin's institutes: Abridged edition* (p. 1). Louisville, KY: Westminster John Knox Press.

Chambless, D. L., & Hollon, S. D. (1998). Defining empirically supported therapies. *Journal of Consulting and Clinical Psychology, 66*, 7-18.

Chambless, D. L., & Ollendick, T. H. (2001). Empirically supported psychological interventions: Controversies and evidence. *Annual Review of Psychology, 52*, 685-716.

Crabb, L. J., Jr. (1977). *Effective biblical counseling*. Grand Rapids, MI: Zondervan.

Ellis, A. (1962). *Reason and emotion in psychotherapy*. New York: Lyle Stuart.

Hawkins, R. S., Tan, S.-Y., & Turk, A. A. (1999). Secular versus Christian inpatient cognitive-behavioral therapy programs: Impact on depression and spiritual well-being. *Journal of Psychology and Theology, 27*, 309-18.

Hodge, D. R. (2006). Spiritually modified cognitive therapy: A review of the literature. *Social Work, 51*, 157-66.

Hook, J. N., Worthington, E. L., Jr., Davis, D. E., Jennings, D. J., II, Gartner, A. L., & Hook, J. P. (2010). Empirically supported religious and spiritual therapies. *Journal of Clinical Psychology, 66*, 46-72.

Johnson, W. B., DeVries, R., Ridley, C. R., Pettorini, D., & Peterson, D. R. (1994). The comparative efficacy of Christian and secular rational-emotive therapy with Christian clients. *Journal of Psychology and Theology, 22*, 130-40.

Johnson, W. B., & Ridley, C. R. (1992). Brief Christian and non-Christian Rational-Emotive Therapy with depressed Christian clients: An exploratory study. *Counseling and Values, 36*, 220-29.

Jones, S. L., & Butman, R. E. (2011). *Modern psychotherapies: A comprehensive Christian perspective* (2nd ed.). Downers Grove, IL: InterVarsity Press.

Mahoney, M. J. (1974). *Cognition and behavior modification.* Cambridge, MA: Ballinger.

McCullough, M. E. (1999). Research on religion-accommodative counseling: Review and meta-analysis. *Journal of Counseling Psychology, 46,* 92-98.

McMinn, M. (1991). *Cognitive therapy techniques in Christian counseling.* Dallas, TX: Word.

McMinn, M. R., & Campbell, C. D. (2007). *Integrative psychotherapy: Toward a comprehensive Christian approach.* Downers Grove, IL: InterVarsity Press.

Meichenbaum, D. (1977). *Cognitive-behavior modification: An integrative approach.* New York: Plenum.

Nielsen, S. L., Johnson, W. B., & Ridley, C. R. (2000). Religiously sensitive rational emotive behavior therapy: Theory, techniques, and brief excerpts from a case. *Professional Psychology: Research and Practice, 31,* 21-28.

Pecheur, D. (1978). Cognitive theory/therapy and sanctification: A study in integration. *Journal of Psychology and Theology, 6*(4), 239-53.

Pecheur, D. R., & Edwards, K. J. (1984). A comparison of secular and religious versions of cognitive therapy with depressed Christian college students. *Journal of Psychology and Theology, 12,* 45-54.

Propst, L. R. (1980). The comparative efficacy of religious and nonreligious imagery for the treatment of mild depression in religious individuals. *Cognitive Therapy and Research, 4,* 167-78.

Propst, L. R. (1988). *Psychotherapy in a religious framework: Spirituality in the emotional healing process.* New York: Human Sciences Press.

Propst, L. R., Ostrom, R., Watkins, P., Dean, T., & Mashburn, D. (1992). Comparative efficacy of religious and nonreligious cognitive-behavioral therapy for the treatment of clinical depression in religious individuals. *Journal of Consulting and Clinical Psychology, 60,* 94-103.

Smith, T. B., Bartz, J., & Richards, P. S. (2007). Outcomes of religious and spiritual adaptations to psychotherapy: A meta-analytic review. *Psychotherapy Research, 17,* 643-55.

Tan, S.-Y. (1987). Cognitive-behavior therapy: A biblical approach and critique. *Journal of Psychology and Theology, 15,* 103-12.

Tan, S.-Y. (2007). Use of prayer and Scripture in cognitive-behavioral therapy. *Journal of Psychology and Christianity, 26,* 101-11.

Tan, S.-Y., & Johnson, W. B. (2005). Spiritually oriented cognitive-behavioral therapy. In L. Sperry & E. P. Shafranske (Eds.), *Spiritually-oriented psychotherapy* (pp. 77-103). Washington, DC: American Psychological Association.

Tan, S.-Y., & Ortberg, J., Jr. (2004). *Coping with Depression* (2nd ed.). Grand Rapids, MI: Baker.

Wade, N. G., Worthington, E. L., Jr., & Vogel, D. L. (2007). Effectiveness of religiously tailored interventions in Christian therapy. *Psychotherapy Research, 17,* 91-105.

Worthington, E. L., Jr. (1982). *When someone asks for help: A practical guide for counseling.* Downers Grove, IL: InterVarsity Press.

Worthington, E. L., Jr., Hook, J. N., Davis, D. E., & McDaniel, M. A. (2011). Religion and spirituality. *Journal of Clinical Psychology: In Session, 67,* 204-14.

6

Christian-Accommodative Trauma-Focused Cognitive-Behavioral Therapy for Children and Adolescents

Donald F. Walker, Heather Lewis Quagliana,
Morgan Wilkinson and Dana Frederick

In this chapter, we describe a Christian-accommodative approach to trauma-focused cognitive-behavioral therapy (TF-CBT) for children and adolescents who have been physically or sexually abused. We begin by briefly reviewing the historical development of TF-CBT. Next, we present an overview of the treatment modules involved in TF-CBT, followed by a presentation of a Christian-accommodative approach to TF-CBT that we have used in our clinical practice. Afterward, we discuss the results of an initial clinical trial utilizing a Christian-accommodative approach to TF-CBT. We conclude the chapter by presenting several case studies illustrating our Christian-accommodative approach.

HISTORICAL DEVELOPMENT OF TF-CBT

Trauma-focused cognitive-behavioral therapy in its secular form was originally developed by Dr. Judith Cohen and Dr. Anthony Mannarino at the Allegheny Center for Traumatic Stress. Since its development, TF-CBT has been subjected to a number of treatment studies and subsequent refinements to its original proposed protocol. Today it is arguably the most empirically supported treatment method for children and teens who have been victims of childhood physical and sexual abuse.

Perhaps as a result of the body of work attesting to the efficacy of TF-CBT, the secular treatment protocol for TF-CBT has also been widely implemented in child and adolescent treatment settings across the country. For example, practice guidelines from the International Society for Traumatic Stress Studies recommend the use of TF-CBT in comparison to other treatments for childhood physical and sexual abuse (Cohen et al., 2009). The National Child Traumatic Stress Network considers TF-CBT to be a leading treatment for treating childhood trauma. In 2005, as the result of federal grant funding, the Medical University of South Carolina began a free, online training in TF-CBT for psychotherapists and counselors (available online at http://tfcbt.musc.edu) used by over thirty thousand professionals around the world (Cohen et al., 2009).

TOWARD A CHRISTIAN-ACCOMMODATIVE APPROACH TO TF-CBT

In the past several years, a team of researchers led by Walker (the first author of this essay) have begun to consider the potential efficacy of addressing religion and spirituality in trauma-focused treatment for children and teens (Walker, Reese, Hughes & Troskie, 2010; Walker, Reid, O'Neill & Brown, 2009). Our research and clinical experience has indicated that regardless of the age of the survivor, trauma often produces changes in a trauma survivor's personal religious and spiritual faith. Some children and teens respond to abuse by becoming angry or disappointed with God. Other childhood victims of abuse turn to God for comfort and become closer to God as a result of their experience. Still others find parts of their personal faith damaged while other parts grow stronger. For example, some childhood victims of abuse report having difficulty attending church for organized services, while simultaneously growing closer in their relationship to God.

All of these potential reactions to childhood abuse depend in part on the circumstances surrounding the abuse itself. For example, research suggests that survivors of religion-related abuse (in which some aspect of religious faith was used to perpetrate the abuse itself) experience profound damage in their relationship to God. This is particularly the case in instances where a clergy member perpetrated the abuse. Research has demonstrated that survivors of clergy sexual abuse in particular often report that God is angry, distant and less loving than survivors of other kinds of abuse (Walker et al., 2009).

Conversely, our experience as psychotherapists and relevant research suggest that for children who have a secure relationship with God prior to an experience of abuse, their relationship with God serves as a foundation to cope with and make meaning of the abuse experience. For example, we have previously described a case study of a seventeen-year-old girl named Isabel, who was raped by a stranger outside of her home. Isabel had been raised in a devout Christian home; perhaps as a result, she was able to use spiritual practices from her faith (such as reading Scripture and praying) to cope with mental health symptoms (such as anxiety) that she experienced after the abuse. Her therapist was intentional about incorporating these spiritual resources into treatment and felt that making use of Isabel's faith in this way helped to make her therapy more effective (for a complete discussion, see Walker et al., 2010).

As a result of these observations from our clinical experience and from the results of research, we have developed a Christian-accommodative approach to TF-CBT to address these kinds of religious and spiritual issues and to use clients' religious and spiritual resources in their treatment. Our approach to TF-CBT emphasizes assessing the potential role of client religion and spirituality at the beginning of treatment as a resource for healing, or conversely, as an outcome variable that could be targeted for intervention during treatment itself.

OVERVIEW OF TF-CBT TREATMENT MODULES

In its secular form, TF-CBT typically takes place over twelve to fourteen sessions. Although the treatment manual for TF-CBT is presented in a linear fashion, the manual is designed to be flexible. Therefore, some clients may not need all of the treatment modules. Furthermore, the manual is intended to be individualized to the child and parent being seen for psychotherapy. This allows for some creativity on the part of the psychotherapist in delivering the treatment. TF-CBT has a number of treatment components, summarized using the PRACTICE acronym. According to Cohen et al. (2009), PRACTICE stands for psychoeducation (P), parental treatment, relaxation (R), affective (A) expression and modulation, cognitive (C) coping skills, trauma (T) narrative and cognitive processing of the trauma, in-vivo (I) desensitization to trauma reminders, conjoint (C) parent-child sessions, and enhancing (E) safety and future development. Treatment is typically preceded by one or more assessment sessions, and is often pre-sented in a linear, session-by-session format. However, these components are intended to be applied flexibly. As Cohen et al. point out, depending on treatment need, some psychotherapists may choose to skip one or more of the modules, or move up a module if necessary. For example, in our clinical experience, we have sometimes found it necessary to move up the safety planning module when our clients are in environments that place them at risk for experiencing abusive episodes.

In a Christian-accommodative approach to TF-CBT, we follow each of the modules in their secular form. However, all of the modules are adapted to explicitly address religious and spiritual issues. Subsequently, some modules now incorporate spiritual interventions such as Scripture or prayer in them. In other modules, we incorporate discussion of religious issues, such as where God was when the traumatic event occurred, and how the client feels about God's presence during and after the trauma. In this next section, we present a Christian-accommodative approach to TF-CBT.

A CHRISTIAN-ACCOMMODATIVE APPROACH TO TF-CBT

Initial assessment. As one might expect, the standard treatment protocol for TF-CBT in its secular form involves assessing the nature of the abuse that the child or adolescent client experienced as well as the effects of the abuse on their mental health (Cohen et al., 2006). This is typically accom-plished using separate individual interviews with both parent and child. In some situations, as when a child has been removed from the care of their biological parent(s), the interview may be conducted with a legal guardian from the Department of Child and Family Services.

Therapists typically assess the nature of the abuse (physical, sexual or both), the frequency of the abuse (single event or chronic abuse) and the relationship of the perpetrator(s) to the child. In addition, therapists also assess the effects of the abuse on the child's mental health and emotional functioning. In particular, therapists look for acute psychiatric symptoms such as suicidal ideation or the presence of psychotic symptoms brought on by the abuse. Therapists then typically proceed to assess for the presence of trauma-related symptoms consistent with post-traumatic stress disorder, depression and anxiety.

Elsewhere we have argued that in addition to assessing the nature of the abuse and its effects, therapists should assess the potential role of religion and spirituality in either exacerbating or assisting clients to resolve their symptoms (Walker et al., 2010). Specifically, we encourage therapists to do this by modifying Richards and Bergin's (2005) Level 1 versus Level 2 approach to assessment specifically for use with children and teens who have been abused. In a typical Level 1 assessment, therapists broadly assess the role of religious and spiritual faith in the client's presenting problems. This can be accomplished through the use of questions such as "What is your religious affiliation?" and "Are there any religious or spiritual issues that you want to talk about in therapy?" Adapting this for use with child abuse victims specifically, we encourage therapists to assess for potential changes in a child abuse victim's religious faith after trauma. For example, therapists can use open-ended inquiries such as "tell me about your faith since the abuse occurred."

In a typical Level 2 assessment of client religion and spirituality, therapists are encouraged more specifically to assess the role of religion and spirituality in the client's presenting problem. Richards and Bergin (2005) encourage therapists to consider using standardized religious measures as well as clinical interviews to assess the role of religion and spirituality in a client's clinical presentation. Adapting this protocol for use with child abuse survivors specifically, we encourage therapists using a Christian accommodative approach to assessment to assess potential damage to a client's faith in a detailed fashion. Abuse survivors often experience spiritual struggles related to anger toward God and questioning how God could allow their abuse to occur. They may also struggle in their relationship with God and their image of God, often having difficulty believing that God still loves them (Walker et al., 2009). Therefore, we encourage therapists to assess more specifically for problems in a child abuse survivor's relationship with God during a Level 2 assessment in this phase of treatment.

Psychoeducation. The psychoeducation module is the first initial treatment module in TF-CBT. Therapists typically educate clients and their parents about common emotional and behavioral reactions to abuse (such as hypervigilance or difficulty sleeping). Therapists also usually provide information about the child's diagnosis and what treatment will entail.

During the psychoeducation phase of treatment, we also encourage therapists to educate children and their parents about common religious and spiritual reactions to abuse. As mentioned above, abuse survivors often experience spiritual struggles related to the abuse, particularly in their relationship with God. We encourage therapists to normalize this for clients by making them aware that this often happens.

Relaxation. The purpose of the next several treatment modules is to assist clients in managing their reactions to the abuse that has occurred and also prepare them for the emotional stress of discussing the abuse during the trauma narrative module. During the relaxation module, clients are taught relaxation training in the form of progressive muscle relaxation and focused breathing involving mindfulness meditation. Training in progressive muscle relaxation is usually done with an age-appropriate script. For example, the training module at the Medical University of South Carolina has a video with a progressive muscle relaxation script for child clients involving imagining that their arms become "as loose as spaghetti" or that they are chewing on a jawbreaker. Focused breathing is taught in which child clients engage in mindful attention to the sensation of the air in their body moving their diaphragm up and down while they breathe, as well as the ensuing feeling of relaxation.

In a Christian-accommodative approach to this module, we encourage clients to pray while engaging in progressive muscle relaxation and focused-breathing exercises. We sometimes encourage clients to pray the Jesus prayer, "Lord Jesus, Son of God, have mercy on me, a sinner," while practicing these forms of relaxation. The client begins by praying "Lord Jesus, Son of God" while inhaling, then exhaling "have mercy on me, a sinner." In our clinical experience, we have found that clients are often naturally drawn to prayer during this treatment module and easily employ it at home when trying to cope with the stress of trauma-related symptoms.

Affective expression and modulation. In this module, children learn to recognize different feeling states and how to regulate their expression of different feelings. Teaching children feeling recognition can occur in several ways. Psychotherapists often use psychotherapeutic games or utilize child drawings in this module. For example, some psychotherapists use the color-your-life technique in which a child chooses different colors to describe different feelings that they have experienced. After picking a color to represent a feeling, children then describe a time in their lives when they felt the feeling that is represented by the color. Another game that is sometimes used to teach feeling identification is to have the child generate a list of feelings within a given time limit (typically one or two minutes) to see how many feelings the child can identify. After identifying a number of different feelings, the psychotherapist then asks the child to describe times when they have felt emotion.

Children are also taught thought interruption during this TF-CBT module. Thought stopping is usually done either through verbal means (by telling a thought to "go away") or by physical means (such as snapping a rubber band against one's wrist when one begins to have an unwanted thought). Afterward, the thought is replaced with a positive image in the form of a special event (such as one's birthday) or experience (such as a time when the child hit a home run or scored a winning basket).

In using an explicitly Christian-accommodative approach to this TF-CBT module, we have incorporated biblical passages, Christian worship songs and biblical stories to help children and teens interrupt their thoughts. For example, a teenage girl who was depressed and struggling with depression reported frequently replaying a time when an abusive parent condemned her, telling her "you're a sinner." This girl continued to replay the image of her abusive parent while repeating this phrase to herself over and over again. We helped the girl identify a Christian song to use to interrupt the thought, and we had her begin to sing this song whenever she started to replay the scene in her mind. In her case, we suggested the song "More" by Matthew West. Specifically, we encouraged her to repeat the chorus (sung from God's perspective about the extent of his love for us) whenever she had disturbing, condemning thoughts about being a sinner.

Cognitive coping and processing I. This treatment component builds on the previous one by teaching clients the relationship between their thoughts, feelings and behaviors—what Cohen et al. (2009) referred to as the cognitive triangle. Children are taught the cognitive triangle using role plays that demonstrate the interrelationship between thoughts, feelings and behaviors. For example, a psychotherapist might role play an ambiguous scenario that takes place at school, such as another child walking by them without saying anything. The psychotherapist then role plays how the child might interpret this situation, and how different interpretations might lead to different feelings, which in turn lead to different behaviors. The psychotherapist might suggest, for example, that a child might think that his or her peer didn't like him or her because the peer didn't say hello. Interpreting the situation in this way might lead the child in the hypothetical role play to feel sad. After feeling sad, the client might, in the role play, walk away from the child who ignored him or her. The psychotherapist might then offer an alternative interpretation to the scenario. For example, "Perhaps the other child was in a hurry, and did not think to stop and say hello." The psychotherapist could then point out that interpreting the situation this way might lead the child client to not feel hurt by the other child's failure to say hello. The client could also then choose to say hello to the other child in the role play to try to initiate a conversation.

In our Christian accommodation of this module, we encourage therapists to help children realize how their thoughts, feeling and behaviors help them to draw nearer to God or farther away. Consider the hypothetical example of the ambiguous situation at school that we provided above. Helping a child to consider an alternative interpretation in this situation probably helps him or her to not feel hurt by the other child's failure to say hello. Behaviorally, he or she might also choose to say hello. Spiritually, however, interpreting the other child's actions in a neutral way is also a more gracious interpretation (not involving an assumption of spite on the part of the other child). Choosing a behavioral response that allows for reconciliation is also more congruent with a Christlike response.

Trauma narrative. During this treatment component, the child or adolescent client will tell the psychotherapist the story of what occurred during the traumatic event. Prior to asking a child to share their trauma narrative, psychotherapists typically prepare the child several sessions in advance that they will be asked to describe the narrative in session with the psychotherapist. When discussing the trauma narrative in advance of the actual session, it has been our experience that it is also helpful to explain the rationale for talking about the trauma with the child. We typically do this by tying the need to discuss the trauma to the child's presenting symptoms using developmentally appropriate, everyday language. For example, it has been our experience that some children have a restricted range of affect in which they feel sad and angry after abuse has occurred. With a child client who is middle-childhood age (somewhere between seven and ten years old), we have explained the need to discuss the trauma narrative by explaining that they have "a lot of sad and mad feelings inside and that talking about what happened will get those feelings out."

In addition to warning the child ahead of time and explaining a rationale for the trauma narrative, we have also prepared child clients for the trauma narrative by asking our clients how long they feel able to discuss the trauma narrative in session. We also typically schedule a joint meeting in which the parent and child are present, and openly warn both the parent and the child that discussing one's trauma narrative is difficult. We inform both the parent and the child that it is common for children to sometimes want to avoid discussing the trauma narrative once the scheduled date of the session occurs, and we encourage the parent to bring the child to psychotherapy when that occurs, so that we can discuss their ambivalence about discussing their trauma narrative, rather than cancelling the appointment. We also reassure clients who express fears about discussing the trauma narrative that we will not force them to discuss it, but that we want to talk with them about their feelings regarding the trauma narrative (rather than the narrative itself) if they find themselves wanting to avoid retelling it in session.

Prior to telling psychotherapists the actual trauma narrative, Cohen et al. recommend that clients describe either a happy event (such as a recent birthday) or a neutral event (such as a recent day at school) to prime children for the task of retelling the traumatic event. Once the actual trauma narrative begins, children are typically asked to describe what was happening before the actual event, what happened when the traumatic event itself occurred, and what happened afterward. Children often tell the trauma narrative while drawing what happened in a scene-by-scene format. However, the point of the telling of the trauma narrative is to help children integrate the experience into their lives and make meaning of the event. Therefore, children are encouraged to describe the event using any medium through which they feel comfortable expressing themselves. Some children draw what happened, whereas others may make up songs or poems about the traumatic event.

To help clients access the memory, they are instructed to tell what someone else would have seen if they had been there. In addition, to help access different sensory memories, clients are also often asked what someone else would have heard, smelled or felt if they had been at the traumatic event as well. Afterward, Cohen et al. also specifically ask children to tell the psychotherapist something that they never thought that they would tell someone else. They also ask clients to describe what advice they would give to other children who have been through a similar experience.

In a Christian-accommodative approach to the trauma narrative, we encourage psychotherapists to consider their role as being witnesses of the client's spiritual struggles and attempts to make meaning out of the trauma narrative. In addition, we encourage psychotherapists to explore parallels to the client's story with biblical narratives. For example, a psychotherapist might ask an older child client if they identify with the story of Job in the Bible.

We encourage psychotherapists to explore spiritual struggles that clients might be experiencing, particularly spiritual struggles involving the client's relationship with and image of God. Specifically, some clients may need to ask God where God was during the trauma and how God could have allowed the trauma to occur, especially in situations involving physical or sexual abuse. Rather than attempting to answer those questions for clients, we encourage psychotherapists to hear clients' attempts to answer them for themselves. Furthermore, we also encourage clients to openly discuss the trauma itself and their feelings about the trauma with God in prayer during the trauma narrative. In addition to prayer, some clients may be helped by using an empty-chair technique during this treatment module, where they alternate between speaking for themselves (from one chair) and attempting to respond from God's perspective (from another chair) about the traumatic event.

Cognitive coping and processing II. During this TF-CBT module, the psychotherapist explores and corrects trauma-related cognitive distortions that the client may be experiencing. In this module, psychotherapists often reread the trauma narrative in order to identify trauma-related cognitive distortions for correction.

Some clients might believe that the traumatic event was their fault. For example, a female teenage client presenting for psychotherapy having been date raped might erroneously believe that she made the rape occur by flirting with her date. Her psychotherapist would label this belief as a thought error and point out that many girls flirt with their dates without getting raped.

We suggest that an explicitly Christian-accommodative approach to this module will only be necessary when the cognitive distortion explicitly involves religious content. This will typically be the case when the trauma itself involves religion, as in cases of religion-related physical or sexual abuse (Bottoms, Nielsen, Murray & Filipas, 2003). For example, a physically abusive parent might have claimed that an oppositional child needed their sin nature beaten out of them, and that the Bible justified their physically abusive parenting practices. In such a case, a psychotherapist would label the belief that the Bible justifies abuse as an error and point out that the Bible describes God as a loving God who wants us to love one another and that we have laws against hurting people.

In vivo sensitization. The purpose of in vivo sensitization is to prevent generalization of anxious reactions to trauma in situations in which an anxious response is maladaptive. In discussing the purpose of this module, Cohen et al. (2009) point out that it is maladaptive to be anxious in response to actual threats to one's physical integrity. Therefore, psychotherapists are encouraged to be discerning in their application of in vivo desensitization. It is adaptive, for example, for a child exposed to community violence to be aware of their surroundings if they might realistically be faced with a mugging or a drive-by shooting. It is also adaptive for a child who has been placed in foster care because their biological mother drank and drove with them in the car to be aware of their surroundings if they are in a situation in which their biological mother might be driving them. Psychotherapists do not want to eliminate anxiety-provoking responses in such instances.

However, it is problematic when a child's reaction to a traumatic event becomes generalized to a nonthreatening situation. For example, a child who was physically abused in the home of a biological parent might become anxious when sleeping in the bedroom of foster parents who are not physically abusive. In this situation, in vivo sensitization could be used to help the child respond calmly when going to bed in his or her new bedroom.

In vivo sensitization involves creating an anxiety hierarchy and then gradually exposing the child to the anxiety-provoking scenarios in the hierarchy while helping the child to practice relaxation as a competing response. As such, this module requires a firm commitment on the part of both the psychotherapist and the child's parent or guardian to completing in vivo sensitization. It is crucial that psychotherapists avoid beginning the process of in vivo sensitization and then stopping before successfully taking the child through all of the situations in their created anxiety hierarchy. Starting the process and then stopping it abruptly could serve to reinforce the child's initial anxious response, as they ultimately are taught that they are indeed too weak or frail to successfully face their feared stimulus.

We suggest that a Christian-accommodative approach to in vivo sensitization could explicitly utilize both prayer and Scripture during the process. For instance, clients could be encouraged to practice in vivo sensitization using Bible verses that emphasize courage and facing one's fears. For example, Joshua 1:9 says "Be strong and courageous. Do not be afraid; do not be discouraged, for the LORD your God will be with you wherever you go." Clients could also be encouraged to pray while undergoing exposure to different anxiety-provoking situations in their anxiety hierarchy. Clients could be taught to pray for strength, courage, peace and the sense of God's presence as they undergo exposure to different things that they fear. In doing so, it is important to avoid reinforcing the child's anxiety in the way that they are taught prayer as a coping technique. Using prayer as part of in vivo sensitization will be most effective if the child is taught prayer while they are in a relaxed state and their experience of prayer is itself relaxing. Engaging in the practice of prayer without rehearsal while undergoing exposure to a feared stimulus could result in anxious prayers that might serve to reinforce the anxiety itself. Children and parents should also be reminded that although it is adaptive to pray during times of stress (such as exposure during in vivo sensitization), the primary purpose of prayer is to worship and enjoy fellowship with God.

Safety planning and future development. Safety planning, as its name implies, involves helping child and adolescent clients to take practical steps toward taking responsibility for their own safety in future situations that could involve exposure to violence. Safety planning is crucial in psycho-therapy cases in which a child client has been physically or sexually abused. As such, this module is sometimes moved to the very beginning of the treatment process, if the situation warrants it (i.e., if the child is at risk for experiencing abuse again in the near future).

During safety planning, the psychotherapist first reinforces steps that the child has already taken to assume responsibility for his or her own safety. As Cohen et al. (2009) point out, many children have taken some strides to do this prior to coming to psychotherapy by reporting the person who abused them to an adult. Praising children for their own efforts to take care of themselves honors their strength and courage.

In this module, the child's psychotherapist helps the client identify triggers that suggest that a situation is going to be unsafe, and then helps the client to identify steps to ensure their own safety. In situations involving abuse or domestic violence, there is often a set of clearly identifiable steps that occur prior to an abuser initiating an act of violence. For example, a child who has witnessed domestic violence by a physically abusive father against his or her mother might be able to identify clear signs that violence is about to occur in a predictable pattern of escalating behaviors. Such behaviors might occur in a chain such that (a) the father comes home from work, slightly agitated, (b) rests for a bit, (c) shows signs of frustration in response to mildly frustrating stimuli, such as the children in the home playing loudly, (d) begins to raise his voice, (e) becomes louder and verbally abusive and (f) moves to strike the child's mother. Children can be helped to identify the steps that occur in such abusive situations by asking them to retell what happens when someone in their family becomes violent and then writing down the events in sequence.

After identifying warning signs that indicate violence could occur, the second aspect of safety planning involves helping the child to identify steps they can take to ensure their own safety. To support the child's autonomy, we encourage children to try to take the lead in identifying these steps. Many times this is overwhelming for the child, and, in those instances, we will suggest specific concrete steps that a child can take, such as (a) calling 911, (b) identifying an "escape route" in the house, (c) identifying a trusted neighbor to run to for help and (d) identifying a trusted friend or neighbor to call for help if there were time to do so.

Planning for future development in this module involves helping the child to integrate the traumatic experience into his or her life. During this treatment component, children should be helped to identify traumatic triggers, particularly those that may occur at different times of year. For example, one of us treated a child who was sexually abused by an extended family member over the Thanksgiving holiday. Since contact with this family member was discontinued, planning for future development involved deciding how to respond to the trigger of celebrating Thanksgiving each year.

Much of this TF-CBT component involves practical planning for safety and considering how to deal with trauma reminders in the future. As a result, there is not much room for Christian accommodation in this module. However, we have typically encouraged parents of children to engage in nighttime prayers with their children if they do not already do so. We have found this practice to be particularly meaningful in promoting a sense of safety among school-aged and younger children with a non-offending parent after abuse.

Summary of Christian accommodation of TF-CBT. Much of a secular TF-CBT approach is congruent with a biblical emphasis on changing one's thoughts in order to simultaneously change feelings and behavior (Prov 23:7). However, our Christian accommodation is unique in its emphasis on assessing the role of client religion and spirituality before treatment either as a possible aid for healing or as an aspect of their spiritual functioning that has been damaged. This assessment guides treatment planning so that therapists can use those aspects of clients' personal faith that are still available as resources if other parts of their faith are damaged. Specifically, our Christian accommodation encourages therapists to openly discuss religious and spiritual issues, pray, and reference Scripture at various points throughout treatment.

DESCRIPTION AND RESULTS OF AN INITIAL CLINICAL TRIAL

Procedures. Five advanced interns pursuing a master's degree in mental health counseling and completing a specialty internship in child therapy were trained in providing Christian-accommodative trauma-focused cognitive-behavioral therapy to child participants. Interns who received case assignments were supervised weekly on their implementation of Christian-accommodative TF-CBT and obtained consent to video record each session. Interns utilized Christian-accommodative TF-CBT checklists in each session to assure standardization of treatment. The scoring of all pre- and post-measures was overseen by the second author (Quagliana).

Participants were recruited from local elementary schools, a local church and incoming clinic referrals. Inclusion criteria for the current study included the following: (1) parent and child identify themselves as religious, particularly practicing Christianity, (2) child or adolescent is between the ages of six and sixteen, (3) the child or adolescent has experienced some type of physical or sexual abuse, and (4) the child or adolescent has not received prior treatment for the physical or sexual abuse. Compensation for the current study was no fee for participation.

Participants. Informed consent was obtained from participants' parent or guardian and assent was obtained from participants. Participants originally included five children; however, three participants dropped out of treatment, or did not follow through with beginning treatment. The sample consisted of two children (one male, one female) whose average age was eight years. One participant had been sexually abused. The other participants had been physically and sexually abused.

Measures. Child Behavior Checklist, 6-18 (CBCL; Achenbach, 2001). The CBCL is a questionnaire administered to parents and caregivers to obtain an overall picture of a child's behavioral functioning. The CBCL contains both internalizing and externalizing behavior scales in addition to a PTSD scale. Parents were administered the CBCL pre- and post- treatment to provide a comprehensive overview of behavioral symptoms.

Trauma Symptom Checklist (for Young Children, TSCYC, Briere, 2005, and Children TSCC; Briere, 1996). The TSCC (Briere, 1996) is self-report measure of PTSD symptoms for children ages eight and over with scales measuring anxiety, depression, anger, posttraumatic stress, dissociation and sexual concerns. The TSCYC (Briere, 1999; 2005) is a parent report measure for children ages three through twelve. For the participant under age eight, a parent completed the TSCYC, which also measures symptoms of PTSD including dissociation, sexual concerns, posttraumatic stress, anxiety and depression.

Results and discussion of initial clinical trial. The pre-intervention and post-intervention results for both remaining clients from the clinical trial are reported in table 6.1. Both clients improved in most areas as a result of treatment. The first client improved significantly in all trauma-related areas as measured by the TSCC. The second client demonstrated modest improvement in several areas.

Table 6.1. Results for Two Clinical Trial Clients

Scale	Client 1		Client 2*	
Trauma Symptom Checklist				
	Pre	Post	Pre	Post
Anxiety	100	60	40	40
Depression	91	43	45	41
Posttraumatic Stress	88	64	50	46
Sexual Concerns	100	50	67	56
Dissociation	86	47	46	43
Anger	78	39	41	41
Child Behavior Checklist				
Total Score	46	36	52	50
Externalizing Score	72	66	44	47
Internalizing Score	68	70	52	43

Note: Client 2 was under eight years old. The scores reported are the Trauma Symptom Checklist for Children—a caregiver report. The posttraumatic stress score reported for client 2 is the posttraumatic stress total score from the Trauma Symptom Checklist for Young Children.

As a research team, we were disappointed with the difficulty we encountered in recruiting and retaining participants. We are encouraged to report that qualitatively, use of religious imagery and reference to Scripture were powerful treatment components during therapy. In this next section, we present a series of case studies demonstrating the application of Christian-accommodative TF-CBT. The first client was seen by the third author (Wilkinson) and has been de-identified to protect client confidentiality. The second and third cases are amalgamated from clients seen by the second and fourth authors (Quagliana and Frederick). These amalgamated case presentations draw on some clinical material from the two clients that completed this initial clinical trial.

Case Studies Illustrating a Christian-Accommodative Approach to TF-CBT

The case of Mary. Mary was a ten-year-old Jamaican female brought into therapy after alleged sexual abuse by an older adolescent at her church. Mary's mother, a single parent, reported that Mary had difficulty sleeping and that her grades were slipping in school. She also reported that Mary no longer wanted to spend time with friends outside of school or church and had become more irritable at home and church.

Assessment. Both the client and her mother reported being very committed to their religion. During this phase of treatment Mary readily discussed wanting to talk about the trauma and stated that she prayed "God would forgive" the alleged perpetrator. Mary also said that she felt angry at God and her perpetrator while also feeling compelled to forgive the perpetrator. In addition, Mary also stated that she felt like she was "damaged" in God's eyes, a specific spiritual struggle that would be addressed in later sessions. Finally, Mary's abuser attended the same church that she attended, and, as might be expected, Mary said that it was very difficult to even imagine going to services at the church again.

Mary's mother needed psychoeducation about the effects of trauma as it related to Mary's discomfort about attending church (where she would see the abuser occasionally if she chose to attend). Her psychotherapist developed a safety plan with Mary and her mother regarding church attendance. Mary's mother did feel her role as a parent and protector as a sacred calling and readily engaged in developing and utilizing the safety plan. Mary's mother also encouraged her to change churches (though not denominations) and Mary was eventually able to attend services at a different location.

Mary reported a high degree of anxiety during the school day and at night when she tried to sleep. Her psychotherapist taught Mary to engage in "belly breathing" and refocus her thoughts. Mary would also often recite psalms or songs like "Jesus Loves Me" in order to relax at school and home.

Mary enjoyed art and drawing, so in order to practice feeling identification, Mary would paint her feelings and process how each color represented her feelings. The amount of a specific color used on the paper also represented the varying degrees of the different feelings she was experiencing. In addition, Mary was also taught thought interruption and positive imagery using the image of God holding her when she felt scared, anxious and alone. She also took comfort in the notion that God was "with her" throughout the day and used that thought as a means of coping self-talk. At this time she also began to process with her psychotherapist how her dysfunctional thoughts about being damaged and unacceptable to God might not be accurate.

Building on the previous stage, Mary was able to process her anger toward God and her perpetrator. Mary was able to process with the therapist and her mother how just because the perpetrator went to her church it did not mean "he was a good person" or that God approved of his behavior. She also processed why God would allow something to happen to her according to her doctrinal upbringing. While the therapist did not comment on why God would allow the abuse, she did help Mary process and ask further questions in addition to asking Mary how she thought God would answer her questions. Because religion seemed to be an important part of Mary's life (not just part of what her family did) several sessions were devoted to this process. Mary also processed whether or not she wanted to discuss the abuse with others at their church. The therapist encouraged Mary to remember that her story was her own to share or not share in those circumstances. Separately, Mary's mother processed reporting the alleged abuse to church leadership.

Trauma narrative. Because Mary was pretty self-aware and high functioning, she easily embraced the trauma narrative. Mary created a book about her trauma story, which included how she felt, how her life is different since the abuse, and how therapy has affected her story. Mary chose to read the story to her mom. Mary was even able to attribute her ability to overcome the trauma to the hand of God.

Cognitive coping and processing II. During this phase the therapist processed trauma-related cognitive errors with Mary. Specifically, Mary struggled with feeling unsafe and with feeling that she should have told someone about the abuse sooner. (The abuse occurred over the course of a year before anyone found out.) The therapist also confronted Mary on her desire to forgive the perpetrator without fully acknowledging that his actions were wrong and unacceptable first. (Part of Mary seemed to dismiss the perpetrators actions instead of acknowledging them.)

In vivo sensitization. Mary had an increase in PTSD symptoms when driving by a specific storefront that triggered abuse memories for her. Using relaxation and in vivo sensitization to process Mary's feelings of fear and anxiety, Mary was able to decrease her PTSD symptoms when driving by the storefront and prevent a further generalization to similar nonthreatening stimuli. Mary would go over her "safety hand" to remind herself who she could call on when she felt unsafe. She also used prayer to self-soothe and feel confident.

Conjoint sessions with parents and children. Mary would have conjoint sessions (or partial sessions) with the therapist and her mother to address issues and process trauma. Mary would engage in activities such as reading her trauma narrative or showing her mother the art she made and the corresponding story or feelings. Mary also took the time to confront her mom about her desire to spend more quality time with her. Mary and her mom lived with her adult older brother and Mary's mom worked full time, often picking up extra weekend shifts. Mary desired to have more one-on-one quality time with her mom. The therapist encouraged an open discussion between Mary and her mom and helped them to create a scheduled "mother-daughter" time each week. Because religion was a priority for the family, Mary and her mother also decided to spend a few minutes praying together each night before bed.

Safety planning and future development. Much safety planning had already taken place throughout treatment, but the therapist continued to process the safety plan previously developed and the newly established prayer time before bed to foster a sense of safety. The therapist also processed with Mary how to pay attention to internal warnings and did role-plays on how to respond in a potentially unsafe situation. The therapist also did some psychoeducation regarding situations when the trauma symptoms may return (i.e. puberty, first date) and how Mary could use the tools she has learned in therapy and through her religious practices to cope.

The case of David. David, a seven-year-old Caucasian male, presented to psychotherapy for both sexual abuse and sexual behavior problems. David had been perpetrated by an older neighborhood friend while playing at home. Following this incident, David exhibited sexual behaviors (inappropriate touching) toward a younger friend, which precipitated the family seeking treatment. David and his family identified as Christians, specifically Baptist. David found comfort in repeating Scriptures from the Bible that he learned through Sunday school and vacation Bible school. As a result, his mother chose David to participate in Christian-accommodative TF-CBT for treatment.

Safety planning. The first concern addressed in treatment was safety planning with David's mother. In order to prevent future victimization of David and to prevent sexual behavior problems, the psychotherapist created a safety plan with her to have him monitored at all times around all children.

Assessment. In the assessment phase of the Christian-accommodative TF-CBT protocol, David reported that even following the sexual abuse and sexual behavior problems, he continued to trust in God and did not blame God for what happened. In fact, he reported praying about the incidents as a coping strategy. David's religious coping strategies were also evident in his use of religious imagery and Scripture when prompted for religious or spiritual coping resources. In the relaxation phase of the TF-CBT protocol, David said that he could "rest in the shadow of God's wings." He revealed to his psychotherapist that he identified God as an eagle. The psychotherapist encouraged David to utilize this imagery and metaphor when feeling anxious and overwhelmed with abuse-related thoughts and feelings. The psychotherapist further encouraged the child by reciting to David the Bible passage of Psalm 91:4, which states, "He will cover you with his feathers, and under his wings you will find refuge; his faithfulness will be your shield and rampart."

Relaxation. Throughout the TF-CBT protocol, David clung to the imagery of God as an eagle and the protection that he could receive from resting in God's wings. David also engaged this imagery in nonverbal ways as the psychotherapist encouraged him to draw pictures of how he viewed God and resting in his wings. Furthermore, David noted that when he feels sad he finds comfort in praying and singing songs to God.

Trauma narrative. David was resistant in discussing his trauma narrative related to both the alleged sexual abuse and sexual behavior problems and in taking any responsibility for alleged sexual behavior problems. However, the psychotherapist engaged the trauma narrative in a variety of methods including art to better understand the emotions experienced by David. He was able to utilize his religious coping when the trauma narrative elicited anxious thoughts and feelings. Again the themes of resting in God's wings and praying when scared brought great comfort to David.

CONCLUSION

In this chapter, we have presented a Christian-accommodative approach to TF-CBT that combines a biblical respect for the role of cognitions in altering feelings and behavior with a consistent research finding that victims of abuse require trauma-focused treatment to overcome it. Although we are disappointed with our initial efforts to recruit clients for a clinical trial, we have enough clinical experience using this approach to know that it works. We have presented several case studies demonstrating this approach. We look forward to the collection of additional data demonstrating its efficacy.

REFERENCES

Achenbach, T. M. (1991). *Integrative guide for the 1991 CBCU 4-18 YSR, and TRF Profiles*. Burlington: University of Vermont, Dept. of Psychiatry.

Achenbach, T. M., & Rescorla, L. A. (2001). *Manual for the ASEBA School-Age Forms and Profiles*. Burlington, VT: ASEBA.

Bottoms, B. L., Nielsen, M., Murray, R., & Filipas, H. (2003). Religion-related child physical abuse: Characteristics and psychological outcomes. *Journal of Aggression, Maltreatment & Trauma, 8* (1-2), 87-114.

Briere, J. (1996). *Trauma Symptom Checklist for Children (TSCC)*. Odessa, FL: Psychological Assessment Resources.

Briere, J. (1999, 2005). *Trauma Symptom Checklist for Young Children (TSCYC)*. Odessa, FL: Psychological Assessment Resources.

Cohen, J. A., Mannarino, A. P., & Deblinger, E. (2006). *Treating trauma and traumatic grief in children and adolescents*. New York: Guilford Press.

Cohen, J. A., Mannarino, A. P., Deblinger, E., & Berliner, L. (2009). Cognitive-behavioral therapy for children and adolescents. In E. B. Foa, T. M. Keane, M. J. Friedman & J. A. Cohen (Eds.), *Effective treatments for PTSD: Practice guidelines from the International Society for Traumatic Stress Studies* (pp. 223-44). New York: Guilford Press.

Richards, P. S., & Bergin, A. E. (2005). *A spiritual strategy for counseling and psychotherapy* (2nd ed.). Washington, DC: American Psychological Association.

Walker, D. F., Reese, J. B., Hughes, J. P., & Troskie, M. J. (2010). Addressing religious and spiritual issues in trauma-focused cognitive behavior therapy with children and adolescents. *Professional Psychology: Research and Practice, 41,* 174-80.

Walker, D. F., Reid, H. W., O'Neill, T., & Brown, L. (2009). Changes in personal religion/spirituality during recovery from childhood abuse: A review and synthesis. *Psychological Trauma: Theory, Research, Practice, and Policy, 1,* 130-45.

7

Evidence-Based Principles from Psychodynamic and Process-Experiential Psychotherapies

Keith J. Edwards and Edward B. Davis

Psychotherapy commonly centers on treating clients with emotional, relational and identity difficulties. Psychodynamic and process-experiential (PE) psychotherapies are frequently used for treating such problems, but among scientists and practitioners alike, there is a pervasive and popularized notion that these psychotherapies lack empirical support (Elliott, 2002; Shedler, 2010). Such a notion may in part emanate from what Shedler (2010) described as "lingering distaste" for the psychoanalytic community, based on that community's "past arrogance and authority" (p. 98). It may also reflect a response to the historically dismissive stance that the psychodynamic and PE communities have taken toward research. Nonetheless, the growing demand for time-efficient and evidence-based treatments has resulted in the development of psychodynamic and PE approaches that are both short-term and evidence-based (Elliott, Watson, Goldman & Greenberg, 2004; Shedler, 2010).

ADDRESSING PROBLEMATIC WORLDVIEW ASSUMPTIONS

Many Christian counselors and psychotherapists have worldview-related reservations about psychodynamic and PE approaches based on inconsistencies between these traditions' underlying worldview assumptions and those of traditional Christian theology. For example, both psychodynamic and PE psychotherapies emphasize ideals of autonomy, self-determination and personal fulfillment, whereas traditional Christian theology emphasizes ideals of depending on God, being led by the Holy Spirit and finding fulfillment through Christlike service.

Indeed, for Christian mental-health professionals, there are myriad worldview-conflicts between psychodynamic/PE models and orthodox Christian doctrine. We do not have the space to address all such conflicts. Instead, we will briefly comment on why it makes sense for Christian counselors and psychotherapists to appropriate some principles from psychodynamic and PE treatments in the service of Christ, his church and his kingdom.

APPROPRIATING PRINCIPLES FROM PSYCHODYNAMIC AND PROCESS-EXPERIENTIAL PSYCHOTHERAPIES

There are several reasons for Christian counselors and psychotherapists to appropriate principles from psychodynamic and PE psychotherapies. For instance, Christianity is an experientially focused religion in which positive transformation occurs primarily through loving relationships with God and others. Similarly, psychodynamic/PE treatments are chiefly dedicated to providing clients with corrective emotional experiences in the therapy relationship (Moriarty & Davis, 2012; cf. Norcross, 2011). For this reason, a Christian counselor or psychotherapist can use these techniques to facilitate deep-level, sanctifying transformation in clients' relationships with God, others and themselves.

In this chapter, we discuss evidence-based psychodynamic and PE strategies that can be used in Christian counseling and psychotherapy. Toward that end, we argue that the worldview-conflicts between psychodynamic/PE models and Christian theology can be reconciled by distinguishing between content and process. For example, one can use emotionally evocative communication strategies (same process) to either preach the gospel of Jesus or propagate the philosophy of Marxism (different contents). Similarly, despite the worldview conflicts between psychodynamic/PE models and Christian theology, Christian counselors and psychotherapists can use psychodynamic/PE strategies to promote the positive growth of Christian clients.

In fact, psychodynamic/PE treatments actually *privilege* process—particularly emotionally rich experiential processing. Therapists skilled in using psychodynamic/PE techniques must be process experts who are able to facilitate the client's deep emotional engagement and experiencing, because these processes are the presumed mechanisms of change. It is this type of processing that can reveal the rich layers of client's experiences, opening up possibilities for increased insight and for growth-promoting meaning making (Greenberg, 2011).

When using psychodynamic/PE techniques, the task of meaning making is where process and content are integrated. Within the context of Christian counseling and psychotherapy, because the clinician and the client share a common meaning-making framework (i.e., a Christian worldview), theologically informed transformation is perhaps especially possible.

Unfortunately, there are as of yet no randomized controlled trials examining the efficacy of Christian-accommodated psychodynamic or PE treatments. However, we hypothesize that *all* Christian counselors and psychotherapists can benefit from appropriating the evidence-based principles of psychotherapeutic change that are emphasized within the psychodynamic and PE traditions—namely the adept tracking and directing of therapeutic process. In other words, we believe all Christian clinicians can become more effective if they cultivate process expertise (e.g., through becoming competent in using psychodynamic and PE interventions).

The remainder of this chapter is divided into two parts. First, we review the empirical evidence supporting the efficacy of psychodynamic and PE psychotherapies. Next, we describe a three-phase model of experiential therapy, integrating psychodynamic and PE approaches (Greenberg & Watson, 2006). At various places, we discuss ways that Christian counselors and psychotherapists can use these types of interventions in their work with Christian clients.

EMPIRICAL SUPPORT FOR TREATMENT EFFICACY

The efficacy of psychodynamic psychotherapy. Perhaps the best available research on the efficacy of psychodynamic psychotherapy is Gerber et al.'s (2011) review-article, the culminating report of their ad hoc subcommittee for evaluation of the evidence base for psychodynamic psychotherapy. This committee was comprised of five expert psychotherapy researchers—three who espoused a psychodynamic theoretical orientation and two who espoused a nonpsychodynamic one. They examined fifty-four randomized controlled trials (RCTs) that were deemed to be of at least *adequate* methodological quality. The RCTs included a total of sixty-three comparisons between psychodynamic psychotherapy and either an *active* comparison group ($n = 39$ comparisons; i.e., a group who received an evidence-based treatment or a specific/presumed-effective treatment) or an *inactive* comparison group ($n = 24$ comparisons; i.e., a group that received no treatment, treatment as usual, or a minimal/presumed-ineffective treatment). Relative to *active* comparators ($n = 39$), psychodynamic treatments evidenced better outcomes in six comparisons (15%), poorer outcomes in five comparisons (13%), and statistically equivalent outcomes in twenty-eight comparisons (72%). In contrast, relative to *inactive* comparators ($n = 24$), psychodynamic treatments evidenced better outcomes in eighteen comparisons (75%) and statistically equivalent outcomes in six comparisons (25%; Gerber et al., 2011). In sum, Gerber et al. (2011) concluded that the empirical support for psychodynamic psychotherapy is *promising* but mainly suggests that psychodynamic psychotherapy is more efficacious than an inactive comparator. Relative to other active treatments (e.g., CBT), the evidence suggests statistically equivalent efficacy.

At the time of writing this chapter (May 2013), no psychodynamic treatments have received enough empirical support to be consensually deemed *well-established* as per Chambless et al.'s (1998) gold-standard criteria for classifying evidence-based treatments. Only two have received enough to be considered *probably efficacious:* (a) short-term psychodynamic psychotherapy for depression and (b) psychodynamic treatment for panic disorder (for a regularly updated list of evidence-based treatments, see www.psycho logicaltreatments.org).

Before proceeding, it is important to summarize Shedler's (2010) controversial review of meta-analytic research on the efficacy of psychodynamic psychotherapy. Of the meta-analyses Shedler (2010) reviewed, the two most methodologically rigorous were (a) Abbass et al. (2006) and (b) Leichsenring, Rabung and Leibing (2004). Both meta-analyses examined only the highest-quality RCTs ($n = 23$ and 17 RCTs, respectively, with eight overlapping) of short-term psychodynamic psychotherapy (i.e., forty hours or less; $M = 15$ and 21 sessions, respectively), relative to inactive comparators. These meta-analyses synthesized the RCT findings into a quantifiable common metric: an *effect size* (ES)—that is, the standardized mean difference between comparison groups (i.e., the group-mean difference, expressed in standard-deviation units). (Conventional interpretive guidelines suggest that an ES of 0.8 indicates a large effect, 0.5 indicates a moderate effect, and 0.2 indicates a small effect.)

Abbass et al. (2006) found that, for general psychiatric symptoms, short-term psychodynamic psychotherapy evidenced a between-groups, control-referenced ES of 0.97 at therapy termination and of 1.51 at long-term follow-up (>9 months post-therapy). Leichsenring et al. (2004) found that for *general psychiatric symptoms* short-term psychodynamic psychotherapy (*n* = 15 RCTs) demonstrated a between-groups, control-referenced ES of 0.90 (*SD* = 0.48) at therapy termination and of 0.95 at follow-up (*M* = 14 months); for *presenting problems* (*n* = 17 RCTs), 1.39 (*SD* = 0.83) and 1.57 (*SD* = 0.88), respectively. Notably, when the outcomes of short-term psychodynamic psychotherapy and active comparators (e.g., CBT) were compared, the respective therapy-termination and follow-up data were statistically equivalent, both for general psychiatric symptoms (*n* = 14 RCTs at therapy-termination and 12 at follow-up) and for target problems (*n* = 15 and 14 RCTs, respectively; Abbass et al., 2006), supporting Gerber et al.'s (2011) conclusions. Importantly, these data *contradict* Shedler's (2010) claims that (a) psychodynamic psychotherapy uniquely leads to benefits that increase over time and (b) the benefits of nonpsychodynamic treatments tend to decay. Indeed, Shedler's article has received a number of worthy criticisms (e.g., Anestis, Anestis & Lilienfeld, 2011).

The efficacy of Christian-accommodated psychodynamic treatments. Only two outcome studies have examined the efficacy of Christian-accommodated psychodynamic treatments: Tisdale et al. (1997) and Thomas, Moriarty, Davis and Anderson (2011). However, these studies offer only pilot data, because each study lacked a control group and included other types of treatment (e.g., pharmacotherapy, psychoeducation). Tisdale et al. (1997) examined the change experienced by clients who participated in an object-relations oriented, multimodal program for adult psychiatric inpatients. The treatment program involved an integration of object relations theory with theological principles, as described in books by Cloud and Townsend (e.g., 2004). Relative to admission scores, participants' discharge scores evidenced statistically significant improvements in god images (i.e., the mental/neural representations that underlie a person's embodied, emotional relationship with God; Davis, 2010) and self-images (i.e., the mental/neural representations that underlie a person's thoughts and feelings about themselves). However, only the latter were large enough to be considered clinically meaningful. Of note, the evidenced changes in self-images *increased* over the twelve-month follow-up period, while the changes in god images endured but did not improve further.

In another pilot study, Thomas et al. (2011) used a Christian-accommodated, psychotherapy-integrationist oriented, eight-week, manualized protocol to treat adult outpatients in a group-psychotherapy format. This protocol was designed for use with individuals seeking treatment for god-image difficulties. At admission and termination, a variety of self-report outcome measures were administered, and scores on these measures evidenced statistically significant improvements on all nine god-image variables; all but one of these improvements were large-sized and thus clinically meaningful. Specifically, participants reported experiencing God emotionally as *less* distant (within-subjects, pre-post change ES = 1.73), disapproving (ES = 1.39) and harsh (ES = 0.88), and as *more* accepting (ES = 1.23), intimate (ES = 1.13) and supportive (ES = 0.79). Furthermore, they reported experiencing *less* god-attachment anxiety (ES = 0.70) and god-attachment avoidance (ES = 0.43), as well as *more* congruence (ES = 1.30) between their emotional experience of God (god images) and their theological beliefs about God (god concepts; Davis, 2010). When asked to specify the change mechanisms that led to their psychotherapeutic benefits, participants most commonly mentioned (a) two mechanisms of group-member influence (interpersonal input and output [n = 13] and universality [n = 10]) and (b) three psychotherapeutic interventions (allegorical-bibliotherapy, a cognitive-restructuring exercise and a psychodynamic exercise [ns = 9 for all three]).

The efficacy of process-experiential psychotherapy. Unfortunately, there are as of yet no studies examining the efficacy of Christian-accommodated PE treatments, although some authors have hypothesized that narrative-experiential interventions may be particularly potent in effecting positive god-image change (Davis & Badenoch, 2010; Moriarty & Davis, 2012). In contrast, within the secular psychotherapy-research literature, there are dozens of studies on the efficacy of PE psychotherapy, relative to both in-active and active comparators (Elliott, 2002).

Perhaps the best available research in this area is Elliott's (2002) review chapter, a meta-analysis of eighty-six published outcome studies of PE psy-chotherapies. This meta-analysis evaluated comparisons between PE psy-chotherapy and either an inactive comparator (no treatment or waitlist control; $n = 36$ comparisons) or an active comparator (a non-PE treatment; $n = 48$ comparisons). Relative to *inactive* comparators, PE treatments evi-denced a between-groups, control-referenced ES of 0.72 ($SD = 0.53$). The within-subjects, pre-post change ES was 1.03 ($SD = 0.59$) at termination, 1.26 ($SD = 0.71$) at early follow-up (i.e., one to eleven months), and 1.15 ($SD = 0.55$) at late follow-up (i.e., ≥ twelve months). In contrast, relative to *active* comparators, PE treatments evidenced statistically equivalent outcomes to those of non-PE treatments, with a between-groups, comparative ES (i.e., differences between the pre-post change ESs of the two treatment groups) of 0.0 ($SD = 0.44$; Elliott, 2002). Of note, at this time no PE treatments have received enough empirical support to be deemed *well-established*, and only two have received enough to be considered *probably efficacious:* (a) emotion-focused therapy for depression and (b) emotion-focused therapy for moderately distressed couples (Greenberg, 2011).

Shared Assumptions of Psychodynamic and Process-Experiential Psychotherapies

Psychodynamic and PE therapies have very different historical origins, and they each have distinctive ideas about human personality, psychopathology and psychotherapy. However, there have been increasing efforts to inte-grate these and other approaches into a common theoretical and psycho-therapeutic framework (e.g., www.unifiedpsychotherapyproject.org). As it relates specifically to integrating psychodynamic and PE therapies, such efforts are largely based on consilient advancements in the fields of at-tachment and interpersonal neurobiology. The integration of these two therapies is based on shared assumptions that (a) relationships are the cru-cible of human development, (b) emotions are the primary motivational system, and (c) implicit (nonconscious) mental processes matter (Cozolino, 2010; Siegel, 2012).

Relationships are the crucible of human development. It is now well-established that, across the lifespan, close relationships impact and modify humans' mental models of self and others. In attachment relationships, our embodied mind can be transformed in positive ways, through experiential engagement with another embodied mind that is experienced as safe, attuned, empathic and responsive (Cozolino, 2010; Siegel, 2012).

Emotions are the primary motivational system. Psychodynamic and PE psychotherapies also emphasize the primacy of affect. The human brain-body system is viewed as genetically predisposed to be goal-seeking, adaptational and self-organizing. Emotions are seen as the primary motivational system that guides humans' adaptation to the environment, because emotions are the main mechanism by which experiential memories are stored and the chief lens through which subjective experiences are appraised. In addition, emotions guide humans' coping and adaptation efforts, and they provide the self with feedback regarding the status of one's goals and relationships. Furthermore, emotions are the primary mechanism of interpersonal communication and attachment bonding (Greenberg, 2011).

Implicit (nonconscious) mental processes matter. Last, there is now widespread recognition that a substantial amount of energy and information is processed at an implicit level (i.e., outside of conscious awareness). For instance, nonconscious mental processes help explain why our head and heart knowledge are not always congruent (e.g., god images and god concepts, respectively; Davis, 2010). Psychodynamic and PE approaches affirm that the brain largely processes energy and information at a nonconscious level, implicitly shaping our perceptions, feelings and thoughts (Cozolino, 2010; Siegel, 2012).

AN INTEGRATIVE MODEL OF EXPERIENTIAL THERAPY

Next, we describe a three-phase model of experiential therapy based on the work of Greenberg and Watson (2006) that integrates psychodynamic and PE approaches. Within this model, the goals of therapy are (a) to co-construct reflective awareness of deeper emotional dynamics, (b) to overcome defensive avoidance of these dynamics, and (c) to facilitate transformative experiencing of new emotional dynamics. These goals are pursued as the therapist establishes emotional engagement through attunement, resonance and empathy; fosters awareness through active, reflective exploration; overcomes avoidance through sensitive exploration of client vulnerabilities; builds clients' self-efficacy through confirmation of client strengths; and facilitates transformative experiences through the use of certain process-skills, none of which is unique to experiential therapy. Here we describe a few of these skills.

Crucial process skills. Developing and maintaining a good working alliance. In the psychotherapist's toolbox, perhaps the most important process skill is developing and maintaining a good working alliance. Indeed, it is now well-established that, across all psychotherapy formats (individual, family and group), the working alliance is demonstrably effective in promoting positive psychotherapeutic outcomes (Norcross, 2011). The working alliance is especially emphasized within the context of psychodynamic and PE psychotherapies, because it is the basis for everything else that happens in therapy (Greenberg, Rice & Elliott, 1993; Norcross, 2011).

Empathic attunement and resonance. Another important process skill is empathic attunement and resonance with the client's immediate and unfolding emotional experience. Throughout all phases of treatment, experiential therapists are guided by their moment-to-moment "process assessment" of the client's current emotional state (Elliott et al., 2004). Siegel (2010) has described the psychotherapist's in-session practice of mindfulness (i.e., purposeful awareness of here-and-now experiences, with an attitude of curiosity, openness, acceptance and lovingkindness) as one effective way to be fully present, attuning and resonating with the client's experiences as they unfold. This type of empathic attunement and resonance is the soil within which secure attachment and positive transformation occur (Cozolino, 2010; Greenberg, 2011).

Empathic understanding and validation. Communicating empathic understanding of the client's emotional experience is another key component of fostering secure attachment and transformation. Here again the goal is to help the client experience the therapist's attunement and resonance. For example, the therapist might say: "You feel so overwhelmed by your own feelings that you find it hard to even make sense of your husband's response. Everything seems confusing and overwhelming. Is that it?" This final question indicates tentativeness, thereby communicating the therapist's collaborative intent (described below; Greenberg, 2011).

Empathic validation is the complement to understanding. In a validation statement, the therapist implicitly communicates: "You make sense to me." With such an intervention, the goal is to support clients' sense of coherence and to promote continued exploration of their experiences and behavior. An example is: "You feel so alarmed that you can't focus. It makes sense that when you're terrified, you can't even concentrate." Empathic validations are especially effective when helping clients confront emotions they find confusing or disorienting. At such times, a therapist's validation can strengthen the client's ability to tolerate emotional engagement and to become more open to exploring their experiences (Greenberg, 2011).

In attachment terminology, the collective goal of empathic attunement, resonance, understanding and validation is to help clients "feel felt." For example, Christian clients who present with significant spiritual struggles (e.g., questions about how things "should" be for believers) often benefit from having their spiritual struggles empathized with and validated. Thus, a Christian client who is dealing with unresolved anger toward an abusive parent may believe that expressing anger toward that parent is "sinful." It can be effective to empathize with and validate both the client's anger and the spiritual struggle over expressing that anger.

Collaborative intent. Another important process-skill is communicating collaborative intent. That is, it is crucial to routinely invite clients' input and to facilitate clients' mutual involvement in therapy's overarching goals (i.e., aims) and tasks (i.e., the global and specific strategies for achieving those aims; Norcross, 2011). Also, it is important to communicate tentativeness when offering an empathic understanding or validation. Communicating tentatively fosters a sense of safety, which is critical to supporting client exploration and maintaining a good working alliance (Greenberg et al., 1993). Collaboratively inviting client feedback is also a demonstrably effective element of the therapy relationship (Norcross, 2011).

Phase 1: Accessing and allowing emotional experience. In the three-phase model described here, clients are guided to seek answers to four questions about their subjective experiences: "What are my feelings?" "What are my feelings telling me?" "What needs underlie these feelings?" "What do I need to do?" (Greenberg & Watson, 2006). (Note that experiential therapy proceeds according to the principle that all feelings should be attended to, but not all feelings should be acted on.) In the first phase, clients are encouraged to explore, discuss and express the full range of their emotional experiences, especially feelings that are contradictory, threatening or distressing (Shedler, 2010). Several interventions can help clients access and allow their emotions (Greenberg, 2011).

Clarification. In experiential therapy, the first task is to facilitate experiential awareness, and clarification is one way to evoke clients' emotional experience. Clarification involves asking for specific examples of the problem the client is describing; the goal is to seek details. For example, when a college-student client reports she is having a lot of conflict with her mother because her mother is so controlling, you might use clarification by asking, "What's an example of a recent situation when your mom was being controlling and it really upset you?" As the client searches her memory and recounts the event, the experiential therapist attends to the client's emotional states. The more detailed the description, the more likely the client will relive the emotions of the event. Client defenses are often manifested in the form of vagueness or lack of details, or they are reflected in the client's minimization or avoidance of vulnerable feelings. Persistent, sensitive and empathically attuned clarification is a gentle but effective way to access clients' emotions, bypass their defenses and overcome their avoidance (Frankland, 2010).

Evocative question/experiential focus. Evocative questions are also effective. These open questions are designed to evoke clients' attention to and exploration of their internal experience. Evocative questions help clients differentiate between external events and their internal responses to those events. For example, the therapist may probe for the client's subjective experience: "What's happening right now, as you say that?" Or the therapist can use Siegel's (2010) SIFT-the-mind question: "As you reflect on your own internal experience, what sensations, images, feelings and thoughts come to mind?" Two other examples are "What did you feel when you heard your husband say that he *does* care?" or "Where in your *body* do you feel the fear?" Evocative questions are also useful for probing the client's experience of the therapist and for making the relationship experientially salient. For instance, the therapist can ask: "What is it like for you to tell me about your struggle with masturbation?" In short, evocative questions increase clients' internal attending, which deepens and helps them put words to their embodied, emotional experiences. Indeed, Lieberman et al. (2007) have shown that putting feelings into words (i.e., affect labeling) helps down-regulate negative emotions.

Empathic conjecture. Empathic conjecture is another experiential intervention. Here the goal is to offer a tentative understanding of the tacit meaning embedded within the client's experience, by probing for feelings that are as-yet unacknowledged or that are at the edge of the client's awareness. An example is: "You say you are frustrated with the way things have gone, and I can understand that. It also seems you're feeling sad and alone. Does that fit?" Empathic conjectures can help clients symbolize experiences they are having difficulty putting into words, especially when those experiences involve contradictory, threatening or distressing feelings. These conjectures must be offered tentatively, with collaborative intent, because the therapist is essentially speaking for the client, verbalizing as-yet unarticulated experience (Greenberg, 2011).

Slowing the narrative pace and heightening client experience. In addition, it is helpful to slow down the client's narration of experiences (e.g., through probing for clarifying details). Doing so fosters increased self-awareness and deeper experiential processing. Furthermore, the therapist can heighten the client's emotional experience by using repetition, images, metaphors or enactments. For example, during an empty-chair dialogue (discussed below), the therapist might say: "So could you say that again, directly to her . . . that you shut her out?" "Slow down a minute and describe what happened inside you as she said 'I never *did* love you.'" "Can you say that again, 'I feel so abandoned by God . . . so alone'?" Because experiential exercises can make clients feel self-conscious and uncomfortable, the therapist needs to be willing and able to empathically and courageously enter the client's subjective world. One way to navigate this sacred space is to use sensitive language that invites the client's feedback and collaboration (e.g., "I wonder if . . . ," "I'm sensing that . . ." or "Does that fit for you?" Greenberg, 2011).

Overcoming avoidance of emotion. The primary way clients cope with problematic emotions is through avoidance. McCullough et al. (2003) has conceptualized such avoidance as reflecting an *affect phobia.* Experiential therapists actively but sensitively explore and challenge clients' attempts to avoid distressing feelings and thoughts. The clinician guides the client toward and deeper into difficult-to-face feelings and thoughts. In the context of a safe, empathic, trusting therapy relationship, the client is exposed to previously avoided feelings and thoughts. Using graded exposure (to avoid flooding), the therapist seeks to promote coregulatory expansion of the client's window of affect tolerance (Cozolino, 2010; Siegel, 2012).

The process of overcoming avoidance progresses in three steps. First, clients become aware *that* they are avoiding. Next, they become aware of *how* they are avoiding. Finally, they become aware of *what* they are avoiding. For example, a fictitious Christian client named Omar idealized his father (a minister) but described long periods of being alone, without his father's presence. The therapist noted that Omar's narration was oddly devoid of emotion. In particular, Omar rationalized his experiences, offering the excuse that his father was a minister who had extensive godly responsibilities. By using a story about a son's longing for contact and closeness with his father, the therapist empathically validated Omar's perspective but also confronted his rationalization. The therapist then made an empathic conjecture about Omar possibly feeling lonely and abandoned. Omar was able to enter into his feelings of sadness and longing, opening the door for exploring how his father's absence has vastly impacted his adult functioning.

With Christian clients, it is especially important to explore their attempts to avoid distressing feelings and thoughts that manifest in their embodied, emotional relationship with God. For instance, there often is a large discrepancy between Christians' head and heart knowledge of God, with a need to overcome the defense mechanisms blocking the integration of these two modes of knowledge (Davis, 2010).

Phase 2: Relational processing and making sense of emotional experience. Coregulating the client's emotional arousal. Clients avoid painful and difficult emotions for a reason: they are distressing and hard to regulate. There are a variety of ways that therapists can help clients approach and regulate these types of emotions. For example, therapists can help clients build their capacity to experience and tolerate difficult emotions by learning and practicing affect-regulation skills (e.g., deep breathing, muscle relaxation, Christian contemplative prayer/meditation), both during and in between therapy sessions. Therapists also can encourage clients to adopt a safe, "working-distant" stance, separating themselves from the emotion's intensity by reflectively exploring its meaning and implications. Another way the therapist can coregulate the client's emotional arousal is to maintain an experientially mindful presence through a warm and gentle vocal tone, a kind and empathic facial expression, and a calming and respectful silence (Greenberg, 2011; Siegel, 2010). Also, it is helpful for the therapist to validate the difficulty of experiencing painful emotions and to affirm clients' efforts to regulate their affect and self-soothe (regardless of whether such efforts are successful).

In experiential therapy, clients who have experienced trauma and abuse are especially at risk for becoming affectively dysregulated. It is now well established that, for traumatic memories to be transformed, they need to be activated and experientially accessed. However, for this processing of traumatic emotions to be effective, the level of emotional arousal needs to be at a moderate and manageable level, until distress subsides. This processing of difficult or avoided emotions is the experiential version of gradual desensitization to feared stimuli (Cozolino, 2010; Harwood, Beutler, Williams & Stegman, 2011; McCullough et al., 2003).

Using confrontation. Another way to help clients process and make sense of their emotional experience is to use confrontation, which involves the therapist reflecting back to a client something the therapist observes, thereby raising awareness of it and directing attention toward it. Confrontation may involve raising awareness of an aspect of the client's behavior or emotional state, in an effort to enhance the client's experience (e.g., "You seem to be really enjoying telling me about your son's award"). It may involve directing clients' attention toward something of which they are already aware (e.g., "I notice you have been ten minutes late for the last two sessions"). Or it may raise awareness of something that clients are avoiding or of which they are not consciously aware. Indeed, clients often communicate far more meaning implicitly than explicitly, and confrontation can be used to focus the client's attention on tacit nonverbal cues that are pregnant with meaning (e.g., changes in vocal tone, body posture or physiological state). For instance, confrontations can be used to highlight inconsistencies between clients' verbal report and affective display (e.g., smiling while describing a painful experience). Even so, when therapists offer confrontations, they must conjointly communicate collaborative intent, through such means as inviting client feedback (Frankland, 2010).

Exploring problematic reactions. Clients often report experiencing upsetting or puzzling reactions to events or people. Exploring problematic reactions can help clients make sense of their experiences and gain self-understanding (e.g., about the ways they habitually experience and interpret life events). Here the therapist invites the client to re-enter and systematically re-experience the situation. The overarching goal is for clients to become aware of the deeper meanings embedded within their experience, especially the ways their problematic reaction may reflect a recurring theme in their lives or a typical way they construe situations or people. Elliott et al. (2004) have called this intervention *systematic evocative unfolding.*

Note that systematic evocative unfolding is not a conceptual analysis of the situation; it is an experiential re-entry, involving clients systematically describing what they are experiencing (or rather, re-experiencing) as the problematic episode unfolds in their narrative. For example, Greenberg and Watson (2006) described a female client who reported a disturbing experience of depression following an important exam at school. During the exploration of the experience, the client realized she was angry at the teacher because he included questions about material that was never covered in class. As a child, this client experienced recurrent emotional and physical abuse from her father; now, as an adult, whenever she encountered unfair treatment from an authority figure, she withdrew into depression. Through experiential therapy, the client was able to change this pattern, largely via empty-chair dialogue (discussed below).

Identifying and exploring recurring themes and patterns. One of the goals of experiential therapy is to provide the client with new self-understanding. This goal can largely be accomplished by helping clients identify and explore themes and patterns that recur across their feelings, thoughts, behaviors and relationships (Shedler, 2010). Such an enterprise often involves co-constructing coherent, textured, growth-promoting life narratives (Cozolino, 2010).

A well-recognized feature of experiential therapy is the discussion of past relational experiences with a developmental focus. This developmental focus needs to center on exploring early-childhood experiences of caregivers and how those experiences are related to and reflected in the client's current emotional and relational life. The goal here is to assist clients in freeing themselves from internalized past experiences, so they can more fully and flexibly live in and enjoy the present (Shedler, 2010).

Clients often resist exploring the past for a number of reasons. With Christian clients, two of the most commonly cited reasons are the biblical principles that Christians should (a) forget the past and move on (e.g., Phil 3:13) and (b) refrain from blaming their parents for their current problems. The therapist can counter such objections by highlighting that, in experiential therapy, the focus is on one's own experiences—how subjective experiences in the past impact subjective experiences in the present. Exploring significant childhood memories is thus a way to activate emotionally salient but nonintegrated parts of oneself, toward the goal of transforming one's self-functioning. For instance, my (Edwards) father was an alcoholic, and when he was drunk he violently physically abused my mother. I frequently witnessed this explosive violence, and my traumatic experiential memories needed integration and transformation. Indeed, through psychotherapy and personal reflection, I have spent a lot of time understanding and resolving the impact my father's drinking and violence has had on my self-functioning.

Experiential therapists also focus on current interpersonal relationships and attachment dynamics. In-session experiential processing is used to explore the clients' self- and other-representations, attachment tendencies and interpersonal patterns of behavior (Davis, 2010; Siegel, 2012). In addition, clients are encouraged to cultivate and draw on their social support network, partly as a way to enhance the likelihood of a positive psychotherapeutic outcome (Harwood et al., 2011).

With Christian clients, explorations of emotional experience of God may also help illuminate any transference/countertransference dynamics that are emerging. Such explorations can include discussions of how God may desire to bring healing and sanctification in the client's mind, brain and relationships, via experiences in psychotherapy (Moriarty & Davis, 2012).

Furthermore, the client's general patterns of relating will manifest in the therapy relationship. Thus it is important for the therapist to use confrontation to point out these patterns and to use interpretation to elucidate their connection to past relationships (Frankland, 2010; Shedler, 2010). However, such explorations may evoke client shame, self-consciousness, resistance or defensiveness, and it can be a challenge to collaboratively and safely process these dynamics. Sometimes it is possible to empathically reflect, confront or process these dynamics in real time, but at other times it may be necessary to wait until the events have passed and can be explored in retrospect. For example, Levenson (2010) described a male client who could not answer a direct question regarding his feelings about lending money to his daughter. Several sessions later, the client disclosed that his therapist's request for more information had irritated him. Because he had previously experienced his therapist as safe and understanding, the client assertively verbalized his anger, without fearing he would be rejected. Gradually, the client's recurrent positive experiences in the therapy relationship empowered him to assert himself in other relationships (i.e., outside therapy).

Facilitate optimal levels of experiential processing. In experiential therapy, a centrally important activity is clients' active processing of their emotional experiences, while relating with the therapist. The therapist facilitates active processing by evoking clients' verbal description of their internal, subjective experience. In other words, it is not enough for clients to merely have a deep emotional experience; for the experience to be therapeutically beneficial, clients must also put words to that experience (i.e., it must be symbolized; Greenberg, 2011; Siegel, 2010).

Here the therapist must focus on keeping clients' arousal level in an optimal window (i.e., mild-to-moderate arousal)—neither so high that clients are overwhelmed nor so low that they are languishing. Stated differently, the therapist needs to facilitate optimal levels of experiential processing (vs. conceptual processing), thereby (a) expanding the client's window of affect tolerance and regulation and (b) fostering integration of different aspects of the client's emerging experience (Cozolino, 2010). Indeed, facilitating clients' verbal articulation of their subjective state is one way to coregulate their level of arousal, keeping it at an optimal level. Thus, when an intense emotional experience emerges in the session, the therapist should shift the focus to experiential, verbal processing of that upsetting reaction. Initially, affect-regulation techniques (e.g., deep breathing) may need to be used, but the goal is to help clients verbalize their internal experiences, thereby helping them integrate and regulate their affect (cf. Lieberman et al., 2007).

Freely explore fantasies, dreams and wishes. Much of human experiential processing occurs outside of conscious awareness, especially when it comes to affective and relational experiences (Cozolino, 2010). Hence, when using experiential techniques, the psychotherapist needs to provide ample time and space for implicit (nonconscious) aspects of the client's experience to emerge. Free association should be encouraged, especially the exploration of fantasies, dreams and wishes. Here the goal is facilitating insight into what underlies the client's emotional and relational difficulties (Shedler, 2010). For example, to fully access the underlying meaning of an emotional experience, have the client explore the unacceptable behaviors (e.g., fantasies and wishes) they might like to enact in the situation. A client struggling with anger toward an abusive boss can be asked: "I know that actually confronting your boss might put your job at risk, but what do you wish you could say to him?" Exploring fantasies or wishes is very effective with Christian clients who consider angry thoughts or impulses morally unacceptable.

Phase 3: Transformation and restructuring of emotional experience. The first two phases of experiential therapy are focused on accessing and making meaning of clients' subjective self-states. The interventions we have described in these prior phases are largely designed to promote enhanced awareness, relational processing and self-integration (at conscious and nonconscious levels). This last phase of experiential therapy—emotional transformation—actually takes place over the entire course of therapy, especially during the middle phase. This transformation also happens outside therapy, as clients act on the emotional-awareness and regulation-skills they have developed in therapy sessions. Experiential therapists actively track and guide clients' extra-therapy enactments, to support more complete, generalized transformation (Greenberg, 2011). Nonetheless, transformation is of course facilitated in therapy as well, and here we describe two techniques for accomplishing that task.

Interpretations and narrative integration. Again, new self-understanding is one important outcome of experiential therapy, and interpretations are an effective way to promote such understanding. Frankland (2010) has defined an interpretation as "a statement or question (often involving information gathered from clarifications and confrontations) that is designed to help the patient understand and appreciate an internal issue or struggle that is outside of her awareness" (p. 56). Interpretations link current functioning with significant developmental experiences that the client has described previously. For example, a fictitious client named Tanya presented with distress about her romantic relationship with a man who often ignored her and was unresponsive to her legitimate needs. Tanya was afraid to be assertive regarding her needs, because she feared losing the relationship. The therapist sensitively commented that, earlier in therapy, Tanya alluded that a similar pattern of fearful nonassertion characterized her reverse-caretaking role with her alcoholic mother. This interpretation led to deeper exploration of Tanya's pattern of nonassertion—a pattern that often left her with unmet needs. With the support of her therapist, Tanya began to risk being more assertive with her friends and boyfriend.

The interpretations employed in phase 3 seek to promote deeper processing of emotional meaning, with a goal of integrating that meaning into the client's life narrative. During this phase, the emotional significance of clients' beliefs and assumptions are made more explicit, and the developmental roots of their difficulties are identified and integrated with their current experiences. Cognitive and emotional restructuring occurs largely via the process of narrative integration, which involves linking various components of the client's life into a coherent story (Cozolino, 2010). For example, Davis and Badenoch (2010) have suggested that narrative integration is an important treatment goal when working with religious/spiritual individuals who espouse a relationship with God. God-image narrative therapy (see Davis, 2009, for a treatment manual) is one experiential treatment that can be used to explore the connections among these clients' experiences in relationship with God and others. Here the goal of narrative integration is threefold: (a) the integration of clients' spiritual narrative, (b) the integration of clients' life narrative and (c) the integration of clients' spiritual narrative with their life narrative.

The following fictitious case illustrates this transformation process. Sally, a Christian missionary nurse, habitually overworked herself. If she took time off, she was afraid her fellow missionaries would criticize her and the locals would think less of her faith. In fact, Sally's fellow missionaries praised her for her tireless dedication, and the locals expressed admiration and gratitude. As a result, she felt like a failure whenever she could not help her constituents in all the ways they needed help. Sally habitually redoubled her nursing efforts, to avoid feelings of failure. In short, her maladaptive pattern was self-defeating and gradually led her to the point of burnout. Through psychotherapy, Sally came to recognize how her critical and demanding father had been internalized in the form of her harsh introject, which drove her to compulsively achieve. She was able to experience and express anger at her father's harsh treatment. She was also able to mourn the loss of a more loving and grace-filled childhood. Through experiencing her psychotherapist's compassion, kindness and grace, Sally was able to experience God, others and herself in similar ways. She developed a more self-compassionate introject and restructured her life in ways that were more healthy and life-giving for her.

Facilitation of task resolution. Experiential therapy involves adeptly facilitating the client's completion of therapy tasks, while maintaining a relationship-focus (see Elliott et al., 2004; Greenberg, 2011, for reviews). Here we describe one application of a popular, well-researched task for promoting emotional transformation—the empty chair technique.

The empty-chair task is usually proposed when a client accesses and explores unresolved negative feelings toward a significant other person (usually a parent). The goal of this task is to facilitate experiential processing and resolution of the client's negative feelings. The therapist first clarifies the nature of the unresolved feelings, proposes the task, sets an empty chair across from the client and invites the client to visualize the person as seated in that chair. The chair in which the client is currently sitting is dubbed the "self-chair." The therapist typically has clients start by staying in the self-chair and expressing their feelings and thoughts to the imagined other person. When clients have expressed sufficient emotions (i.e., evidencing optimal experiential processing), they are asked to switch to the empty chair and experience these complaints in the role of the "other." At that point, the client may say something such as "I don't know how he would feel or what he would say." The therapist then offers the process directive (e.g., "Be the father in your head"), to facilitate emotional identification with the client's introject of the other person. The end of the empty-chair dialogue task is usually marked by a sequence of two adaptive emotions: first anger (e.g., holding the other person responsible) and then sadness (e.g., for the loss that the unresolved negative feelings represent). This sequence is prototypically activated by asking clients (seated in the self-chair) to express their adaptive, underlying, unfulfilled needs (e.g., "Tell your father what you needed from him"). Then these needs become experientially associated with adaptive emotions and action tendencies. Full resolution may result if the other person takes responsibility and apologizes, or if the self forgives the other person; partial resolution may result from setting a boundary, distancing or letting go.

SUMMARY AND CONCLUSION

In this chapter, we have summarized the psychodynamic and PE outcome research, which has revealed that each of these psychotherapies is more efficacious than inactive comparison groups (e.g., control groups) and is as efficacious as other active treatments (e.g., evidence-based treatments). We also have described a three-phase model of experiential therapy (Greenberg & Watson, 2006) and have discussed interventions that can be employed in each phase, including examples of how to use experiential interventions in Christian counseling and psychotherapy.

As we conclude this chapter, we want to make it clear that we are not suggesting that experiential interventions are more effective than other interventions or are uniformly effective with all clients. In fact, we recommend that psychotherapists routinely practice *informed theoretical/technical pluralism* and *patient-treatment matching*. That is, we recommend that psychotherapists cultivate a habit of thoughtfully drawing on a broad range of theories and techniques, with an attitude of flexibility, openness and humility (informed theoretical/technical pluralism; Moriarty & Davis, 2012) and of making strategic, research-informed clinical decisions that integrate client, relationship and technique factors (patient-treatment matching; Harwood et al., 2011). With regard to the latter, the evidence-based principles of systematic treatment selection prescribe that insight-oriented, relationship-focused interventions (e.g., the interventions we describe in this chapter) are most likely to be effective with individuals who have an internalizing coping style (i.e., tend to internalize blame, be introverted and cope by turning inwardly). In contrast, skill-building and symptom-removal interventions (e.g., CBT) are more likely to be effective with individuals who have an externalizing coping style (i.e., tend to externalize blame, to be extroverted and to cope by acting outwardly; Norcross, 2011).

In conclusion, the take-home evidence-based practice recommendation of this chapter is that, within Christian counseling and psychotherapy, psychodynamic and PE interventions are most likely to be effective with Christian clients who have an internalizing coping style. With such clients, use the interventions we have described, accommodating them by incorporating religion/spirituality into therapy goals and tasks and by emphasizing experiential processing not only of clients' human relationships but also their emotional relationship with God. In time, we hope that Christian-accommodated psychodynamic and PE techniques will be thoughtfully developed and empirically examined, so that such interventions can be selected and utilized with confidence, in the context of evidence-based Christian counseling and psychotherapy.

REFERENCES

Abbass, A. A., Hancock, J. T., Henderson, J., & Kisely, S. (2006). Short-term psychodynamic psychotherapies for common mental disorders. *Cochrane Database of Systematic Reviews,* Issue 4, Article No. CD004687.

Anestis, M. D., Anestis, J. C., & Lilienfeld, S. O. (2011). When it comes to evaluating psychodynamic therapy, the devil is in the details. *American Psychologist, 66,* 149-50.

Chambless, D. L., Baker, M. J., Baucom, D. H., Beutler, L. E., Calhoun, K. S., & Crits-Christoph, P., et al. (1998). Update on empirically validated therapies, II. *The Clinical Psychologist, 51,* 3-16.

Cloud, H., & Townsend, J. (2004). *How people grow: What the Bible reveals about personal growth.* Grand Rapids, MI: Zondervan.

Cozolino, L. (2010). *The neuroscience of psychotherapy: Healing the social brain* (2nd ed.). New York: Norton.

Davis, E. B. (2009). *God image narrative therapy: A treatment manual.* Unpublished manuscript, School of Psychology and Counseling, Regent University, Virginia Beach, VA. Retrieved from www.drwarddavis.com/resources.html.

Davis, E. B. (2010). *Authenticity, inauthenticity, attachment, and god-image ten-*

dencies among adult evangelical Protestant Christians. (Doctoral dissertation). Retrieved from www.drwarddavis.com/resources.html.

Davis, E. B., & Badenoch, B. (2010). Storying god images: Bringing narrative integration to our experience of the divine. *Winter 2009 GAINS Quarterly* (pp. 14-24, 63-65). Retrieved from www.drwarddavis.com/resources.html.

Elliott, R. (2002). The effectiveness of humanistic therapies: A meta-analysis. In D. J. Cain (Ed.), *Humanistic psychotherapies: Handbook of research and practice* (pp. 57-81). Washington, DC: American Psychological Association.

Elliott, R., Watson, J. C., Goldman, R. N., & Greenberg, L. S. (2004). *Learning emotion-focused therapy: The process-experiential approach to change.* Washington, DC: American Psychological Association.

Frankland, A. (2010). *The little psychotherapy book: Object relations in practice.* New York: Oxford University Press.

Gerber, A. J., Kocsis, J. H., Milrod, B. L., Roose, S. P., Barber, J. P., & Thase, M. E., et al. (2011). A quality-based review of randomized controlled trials of psychodynamic psychotherapy. *American Journal of Psychiatry, 168,* 19-28.

Greenberg, L. S. (2011). *Emotion-focused therapy.* Washington, DC: American Psychological Association.

Greenberg, L. S., Rice, L. N., & Elliott, R. (1993). *Facilitating emotional change: The moment-by-moment process.* New York: Guilford Press.

Greenberg, L. S., & Watson, J. C. (2006). *Emotion-focused therapy for depression.* Washington, DC: American Psychological Association.

Harwood, T. M., Beutler, L. E., Williams, O. B., & Stegman, R. S. (2011). Identifying treatment-relevant assessment: Systematic Treatment Selection /InnerLife. In T. M. Harwood, L. E. Beutler & G. Groth-Marnat (Eds.), *Integrative assessment of adult personality* (3rd ed., pp. 61-79). New York: Guilford Press.

Leichsenring, F., Rabung, S., & Leibing, E. (2004). The efficacy of short-term psychodynamic psychotherapy in specific psychiatric disorders: A meta-analysis. *Archives of General Psychiatry, 61,* 1208-16.

Levenson, H. (2010). *Brief dynamic therapy.* Washington, DC: American Psychological Association.

Lieberman, M. D., Eisenberger, N. E., Crockett, M. J., Tom, S. M., Pfeifer, J. H., & Way, B. M. (2007). Putting feelings into words: Affect labeling disrupts amygdala activity in response to affective stimuli. *Psychological Science, 18,* 421-28.

McCullough, L., Kuhn, N., Andrews, S., Kaplan, A., Wolf, J., & Hurley, C. L. (2003). *Treating affect phobia: A manual for short-term dynamic psychotherapy.* New York: Guilford Press.

Moriarty, G. L., & Davis, E. B. (2012). Client God images: Theory, research, and clinical practice. In J. Aten, K. O'Grady & E. Worthington Jr. (Eds.), *The psychology of religion and spirituality for clinicians* (pp. 131-60). New York: Routledge.

Norcross, J. C. (Ed.). (2011). *Psychotherapy relationships that work: Evidence-based responsiveness* (2nd ed.). New York: Oxford University Press.

Shedler, J. (2010). The efficacy of psychodynamic psychotherapy. *American Psychologist, 65,* 98-109.

Siegel, D. J. (2010). *The mindful therapist.* New York: Norton.

Siegel, D. J. (2012). *Pocket guide to interpersonal neurobiology: An integrative handbook of the mind.* New York: Norton.

Thomas, M. J., Moriarty, G. L., Davis, E. B., & Anderson, E. L. (2011). The effects of a manualized group-psychotherapy intervention on client god images and attachment to God: A pilot study. *Journal of Psychology and Theology, 39,* 44-58.

Tisdale, T. T., Key, T. L., Edwards, K. J., Brokaw, B. F., Kemperman, S. R., & Cloud, H., et al. (1997). Impact of treatment on God image and personal adjustment, and correlations of God image to personal adjustment and object relations development. *Journal of Psychology and Theology, 25,* 227-39.

Part Three

EVIDENCE-BASED PSYCHOTHERAPEUTIC TREATMENTS FOR COUPLES AND GROUPS

8

Preparing Couples for Marriage

The SYMBIS Model

Les Parrott and Leslie Parrott

As codirectors of the Center for Relationship Development at Seattle Pacific University, we emphasize marriage preparation and early marriage mentoring. A psychoeducational approach that incorporates essential skills and highlights up-to-date information about contemporary marriage is crucial to correcting faulty information and equipping couples with an accurate understanding of themselves and what they bring to the relationship for a successful marriage. The marriage mentoring component complements the psychoeducational approach by allowing the couple to receive personal encouragement and learn through marriage models. A marriage mentor is defined as a relatively happy, more experienced or seasoned couple who empowers a newly married couple through sharing resources and relational experiences, particularly throughout the first year of marriage.

The Center for Relationship Development (CRD) was established in 1992 with the overarching goal of nurturing healthy relationships through preventative interventions. In conjunction with the University's Department of Psychology, CRD sponsors curricular offerings that are academically rigorous and based on solid theoretical and applied research. Currently, these offerings consist of two psychology courses in relationship development. The first course focuses on practical principles for building healthy relationships in general (family, friendships, dating, etc.). The second course is more advanced and presents practical tools for marriage and family rela-

tionships over the life cycle. Students must complete the first course and
have advanced status to enroll. More than one thousand upper division students have completed this course. The relevance of these relationships
courses to our marriage preparation model is readily apparent. An issue of
American Demographics reported that two-thirds of college students say
that "having close relationships with other people is always on their minds"
and ranks highest as a "personal value" (Walker & Moses, 1996, p. 36; also
Owen, Rhoades, Stanley & Fincham, 2008). By tapping into this felt need,
rapport is established for those individuals who eventually become engaged
to be married and, as a result of the course content, understand the need for
quality preparation for marriage.

Therefore, in addition to the relationship development courses, CRD
sponsors an ongoing marriage preparation model titled "Saving Your Mar-
riage Before It Starts" (SYMBIS, 1995; updated and revised 2006) or "Saving
Your Second Marriage Before It Starts" (SYMBIS-2; Parrott & Parrott, 2001).
Over the past several years, several thousand couples have participated in
SYMBIS. A unique feature of this program includes the Marriage Mentor
Club, which links newlyweds with a seasoned married couple throughout
the first year of marriage (Parrott & Parrott, 2005).

We believe deeply in the impact of preventive interventions on the per-
manence, intimacy and satisfaction of marriage. Research has underscored
a tendency for minor problems in marriage to escalate into major rifts if
they are not addressed promptly. In fact, half of all serious marital problems
develop in the first two years of marriage (Huston et al., 2001; Lasswell,
1985). Our experiences in marriage and family therapy are consistent with
this prognosis and have shaped our emphasis on treating marriages in their
early phase.

Theoretical Underpinning

The overarching modality of the SYMBIS program is shaped by the family-
systems approach, particularly by family-systems theory as presented by
Bowen (1978) in his seminal work *Family Therapy in Clinical Practice*. It has
also been influenced by the contributions of Friedman (1985), a former
student of Bowen, who has been a pioneer in applying systems theory to
religious congregations and families within the church and synagogue.

Other significant influences on our approach to marital preparation and therapy are Carter and McGoldrick (1989), systems therapists who emphasize the importance of the family life cycle in marital therapy.

The SYMBIS model attempts to weave into its fabric the Bowenian concepts of self-differentiation (i.e., separating one's own intellectual and emotional functioning from that of the family) and viewing the couple in the context of their transgenerational family system—especially in the first few counseling sessions. For example, the Bowenian theory suggests that extended family dynamics transfer relationship and communication patterns (myths, secrets and legacies) into the marital system. We believe that a crucial element of marriage preparation is the identification of the family legacy each marriage partner unconsciously brings into the marriage, specifically in uncovering unspoken rules and unconscious roles that shape each partner's expectations for marriage. Bringing both of these aspects out into the open is an important step in marriage preparation and can be accomplished through constructing a family genogram (i.e., a pictorial display of a person's family relationships and history, noting psychological patterns that punctuate relationships) as well as through a variety of exercises.

Helping couples who progress through the SYMBIS model to become aware of their own unspoken rules gives them the freedom to accept, reject, challenge or change those rules from their family of origin for the sake of their own relationship. Identifying unconscious roles is equally important. Without knowing it, a bride and groom are drawn into acting out roles (e.g., the navigator, money manager, decorator, etc.) that they form from a blend of their personal dispositions and family system dynamics. Once partners become aware of the assumed and prescribed roles that each partner tends to take, they can then discuss how to write a new script together.

In addition, as the couples move through the developmental passages of the family life cycle (marriage, birth, raising children, launching young adults, retirement and death), these transitions dynamically impact the extended family system. Symptoms or problems may occur in healthy marriages when there is extraordinary developmental stress (untimely death, chronic illness, birth of a handicapped child). However, even minor developmental stressors can cause problems for a family that is coping with dysfunctional extended-family relationship dynamics (Carter & McGoldrick, 1989).

The role of the family of origin is central to marriage counseling from our perspective. In other words, the couple cannot be considered in isolation from the extended families of origin of both partners. Friedman (1985) eloquently states,

> The position we occupy in our families of origin is the only thing we can never share or give to another while we are still alive. It is the source of our uniqueness, and hence, the basic parameter for our emotional potential as well as our difficulties. . . . The more we understand that position, therefore, and the more we can learn to occupy it with grace and savvy, rather than fleeing from it or unwittingly allowing it to program our destiny, the more perfectly we can function in any other area of our life. (p. 34)

From our family systems perspective, there are three significant measures of marital health: (a) the marriage relationship (how much conflict and distance is present); (b) the physical and emotional health of each marriage partner, including evidence of an over-functioning-under-functioning reciprocity (i.e., attempting to make one self out of two); and (c) the emotional and physical health of each of the children, including relationships with each of the parents and with the siblings that might indicate the presence of entrenched relational triangles (i.e., the two-person system of husband and wife drawing in a third to stabilize, creating a three-person system of two-against-one or two-helping-one). Marriages are considered to be healthy to the extent that the entire family system is symptom free. It would be impossible to measure the health of the marriage without an understanding of the entire nuclear family. From a family-systems perspective, difficulties in marriage have less to do with the differences between marriage partners than with what is causing the differences to be highlighted at the present time (Friedman, 1985).

Also stemming from the Bowenian perspective is the idea of fostering true marital intimacy through strengthening self-differentiation. Self-differentiation, according to Bowen, is the ability to have well thought-out life values, principles and convictions and to hold on to them in the face of anxiety and pressure for conformity and togetherness. This unswerving authenticity is the capacity to maintain relationships based on emotional separateness, equality and openness (Parrott & Warren, 2003). The self-differentiated person is able to say, "This is who I am, what I believe, what I stand for, and what I will do or will not do, in a given situation." Bowen states, "A more differentiated person can participate freely in the emotional sphere without the fear of becoming too fused with others. A well-differentiated person is not changed by coercion or pressure, or to gain approval, or enhance one's stand with others" (Bowen, 1978; Gilbert, 1992, pp. 193-94). This concept should not be confused with autonomy or narcissism. Differentiation includes the capacity to maintain a non-anxious presence in the midst of anxious systems while taking full personal responsibility for one's emotional well-being (Friedman, 1985). This is critical to marriage preparation because true intimacy is often misunderstood (Oliker, 1989; Larson, 1988; Crosby, 1976). As misguided couples attempt to achieve emotional closeness (i.e., intimacy), they become ensnared by their own need for the relationship to magically complete and improve their own identity and esteem. Relational fusion, which is a lack of differentiation in an attempt to achieve harmony within the system (i.e., masquerading as intimacy), leads to a high level of relational stress and these dependent couples, with low levels of self-differentiation, cultivate an enmeshed relationship, characterized by a general reliance on their spouse for continual support, assurance and wholeness. When either of the fused partners becomes dissatisfied, their stress is defined solely within the relationship and blame is inevitably placed on the other person.

The opposite of an enmeshed marriage (characterized by a lack of relational boundaries and separations) is a relationship of rugged self-reliance, often called the disengaged relationship. Spouses who are attempting to earn their sense of wholeness by relying on no one, not even their marriage partner, also exhibit symptoms of a low level of self-differentiation and the result is gradual frustration and dissatisfaction with marriage. The goal of SYMBIS is to help the couple achieve an interdependent relationship through strengthening self-differentiation. Issues that involve high levels of anxiety and emotional reactivity of the couple are reframed as opportunities for further self-differentiation within the extended-family context and within the marital dyad.

Gilbert (1992) suggests the following features in relationships characterized by self-differentiation: (a) emotional calm (a non-anxious presence); (b) intellectual objectivity (the ability to observe self in a relationship pattern and make changes without expectations of the other); (c) maintaining one-to-one relationships with one's spouse and the individuals in one's extended family; (d) viewing others as anxious or fearful (rather than malicious or manipulative) during conflict; (e) the ability not to react in kind to anger or anxiety of others; (f) the ability to make choices or define positions that may jeopardize love, approval, acceptance and nurturing; (g) focusing more on personal responsibility than on the behavior of others in the relationship; and (h) calm and thoughtful decision-making. Our goal in marriage preparation and marital therapy, and all therapy in general, is to enable the person or the individuals within a couple to move toward self-differentiation and a more authentic, healthy intimate connection.

INTERVENTION MODEL

The SYMBIS model is designed to support a couple in building a successful marriage through a series of sessions, each with a distinct goal: (1) confronting common marital myths and developing healthy expectations for marriage; (2) developing a realistic concept of love and its malleability; (3) cultivating an attitude and outlook toward life that will sustain marriage in spite of unforeseen difficulties; (4) teaching effective communication skills; (5) accurately understanding and accepting gender differences; (6) teaching effective skills for resolving marital conflict; and (7) exploring the value of a spiritual foundation and the ways couples can build one. In addition to exercises and discussion on each of these seven topics (see table 8.1), the SYMBIS model also includes administration and interpretation of an assessment such as the PREPARE assessment (Olson, Fournier & Druckman, 1987) or the L.O.V.E. style assessment (Parrott & Parrott, 2009). This typically requires about ten sessions.

Critical to the SYMBIS model is the facilitation of a year-long relationship with a marriage mentor couple. Once a couple marries, many issues arise in the relationship that were never imagined during the engagement period. In addition, issues that were explored during premarital counseling suddenly become more salient. Research regarding commitment in marriage indicates that the first year of marriage is the time

Table 8.1. SYMBIS Session Goals and Methods

Session	Goal	Sample of Methods
1	Establish rapport and begin initial assessment	• Administer assessment • Develop a preliminary family genogram
2	Expose common marital myths and develop healthy expectations of married life	• Exercises: "Your Personal Ten Commandments" and "Making Your Roles Conscious"
3	Establish a realistic understanding of love and its fluidity	• Exercises: "Defining Love" and "Your Changing Love Style"
4	Cultivate a life-attitude that will sustain marriage (free from blame, self-pity and resentment)	• Exercises: "Avoiding the Blame Game" and "Adjusting to Things Beyond Your Control"
5	Cultivate the personal qualities and teach the specific skills of healthy communication	• Self-test: "How Well Do You Communicate?" • Role play: clarifying content and reflecting feeling
6	Explore and bridge common gender differences while reviewing communication skills	• Exercise: "Your Top Ten Needs" • Role play: communication skills within gender context
7	Teach, model and practice effective conflict resolutions skills	• Exercise: "Mind Reading" • Role play: "Sharing Withholds" and other skills
8	Explore faith journeys and provide tools for melding spiritual paths	• Exercises: "Your Spiritual Journey" and "Improving Your Serve"
9	Provide couple's strengths and areas for growth	• Assessment debriefing and interpretation
10	Facilitate relationship with marriage mentor couple	• Follow-up sessions

couples are most likely to become disillusioned with marriage (Peters & Dush, 2009; Surrah & Hughes, 1997). Mentoring allows for a connection of a newly married couple with a seasoned, healthy couple that serves as a sounding board and much more as they invest in the newly married couple to sustain them during this often tumultuous period of adjustment. The two couples typically meet a minimum of three times: at three months after the wedding, at seven months, and near the one-year wedding anniversary. The value of marriage mentoring in great part is that it short-circuits unnecessary anxiety by normalizing the experiences of early marriage. It also supports the preventive structure established in the premarital counseling sessions by providing real-life models and opportunities to reinforce insights and skills (e.g., communication and conflict resolution skills) that can keep detrimental patterns from becoming entrenched ways of relating. Marriage mentor couples are recruited, screened and trained in mentoring strategies that support the pre-marriage work. As an aside, they typically report a "boomerang effect" of receiving as much good out of the process as the newlyweds (see Parrott & Parrott, 2001, 2006).

Since we know of no area in marital interaction that has received more astounding results in recent years than regarding conflict resolution, we work to integrate these findings into our approach. Research at the University of Denver, for example, has predicted with 80% accuracy who will be divorced six or seven years after marrying (Stanley, Markman & Whitton, 2002). Research at the University of Washington has established a 94% accuracy rate on the prediction of marriage success, again, based solely on conflict in marriage (Gottman, 1994). This preponderance of research has underscored the importance of incorporating conflict resolution skills into our psychoeducational approach. Our goal is to contextualize these findings within the family system and help couples understand both what unhappy couples do wrong and what healthy couples do right. In a didactic fashion, we explore the disastrous ways of arguing that will sabotage a couple's attempts to resolve conflict and, through role-playing exercise, we work to help couples gain skills to identify and avoid the presence of these saboteurs.

Our intervention model also utilizes Yale psychologist Robert Sternberg's triangular theory of love (Sternberg, 1986). We work to strengthen marital commitment by helping couples understand that love has three essential ingredients: passion, intimacy and commitment (Sternberg, 1986). This is presented in the context of God's covenantal love as the model that shapes and sustains our faithfulness to each other. The bottom line is that we try to help couples understand the fluidity of love and equip them with tools that will cultivate the type of commitment that will sustain their love over the life cycle.

While we will refer to the "counselor" as we describe the implementation of the SYMBIS model, we readily note that in various contexts the leader might technically be a group leader, facilitator, counselor, or psychotherapist or couple therapist.

SPECIFIC METHODS/STRATEGIES FOR INTERVENTION

The SYMBIS model of marriage preparation incorporates a comprehensive marriage preparation curriculum into its ten-session counseling model. The book *Saving Your Marriage Before It Starts* (Parrott & Parrott, 1995, 2006a) addresses seven key relationship areas by posing seven questions (stemming from the theoretical foundations elaborated above): (1) Have you faced the myths of marriage with honesty? (2) Can you identify your love style? (3) Have you developed the habit of happiness? (4) Can you say what you mean and understand what you hear? (5) Have you bridged the gender gap? (6) Do you know how to fight a good fight? (7) Are you and your partner soul mates? The SYMBIS-2 model (for second or subsequent marriages) adds two additional questions to this list: (1) Are you ready to get married again? (2) Do you know how to blend a family?

Companion SYMBIS workbooks (male and female) are used in conjunction with the book to engage the couple in strategic exercises during the counseling process (Parrott & Parrott, 1995b, 2006b). There are twenty-two optional exercises built into the SYMBIS model.

Session 1. The goal of SYMBIS session one is to establish rapport and begin initial assessment with the couple through the administration of an assessment such as the PREPARE or L.O.V.E. Styles (Parrott & Parrott, 2009; www.lesandleslie.com/assessments/l-o-v-e-styles-profile) and possibly constructing a family genogram for each individual. The family genogram incorporates information about family structure, functioning information and critical-life-cycle events. Patterns of conflict and relational triangles will be explored through family myths, rules, roles, relationships and legacies. Particular attention is paid to the level of self-differentiation of each from their parents—giving each person in the couple more objectivity on their family of origin issues. Of course, as this is the first session the emphasis is on establishing rapport with the couple and care must be taken to not overwhelm the couple with information that may be too heavy or burdensome to the couple.

Session 2. The purpose of session two is to expose common marital myths and develop healthy expectations for married life. Some of these myths include: "We expect the same thing from marriage." "Everything good in our relationship will get better." "Everything bad in our relationship will disappear." "My spouse will make me whole." To help couples expose and explore these myths at a personal level, an exercise called "Your Personal Ten Commandments," has them consider "unspoken rules" from their family of origin on such issues as finances, chores, holidays and so on. Another exercise, "Making Your Roles Conscious," has couples consider the role each of their parents played in such matters as providing income, paying bills, maintaining the automobile, making the bed, cleaning, caring for a pet, scheduling social events and so on. Both of these exercises were designed specifically for the task of helping a couple openly discuss their transgenerational family legacy of unspoken rules and unconscious roles and enable partners to create a healthy shared vision for marriage that is unique and fulfilling to the two of them.

Session 3. In session three, the counselor works with the couple to establish a realistic understanding of love and its fluidity. Exercises "Defining Love" and "Your Changing Love Style" have been designed to facilitate this process. Providing accurate and complete information about what love is and how love is experienced over the life-cycle is crucial to this model. "Your Changing Love Style" is based on the triangular model of love developed by Sternberg (1986), which identifies three elements of love—passion, intimacy and commitment. Each partner divides the time course of his or her relationship into three phases, charting a love triangle that best suits each phase of their relationship (allowing for the fluidity of passion, intimacy and commitment over time). The couple then discusses the unique style of love that characterizes their relationship currently and in times past. "Defining Love" allows couples to accept responsibility for cultivating passion, intimacy and commitment in their relationship through identifying, in their own terms, how each partner defines love. They select from a list of twelve attributes most frequently identified with love: acceptance, caring, commitment, concern for the other's well-being, friendship, honesty, interest in the other, loyalty, respect, supportiveness, trust and wanting to be with the other. From this list of attributes, each partner chooses his or her top three and writes a definition of love that incorporates them. The partners compare their priorities and definition with one another to see what differences, if any, emerge when it comes to defining love.

Session 4. The goal of session four is to enable the couple to cultivate a life-attitude that will sustain marriage (free from such toxic attitudes as blame, self-pity and resentment). In a sense, this session is dedicated to programing the mind for a happier marriage. It reveals to the couple that their happiness together will not be a matter of luck but of will. For this reason, we have an exercise called "Listening to Your Self-Talk" that helps each person in the couple tune into their internal dialogue as a starting place for learning to choose their own attitude. And the exercise called "Avoiding the Blame Game" actually has both people in the couple consider how they would respond in three specific scenarios that are typical of marital circumstances. A third exercise, "Adjusting to Things Beyond Your Control," focuses on developing a healthy, differentiated demeanor in the relationship. Using the biblical example of Mary and Joseph, the exercise helps them each ponder how the Christmas story would have been written differently if this young couple had not had the capacity to adjust to circumstances beyond their control. By having each person consider potential challenges they will face and how they are prone to respond to them, this exercise elevates their understanding of how they can better adjust and cope as individuals as well as a couple.

Session 5. Session five focuses on communication: how to say what you mean and understand what you hear. The goal is to cultivate a solid foundation for shared empathy and equip couples with specific communication skills for their relationship. "How Well Do You Communicate?" is a simple and quick self-assessment that is surprisingly revealing and serves as a catalyst for a personal conversation about communication. A primary goal in this session is to help each person "hear" what their partner isn't saying with words. In other words, it is to help each of them listen to the emotions underneath the words and, importantly, reflect that feeling back to their partner. This session, especially, can become more meaningful and im pactful when role-playing scenarios are facilitated by the counselor— narios that ingrain the ability to clarify content (e.g., "Is this what y saying?") and reflect feelings ("I get the sense that you feel . . ."). W' two skills may be seen as elementary to an engaged couple, t' more appreciated by the couple when they attempt to pra role-play.

Session 6. The central task of session six is the ex'

gender differences, particularly in the area of personal needs and communication patterns. In an exercise called "Your Top Ten Needs," each person in the couple is presented with more than a dozen common psychological needs such as admiration, affection, commitment, companionship, honesty, personal space, rootedness and so on. Each person has the same list, but they separately rank how important each quality is to them. The result is an engaging and revealing conversation about some of their deeper needs that men and women often don't recognize about each other since they each value them differently. Another important exercise designed to bridge the gender gap is the "Couple's Inventory." This exercise helps the partners take stock of the role they each play, consciously and unconsciously, in their relationship. This area is a special focus, particularly because of the way each partner is impacted by unconscious roles as a result of their own family-of-origin. The exercise is a list of fifteen sentence stems that each partner completes as honestly as possible. Selected sentences include, "I feel central to our relationship when . . ." "I feel peripheral to our relationship when . . ." "I feel most feminine/masculine in our relationship when . . ." "Our finances are controlled by . . ." "Our social life is planned by . . ." "The role I play as your wife/husband is . . ." and so on. The couple then is asked to compare the statements with each other and discuss how their gender influences the way they responded.

Session 7. Session seven tackles the area of effective conflict resolution. The exercises "Mind Reading" and "Sharing Withholds" engage the couple in effective conflict resolution. "Sharing Withholds" is designed to help the couple keep a clean emotional slate and avoid needless conflicts. This is a key technique for ongoing, effective conflict resolution. We call it "sharing withholds" because it gives couples the chance to share thoughts and feelings that they have withheld from each other. It takes the couple about ten to fifteen minutes. They begin by writing two things the other has done in the last forty-eight hours that they sincerely appreciated but did not tell him or her. For example, "I appreciate the help you gave me in writing my proposal last night." Next, each individual writes one thing the other has one in the last fort-eight hours that irritated them but they did not say ything about. For example, "I didn't like it when you borrowed my umla without telling me." Once each person has written their statement, the couple takes turns sharing. One person shares all three statements one after the other. Then the other person shares his or her three statements. One important part of this exercise is that the person on the receiving end can say only "thank you" after each statement. This rule allows couples to share something that bugs them without fearing a blow-up or a defensive reaction. It also allows couples to receive critiques in the context of affirmation. Once the couple understands the process, this exercise can be done every day to keep repressed feelings from causing damaging and explosive conflicts.

Session 8. The eighth SYMBIS session focuses on an exploration of the faith journeys for the purpose of providing tools to integrate spiritual paths, values and experiences into the relationship. The exercise "Your Spiritual Journey" helps each partner take a more in-depth and reflective look at their spiritual pilgrimage and better articulate it for their partner. It helps them identify significant mile markers in their personal faith and raise a new level of awareness about their spiritual quest together. This exercise also helps the couple align their respective expectations around spiritual matters such as praying together, church attendance, paying a tithe and so on. Ultimately the exercise helps each person in the couple gain new insight into what helps him or her feel closest to God and how that activity might mesh with or distract his or her partner's perspective in relating to God. Another exercise, "Improving Your Serve," guides the couple through a brief process of transcending their own boundaries as a couple to look beyond their own needs to how they might uniquely meet the needs of others around them—as a couple. It helps them consider such pragmatic efforts such as volunteering together in some aspect of ministry, working on a relief effort, or welcoming new people to their neighborhood as they offer the gift of hospitality.

Sessions 9 and 10. Session nine in the SYMBIS model provides concrete information about the couple's strengths and opportunities for growth by revisiting the results of the assessment tool they used in their first session. Depending on the assessment tool and the counselors discretion this may be done in either one or two sessions. At this point we also suggest that the counselor help the couple to become linked with a certified marriage mentor couple, a seasoned couple who will walk alongside them during the first year of marriage, allowing the newlyweds to learn from their successes and challenges (see www.marriagementoring.com). Finally, we suggest that the counselor schedule a session to meet with the couple one last time for a "tune up" at about the three-month mark of their marriage. This is where much of the premarital work becomes more salient for the couple and a tune-up session will help them find answers to questions they may have now that they have crossed the proverbial threshold of marriage.

FORMAT OF APPLICATION

The SYMBIS model specially targets engaged couples but can also be used with about-to-be-engaged and newly married couples. Couples are recruited to participate in the program through the Center for Relationship Development at Seattle Pacific University by regional marketing, pastoral referrals, regional and national media attention, and word-of-mouth referral. Couples range in age from the twenties to the fifties, with the majority of participants in their late twenties to early thirties. While most of the participating couples are anticipating engagement, preparing for a first marriage, or in the early phases of a first marriage, some couples are entering a second marriage. SYMBIS programs have been established nationally at a variety of colleges, universities and churches to serve local college students and congregations. No screening or assessment is required for participation in the SYMBIS program.

QUALITIES AND ROLE OF THE LEADER/
FACILITATOR/PSYCHOTHERAPIST

The SYMBIS model is flexible. It is designed to be used in a wide variety of therapeutic, educational and congregational settings. In its most rigorous and thorough format (individual counseling sessions for engaged couples), SYMBIS requires a master's level couple therapist or pastoral counselor with a basic understanding of family systems dynamics.

As a psychoeducational group experience, the SYMBIS model can be implemented by a facilitator through the use of an eight-session video curriculum for couples, which includes a leaders guide and provides a complete curriculum for the course and the follow-up design for a marriage mentor program. This complete marriage preparation program has been implemented on college and university campuses and in both Protestant and Catholic churches successfully. Couples without a formal facilitator may even use the curriculum on their own by reading the book, viewing the video sessions and completing the exercises (see Jakubowski, Milne, Brunner & Miller, 2004; Parrott & Parrott, 2003; Ripley, Parrott, Worthington, Parrott & Smith, 2001).

Summary and Conclusions

The SYMBIS model affords many areas for improvement. Not least of these is the need for much more empirical research. With a more stable base of research, the SYMBIS model could articulate its effective efforts with greater confidence.

Perhaps the program's major strengths are its relevance and accessibility. The model reaches a felt need of this generation of couples by identifying their most salient issues. The program is also one that is easy for most individuals to access. Because it can be conducted in a variety of settings with varying degrees of rigor, SYMBIS can reach a great number of couples.

When we consider what is important in preparing couples for lifelong marriage, there are many skills and strategies stemming from a variety of modalities that can be incorporated into the SYMBIS model. As a psychoeducational approach continually influenced by new research findings, SYMBIS is in a continual process of being reshaped. The soil of Bowenian family systems provides a stable context for correcting faulty information and equipping couples with an accurate understanding of themselves and what they bring to the relationship.

References

Bowen, M. (1978). *Family therapy in clinical practice*. New York: Jason Aronson.

Carter, B., & McGoldrick, M. (1989). *The changing family life cycle: A framework for family therapy*. (2nd ed.). Needham Heights, MA: Allyn and Bacon.

Crosby, J. F. (1976). *Illusion and disillusion: The self in love and marriage*. (2nd ed.). Belmont: Wadsworth.

Friedman, E. H. (1985). *Generation to generation: Family process in church and synagogue*. New York: Guilford Press.

Gilbert, R. M. (1992). *Extraordinary relationships: A new way of thinking about human interactions*. New York: Wiley.

Gottman, J. M. (1994). *Why marriages succeed or fail*. New York: Simon & Schuster.

Hammersla, J., Parrott, L., & Parrott, L. (1995). *Report on research submitted to Murdock Charitable Trust*, January 25, 1995.

Huston, T. L., Caughlin, J. P., Houts, R. M., Smith, S. E., & George, L. J. (2001). The connubial crucible: Newlywed years as predictors of marital delight, distress, and divorce. *Journal of Personality and Social Psychology, 80,* 237-52.

Jakubowski, S. F., Milne, E. P., Brunner, H., & Miller, R. B. (2004). A review of empirically supported marital enrichment programs. *Family Relations 53*(5), 528-39.

Larson, J. H. (1988). The marriage quiz: College students' beliefs in selected myths about marriage. *Family Relations, 37,* 43-51.

Lasswell, M. (1985). Illusions regarding marital happiness. *Medial Aspects of Human Sexuality, 19,* 144-58.

Markman, H. J., Stanley, S., Floyd, F., Hahlweg, K., & Blumberg, S. (1992). Prevention of divorce and marital distress. In L. E. Beutler & M. Crago (Eds.), *Psychotherapy research: An international review of programmatic studies* (pp. 115-22). Washington, DC: American Psychological Association.

Oliker, S. (1989). *Best friends and marriage*. Los Angeles: University of California Press.

Olson, D. H., Fournier, D. G., & Druckman, J. K. (1987). *Counselor's manual for PREPARE/ENRICH*. (Rev. ed.). Minneapolis, MN: PREPARE/ENRICH.

Owen, J. J., Rhoades, G. K., Stanley, S. M., & Fincham, F. D. (2008). "Hooking up" among college students: Demographic and psychosocial correlates. *Archives of Sexual Behavior, 39*(3), 653-63.

Parrott, L., & Parrott, L. (1995a). *Mentoring engaged and newly married couples*. Grand Rapids, MI: Zondervan.

Parrott, L., & Parrott, L. (1995b). *The marriage mentor manual*. Grand Rapids, MI: Zondervan.

Parrott, L., & Parrott, L. (2001). *Saving your second marriage before it starts*. Grand Rapids, MI: Zondervan.

Parrott, L., & Parrott, L. (2003). The SYMBIS approach to marriage education. *Journal of Psychology and Theology, 31,* 208-12.

Parrott, L., & Parrott, L. (2005). *The complete guide to marriage mentoring*. Grand Rapids, MI: Zondervan.

Parrott, L., & Parrott, L. (2006a). *Saving your marriage before it starts: Seven questions to ask before (and after) you get married*. (Rev. ed.) Grand Rapids, MI: Zondervan.

Parrott, L., & Parrott, L. (2006b). *Saving your marriage before it starts: Workbook for men/women*. Grand Rapids, MI: Zondervan.

Parrott, L., & Parrott, L. (2009). *L.O.V.E.: Putting your love styles to work for you.* Grand Rapids, MI: Zondervan.

Parrott, L., & Warren, N. C. (2003). *Love the life you live.* Wheaton, IL: Tyndale.

Peters, H. E., & Dush, C. M. K. (2009). *Marriage and family: Perspectives and complexities.* New York: Columbia University Press.

Ripley, J. S., Parrott, L., III, Worthington, E. L., Jr., Parrott, L., & Smith, C. (2001). An initial empirical examination of the Parrotts' marriage mentoring: Training the program coordinators. *Marriage and Family: A Christian Journal, 4,* 77-93.

Stanley, S. M., Markman, H. J., St. Peters, M., & Leber, P. (1995). Strengthening marriage and preventing divorce: New directions in prevention research. *Family Relations, 44,* 392-401.

Stanley, S. M., Markman, H. J., & Whitton, S. (2002) Communication, conflict, and commitment: Insights on the foundations of relationship success from a national survey. *Family Process, 41*(4), 659-75.

Sternberg, R. (1986). A triangular theory of love. *Psychological Review, 93,* 119-35.

Surrah, C. A., & Hughes, D. K. (1997). Commitment processes in accounts of the development of premarital relationships. *Journal of Marriage and the Family, 59,* 5-21.

Walker, C., & Moses, E. (1996). The age of self-navigation. *American Demographics, 18,* 36-47.

9

Christian PREP: The Prevention and Relationship Enhancement Program

C. Gary Barnes and Scott M. Stanley

Christian PREP (Prevention and Relationship Enhancement Program) is founded on Christian teaching about marriage and relationships with an integration of solid research on marriage and relationships. The PREP approach has a strong empirical character wherein strategies and techniques are informed by research on marriage, adaptations are rigorously tested in outcome studies, and content is regularly refined based on new scientifically supported insights. CPREP draws from discovered scientific truth and integrates it with scriptural truth, which more deeply informs strategies, goals and purpose regarding marriage.

Christian PREP (or CPREP) may be viewed by some as a Christian-accommodated treatment model. If viewed from initial experience with PREP as a secular intervention, CPREP is easily perceived as a "religiously accommodated intervention" (RAI; Worthington & Sandage, 2001) that incorporates religious themes and practices including prayer and forgiveness, as well as biblical and theological understandings for inspiration, motivation, transformation and commitment. While a detailed history is beyond the scope of this chapter, it is accurate to view CPREP as a Christian accommodation of PREP only with regard to the themes that were present in PREP since the earliest versions of the secular version (e.g., communication, conflict management, expectations, fun, friendship). However, other major themes present in both curricula since the early 1990s arose simultaneously from both empirical and theological insights developed through the 1980s (e.g., commitment and security, emotional safety). Furthermore, important themes in PREP (e.g., forgiveness) actually arose first in CPREP based in Christian theology and teaching rather than empirically or within PREP.

Although not all of PREP arose from a secular tradition and not all of CPREP arose from a theological tradition, both are based in the assumption that there are essential truths about relationships that can be learned by revelation and scientific discovery. As such, PREP is an empirically based intervention informed in aspects by both general and specific revelation and CPREP is not so much an accommodation as an "elaboration" of how PREP may be understood and practiced in a more explicitly Christian manner. In PREP, there is nothing contrary to Christian revealed truth and much that is strongly consistent. But in CPREP there is specific and explicit application of Christian revealed truth as it pertains to marriage and practices for fostering stability, peace, contentment and satisfaction. If, however, one did only consider CPREP as the type of RAI identified above, then based on both specific strategies and existing outcome studies, CPREP might be considered "about 75% along the road to being an empirically supported intervention" (Worthington & Sandage, 2001).

A central theme in Christian theology—especially in the theology of marriage—is the concept of oneness. Oneness is not based on sameness, but this concept that is at the center of CPREP reflects essential truths about intimacy, connection, and identity. Oneness simultaneously reflects both the human desire for intimacy and emotional safety (cf. Gen 2:25) as well as deep truths about the nature of the Trinity and the relationship between Christ and the church (Eph 5:22-23). In human terms, nothing approaching the ideal of this kind of differentiated unity between two spouses is possible unless they have a commitment to achieve such a partnership *and* are able to manage their interactions in ways that make it emotionally safe to preserve connection and work as a team (Eph 4:2, 3; Jas 1:19). While some practices that help marriages thrive are psychologically and theologically complex (e.g., forgiveness), other practices such as communication and problem solving are mundane but essential to oneness. But foundational to those practices is a solid commitment. In CPREP, couples are taught how the depth of intimacy implied in Genesis 2:25 (being naked and unashamed) is nestled in the context of the great emphasis on commitment in verse 24, which emphasizes priority (leaving father and mother), being united in a special and strong bond, and oneness (becoming one flesh).

Among various specific goals, CPREP (like PREP) is designed to teach couples how to reduce the negatives that tear marriages down and protect and deepen friendship, commitment and spiritual connection between mates. While the model is based on a psychoeducational approach that is most typically used in group formats, many of the core strategies are equally usable in counseling. In fact, many of the communication and conflict management strategies that comprised the original nucleus of PREP were drawn from the field of cognitive-behavioral marital therapy, which is one of the primary models of marital therapy with demonstrated effectiveness (Snyder, Castellani & Whisman, 2006).

EMPIRICAL UNDERPINNINGS

While CPREP is founded on scriptural truth and a Christian worldview, the approach was founded on an immense respect for science and the role it can play in building strategies to motivate and help couples. This role for science is embedded in the shared history with PREP. The PREP approach is based on over three decades of scholarship in the field of marital health and success, including studies from the laboratory of Howard Markman and Scott Stanley at the University of Denver, as well as work by a myriad of other scholars (e.g., Bradbury & Fincham, 1990; Gottman, 1994; Mace & Mace, 1980; Noller, 1981). A key goal of PREP and CPREP is to take maximal advantage of the best research available, including both outcome studies on relationship education and marital therapy, as well as basic science studies that can inform the development and revision of the specific strategies employed.

The empirical roots of PREP go back to the mid-1970s when an increasing number of psychologically trained researchers began to study marriage, particularly using new techniques involving the behavioral observation of couples. At Indiana University, Howard Markman and Clifford Notarius teamed up with John Gottman to investigate specific causes of marital distress. Along with other pioneers, such as Robert Weiss, Gottman, Notarius and Markman analyzed the ways in which distressed couples communicated differently from happy couples. Such research highlighted how distressed couples were particularly deficient in their ability to handle conflict and negative emotions effectively. Markman became motivated to develop a preventive approach for couples based in empirical research. He was subsequently joined in this direction by colleagues such as Frank Floyd and Scott Stanley, and later by Susan Blumberg (Markman, Stanley & Blumberg, 2010).

PREP has grown over the years into a continually refined model for work with couples that is based on scientific advances and consistent with a best-practices model for marital education, prevention and intervention (Halford, Markman, Kline & Stanley, 2003). In the broader field, meta-analytic studies suggest that both marriage education (Hawkins, Blanchard, Baldwin & Fawcett, 2008) and premarital education efforts are generally effective (Carroll & Doherty, 2003). However, there are many unanswered questions about aspects of programs that moderate effectiveness (Hawkins, Stanley, Blanchard & Albright, 2012). PREP itself is one of the most extensively researched approaches in the history of relationship education, with many existing outcome studies on variations of PREP (Hahlweg, Markman, Thurmaier, Engl & Eckert, 1998; Markman, Renick, Floyd, Stanley & Clements, 1993; Stanley et al., 2010a).

To our knowledge, PREP is the only relationship education curriculum listed in the US Government's SAMHSA National Registry of Evidence-Based Programs and Practices (NREPP). However, a relatively strong evidence basis does not mean that other approaches are ineffective, or that PREP is always effective, only that PREP and approaches that have similar science traditions (e.g., Halford et al., 2004) have a stronger claim to effectiveness when compared to other options. For an overview of the status of the field, see Markman and Rhoades, 2012.

In addition to being empirically tested, PREP and CPREP (and other derivatives) are empirically informed. Core strategies are based solidly on the findings of basic research on marriage and romantic relationships. For example, learning about what makes or breaks a relationship provides important clues as to what to teach couples in order to help their relationship succeed. CPREP includes attention to risk factors for marital distress and divorce, many of which are well replicated (see Stanley, 2001). Both practitioners using the approach and couples learning it are explicitly encouraged to focus more on *dynamic* risk factors, since they are by definition more plausibly changeable (e.g., poor communication, negative reciprocity and unrealistic expectations), rather than historical, *static* risk factors (e.g., parental divorce).

Sometimes research points in directions that are consistent with Christian teaching but would not have been obvious from those teachings alone. For example, attributions about each other's motives affect perceptions and interactions between partners (Bradbury, Beach, Fincham & Nelson, 1996). Based on this, we attempt to teach partners to be on the alert for making negative interpretations about each other's motivations, which turns ordinary frustrating events into more deeply personal and negative dynamics. Such strategies are entirely consistent with biblical teaching that love bears all things and believes all things (1 Cor 13:7), as well as scriptural warnings against focusing on the speck in another's eye (Lk 6:41). The warning and implications, however, seem more specific and powerful when expressed both as matters of scriptural admonition as well as explanations from research and theory about the destructive power of negative attributions. Hence, in many ways CPREP relies explicitly on both biblical teaching and elaboration based on research.

Sometimes research draws greater attention to patterns that most people know are destructive but lack an appreciation for just how destructive (e.g., negative reciprocity in communication; Gottman, 1994; Markman, Rhoades, Stanley, Ragan & Whitton, 2010). The warnings about such patterns are ubiquitous in Scripture, especially in Proverbs and James, but that that does not mean that even biblically literate couples have noted or taken seriously such admonitions. Furthermore, empirical findings emphasize how chronic parental conflict puts children at substantial risk for long-term emotional and relational problems (e.g., Cummings & Davies, 1994).

The content of PREP and CPREP are continually updated with fresh insights from research, even on well-explicated themes at the core of Christian theology. Crucial marital processes such as forgiveness (e.g., Fincham, Hall & Beach, 2005; McCullough, Worthington & Rachal, 1997), prayer (e.g., Lambert, Fincham, Braithwaite, Graham & Beach, in press), and the nature of sacrifice (e.g., Whitton, Stanley & Markman, 2007) are excellent examples. A detailed example will clarify further.

A growing body of studies demonstrates that not only is sacrifice very good for marriages, but that it may be particularly potent for signaling and thereby reinforcing trust and commitment between partners (Stanley, Whitton, Low, Clements & Markman, 2006; Wieselquist, Rusbult, Foster & Agnew, 1999). Such findings have led us, in recent years, to experiment with a strategy wherein we encourage people to (a) think about small sacrifices, (b) which they can perform any given day or week, (c) which they have strong reasons to believe their partner appreciates, *but* (d) which they are not otherwise likely to do, and (e) to commit to doing more of such things as they identify them. They are encouraged not to tell their partner what things they are choosing to do so as not to encourage an exchange orientation (known to be destructive in marriage). The resulting strategy is theologically sound, empirically based, behavioral and doable, and potentially effective both for countering the salience of negatives in marriage and for reinforcing commitment that builds trust and safety.

We will now turn to explore the CPREP approach in more detail. The most typical use of CPREP is in psychoeducational contexts, so most of the specifics we will describe have this setting in mind. However, as we have noted, the CPREP model has direct application in therapy and counseling as well as educational contexts.

DESCRIPTION

Objectives. Integrationists embrace the "unity of truth" and agree that "all truth is God's truth." However, they also admit that all truth *claims* cannot be true since interpretations of both revealed truth and discovered truth are not without error. Congruence of truth claims within a discipline as well as across disciplines becomes highly significant for confirmation of "true truth." As such, an overarching goal of CPREP is to put truth in front of couples in ways that might change them at a deeper level of the heart, even as they are taught specific strategies they can employ to strengthen their marriages.

The CPREP model strongly affirms that in all marriages outcomes are not so much about *finding* the right person as *being* the right person. The apostle Paul tells husbands and wives in Ephesians 5:21 that they must "submit to one another out of reverence for Christ." This is particularly demonstrated as individual choices are made about how inevitable differences will be handled in order to achieve mutual understanding and mutually agreed on resolutions. In such ways, CPREP is distinct from PREP in its acceptance and use of directly revealed truth, which not only gives it a unique goal and direction, but also a special spiritual dynamic and process for individual and couple transformation.

Specific strategies of CPREP include (a) raising awareness about patterns that undermine marital success; (b) fostering attitudes that give rise to action about commitment and friendship; and (c) equipping couples with skills to facilitate intimacy and talk without fighting. The two primary arenas for application are: (a) strengthening protective factors, such as the ability to talk as friends, do fun activities together and strengthen pathways of spiritual connection (e.g., sharing spiritual struggles or engaging in some act of service together); and (b) lowering risk factors, such as frequent negative escalation and/or threatening commitment to the future during moments of extreme frustration.

Approach and integration. Doubtless because of its shared history with PREP, CPREP has a very strong emphasis on communication, conflict and behavior. Many specific strategies in CPREP are designed to teach couples communication and problem-solving skills that can help inhibit the use of destructive strategies associated with distress and divorce. In terms of theoretical orientation, PREP and CPREP employ techniques consistent with cognitive-behavioral marital therapy (e.g., Epstein & Baucom, 2002; Jacobson & Margolin, 1979) in working toward changes in interaction quality and the ability to stay positively connected. The goal is to empower couples to communicate effectively, work as a team to solve problems, manage conflicts and negative emotions without damaging closeness, and preserve and enhance love, commitment and friendship. In educational settings (e.g., classes, workshops, retreats), an instructor or group leader uses a combination of didactic teaching, video examples and role-plays to teach specific skills. Couples are given time to practice, ideally repeatedly and with enough coleaders or other team members to give couples coaching in skills training that can help them learn to tailor behavioral strategies to their own relationship, style and needs.

Both Scripture and research clearly suggest that certain behaviors are destructive to relationships (e.g., Prov 18:13; Mt 5–7; Gal 5:13-15; and most of the book of James) and other types of behavior are constructive (e.g., Jas 1:19). We acknowledge that the inclusion of insights and warnings about negative behaviors does not mean that Christian Scripture and theology are essentially behavioral in their approach to change—at least not as we think about it in the context of marital therapy or education. In fact, CPREP embraces an assumption of the need for inner change—a true desire to do the right thing in regard to one's partner—but it also contains a behavioral model of change when it comes to dealing with communication and conflict management. We do not argue that scriptural insights lead, necessarily, to a skills-based approach in these domains. At the same time, direct efforts to change behavior certainly seems consistent with biblical goals for greater peace, harmony and care in how two people treat one another. There are, however, countless ways in which people respond to truth with positive behavioral changes.

God, the designer of marriage. That CPREP is built on a deeper understanding than one based on behaviorism is reflected in the way it grounds the purpose and design of marriage in God and not humankind. Specifically, CPREP consistently maintains that God intended something very meaningful for marriage, particularly in what oneness in marriage expresses about the nature of God (Gen 1:27; Jn 17:11). Therefore, a distinct goal of CPREP is to help couples begin, maintain or renew a joyous Christian marriage characterized by the love and oneness of God.

While a number of strategies and objectives of CPREP and PREP remain the same *insofar as both emphasize that* love and oneness will be cultivated or constricted according to the choices that are made in relational interactions, the importance of marriage from a Christian perspective can be a significant motivational factor for those open to this level of thought within their faith. Concern for being in right relationship with God and with one's marriage partner fosters reflection and focus on deeper core beliefs for those open to deeper truths. For example, CPREP presents a model of commitment based on research and the distinction between dedication and constraint, stressing the role of how acts of dedication foster security for attachment (e.g., Stanley et al., 2010b). Dedication is likened to the theological concept of *agape* love, which is robustly defined in 1 Corinthians 13. For couples open to deeper truths, the material leads to reflection on 1 John

4:18, which states that "perfect love drives out fear." This teaching emphasizes the role of acts of dedication as acts of committed love that support deeper oneness in a marriage.

Safety. As already mentioned in various ways, both CPREP and PREP contain an essential belief that thriving marriages have two key types of safety (Stanley, Markman & Whitton, 2002): (a) emotional safety, which relates to how partners interact and connect, such as being able to say what one really thinks, or to convey and receive emotional support; and (b) commitment safety, which relates to a fundamental sense that the marriage has a secure base in commitment. As already discussed, these aspects of safety are implied in the first major teaching in Scripture about marriage in Genesis 2:24-25: "That is why a man leaves his father and mother and is united to his wife, and they become one flesh. Adam and his wife were both naked, and they felt no shame." Emotional safety is powerfully implied in the two being able to be naked without shame.

One major goal in helping people achieve their hearts' desires in marriage is enabling them to remove the barriers to real intimacy, which means helping them develop and maintain safety. CPREP also calls attention to the Genesis 3 narrative, noting that the Fall resulted in fear-based motivations to cover up and hide from each other (behind fig leaves) and from God (among the trees).

One of the fundamental functions of commitment is, arguably, to foster security around romantic attachment so that adults and children can thrive (Stanley et al., 2010b). In CPREP (as in PREP), commitment is not merely assumed to be part of marriage, but themes and strategies related to commitment are directly taught. For example, couples are encouraged to talk regularly about their future together as a way to enhance and reinforce a secure base worthy of a lifetime of investment together.

Protecting emotional safety from corrosive conflict. A key concept underlying CPREP is that various kinds of negative interaction are corrosive to the positive bond between partners over time. While negative patterns may arise from deeper dynamics such as selfishness (Jas 4:1-3), family modeling, or a simple lack of ability to manage negative emotions constructively, the cumulative effect of repeated, negative interactions is distance and erosion of the positive bond. In the simplest expression, "reckless words pierce like a sword" (Prov 12:18 NIV 1984). Such patterns make drawing close fundamentally unsafe. Reducing negative interaction is not merely a goal in its own right—for example to protect children from damaging impacts—but doing so is important for the protection of the positive bond between two spouses (see Notarius & Markman, 1993). There is much evidence that positive connection in marriage is affected over time by how the negatives are managed. (For a discussion of these complex issues, see Markman et al., 2010).

Maintaining positive connection. Along with the use of cognitive-behavioral techniques, PREP and CPREP are designed to teach couples how to preserve and deepen friendship, fun, spiritual connection and sensuality (e.g., Markman, Stanley & Blumberg, 2010; Stanley, et al., 1998), consistent with the trend in the field to help couples develop the positive side of their marriages (e.g., Jacobson & Christensen, 1998). In the frame of prevention, such factors are purely protective factors designed to give couples an edge in building lasting love.

PREP and CPREP promote the concept that falling out of romantic love is not inevitable. While satisfaction and connection decline over time for the average couple (Glenn, 1991), it may not be destiny if two individuals are willing to work to keep their love vibrant (Acevedo & Aron, 2009). Even though it may not be intentional, couples typically allow the cares and duties of life to crowd out time spent doing positive or meaningful things together. Commitment messages encourage couples to work against this, and participants report that acting on these commitment intentions is the one thing they will most likely implement as a result of participating.

Personal responsibility. The Christian community has the distinctive opportunity, privilege and responsibility to reflect Christ not only as individuals but also in our relationships. Furthermore, in the New Testament the *imperative* always follows from the *indicative*. In other words, a Christian approach is "doing follows being" rather than "doing in order to become." As Christians, we have a new standing in Christ and therefore we are to demonstrate Christlikeness in the context of relationships. The apostle Paul teaches that we are to "follow God's example . . . as dearly loved children" and therefore to "walk in the way of love, just as Christ loved us and gave himself up for us as a fragrant offering and sacrifice to God" (Eph 5:1-2).

Jesus contrasts the relationships among his followers with the Gentile rulers who "lord it over" one another. In other words, the world deals with the inevitable differences, problems and conflicts of relationships by exercising control with self-serving power to obtain personal desired outcomes. In contrast, followers of Christ are to demonstrate benevolent power for the sake of oneness while embracing the inevitable differences, problems and conflicts of all relationships. Such a non-controlling process demonstrates that oneness that is not based on sameness. This in turn reflects our trinitarian God (three persons, one being) as we fulfill our greater purpose as image-bearers of God.

Choosing us. I (Barnes) have been experimenting with a conceptual schema designed to help people within the CPREP model to see the many choice-points they have in life. As individuals, they can make choices that either protect or deepen oneness in their marriages or weaken it. Couples are given a handout as depicted in figure 9.1. The highlight shaded bar in the figure represents choices that protect or deepen connection and thereby foster oneness. Such choices create the impact of love in each other. It is not sufficient to intend that the other person feels loved, nor is it sufficient to make efforts for the other person to feel loved. The key is whether or not a partner is actually creating the impact of love in the other. When each person is creating the impact of love in the other, the relationship is enriched and protected.

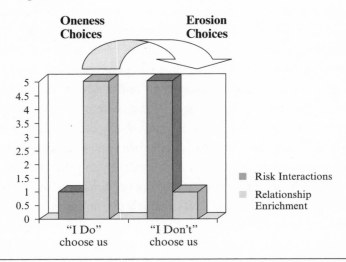

Figure 9.1. How a marriage dies: One common path

Too often in marriage, options to "choose us" (e.g., to make the time to sit and talk with one's mate) are not taken and pathways that undermine "us" or erode oneness are either actively chosen or passively allowed. For example, all couples struggle with discordant desires to one degree or another, but some choose avoidance while others choose or lose control to destructive conflicts. Patterns of how couples handle these inevitable differences, problems and conflicts are associated with relationship outcomes. We add that the degree to which such negative patterns are destiny for couples has likely been overstated in our field for some time. Nevertheless, there is much evidence that communication danger signs as taught in CPREP (e.g., withdrawal, escalation, negative interpretation and invalidation) do real damage to a couple's ability to preserve strong and happy marriages (e.g., Notarius & Markman, 1993). CPREP teaches couples that such negative patterns are common and normal, yet potentially destructive. In fact, not only is this clear from a vast research literature, but warnings about the same patterns are ubiquitous in Scripture. By any standard of truth, nasty, caustic behavior tears relationships down.

The next intentional step in the process of change is to adopt the attitude that even though these danger signs occur naturally and automatically, they can be diminished by strategies taught in CPREP, such as (a) making more benign interpretations of the partner's behavior in the first place, (b) limiting the negative impact of escalation by learning how to use strategies such as time out, and (c) ameliorating damage that has been done through individual steps of humility (such as apologies) and dyadic commitment to a continual process of forgiveness. Finally, actions are taught and practiced (communication skills, conflict management strategies) that can be chosen not only to prevent damage but to allow safe, effective and constructive strategies for understanding issues and managing problems. When these things happen and the goal of mutual understanding is accomplished, then the dark shaded bar in figure 9.1 is low and the risk interaction in the relationship is low.

Most relationships begin with a *oneness profile*, that is, a high rate of oneness interaction choices and low rate of erosion interaction choices (see figure 9.1). Couples who are not experiencing this are not experiencing relationship satisfaction and are therefore not likely to say to each other, "Let's spend the rest of our lives together." Many married couples start out with a oneness profile—though perhaps one limited in depth—but then slide to the *erosion profile*, become dissatisfied and distressed, and end up divorcing. We expect that a smaller number of couples go through that slide-over time but do not divorce, becoming stably distressed. The remaining couples, surely the minority, are characterized by an overall average experience of stability *and* satisfaction, maintaining their oneness profile to some degree. It is not that these couples never experience the erosion profile, but when they do, both partners eventually make the reversible choices for recapturing the oneness profile.

PREP and CPREP were designed as psychoeducational approaches either to help couples prevent what is a common slide in marriage from the oneness profile to the erosion profile or to help couples who may always have had a higher risk profile to learn how to more consistently choose attitudes and behaviors that promote oneness. Either way, the practical goal is to help couples learn and implement strategies that will keep the relationship enrichment bar high and the risk interactions bar low (by dealing with problems without creating new problems in the process). Thus, in CPREP every single learning module is either focused on keeping the risk interactions bar low or the relationship enrichment bar high (again, see figure 9.1).

Implementation. PREP and CPREP are both designed for multiple formats to accommodate the opportunities and limitations unique to each setting. The optimal format is a 12-hour labor-intensive model involving one group leader, who provides lectures, and one coach per couple, who helps them acquire skills (see discussion of dose in Hawkins et al., 2012). There are also new variations of PREP that add group activities in order to increase learning. Many of these new strategies are not yet included in any version of CPREP. The existing twelve-hour model includes fourteen lessons and ten coaching sessions totaling four hours and forty-five minutes for couples to practice skills and exercises for preventing problems and enhancing their relationship. A variation of this model uses one or two people to deliver the lectures and one coach per two couples. Workshops can also happen without coaches as couples are simply given time to practice skills on their own. The twelve-hour model may be presented in a weekend format, once a week in six two-hour sessions, or in a combination of Saturday and two weeknight sessions. Shorter six-hour formats tend to be offered in one day (e.g., Saturday), though we in the field suspect that such formats are not as effective as those that space out learning and skill acquisition and allow for homework (see Hawkins et al., 2012). Within this structured curriculum is the flexibility to use separate modules and to use them with a variety of delivery formats.

The full twelve-hour format follows a very specific curriculum of information, demonstration, practice and feedback. Lessons include topics of oneness, communication danger signs, how to talk safely and with respect, filters in communication, hidden issues in conflict, expectations, strategies for expressing criticism constructively and effectively, fun, problem solving, friendship, ground rules managing conflict and preserving positive bonds, forgiveness, physical oneness, commitment, spiritual oneness and mutual faith practice.

PREP and CPREP are both designed as educational models that foster experiential learning. Throughout the program a basic pattern of learning repeats as a cycle of learning something new and then doing something new. When it comes time to master key skills, a cycle is intensified. Participants learn by the leaders' presentation of new material, followed by demonstration of that material, followed by practicing the new skill, followed by debriefing the experience, followed by more practice to master the skill.

The leader ideally should be someone with a good knowledge base for understanding and helping couples learn skills. Leaders may include psychologists, social workers, clergy, nurses and lay leaders. Anyone with good people skills, organizational skills, and some ability to present material could make a good PREP or CPREP leader. The leader's duties include presenting lectures, directing discussion, answering questions and supervising coaches. When it comes to working with diverse groups and cultures, our accumulated experience tells us that the crucial adaptations are made by instructors who know both the materials and their audience well, especially in terms of common issues, themes and culturally based values and experiences.

The best overall implementation of the PREP and CPREP approaches involves a combination of flexibility and structure. There are many ways couples can learn the PREP and CPREP approaches. Couples can learn on their own using various PREP and CPREP materials. These materials may be viewed and ordered through the PREP Store on the website at www .prepinc.com. There are books, participant manuals, PowerPoint presentations and various small devices for helping couples remember key points or skills. The team at PREP is also actively working on various new avenues for teaching and reinforcing the skills and concepts from PREP in online and smart phone platforms.

Case Study

Meet Bob and Mary. They've had a stable marriage for nineteen years. Their marital satisfaction has varied over the years, mostly correlating with the different demands that the different stages of marriage typically bring. Bob and Mary have two children: Sally, almost sixteen years old, and Billy, fourteen years old. Bob and Mary both work outside the home. Since the kids have reached their mid-teens, life has picked up a more hectic pace. The time they do get together often quickly turns into a frantic business meeting just to be sure that all the logistical bases are covered. When asked how they are doing in their marriage, they both said, "Surviving, barely." In their quiet and more reflective moments, they each thought their marriage had become more of a managed partnership than a team of partners for life. As they'd been "managing" two teens, they seemed to land more often on different sides of the issues their kids brought to their family life.

As their marriage was drifting, Bob noticed a flyer for a couples workshop in their church bulletin. The workshop was based on CPREP, and the ad said it could help you "stop fighting in your marriage, and stop fleeing from fights in your marriage, and start fighting *for* your marriage!" They decided to sign up.

The twelve-hour CPREP program was presented in thirteen instructional lectures along with fourteen coaching sessions and five homework assignments over six two-hour sessions on Wednesday nights. The Saturday before the CPREP program began, Bob overheard Mary talking to Sally about getting her driver's license the week after her sixteenth birthday. Mary told Sally, "Don't worry about Dad, honey, I'll take care of that. You just go ahead and get ready to take your driver's license test like you and I planned on your birthday."

Bob and Mary had been "talking" for three weeks about why Bob thought

Sally should not get her license and why Mary thought that she should. Bob believed that she was not ready and was unsafe as a driver. Mary believed that she was a safe driver and very ready for her license. Discussions went nowhere. Each of them presented more evidence for their positions with no forward movement. In fact, things seemed to be going backwards as the debate degenerated to destructive accusations of Mary being more concerned about convenience than safety and Bob not doing his fair share of chauffeuring and chores around the house.

Bob overheard Mary's alliance with Sally and, given this three-week history, he counterattacked with all of his "skills focused on winning." Not to be outdone, Mary rose to the occasion and proved that she could verbally out-gun Bob. At the end of a three-hour tug of war, Bob ended it by saying, "You think she should have a license for convenience, and I am not going to let that happen!" At this point, Bob may have been thinking, "Now that's spiritual leadership! So let it be written, so let it be done!" Bob also figured that it was time to hide out to cool down the conflict, so he spent the rest of the day working in the garage. Bob and Mary had no further words with each other for the rest of the day or night. Sunday morning, they remained distant and silent, but still went to church. They enjoyed conversation with others and they looked so good as they sang hymns next to each other from their familiar pew. Yet, inwardly, both knew that their "Christian" oneness was only for show and that with all of their unresolved differences, they were losing hope of ever being one again.

Bob and Mary agreed to follow through with the CPREP couples workshop, and both showed up for the Wednesday night meetings. The fourth Wednesday proved to be a significant turning point. Something had been shifting inside each of them by what they had already learned. While neither would say it openly yet to the other, each was being challenged inwardly by several key themes taught so far in their workshop. First, both had felt the stirring of regret and loss as they thought about the kind of intimacy—the deep sense of acceptance and connection reflected in the idea of being naked and unashamed and without fear of rejection—that they used to have. They had not merely grabbed a few fig leafs. They had grown a forest of fig trees and could no longer find each other in it. They felt the hurt of this loss. Second, they both knew that they had recklessly hurt the other, deeply and repeatedly, by the things that had been said in numerous nasty spats over the years. Both were feeling some conviction about how easy it was to say such hurtful things to each other, and the clarity of Scripture on this subject was rather startling to them. Feelings of longing and loss were fueling a growing desire to heal their marriage.

Both Bob and Mary knew that they had been arguing at the wrong level of facts and events when there was a more important, deeper level of concern. The speaker/listener technique (a core strategy of PREP designed to help couples learn how to talk more openly and safely and to counteract the danger signs) helped them create a structured, safer and more accurate way of talking without fighting. It had become so hard for Bob and Mary to talk about things together, but this tool provided a pathway. While the skills seemed unnatural to them at first, they soon found that they each felt a lot safer emotionally. They talked slower and they took turns talking. They both still did the two tasks of speaking and listening. However, with the speaker/listener technique they agreed to do only one task at a time. The rules for the speaker's task were: (1) Speak for yourself, don't mind read. (2) Keep statements brief, don't go on and on. (3) Stop to let the listener paraphrase. The rules for the listener's task were: (1) Only paraphrase what you hear, don't introduce new information. (2) Focus on the speaker's message, don't rebut.

Bob and Mary also learned the bigger picture of fighting for their marriage rather than fighting in their marriage or fleeing fights in marriage. They learned that a more structured way of talking can be very useful for times of moderate emotional intensity or when what they needed to talk about just didn't feel like a safe topic. When intensity levels are low, their normal unstructured way of talking may still adequately move them forward in the conversation. Their desire to reconnect was all they needed to start making those connections happen again. They also learned that times when intensity levels are very high are not good for any kind of talking, but for moving toward protecting their marriage by taking a time out to cool down. Even if only one person feels the need for a time out, the other person is encouraged to agree to it. It is also helpful if the time-out person is also the person who calls "time in," and that this is done within an agreed-on timeframe. As in sports, the purpose of the time out is not to escape the game. It is to get back into the game in a better way—and on the same team.

As Bob and Mary continued to be coached in the use of the speaker/listener technique, they began to acquire a new rhythm and climate of conversation. With the new technique they were able to set aside their old win/lose dynamic where they each used their own strategies of control, persuasion or manipulation in an attempt to win the outcome they desired. With this new strategy they set aside the goal of first trying to solve the problem and adopted the new goal of mutual understanding. Once the structure broke them out of their "autopilot" mode they became free to understand each other even when they still disagreed with each other. Their voluntary submission to the structure not only facilitated accurate communication, but also prevented the natural and automatic occurrence of the four danger signs of withdrawal, escalation, negative interpretation and invalidation. Most importantly, the structure gave them a sense of respect and safety which freed them up to move to deeper, more important personal issues underneath the facts and events. For Bob and Mary, a simple communication tool—the speaker/listener technique—yielded a profound outcome.

But how can something simple and behavioral move a couple in such deep ways? Of course, very often, nothing any of us does seems to help a particular couple. But a technique can be useful in releasing something really powerfully, spiritually, if it helps two willing hearts to overcome the fear that has been keeping them apart. On the fifth Wednesday night, one of the group leaders, Karen, was coaching Bob and Mary during a time to practice the skills. Bob observed to Karen that he could see they were making real progress with the technique, but, in some way, this felt kind of silly to him. "Why should such a simple technique make any difference?" Karen reflected for a moment, and then said something that changed Bob's view of how he talked with Mary forever. "Bob, that's a great question. This technique is nothing special. It's a means to an end. In fact, that's why we encourage you to try it and practice it, but then develop the pattern that works best for the two of you from it. The technique doesn't have any magical powers. The power is in safety. You two are tearing down the barriers, and the power of that is in the way you are each trying to make it safe for the other to come home to the oneness you used to have. That's acting out the perfect love that casts out fear."

Bob and Mary both began to understand what the driver's license issue meant to each other. Safety contributed to understanding of each other's thoughts, feelings, needs and expectations. This mutual understanding opened the door for deeper sharing and deeper understanding. Mary learned how the fact that Bob used to be a state trooper was feeding intense worry about their daughter driving—but that's not what had been coming out before it was safe. While she knew this about him on some level, he explained the pain of having to make phone calls to parents about their daughters' accidents, and he was very afraid of receiving such a call about their daughter. He felt afraid and desperate to regain control of the situation that was escaping him and endangering his daughter. That fear was hidden in the negative patterns they had been employing, but it was something he could express openly when they were able to talk without fear. Once Mary understood this and Bob knew she got it, the power struggle of who wins was diminished. Their mutual understanding at the deeper level freed them up to arrive at a mutually agreed upon solution.

Bob and Mary's progress in emotional safety was matched by growth in a sense of deeper security in commitment. In fact, in this regard, their participation in CPREP had a potent, non-specific effect on their relationship. They understood each other's willingness to attend a marriage workshop together as a clear sign of their mutual commitment to the marriage. In addition, by participating in CPREP they learned various strategies to act on this commitment. For example, they learned the importance of making time for positive connection by setting aside more time for friendship and fun as well as spiritual connection. Making time for the relationship of a marriage is an act of commitment. Further, Bob and Mary learned the importance of keeping issues and problems off-limits during such positive times, but instead setting aside other times for these discussions in order to protect their reviving positive connection through this simple behavioral discipline. But on a deeper level, these behavioral practices only really mattered because both were being changed inside. Not only were they coming back alive to the desire to be close, they realized that their marriage mattered to God. They accepted how they were called to love each other deeply as Christ loved them.

Conclusions

CPREP is an educational prevention, growth and development approach that may be the most valuable tool for the largest and most diverse group of people within the Christian community who are already attempting to impact marriages positively. CPREP is a "user friendly approach" that does not require mental health professional credentialing even though many of its strategies and tools are often used by mental health and marital therapy professionals who work with distressed couples. CPREP offers three-day instructor training to prepare pastors, Christian professionals, lay leaders, and professional counselors to become strategically effective for preventing problems and enriching Christian marriages. Those who are unable to attend CPREP training may find the book *A Lasting Promise*, which is based on CPREP, to be helpful in the work they do with couples (Stanley, Trathen, McCain & Bryan, 1998).

CPREP also provides powerful examples of the validity of using a cognitive-behavioral strategy for deeper personal and relational transformation, as opposed to merely superficial behavioral change. It demonstrates that simple tools and strategies may have a profound impact when they alter the way we automatically make cognitive and behavioral choices. These upper-level changes free us from defenses so that we may work at the deeper tasks of reflecting on our feelings and connecting core beliefs. As we "speak the truth in love" (Eph 4:15) to ourselves and others, and as we disclose and receive feedback, our relationships become "relational working labs" for new levels of personal and relational transformation. While there is no research that has tested whether CPREP leads to spiritual changes as well as changes typical of cognitive-behavioral (or other) interventions for couples, this is certainly a desired end and would make for a highly valuable research project.

Approaches such as CPREP desire to help couples develop marriages that more explicitly and authentically display Christian character in terms of how partners treat each other. As such, they are examples of "the praxis of practical theology" or "the reflective action that is laden with belief" (Anderson, 2001). CPREP helps couples intentionally live out their beliefs, bringing their practice in line with their stated theology. The hope is that Christian marriages will exemplify oneness that is not based in sameness and thereby testify to the reality of Christ in the world (Jn 17:20-21). It is in this tangible experience and expression that they become "image bearers of God" as they live lives of love (Eph 5:1-2).

REFERENCES

Acevedo, B. P., & Aron, A. (2009). Does a long-term relationship kill romantic love? *Review of General Psychology, 13* (1), 59-65.

Anderson, R. S. (2001). *The shape of practical theology: Empowering ministry with theological praxis.* Downers Grove, IL: InterVarsity Press.

Bradbury, T. N., Beach, S. R. H., Fincham, F. D., & Nelson, G. M. (1996). Attributions and behavior in functional and dysfunctional marriages. *Journal of Consulting and Clinical Psychology, 64,* 569-76.

Bradbury, T. N., & Fincham, F. D. (1990). Attributions in marriage: Review and critique, *Psychological Bulletin, 107,* 3-33.

Carroll, J. S., & Doherty, W. J. (2003). Evaluating the effectiveness of premarital prevention programs: A meta-analytic review of outcome research. *Family Relations, 52,* 105-18.

Cummings, E. M., & Davies, P. (1994). *Children and marital conflict.* New York: Guilford.

Epstein, N. B., & Baucom, D. H. (2002). *Enhanced cognitive-behavioral therapy for couples: A contextual approach.* Washington, DC: American Psychological Association.

Fincham, F. D., Hall, J. H., & Beach, S. R. H. (2005). 'Til lack of forgiveness doth us part: Forgiveness in marriage. In E. L. Worthington Jr. (Ed.), *Handbook of forgiveness* (pp. 207-25). New York: Wiley.

Glenn, N. D. (1991). The recent trend in marital success in the United States. *Journal of Marriage and the Family, 53,* 261-70.

Gottman, J. (1994). *What predicts divorce? The relationship between marital process and marital outcomes.* Hillsdale, NJ: Erlbaum.

Hahlweg, K., Markman, H. J., Thurmaier, F., Engl, J., & Eckert, V. (1998). Prevention of marital distress: Results of a German prospective longitudinal study. *Journal of Family Psychology, 12,* 543-56.

Halford, K. W., Markman, H. J., Kline, G., & Stanley, S. M. (2003) Best practice in couple relationship education. *Journal of Marital and Family Therapy, 29*(3), 385-406.

Halford, W. K., Moore, E. M., Wilson, K. L., Dyer, C., & Farrugia, C. (2004). Benefits of a flexible delivery relationship education: An evaluation of the Couple CARE program. *Family Relations, 53,* 469-76.

Hawkins, A. J., Blanchard, V. L., Baldwin, S. A., & Fawcett, E. B. (2008). Does marriage and relationship education work? A meta-analytic study. *Journal of Consulting and Clinical Psychology, 76,* 723-34.

Hawkins, A. J., Stanley, S. M., Blanchard, V. L., & Albright, M. (2012). Exploring programmatic moderators of the effectiveness of marriage and relationship education programs: A meta-analytic study. *Behavior Therapy, 43*(1), 77-87.

Jacobson, N. S., & Christensen, A. (1998). *Acceptance and change in couple therapy: A therapist's guide to transforming relationships.* New York: W. W. Norton & Company.

Jacobson, N. S., & Margolin, G. (1979). *Marital therapy: Strategies based on social learning and behavior exchange principles.* New York: Brunner/Mazel.

Lambert, N. M., Fincham, F. D., Braithwaite, S. R., Graham, S., & Beach, S. R. H. (in press). Can prayer increase gratitude? *Psychology of Religion and Spirituality.*

Mace, D., & Mace, V. (1980). Enriching marriages: The foundation stone of family strength. In N. Stinnett, B. Chesser, J. DeFrain, & P. Knaub (Eds.), *Family strengths: Positive models for family life* (pp. 89-110). Lincoln, NE: University of Nebraska Press.

Markman, H. J., Renick, M. J., Floyd, F., Stanley, S., & Clements, M. (1993). Preventing marital distress through communication and conflict management training: A four and five year follow-up. *Journal of Consulting and Clinical Psychology, 62,* 70-77.

Markman, H. J., & Rhoades, G. K. (2012). Relationship education research: Current status and future directions. *Journal of Marital and Family Therapy, 38,* 169-200.

Markman, H. J., Rhoades, G. K., Stanley, S. M., Ragan, E., & Whitton, S. (2010). The premarital communication roots of marital distress: The first five years of marriage. *Journal of Family Psychology, 24,* 289-98.

Markman, H. J., Stanley, S. M., & Blumberg, S. L. (2010). *Fighting for your marriage.* San Francisco: Jossey-Bass.

McCullough, M. E., Worthington, E. L., Jr., & Rachal, K. C. (1997). Interpersonal forgiving in close relationships. *Journal of Personality and Social Psychology, 73,* 321-36.

Noller, P. (1981). Gender and marital adjustment level differences in decoding messages from spouses and strangers. *Journal of Personality and Social Psychology, 41,* 272-78.

Notarius, C., & Markman, H. J. (1993). *We can work it out: Making sense of marital conflict.* New York: Putnam.

Snyder, D. K., Castellani, A. M., & Whisman, M. A. (2006). Current status and future directions in couple therapy. *Annual Review of Clinical Psychology, 57,* 317-44.

Stanley, S. M. (2001). Making the case for premarital education. *Family Relations, 50*, 272-80.

Stanley, S. M., Allen, E. S., Markman, H. J., Rhoades, G. K., & Prentice, D. (2010a). Decreasing divorce in Army couples: Results from a randomized clinical trial of PREP for Strong Bonds. *Journal of Couple and Relationship Therapy, 9*, 149-60.

Stanley, S. M., Markman, H. J., & Whitton, S. (2002). Communication, conflict, and commitment: Insights on the foundations of relationship success from a national survey. *Family Process, 41*(4), 659-75.

Stanley, S. M., Rhoades, G. K., & Whitton, S. W. (2010b). Commitment: Functions, formation, and the securing of romantic attachment. *Journal of Family Theory and Review, 2*, 243-57.

Stanley, S., Trathen, D., McCain, S., & Bryan, M. (1998). *A lasting promise*. San Francisco: Jossey Bass.

Stanley, S. M., Whitton, S. W., Low, S. M., Clements, M. L., & Markman, H. J. (2006). Sacrifice as a predictor of marital outcomes. *Family Process, 45*, 289-303.

Whitton, S. W., Stanley, S. M., & Markman, H. J. (2007). If I help my partner, will it hurt me? Perceptions of sacrifice in romantic relationships. *Journal of Social and Clinical Psychology, 26*, 64-92.

Wieselquist, J., Rusbult, C. E., Foster, C. A., & Agnew, C. R. (1999). Commitment, pro-relationship behavior, and trust in close relationships. *Journal of Personality and Social Psychology, 77*, 942-66.

Worthington, E. L., Jr., & Sandage, S. J. (2001). Religion and spirituality. *Psychotherapy, 38*, 473-78.

10

The Hope-Focused Couples Approach to Counseling and Enrichment

*Jennifer S. Ripley, Vickey L. Maclin,
Joshua N. Hook and Everett L. Worthington Jr.*

Couple counseling is difficult work. As couple therapists, we are expected to address what appear to be intractable relationship problems in a short amount of time; not take sides with either party; address underlying psychopathology; integrate diversity, race and religion issues into treatment to be sensitive to their needs; use empirically supported treatments in a way that will (if we are able to get their approval) keep insurance companies happy but still pay our bills; and not get discouraged because no-fault divorces are so prevalent and easy to come by that the couple might just give up. If you have experienced this challenge in your work, we hope that this chapter will assist you by introducing the hope-focused couples approach (HFCA) as an empirically supported flexible religion-accommodative treatment approach (Worthington et al., 1997; Worthington, 2005).

EMPIRICAL SUPPORT

The HFCA as couple enrichment. The HFCA was developed through private practice and refined through research at a clinical research lab across decades. The existing research on HFCA is summarized in table 10.1. The approach has been independently evaluated to meet the standards of an empirically supported treatment (Jakubowski, Milne, Brunner & Miller, 2004) for marriage enrichment. This means that it has been investigated at

Table 10.1. Results of Empirical Studies of the Hope-Focused Couples Approach

Author (Year)	Participants	Analyzed Measures	Intervention	Design	Results
Worthington et al. (1995)	48 couples from psychology classes	DAS Commitment Inventory PAIR	Assessment and feedback only delivered dyadic. 1 hour.	Random assignment to 2 conditions: intervention vs. assessment only. 4 week follow-up.	Small effect sizes for this component of intervention. Dyadic satisfaction was largest effect size, .28 at post-treatment and .42 at follow-up.
Worthington et al. (1997)	51 couples from psychology classes	DAS CARE Relationship Commitment PAIR	HFCA enrichment delivered dyadic. 5-6 hours.	Random assignment to two conditions: HFCA or wait-list. 3-week follow-up.	HFCA was effective with large effect size of Cohen's d = .95 for the DAS at post-treatment and 1.20 at follow-up. Relationship skills had large effect sizes, .77 & 1.26. Commitment and global attraction had low effect size.
Ripley & Worthington (2002)	43 couples from psychology classes (6) and community (37)	DAS CARE GRCISS coding system RDS TRIM	HFCA or FREE enrichment delivered in groups. 6 hours.	Random assignment to 3 conditions: HFCA group, FREE group or wait-list. 3-week follow-up.	HFCA was effective but FREE was not effective in group setting. Wait-list improved. Effect size small for self-report but large for observational measures.
Ripley et al. (2002)	14 married community couples	CARE; KMS; one item from DAS; intimacy scaling; stage of change questionnaire	Assessment and feedback in distance format (phone contact only). Less than one hour.	Random assignment to treatment or wait-list control group.	No change in relationship measures. There was positive movement in stage of change with intention to change for most participants.
Burchard et al. (2003)	20 community couples	Quality of Life Inventory; Trait Forgiveness Scale; Religious Commitment Inventory	Hope-focused or FREE program. 9 hours.	Random assignment to 3 groups: treatments or wait-list. One-month follow-up.	HFCA improved significantly more than control group. FREE program approached significance.
Worthington, Mazzeo & Canter (2005)	1 couple. Case Study	RCI; BFI; TNTF; TFS; stress scaling; Brief Symptom Inventory; DAS; single item forgiveness; CTS; intimacy scaling	Forgiveness-focused Couples intervention (revision of FREE). 8 hours.	Case study with 11-month follow-up assessment.	Wife's score changed from distressed to adjusted, while husband maintained adjustment. Anger and unforgiveness decreased. Various forgiveness measures increased for both partners in general.
Turner & Ripley (2007)	Case Study	marital and sexual satisfaction; commitment, dyad adjustment, partner forgiveness, values, attachment style, stressors, conflict resolution, depression, religious values	3 sessions of marriage enrichment with hope-focused couples therapy delivered as co-therapy.	Case study. No follow-up.	Couple reported improvements, and co-therapists and supervisor indicated positive movement for the couple. The couple especially responded positively to videotaping of their communication and watching the tape, followed by learning some communication skills.

Table 10.1. Results of Empirical Studies of the Hope-Focused Couples Approach (Continued)

Author (Year)	Participants	Analyzed Measures	Intervention	Design	Results
Ripley et al. (2008)	87 couples at intake, 59 at follow-up	RDAS; Commitment scale; Gordon-Baucom Forgiveness; IDCS; Couples self-rate video; spatial scaling of intimacy; heart rate, blood pressure	Hope-focused couples therapy-integrating communication and forgiveness. Religion accommodative or standard versions. 8 hours.	Random assignment to religion accommodative or standard Hope. Small wait list. 6-month follow-up.	No difference on measures for religion accommodative or standard treatment. There were significant positive changes for adjustment, forgiveness, most ratings of IDCS behavioral coding, couples self-rating of the video. No change for commitment, spatial scaling, heart rate or blood pressure. Effect sizes for significant changes were moderate to large.
Ripley et al. (2010)	76 couples	RDAS; Relationship Efficacy Scale; Gordon-Baucom forgiveness; Manifestations of God scale; Couples self-rate video; IDCS	Hope focused couples therapy-integrating communication and forgiveness. Client selected religious or standard versions. 8-14 hours.	Non-random assignment to religion accommodative. 6-month follow-up.	Effect size of treatment was moderate to large. Effect size over .70: RDAS, RES, impact stage of forgiving, IDCS codes of negative affect, problem solving skills, conflict and communication skills. Effect size over .40: moving on stage of forgiving, MOG scale; IDCS positive affect.
Kiefer et al. (2010)	27 parents from the community (not necessarily as couples)	TRIM; Single item forgiveness; Batson's empathy adjectives; care-giving partner forgiveness rating; parenting stress index	FREE intervention, workshop setting. 8-9 hours.	Random assignment to treatment or wait-list. 3-week follow-up.	FREE intervention increased forgiveness of their partner for an event. No change in empathy or forgiveness for past offenses in general. No change in parenting stress.
Worthington et al. (2012)	145 couples	DAS RCS TRIM BEA Anger Cortisol Behavioral ratings of partner in videotaped discussion	Couples randomly assigned to either HOPE or FREE 9 hours, 4 sessions.	Random assignment to 1 of 3 conditions: HOPE, FREE, control. Follow-up at 1 month, 3 months, 6 months and 12 months.	Both FREE and HOPE were effective when compared to a control condition for general couple satisfaction variables FREE was more effective than HOPE for most forgiveness variables. HOPE couples showed reductions in cortisol but only for those who began with high levels of cortisol. Both HOPE and FREE couples had more improvement than control on videotaped interactions.

multiple laboratories with various researchers in several controlled clinical trials, and it has demonstrated consistent efficacy. In addition to using the HFCA with couple enrichment at Virginia Commonwealth University, current research at the lab and clinic at Regent University has demonstrated efficacy with moderate to large effect sizes in couples counseling as well (Ripley et al., 2008; 2010). The approach has been investigated in group (Ripley & Worthington, 2003) and dyadic formats. It has had demonstrated efficacy in component analysis research on the intake and feedback portion of the approach (Ripley et al., 2002; Worthington et al., 1995).

Some research has used clinical trial design with control groups (Ripley & Worthington, 2002; Worthington et al., 2003) and other research has used clinical field study design (Burchard et al., 2003; Kiefer et al., 2010; Ripley et al., 2010). Almost all studies have included some follow-up measurements, and they have demonstrated maintenance of gains achieved during treatment. Several studies have used psychometrically supported behavioral rating systems and demonstrated improvements in videotaped communication (Ripley et al., 2008; Ripley et al., 2010; Ripley & Worthington, 2002; Worthington et al., 2003). There is more research on the communication and conflict resolution components of the intervention than the forgiveness-focused treatment, but both components have demonstrated efficacy (see table 10.1). One study also found that the HFCA intervention lowered levels of the stress hormone cortisol for couples who began the study with high cortisol levels (Worthington et al., 2010); however, there have not been consistent effects of the intervention on heart rate and blood pressure (Ripley et al., 2008, 2010). Even brief studies with few hours of intervention demonstrate positive effects in keeping with expectations for brief interventions. Across all the studies, the story is consistent: couples who participate in the HFCA intervention improve their relationship over time.

Research on religion-accommodative counseling for couples. Research on the religion-accommodative version of the HFCA has demonstrated equivalent outcomes to a standard non-religiously accommodative treatment (Ripley et al., 2010) in considering couple therapy (rather than couple enrichment). Couples seeking counseling were randomly assigned to a religious-accommodative treatment or standard treatment and no differences were found for general relationship outcomes.

These findings are similar to other research on religion-accommodative treatments—mostly individual, but also investigating some group and couple therapies (Worthington, Hook, Davis & McDaniel, 2011). There are two important stipulations to these results:

1. For religious variables (i.e., manifestation of God, religiosity variables), in most studies religion-accommodative treatments demonstrated more efficacy at improving the client's religiosity (Ripley et al., 2010) than have secular treatments.

2. When given the option for religious or nonreligious treatment, most couples self-select religion-accommodative treatment (72% in Ripley et al., 2010). This is not surprising given that most Americans self-identify as religious. We believe that most therapists do not consider or assess whether this is a "value added" option.

It is important to note that even if the research demonstrates little or no difference on relationship outcome variables, there is an ethical obligation to consider faith as a diversity aspect of treatment. For example, if a couple was struggling over the issue of religious heterogamy, then treatment that competently addresses their religious differences in an accommodative way would be ethical and may be more effective. This hypothesis has not been directly researched in clinical studies.

Evidence bearing on mechanisms of change. Recently David and Montgomery (2011) observed that it was possible for a treatment to be efficacious without being scientifically true. They offered the example of an early treatment for malaria. A preventative treatment that was somewhat effective was to shut the windows, which presumably would stop the bad air from circulating. Given that malaria was actually spread by mosquitos, closing windows could be an effective preventative intervention. However, the scientific theory on the mechanism for change on which the treatment was based was incorrect. The next step in research in a clinical intervention is to determine the mechanism for change.

Research on hope is plentiful and supportive with numerous studies summarized in a book by Snyder (1994). The hope approach is theorized to affect motivation to change and thereby to affect couple adjustment and commitment—the two primary indices of the quality of a couple relationship.

Second, the strategy that is taught to couples—to love (i.e., to value the partner), to work (i.e., to exert effort and time at bettering the relationship), and to have faith in God (if religious), each other, therapy, and the therapist as change agents—permeates the literature on the therapeutic relationship. There is little evidence directly investigating these mechanisms of change, but there is much evidence on the role of *love* in couple relationships (e.g., Graber, Laurenceau, Miga, Chango & Coan, 2011), *work* as the impact of homework in couple counseling or dose-response relationships in psychotherapy (e.g., Dattilio, Kazantzis, Shinkfield & Carr, 2011), and *faith* if we consider it to be demonstrated by the placebo effect of expectancy. The HFCA capitalizes on this research and applies it to couples intervention.

Third, making change sensible (i.e., using tangible objects and acts instead of mere discussion) is thought to affect willingness of partners to collaborate with each other and improve memory for in-session changes.

There is empirical evidence that creating an environment of hope, communication training, conflict-resolution training, intimacy training, forgiveness training and reconciliation training is effective in promoting change. However, direct evidence within couple enrichment or counseling contexts is needed to demonstrate specific efficacy for the mechanisms for change.

Overall assessment of the evidence base for the HFCA treatment. We suggest that research supports that the HFCA has a strong empirical base. First, Hook and Worthington (2009) found in a national survey of religious counselors that it was one of the most used approaches in couple counseling. Second, the controlled clinical-trial research suggests that it has been effective as an empirically supported treatment (Jakubowski et al., 2004) for couple enrichment in its secular form, and Ripley et al. (2010) found it to be as effective for couple therapy in its Christian form. Third, the evidence supporting mechanisms of change is strong but not conclusive.

DESCRIPTION OF THE HOPE-FOCUSED COUPLES APPROACH

Strategic hope-focused theory. HFCA is a strategic couples therapy approach. Couple treatments from the strategic approach (Haley & Richeport-Haley, 2007) identify and target key behaviors, beliefs or dynamics that maintain relationship dysfunction. Strategic family therapies are short-term approaches in which solvable problems are addressed using interventions tailored to the family (or in this case couple) to create healthier patterns of relating.

There are many differences of HFCA from classic strategic couple therapies. While classic strategic couple therapies may not focus on past relationship attachments, HFCA has incorporated more recent research on the importance of attachments in intimate partnerships (Schnarch, 2009). The problems in relationship are often not communicated or understood as attachment problems; however, attachment is taken into consideration as a constraint to achievable treatment goals. Improving the couples' bond is a primary strategic goal, informed by attachment theory. That bond is achieved through the use of strategic interventions. In the tradition of strategic approaches, HFCA maintains a present-focused, planned, pragmatic, short-term (five- to twenty-session) approach to treatment.

The positive psychology movement contributed to the HFCA primarily through the influence of hope theory (Snyder, 1994). Snyder conceptualized hope as containing two aspects: agency and pathways (Snyder, 1994). Agency involves cognitive motivation for a goal with a sense of efficacy for that change. Pathways are the means by which the goal is achieved. HFCA also adds "waitpower," which is based on theology by Gabriel Marcel (1962) regarding waiting on God's sovereign action. It encourages the couple to be patient for the full effects of treatment to be realized over time. For religious couples, this may include "waiting on the Lord" as a spiritual development tool for developing patient endurance.

Forgiveness. One of the central components of HFCA is the use of confessions and forgiveness as a means of restoration of the relationship after a relationship injury. Forgiveness, as an area of research, has reached relative maturity in social psychology, brain research, emotions and cognitive research (Worthington, 2005). The direct research on forgiveness in intimate partnerships is an active area of inquiry (Fincham, Hall & Beach, 2006). The upshot of this research is that partners who forgive are often able to restore damaged emotional bonds, suggesting vibrant relationships even if troubles are being momentarily experienced. Consequently, the focus on forgiveness in HFCA has increased as the research has demonstrated efficacy in component studies of HFCA (see table 10.1) and basic research on forgiveness.

The forgiveness component of HFCA is believed to be the most important for long-term maintenance of the results of treatment (see Worthington et al., 2003), but this is based on case examples and an unpublished conference presentation and thus we treat it circumspectly at this point. In the HFCA, couple therapists work with couples in the forgiveness components of HFCA through a cluster of interventions that focus on apologies, empathy, humility, altruism, forgiveness and reconciliation. Couples are taught the difference between deciding to forgive as a cognitive effort and emotionally forgiving as a time-sensitive work of reconciling and restoration of the relationship. The end goal of forgiveness interventions for couples is to fully experience a restored relationship after offenses have occurred, and to learn how to restore their relationship in the future.

Christian counseling integration. While HFCA can be used with any couple as a general positive psychology and psychotherapy intervention, it is readily applied as a Christian approach to counseling with numerous aspects of the approach influenced by Christian thought. HFCA retains ethical integrity by allowing for adaptation to couples with varying beliefs and values.

Inspiration: Faith, work and love. The Christian inspirational foundation of the HFCA is essential. For example, the central ideas communicated with couples are that relationships are maintained by a healthy combination of faith, work and love. Faith is the belief in things not yet seen. Couples strive to develop faith that they can work together to achieve their goal. Couples can also have faith in their therapists' ability to help them with their goals. And, for Christian couples, they can also have faith in God to support their relationship. Work is the effort or energy devoted to the restoration or maintenance of the relationship. Finally, love is defined as valuing one's partner and refusing to devalue each other.

Striving for virtues. The HFCA also works with an assumption that Christian virtues are healthy for relationships (Worthington & Berry, 2005). As such there is an emphasis on becoming a more virtuous person throughout treatment. This is more of an assumption rather than a direct teaching in the approach. Examples of virtues that are encouraged in HFCA include encouraging couples to become more capable of *forgiving* each other, taking an attitude of *humility* (Davis, Worthington & Hook, 2010), *patiently* waiting on the work to create change, demonstrating *love* in a way that one's partner can accept, exhibiting *grace* in resolving conflicts and communicating with softness or *gentleness* about difficult issues.

Striving for sanctification in and through marriage. In research there is a perception among many couples that the couple relationship, especially for married couples, is a sanctified relationship (Mahoney, Rye & Pargament, 2010). Sanctification in this research is the process by which a person ascribes sacred qualities to something in their lives. Even if not religious in other areas of living, some couples still view their marriage relationship as sanctified by God.

Striving for covenant marriage. A covenant is a historical religious concept that prioritizes the needs of the family and marriage, uses vows and promises to restore a relationship, and assumes that both parties will do all they can for the good of the relationship (Ripley, Worthington, Bromley & Kemper, 2005). By describing relationship goals in terms of a covenant the couple therapist works in tandem with the couple's belief system toward healthy relationship principles.

TREATMENT IMPLEMENTATION

Explicitly Christian interventions. There have been a number of recent articles and books on the use of explicitly Christian interventions with therapy in general and couples in particular (see, for instance, the special issue of the *Journal of Social and Clinical Psychology, 27*[7]). Generally the debate has been lively with a good deal of criticism that prayer or similar spiritual interventions are (a) not powerful enough to create transformative change in relationships, (b) impractical for use in counseling, or (c) could create intractable cognitions where partners' prior relationship problems are now layered with spiritual judgments (Beach, Fincham, Hurt, McNair & Stanley, 2008). However, it is also true that many couples seek spiritually informed couples treatment where explicitly Christian interventions are desired (Ripley et al., 2010). There is some data to support the use of religious interventions, such as prayer, as effective means of intervention if fully incorporated into treatment (Beach et al., 2008).

Both religious and nonreligious professional organizations agree that the imposition of religion or spiritual ideologies on clients is unethical

(APA ethics principle E; Hathaway & Ripley, 2009). The goal of psychotherapy, whether Christian or secular counseling, is not to influence clients in directions they do not want to go. However, it is also unethical to ignore and minimize the religious beliefs and strivings of clients. Therefore an ethical therapist begins treatment with a thorough assessment of relevant religious beliefs and strivings.

Prayer as an exemplar spiritual intervention. Prayer is perhaps the most commonly used Christian intervention in treatments (Beach et al., 2008) and therefore will be used as an exemplar for Christian interventions in general. The HFCA has a variety of other interventions tailored to the religion of the couple, as ethically appropriate. The religious accommodative interventions and alternative standard treatments are described in table 10.2.

Table 10.2. Christian Interventions and Correlating Standard Interventions

Christian Interventions	Standard Interventions
In depth assessment of religion, role of religion in marriage and religious values.	Assessment of religion. If unimportant then assess existential meaning as relevant.
Use of religious language in feedback report, treatment discussions, homework worksheets.	Use of psychological language.
Use of scriptures, especially a key scripture of "faith expressing itself through love" (Gal 5:6).	Use wise quotes from secular sources.
Use of prayer in session, especially as a "blessing" prayer for the couple.	Well-wishing statements.
Use of a prayer journal as option for couples to pray for their partner, their relationship and their own character development.	Use of general journal of gratitude and relationship issues.
Frame of efforts as improving both the relationship and their spiritual growth.	Frame of efforts as improving the relationship and personal growth.
Use of a "Joshua memorial" at termination as a means of remembering positive changes.	Use of a "graduation memorial" at termination to remember positive changes.

Beach et al. (2008) have outlined a framework for the use of prayer in psychotherapy "when culturally appropriate" and "for spouses who already engage in prayer" (p. 646). Their approach communicates research that works to legitimate the use of prayer in general in couple therapy based on the general population's use of prayer. For explicitly Christian psychotherapists, there is typically little need to legitimize the general use of prayer with clients who use prayer already.

Prayer can be used as an alternative intervention to standard psychological interventions. Beach et al. (2008) offered four prayer-based alternatives to standard psychological interventions for couples: meditative prayer in place of perspective taking, prayer to interrupt grievance rehearsal in place of breaking thought cycles, prayer to self-soothe in place of relaxation techniques, and finally, colloquial prayer in place of supportive dialogue.

Brief therapy. Research on therapy efficacy has demonstrated that more therapy generally improves various outcomes of treatment, but there is a "leveling off" of treatment effects somewhere between eight and thirty sessions (Wampold, 2001). This led to some of the decisions by managed care as to when to slow down or cut off sessions for psychotherapy. Managed care and insurance have generally put limits on the number of sessions clients can have covered in a year as well. However, the most difficult hurdle for long-term treatment is that the general public does not intend to enter psychotherapy for long-term treatment.

HFCA takes the constraints of insurance (for those couples where insurance covers treatment), the cost of self-pay, and couples' competing obligations for time as a given. Treatment generally lasts five to twenty sessions, with the HFCA lab-studies typically eight to twelve sessions lasting seventy-five to ninety minutes per session. The shorter treatment options of five to seven sessions would be targeted for couple enrichment or for premarital couples. Moderate-length treatment (eight to twelve sessions) is the normal protocol for HCFA. Longer treatment (over twelve sessions) is an option utilized with couples who need more extensive change to reach their goal, have resistances that slow goal attainment, or are inclined toward longer term treatment.

Quick demonstrable change. A principle of HFCA is to create early intervention that demonstrates that change is occurring within the first few hours of treatment. The demonstrable aspects of treatment are maintained throughout therapy whenever possible. One example of this includes intake and feedback (Worthington, McCullough, Shortz, Mindes, Sandage & Chartrand, 1995).

The intake and feedback component of HFCA is an essential and necessary ingredient in the treatment of couples. The Hope lab at Regent University uses extensive online secure questionnaires that couples complete prior to scheduling their intake appointment as an efficient means of collecting information and encouraging the couple to reflect on the state of their relationship. At intake, the couple therapist meets with both partners together for approximately forty-five minutes in which the couple therapist explores the couple's history, perceived strengths and weaknesses, primary goals explored through the miracle question (deShazer, 1988), diversity variables, and religious identity and preferences for religion-accommodative treatment. After the couple intake, the couple therapist conducts thirty-minute intakes with each partner individually to screen for psychopathology and factors that are counterindicative of brief couples treatment (e.g., recent or current affair, moderate to severe violence, significant untreated psychopathology or untreated substance abuse). Couples may create a ten-minute communication videotape and watch, process and rate the tape themselves on positivity and negativity. Finally, couples are given homework to look for ways to increase positivity in their relationship and schedule a positive date together. The intake ends with prayer for religious couples or well-wishing for non-religious couples.

The following week all of the information garnered online and in person is synthesized into a brief report written for the couple (Ripley et al., 2010; Worthington, 2005). The report is written in a format and language that is easy for the couple to understand and a copy is given to each spouse during discussion. Principles of faith, work and love are introduced as the cause of and solution to relationship problems. Key aspects of the relationship are graphed for the couple as a baseline measure of functioning in terms of commitment, communication, conflict resolution, confession/forgiveness, central values, hope and closeness. Couples are then given a tentative treatment plan as an agency pathway (Snyder, 2004) to reach their goals with the strategy of change focused on the key areas of their relationship.

TIPS FOR PRACTICAL APPLICATION

The text *Hope-Focused Marriage Counseling* (Worthington, 2005) and the manuals for the approach (Ripley, Leon, Davis & Worthington, 2010, available at www.hopecouples.com; see also Worthington, 1998, available at www.people.vcu.edu/~eworth) focus on practical application tips with hundreds of interventions that can be implemented and tailored to the needs of the couple. For the purposes of this chapter we have selected a few of the most commonly used HFCA interventions in our laboratories and clinical practices.

Family therapists often use physical space in the room to demonstrate family dynamics, changing alliances and interpersonal stances between partners. Making change concrete ensures that change cannot be easily denied later, and acts as a reinforcing encouragement to the couple (Worthington, 2005). Four examples of the use of physical space in HFCA are the TANGO communication technique, scaling techniques, the empty chair technique and sculpting during forgiveness exercises.

TANGO. There are a number of communication skills training programs that teach steps to communication for couples, focusing on reflective listening and full disclosure of feelings and thoughts around an issue. Miller's awareness wheel (Miller, Nunnally & Wackman, 1976) and the speaker-listener technique in the PREP program (Markman, Whitton, Kline, Stanley, Thompson, St. Peters et al., 2004) have inspired the TANGO intervention in HFCA. The acronym TANGO stands for tell (T) what happened, explain how it affected (A) you, be nurturing (N), check out if you "got it" (G) by reflecting, and observe (O) patterns of communication. The TANGO intervention is intended to be a parsimonious way to create communication rules and boundaries so couples can have the experience of positive communication with each other. The focus of the intervention is not on communication skills, but on learning the principles of communicating and breaking up negative reciprocity patterns. A full description of the approach is available in the hope-focused treatment manual (Ripley, Leon, Davis & Worthington, 2010, www.hopecouples.com).

Scaling. Scaling is a simple measurement of relationship closeness that uses physical space in the therapy room as a means of demonstrating closeness (deShazer, 1988). The couple is asked to stand in the room and stand apart from each other in a way that demonstrates how close or far apart they feel toward each other at that moment. When partners do not agree about how close they feel in the relationship, they often negotiate a solution there in the therapy room, giving the therapist a good picture of how they might try to resolve conflicts. Then the couple is asked to stand how close they would like to be at the end of counseling. Any informal negotiation, which we refer to as a "dance," can be processed with the couple to discuss their different needs for closeness in the relationship with some communication of acceptance of different needs in this domain.

Empty chair in forgiveness. The empty chair technique in HFCA is used as a method for emotionally softening the couple toward each other to increase their bond, increase empathy and prepare them for future forgiveness interventions. Greenberg, Warwar and Malcolm (2008) described an empty chair technique as a forgiveness intervention. Couples who lack insight or have Axis II traits generally do not benefit from this intervention, but most couples can identify some past experiences that have caused them to become guarded, be easily upset or have other unhealthy reactions in their current relationship. A key principle in this intervention is that the offender cannot be the partner but must be someone else in the client's life who has hurt him or her.

The partner's objective is to listen carefully while the empty chair technique is being used, as coached by the therapist. Then the partner is coached to come alongside his or her partner in his or her hurt and express understanding and empathy for his or her past hurt. For Christian counseling the imagery of a perfect and safe sanctuary can be utilized, and the therapist and couple can discuss God's response to their expression of pain from their past.

Sculpting for intimacy. Sculpting is a dramatic technique that uses physical space as a metaphor for communication and closeness in the relationship (Worthington, 2005). For example, a couple that is entrenched in a demand-withdraw communication pattern might, after discussing the pattern, physically demonstrate the pattern by having one partner stand and lean toward their partner pulling on her arm while the other partner turns away. The purpose of the intervention is to help make the pattern clear and authentically experienced for the couple. Worthington demonstrated a sculpting technique during a forgiveness intervention with a couple in a video (see www.hopecouples.com for video) where sculpting was used repeatedly to illustrate the couple's movement from the shock of discovery of the offense, to dealing with the aftermath, to increased empathy and finally to reconciliation over the offense. This makes the event more memorable for the couple, allows them to communicate their position and experience through movement, and gives clear goals for change toward a more open and healthy stance.

CASE STUDY

Mitchell and Rebecca James are an African American couple who have been married for eight years. Mitchell is a thirty-eight-year-old bank branch manager and Rebecca is a thirty-six-year-old lawyer at a prominent law firm. Mitchell indicates that they have come to therapy because, "All we do is argue, all the time." They both are actively involved in their children's lives (ages three and five) even though they both have busy work schedules. Rebecca and Mitchell inform you that they both really enjoy their jobs but that when they got married they made a commitment to each other not to let their jobs come between them. They report that even when the children were born they continued to spend time out alone without the children. They indicate that they have several couples that they are good friends with, and in fact are in a weekly small group Bible Study with a few of them. They report that they have a strong commitment to their faith and attend church weekly.

Rebecca tells you that their arguments are primarily about Mitchell being angry with her because she is not available to spend time with him after the children go to bed. She reports that she feels guilty about not being able to be as available to him. She insists that they used to go out once a week either with friends or alone, but she admits that for the past few months she has brought work home and has not been able to spend as much time with him. She reports that Mitchell does not seem to be willing to wait until the workload lightens and she can once again spend more time with him.

Rebecca and Mitchell complete some measures that give you a base rate of the nature of the relationship overall. Based on the responses and the interview you are able to establish a treatment plan and meet with the couple to give them feedback in a written report. In the following session you talk with Rebecca and Mitchell about the nature of their relationship problems and review their treatment plan with them. They are motivated to improve communication so treatment starts with communication skills. You begin by asking them to participate in a scaling exercise. You ask them to stand apart from each other in a way that demonstrates how close they feel to each other. Mitchell goes all the way to one side of the room and faces the wall, but Rebecca stands facing Mitchell about midway from the wall that Mitchell is facing. You then ask them to stand how close they would like to be with each other at the end of counseling. Mitchell faces her and walks up to her and reaches out to take her hand, and Rebecca responds by taking his hand and moves closer to him.

During the next session Mitchell indicated that one of the arguments that they had was about him not feeling that Rebecca had kept her word about not letting work come between them. The TANGO intervention is utilized to give some structure to the conversation and allow them to fully express their thoughts and feelings about the issue. They make good progress and they are encouraged to use the principles of the TANGO at home to discuss a desire to be closer with each other again. The couple practices various communication and conflict-resolution exercises in sessions for several weeks to establish safety.

In a session devoted to the empty-chair technique, Rebecca explores her anxieties of failing at work and how these were related to her mother's failures in life. Mitchell explored his anxieties about being ignored or abandoned by Rebecca. Despite good progress in the next meeting, however, Mitchell expresses feeling wounded by Rebecca for not being attuned to him. At this point you introduce forgiveness as an intervention, explain it, and encourage Mitchell and Rebecca to prepare for and undergo a session focused on forgiveness. A positive forgiveness session using the REACH model (Worthington, 2005) follows. The couple establishes safe behaviors, soften emotionally, and become ready to apologize and forgive. As they approach the end of their ten contracted sessions, Rebecca and Mitchell decide to finish treatment and focus on what they had learned about each other in a Joshua memorial (Worthington, 2005).

This case study offers a brief overview of how the HFCA can be utilized with a couple experiencing difficulties in their marriage that are disrupting the relationship if the couple is willing to do the work to change the direction the relationship is moving. While the results of the sessions will be different for each couple, when couples are working outside of session and demonstrate a commitment to improve and change, the HFCA brief therapy can prove to be beneficial in helping them make incremental changes in their marriage.

CONCLUSION

The HFCA is a Christian couple treatment in a short-term strategic tradition with a focus on developing hope for the couple, so that the partners can discover a sense of efficacy and use previously unused pathways to change their relationship. The HFCA has a history of direct research, which has involved studies both on the entire approach as well as on its component parts. It has been evaluated by an independent team of reviewers as meeting the criteria for being an empirically supported couple-enrichment intervention (Jakubowski, Milne, Brunner & Miller, 2004) with some additional support for the counseling version of the approach (Ripley et al., 2008, 2010). The HFCA appears to be most effective in changing general relationship adjustment, communication skills and sense of efficacy in the overall format that includes a variety of general relationship interventions with forgiveness integrated into the treatment. The forgiveness-focused program (FREE) has yet to be fully researched with couples. Existing research shows limited positive effects. The approach also has demonstrated improvements in spiritual functioning for couples in one study (Ripley et al., 2010). Overall, we conclude that HFCA program is poised for widespread dissemination for both couple enrichment and counseling (McHugh & Barlow, 2010). It has research support overall, on its various components, and on its theory of change. It has written training texts, manuals and video materials that may be used to educate and train new therapists. As the research shows, for couple enrichment and couple counseling, the hope-focused couples approach can make a contribution to better marriages for Christian or nonreligious couples.

REFERENCES

Beach, S. R. H., Fincham, F. D., Hurt, T. R., McNair, L. M., & Stanley, S. M. (2008). Prayer and marital intervention: A conceptual framework. *Journal of Social and Clinical Psychology, 27*(7), 641-69.

Blow, A. J., Morrison, N. C., Tamaren, K., Wright, K., Schaafsma, M., & Nadaud, A. (2009). Change processes in couple therapy: An intensive case analysis of one couple using a common factors lens. *Journal of Marital and Family Therapy, 35*(3), 350-68.

Burchard, G. A., Yarhouse, M. A., Worthington, E. L., Jr., Berry, J. W., Kilian, M. K.,

& Cantor, D. E. (2003). A study of two marital enrichment programs and couples' quality of life. *Journal of Psychology and Theology, 31*(3), 240-52.

Dattilio, F. M., Kazantzis, N., Shinkfield, G., & Carr, A. G. (2011). A survey of homework use, experience of barriers to homework, and attitudes about the barriers to homework among couples and family therapists. *Journal of Marital and Family Therapy, 37*(2), 121-36.

David, D., & Montgomery, G. H. (2011). The scientific status of psychotherapies: A new evaluative framework for evidence-based psychosocial interventions. *Clinical Psychology: Science and Practice, 18*(2), 89-104.

Davis, D. E., Worthington, E. L., Jr., & Hook, J. N. (2010). Relational humility: A review of definitions and measurement strategies. *Journal of Positive Psychology, 5*(4), 243-52.

deShazer, S. (1988). *Clues: Investigating solutions in brief therapy*. New York: W. N. Norton.

Fincham, F. D., Hall, J., & Beach, S. R. H. (2006). Forgiveness in marriage: Current status and future directions. *Family Relations, 55*, 415-27.

Graber, E. C., Laurenceau, J.-P., Miga, E., Chango, J., & Coan, J. (2011). Conflict and love: Predicting newlywed marital outcomes from two interaction contexts. *Journal of Family Psychology, 25*(4), 541-50.

Greenberg, L. J., Warwar, S. H., & Malcolm, W. M. (2008). Differential effects of emotion-focused therapy and psychoeducation in facilitating forgiveness and letting go of emotional injuries. *Journal of Counseling Psychology, 55*, 185-96.

Haley, J., & Richeport-Haley, M. (2007). *Directive family therapy*. New York: Haworth Press.

Hathaway, W., & Ripley, J. S. (2009). Ethical concerns around spirituality and religion in clinical practice. In J. Aten & M. Leach (Eds.). *Spirituality and the therapeutic process: A comprehensive resource from intake to termination* (pp. 25-52). Washington, DC: APA Books.

Hook, J. N., & Worthington, E. L., Jr. (2009). Christian couple counseling by professional, pastoral, and lay counselors from a Protestant perspective: A nationwide survey. *American Journal of Family Therapy, 37,* 169-83.

Jakubowski, S. F., Milne, E. P., Brunner, H., & Miller, R. B. (2004). A review of empirically supported marital enrichment programs. *Family Relations, 53*, 528-36.

Kiefer, R. P., Worthington, E. L., Jr., Myers, B., Kliewer, W. L., Berry, J. W., Davis, D. E., Kilgour, J., Jr., Miller, A. J., Van Tongeren, D. R., & Hunter, J. L. (2010). Training parents in forgiveness and reconciliation. *American Journal of Family Therapy, 38*, 32-49.

Mahoney, A., Rye, M. S., & Pargament, K. I. (2005). When the sacred is violated: Desecration as a unique challenge to forgiveness. In E. L. Worthington Jr. (Ed.), *Handbook of forgiveness* (pp. 57-72). New York: Brunner-Routledge.

Marcel, G. (1962). *Homo Viator: An introduction to the metaphysics of hope.* New York: Harper & Row.

Markman, H. J., Whitton, S. W., Kline, G. H., Stanley, S. M., Thompson, H., St Peters, M., Leber, D. B., Olmos-Gallo, P. A., Prado, L., Williams, T., Gilbert, K., Tonelli, L., Bobulinski, M., & Cordova, A. (2004). Use of an empirically based marriage education program by religious organizations: Results of a dissemination trial. *Family Relations: Interdisciplinary Journal of Applied Family Studies, 53,* 504-12.

McHugh, R. K., & Barlow, D. H. (2010). The dissemination and implementation of evidence-based psychological treatments: A review of current efforts. *American Psychologist, 65*(2), 73-84.

Miller, S., Nunnally, E. W., & Wackman, D. B. (1976). A communication training program for couples. *Social Casework, 57,* 9-18.

Ripley, J. S., Borden, C. R., Albach, K., Barlow, L. L., Kemper, S. D., Valdez, S., Babcock, J., Smith, C., & Page, M. (2002). Providing personalized feedback for marriage enrichment through distance formats: A pilot project. *Marriage and Family: A Christian Journal, 5,* 215-28.

Ripley, J. S., Leon, C., Davis, E., Smith, A., & Worthington, E. L., Jr. (2008, August). *Hope-focused couples therapy clinical trial: Does religion matter?* Paper presented at the meeting of the American Psychological Association, Boston.

Ripley, J. S., Maclin, V. L., Pearce, E., Tomasulo, A., Smith, A., Rainwater, S., et al. (2010, August). *Religion accommodative couple therapy: Process and outcome research.* Presented at the 118th Annual American Psychological Association National Conference, San Diego.

Ripley, J. S., & Worthington, E. L., Jr. (2002). Comparison of hope-focused communication and empathy-based forgiveness group interventions to promote marital enrichment. *Journal of Counseling and Development, 80,* 452-63.

Ripley, J. S., Worthington, E. L., Jr., Bromley, D. G., & Kemper, S. D. (2005). Covenantal and contractual values in marriage: Marital Values Orientation toward Wedlock or Self-actualization (Marital VOWS) Scale. *Personal Relationships, 12,* 317-36.

Schnarch, D. (2009). *Intimacy and desire: Awaken the passion in your relationship.* New York: Sterling Productions.

Snyder, C. R. (1994). *The psychology of hope.* New York: The Free Press.

Turner, P., & Ripley, J. S. (2007). Applying hope focused marriage therapy to conflict resolution in marriage: A case study. *Journal of Psychology and Christianity, 26,* 65-67.

Wampold, B. E. (2001). *The great psychotherapy debate: Models, methods, and findings.* Mahwah, NJ: Lawrence Erlbaum Associates Publishers.

Worthington, E. L., Jr. (2005). *Hope-focused marriage counseling: A guide to brief therapy.* Downers Grove, IL: InterVarsity Press.

Worthington, E. L., Jr., & Berry, J. W. (2005). Virtues, vices, and character education. In W. R. Miller & H. D. Delaney (Eds.), *Judeo-Christian perspectives on psychology: Human nature, motivation, and change* (pp. 145-64). Washington, DC: American Psychological Association.

Worthington, E. L., Jr., Berry, J. W., Miller, A. J., Sharp, C. B., Canter, D. E., Hook, J. N., Davis, D. E., Scherer, M., Campana, K. L., Wade, N. G., Yarhouse, M., & Ripley, J. S. (2003). *Relative efficacy of interventions to promote forgiveness-reconciliation and communication-conflict-resolution versus retested conrols in early married couples.* Paper presented in the International Conference on Forgiveness Research, Atlanta.

Worthington, E. L., Jr., Hight, T. L., Ripley, J. S., Perrone, K. M., Kurusu, T. A., & Jones, D. R. (1997). Strategic hope-focused relationship-enrichment counseling with individual couples. *Journal of Counseling Psychology, 44,* 381-89.

Worthington, E. L., Jr., Hook, J. N., Davis, D. E., & McDaniel, M. E. (2011). Religion and spirituality. *Journal of Clinical Psychology: In Session, 67(2),* 204-14.

Worthington, E.L., Jr., Mazzeo, S.E., & Canter, D. E. (2005). Forgiveness-promoting approach: Helping clients REACH forgiveness through using a longer model that teaches reconciliation. In Len Sperry and Edward P. Shafranske (Eds.), *Spiritually-oriented psychotherapy* (pp. 235-57). Washington, DC: American Psychological Association.

Worthington, E. L., Jr., McCullough, M. E., Shortz, J. L., Mindes, E. J., Sandage, S. J., & Chartrand, J. M. (1995). Can marital assessment and feedback improve marriages? Assessment as a brief marital enrichment procedure. *Journal of Counseling Psychology, 42,* 466-75.

Worthington, E. L., Jr., Ripley, J. S., Hook, J. N., Miller, A. J., Lin, Y., Lavelock, C., & Crawford, S. (2012). Hope-focused couple approach: Research on efficacy and analysis of why it might be effective. In A.J. Lancaster & O. Sharpe (Eds.), *Psychotherapy: New research* (pp. 1-28). Hauppauge, NY: Nova Science Publishers.

11

The Relational Conflict Restoration Model

Empirical Evidence for Pain-Defense and
Grace-Trust Patterns in Couple Reconciliation

James N. Sells

Dancing is the art of movement. The word conjures images of elegance, style and sophistication. Fred Astaire and Ginger Rogers are iconic. Dance is the creative display of action and reaction. One person steps, then the other. Movement is romantic, playful, separated and independent, then unified and harmonized. Like choreographers, marital scholars, psychologists and therapists also study the way couples dance, not in the ballroom or the stage, but in the context of their lives. Dance is a metaphor for the quality of relational movement. They study how partners move together as an effective, intimate team, and how they fail.

The study of marital conflict, in essence a "dance gone bad," has been a primary focus for social science research (Heavey, Christensen & Malamuth, 1995; Roberts, 2000; Shi, 2003). Findings from these studies suggest that the way that a couple "dances" through conflict is the best predictor of long-term relational success (Gottman, 1994). Furthermore, just as there is a pattern to dance, it is known that couples fight in patterns. Their "movements" are cyclical, that is, couples follow anticipated steps that make components of relational conflict predictable (Bradbury, Fincham & Beach, 2000; Gottman, 1994; Shi, 2003). The effect of these patterns is that "couples often selectively interpret each other's behavior and responses in ways that perpetuate their distress" (Johnson, Makinen & Millikin, 2001, p. 148).

This chapter describes a model that can be used to disrupt couples' conflict patterns, and to teach them steps toward a more elegant dance. The model is grounded in traditional Christian thought and current family systems theory. Christian theology functions as a conceptual foundation—as the "big idea." Family systems theory and empirical findings serve as the method, applying the big idea to the task of couple restoration.

The Christian Foundation for Couple Restoration

Key constructs used in the relational conflict restoration model (RCRM) have their conceptual origin and theoretical underpinnings imbedded within Christian thought and its application. The components of the model—which include the initial understanding of marital commitment and the individual relational characteristics, such as grace, justice, compassion/empathy, trust/faith and forgiveness/reconciliation—are themes to be understood through a religious paradigm. These constructs possess unique meaning within the Christian context. It is in the understanding and application of those ideas, using techniques created in family systems and marital/couples therapy research, that the Christian concepts can provide value to the counselor.

It is legitimate to question whether there exists a Christian therapy for couples, families or individuals, and whether the model described in this chapter is a "Christian" approach. Using an "ends and means" argument, the "end"—that is, a marriage that espouses beliefs and behaviors characterized by the Christian tradition—carries distinctions that are not found with equal degree and commitment outside of the Christian tradition. There is a culture formed through the Christian tradition that shapes the characteristics of relationship for those within the culture. Individuals who are committed to live within the Christian culture and who create marriages compliant with the Christian culture develop values, priorities and lifestyles that are distinct from those who are not influenced by the culture. These values exist outside of the Christian tradition, but the order, prevalence and frequency of the values are unique. If the end—that is, the Christian marriage—is distinct from other marital manifestations, then the means to enhance, restore or encourage relational functionality must also be distinct.

Finally, I believe that the therapies designed to enhance Christian marriage have application to marriages outside of the Christian tradition. A "good idea" within a small original context has potential to be a "great idea" if it holds value and benefit for the larger society. The RCRM approach (along with other Christian approaches) is developed from the definitions, priorities, values, commitments and life patterns of those who adhere to the Christian tradition. My hope is that those who do not share these Christian commitments will still find the approach helpful.

THEORETICAL FOUNDATION OF EMPIRICAL SUPPORT FOR THE RCRM

The theories and techniques that undergird RCRM are emotion-focused couple therapy (EFCT; Greenberg & Johnson, 2010) and contextual family therapy (CFT; Hargrave & Pfitzer, 2003). The RCRM utilizes components established in EFCT and CFT therapies and constructs associated with Christian relational principles to form a therapeutic objective and specific interventions for couples in conflict. The effect of threats to EFCT's attachment or CFT's assaults on justice is to cause protective acts by individuals from perceived threats. An unintended consequence is that a self-sustaining pattern of detachment or mistrust is established.

Emotion-focused couple therapy (EFCT). EFCT was developed by Greenberg and Johnson as a response to the identified need for (a) empirical evidence of treatment of couples, and (b) integration of affective components of the humanistic and psychodynamic traditions into couples therapy as an alternative to the near exclusive focus on behavior change (Johnson, Hunsley, Greenberg & Schindler, 1999). For the EFCT clinician, the focus of the approach is attachment, using Bowlby's (1969) developmental psychodynamic theory of human growth as the basis for a theory of adult attachment and intimacy. Greenberg and Johnson (2010) used the concept of attachment as the basis to understand intimate bonds.

EFCT theory holds that individuals conduct life and form attachments through internal models of relationship in which the world is seen through a variation of safe and trustworthy images and dangerous and uncertain images (Shi, 2003). Conflicted relationships emerge from unstable or incomplete attachments (Greenberg & Johnson, 2010). These insecure attachments create instability in the space between partners. When an individual experiences vulnerability and/or potential harm to the attachment bond, which normally is a source of security, a protective response is created to defend the self and the relationship. EFCT is comprised of four basic postulates. First, intimacy and conflict exist in reciprocal nature between partners with both internal affective responses and relational interactions. Second, intimate partners can become mired in negative relational patterns derived from insecure bonds. Third, relationships are first and foremost maintained in an emotional dimension, with cognitions and behaviors emerging subsequent to affective bonding. Finally, interventions in couples therapy target the way attachments are formed, maintained and developed (Johnson et al., 1999).

Contextual family therapy (CFT). A second theoretical influence of the RCRM is contextual family therapy (CFT). The theory originator, Ivan Boszermenyi-Nagy, saw couple/family bonds through the sharing of essential physical and psychological resources. Families succeed when sacrifices are made for one another, but these sacrifices must be mutual over time. The formation of conflict occurs when the balance of giving and taking is not mutual or reciprocal (Boszermenyi-Nagy, 1987).

Contextual theory focuses on the nature of the space between intimate partners and family members. Using midbrain research, particularly the activity of the amygdala during experiences of stress and threat, Hargrave and Pfitzer (2003) argue that it is noncognitive affective responses to violations of love and trust that guide and direct individual behavior within relationship. They describe relational balance of an outgrowth of an innate sense of justice or fairness. The basis for the creation of trust and for the expression of love emerges from the perceived sense of fairness emanating from the relationship.

Boszormenyi-Nagy applied Buber's (1970) idea of "I-Thou" to family processes to form the foundation to build trust. In this paradigm mature relationships are demonstrated by a fair exchange of regard and respect. Negative emotions (anger, resentment, envy, shame, rage) are indicators of perceived interference in the balance of I-Thou relationships, which prompt the amygdala to exercise its "fight or flight" protective response (Adolphs, Tranel, Damasio & Damasio, 1995).

Empirical basis for RCRM. The RCRM is a relatively new intervention.

Published empirical studies have focused on validation of the model and the relative value of each construct. There are a handful of empirical investigations on the model and its components. Sells, Giordano and King (2002) published the first outcome study of the model. Twelve married adults participated in an eight-week marital intervention group and a week-twelve follow-up. The couples completed measures of marital satisfaction, forgiveness, state-trait anger and a symptom assessment at intake, completion and follow-up. Findings indicated that there was significant change toward marital satisfaction, maturation of forgiveness, and reduction of state anger and mental health symptoms and the time of group completion. At the follow-up there were still significant differences but with attrition toward baseline outcomes.

Bokar, Sells, Giordano and Tollerud (2011) extracted the principle components of the marital process identified by the Sells et al. (2002) study and validated the components of the pain cycle: pain, defense and injury. Participants included 215 heterosexual couples, who completed surveys that measured responses to pain. Defense was measured by the Defense Style Questionnaire. Injury was assessed through the Positive and Negative Affect Schedule. The study indicated that the relationship between pain and defense was significant for both men and women. Pain was correlated highest with immature defenses, as hypothesized. The relationship between defensiveness and injury to the spouse was mixed, with women's injury not being correlated with men's neurotic defense.

McCarthy (2012) replicated Bokar's original work and examined the component of grace as an intervening variable in the conflict process. He found support for the RCRM model and confirmed that high levels of grace predicted reduced conflict, pain and defensiveness. He also found that when conflict escalates and satisfaction wanes, then defense responses escalate and distress ensues, the ability to give and receive grace plummets, and the ability of the couple to successfully resolve conflict is compromised.

Finally, Patrick, Beckenbach, Sells and Reardon (2012) conducted a path analysis with 237 subjects who completed measures of the constructs in the RCRM. The path model theorized that grace, justice, empathy, trust and forgiveness would lead to relationship satisfaction. The path analysis was robust and supported the relationships between these variables.

Empirical Theoretical and Applied Elements of RCRM: A Ten-Step Description of Therapy

Graphically, the RCRM consists of concentric circles with the components on the interior circle comprising the "conflict cycle" and the components on the exterior path containing the "restoration cycle." The cycle is divided hemispherically with each side mirroring the other and representing one of the spouses' experience within the marriage (see figure 11.1).

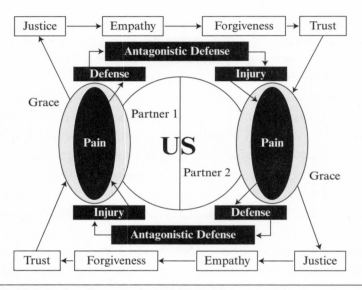

Figure 11.1. Relational conflict restoration model (Sells & Yarhouse, 2012)

Step 1: Goal identification/US designation. US is a relational construct that serves as the core of the RCRM (Sells, Beckenbach & Patrick, 2009). Hargrave (2000) created the term US to describe the priority of "I" and "Thou" in relationship. US is an externalized representation of a couple's values, ideals, purposes and aspirations. While the complimentary cycles of conflict and restoration help identify self-reinforcing behaviors that maintain injury, and alternative corrective means for restoration function as the actual "dance," the US is the motivation, inspiration and goal for the behaviors.

The initial task of the counselor is to form a purpose or goal for therapy. Restoration or re-creation of a marital US is my targeted goal—even if it is beyond their expressed purpose or intent. Toward this end the first step is to initiate conversation regarding the imagined or desired US held by both spouses. The questioning typically includes items such as

- What is your dream of the ideal marriage?
- What are the characteristics of husband and wife within that relationship?
- You once had aspirations for marriage—an image of life together—describe it.
- How does your faith tradition help you define what marriage is?
- What sacrifices have you made in moving from a "me" to an "US"?
- How will "US" be different from the current status of "you and me"?
- What do couples in successful relational partnerships do to make them work?

This process of US identification is drawn from an EFCT concept of attachment. Spouses are not just attached to a person, but to an idea, and that idea is imputed to a person who fails to meet the expectations and qualifications of the imagined marital image. Rather than dismiss those marital ideals as unrealistic, unfair or unreasonable, it is recommended that they continue to be held as relational goals that couples seek to achieve. For example, for the spouse who says, "I always dreamed that I would be married to my best friend," the counselor can encourage that as an excellent goal. "Yes, I want you to build friendship with your spouse. I am hearing that friendship building will need to be an important part of our work together." The goal of US identification is for couples to identify a common purpose in working together to build the marriage, and that at the onset of therapy they are taught to aspire toward a important, valued and desired marital hope. While they likely have come to reduce a destructive presence (conflict), they will simultaneously nurture and develop a positive force—an intimate, self-sustaining US.

Step 2: Pain exhibition. Having established a working goal or rebuilding the marital US, pain is the starting point in understanding the dance of conflict within the marriage. From contextual therapy we know that "pain, hurt, vulnerability or threat is the felt experience of perceived or real imbalance in relationship. Pain is experienced as any assault, injury, or psychological violation resulting in humiliation, shame, guilt, exhibition or perception of injustice" (Yarhouse & Sells, 2008, p. 351). In other words pain is that thing you feel when something is not right (e.g., the throbbing of a tooth, the long line at the post office, the rise in gas prices fifty cents per gallon in the past week). Events that we perceive to be not right or unfair are experienced as pain. Therefore, the RCRM is introduced by starting with the concept of pain. Individuals are asked to explain first minor and then significant painful experiences throughout life. Minor pains may include irritation from traffic or the failure to earn a position on the varsity bowling team. Major pain could be significant losses, tragedies, trauma or crises that have been addressed in childhood, adolescence or adulthood.

The purpose of the question is to prompt the married individuals to their pain-defense response. Each person has a plurality of reactions to aversive, uncomfortable, difficult and/or tragic events. Spouses are invited to describe their annoyances toward life. The intention is to encourage dialogue about general, not marital, annoyers and sources of pain, as opposed to specific acts of injustice that have caused pain in the marriage. Counselors often must block that type of dialogue. Spouses are frequently too willing to articulate with an attitude of blame the history of injustice experienced at the hands of their spouse. Later in the model, there is opportunity to express and receive such conversation. The purpose of this line of questioning is not to uncover the history of painful incidents but to establish the natural link between the experience of pain and the manifestation of defenses.

Step 3: Defense manifestation. Once a plurality of pain circumstances are identified, the couple is set to ask how each individual responds to his/her pain to reduce, manage, eliminate or deny it. Relational defense is any effort to mitigate painful or aversive experiences. Vangelisti and Crumley (1998) examined ways couples respond to pain and identified ten responses including silence, crying, attacking, defending, sarcasm, inquiry, ignoring, conceding, laughing and apologizing. Most frequent among them were silence, attacking, defending and conceding.

Gottman conducted extensive research on the defensive responses of couples. He found stonewalling, criticism, defensiveness and contempt to be characteristics evident in highly conflicted relationships. These he ominously labeled "the four horsemen of the Apocalypse" (Gottman, 1994), indicating that the presence of these four patterns in couple conflict were stable predictors of divorce. Gottman's "four horseman" hold that an injured person may justify his or her actions because of previous painful experiences. The previous injury serves as justification for subsequent actions that may be injurious to the spouse. It is as if the pain from previous violations, both recent and historical, distorts the injured person's sense of relational fairness so that it becomes a perversion of the "eye for an eye" mentality. The guiding moral principle becomes, "Do unto others before they have a chance to do unto you!" In essence, relational defenses indicate the patterns employed to protect individuals from real or perceived injury from their partner. Defenses are efforts to protect from injustice and to detach while simultaneously expressing an intent to build relational intimacy.

The purpose of the defense-manifestation step is to identify specific behaviors that are manifested in the presence of various painful, uncomfortable, frustrating or aversive situations. Couples identify four to six common responses, which may include

- "I am a yeller. When I get frustrated, I scream."
- "I sulk. I just want to collapse on the inside."
- "I go to bed. Sometimes for a long time. I avoid things with a nap."
- "I go running. I get my tension out by a good long run."
- "I eat. The more I hurt the more I eat. I don't do it too much. I am not too overweight."
- "I just cry. I get emotional and get it all out."

With the pain and defense pattern articulated and recorded on the pain cycle, the counselor can validate the reasonable processes exhibited or validate each person's expression of unreasonable processes. For example, to the person who says, "When I have a bad day I drink. I know I shouldn't and I know that it is dangerous, but it's the fastest and most effective way that I know to not feel the hurt that I am feeling." The counselor can validate the insight that such defenses are both effective in relieving pain and potentially devastating. Completion of the pain-defense response pattern for both spouses permits the counselor to move away from individual expression to more interactive engagement with the injury provocation.

Step 4: Injury provocation. Injury provocation refers to the thought processes that are employed when a spouse experiences or observes the defensive manifestations of the other. Leary and Springer (2001) examined relational injury as a construct distinct from other negative emotions such as anxiety, anger, depression, loneliness and shame. They found that relational injury is a distinct emotional experience that cannot be reduced to other negative emotions. Furthermore, Leary et al. (1998) found that a form of injury called relational devaluation was a common outcome when a relational partner perceives the other as acting in disregard toward the marriage.

Vangelisti and Crumley (1998) report that injury emerging from hurtful messages involved negative evaluations, accusations and negative disclosures of information. Individuals who have hurt feelings experience two emotions: sadness over having been wounded by a person he or she values and fear of being vulnerable to harm. Injury arising from relational conflict emerges out of how an individual assesses or appraises the communication occurring within the relationship. When messages render threat, devaluation or resource extraction, then injury and hurt feelings result. They report that hurt/injury, more than anger or guilt, is associated with increased interpersonal conflict.

Questions posed to both spouses involve a crossover of experiences:

- When you see your husband/wife acting like X, what do you think?

- How do you interpret your husband/wife's behavior when he/she _____?

Typically the responses given are

- "There he goes again. Just off leaving me to pick up the pieces."

- "She's after me. She won't give me a break or let it rest."

- "I gotta have space."

- "I think, *He does this to make me mad.* So I tell him what I think—that I am mad. Really mad."

- "Here I am alone again. Mom was right. I shouldn't have married him."

A key assumption error occurs at this juncture in the relationship conflict process. Couples usually assume that they are justified in their interpretation of the intention of their spouse's act. Conflict becomes perpetuated due to an attribution error. Insight into that mistake is essential in diverting couples from a pattern of perpetual conflict to the restoration cycle.

Step 5: Pain-cycle articulation. Steps one through four function as a data-gathering experience, which may occur during one session or evolve through multiple sessions, depending on the nature and degree of the couple's conflict and their ability to work together as a team in understanding their conflict process. Once the parts of the cycle are complete—literally written out in the presence of the couple—then the counselor can pull observations about the pain-defense cycle for the couple. Imagine Linda and Mike Johnson as a couple working this stage with their counselor. The dialogue represents a typical process:

> **Counselor:** *I have some important questions for you both. You can see the cycle that you both have described in this chart. Linda you feel pain of anger, abandonment and isolation. You address that pain with a defense of dialogue. Talking out loud helps you process your thinking and it brings you back to earth, so to speak. Mike, you tend to react to Linda's expectation to talk as one of control. The interpretation that Linda is trying to control you prompts a host of painful stuff—frustration, anger, you feel like you are going to "pop." So, Mike you manage that pain by creating space—if you don't come home right away, you won't feel controlled—so you go work out in the gym, have the oil changed in your car, run errands, anything necessary to keep yourself from having to go home. Linda picks that up and feels the injury of abandonment, which she soothes by seeking dialogue and conversation. Does that accurately depict the cycle that occurs in the Johnson home?*

> **Mike:** I think that pretty well catches us.

> **Linda:** Yes, it's pretty ugly, isn't it?

> **Counselor:** *I wouldn't say that it is ugly at all, not in a pessimistic sense. Rather, I'd describe it as needless. Here is what I mean. Mike, you knew Linda for three years before you were married and*

have seen her interactions with others for an additional eleven years of marriage. So for fourteen years you have watched her manage pain. This "got to talk it out" thing that she does that prompts you to think that she is trying to invade your space and take away your freedom—is this something that just occurs with you, or does she seek conversation with Mom, sister, sister-in-law, best friends, neighbors and others?

Mike: Oh, no, she does that with just about everybody.

Counselor: *Humm, really? And Linda, what about Mike? Was this, "gotta be by myself" thing new, or have you seen it before?*

Linda: Oh, no, it's not new. Mike was always a pretty independent guy. Like before we were married he would do these solo trips into the mountains—we met in Colorado—where he would be gone for two or three days all alone.

Counselor: *Wow. So here is the point. You both interpret the actions of the other—the way that they manage pain—as being intentional shots taken at you. However, what you are actually saying is that they are not so much about you as about him or her. You each take offense to the main management tool used by your partner.*

It is common for couples to articulate a sense of relief at this point in the therapeutic process. When a pattern of conflict is identified, and it is recognized as not a random process but as one that can be managed and even altered, there is a profound sense of hope: "We realize that we can do something about this." At this point, the counselor can change the focus of therapy from identification of the conflict pattern to formation of a restoration pattern.

Step 6: Grace introduction and expression. Sells, Beckenbach and Patrick (2009) identified grace as a transitional construct that has the potential to serve as a bridge from destructive relational patterns to mature relational enhancing behaviors. Grace has varied definitions drawing from religious to secular literature. Its commonality in psychology, counseling, and marriage and family therapy literature is limited. Ortberg (1982) drew the religious idea of grace into the mental health dialogue. He wrote of the human quality of loving others in spite of their faults. "This idea is talked about in therapy as unconditional acceptance, and in theology as unmerited grace" (p. 45). Pruyser (1976) defined grace as reception of unearned generosity. It is this "gratitude response" that seems parallel to grace as a facilitating factor with potential to counter the pain-defense-injury cycle of conflict (Sells, Beckenbach & Patrick, 2009). Maintaining the central thought of an unmerited gift, we define relational grace to be any act of kindness, mercy or goodness that has neither the obligation nor the expectation of reciprocal compensation within the context of marriage or partnership (Sells, Beckenbach & Patrick, 2009; Yarhouse & Sells, 2008). Grace is an act of compassion that is given without duty to respond as a preconceived requirement.

Grace is often a difficult topic to teach in a counseling setting. Those coming from a Christian tradition are familiar with its meaning theologically. This is usually helpful. Those from other faith traditions frequently understand it in very simplistic form, such as the title to a popular "folk song," what religious people say before dinner, or a woman with Audrey Hepburn–like class descending a curved staircase in an elegant evening gown. A simple illustration to convey its meaning in relational contexts is demonstrated in the following dialogue:

Counselor: *Mike and Linda, you both understand grace from childhood Sunday school as God's gift for which work or merit is not expected. Similarly, I want you to think back to childhood to someone who just loved you, cared for you, did good to you. It could be a favorite aunt or uncle, a grandparent, a neighbor, coach or youth pastor.*

Mike: For me it would be my uncle Mike. I am named after him. He lived in Texas on a ranch. When I went there in the summer he would always take me fishing for catfish in the pond in the pasture. We would be there every morning.

Counselor: *Perfect. Did you ever pay him for the worms, the tackle, the time? Did you do the same thing when he would come to your house—host him on a fishing trip?*

Mike: I never did anything for him.

Counselor: So why did Uncle Mike take you fishing? Sure, he loved you. But he loved you whether you fished or not. Was it fun, meaningful, a great time for Uncle Mike to get up early and fish with a middle school kid?

Mike: I am sure it wasn't. He just did it.

Counselor: I am glad you have an "Uncle Mike" in your childhood. That was a grace relationship. He cared for you without the expectation that you would care for him back. So you both know what it is like to give and to receive without the expectation of the other giving and receiving first. You can see the obvious stalemate that is produced: if both insist that the other does good before you do good, then no one will do good. We are stuck! Grace says, "I will do good."

Step 7: Justice obligations. "No justice, no peace!" is the cry of both the social change agent and the spouse in a bad marriage. In its role as a component of RCRM, justice is tied with relational grace as a "detour" experience from the pain-defense-injury cycle. Boszormenyi-Nagy (1987) considered justice to be a fundamental requirement for human survival. He refers to the "matrix of justice" in which a contract must exist within and between generations, including partnered or married couples. The use of justice in RCRM entails that couples engage in dialogue to ensure fairness between intimate partners. Both hold justice as a principle to which they submit as though it were a law requiring obedience within any civil society. Justice requires that a couple attend to problem solving, weighing alternatives and charting a course that is fair, balanced and mutual. The assumption of responsibility, the declaration of mutual violations, and the pursuit of mutual fairness promote integrity in the relationship (see Hargrave, 1994, 2000; Hargarve & Pfitzer, 2003). The principle of justice flows directly from the understanding of grace discussed above, as is illustrated by the following dialogue.

Counselor: Mike, when you accept Linda's grace commitment to you—she is going to give out of a desire to see you flourish, without

> *the demand that you will respond to her first before she will*
> *be good to you. How long will she be able to sustain that com-*
> *mitment before she begins to feel that she is being "taken for*
> *a ride."*

Mike: Oh, I don't really know, but I would assume that it would happen pretty quick.

Counselor: *Right. Unlike God's grace, human-to-human, relational grace*
cannot be sustained forever. Grace requires fairness in order to
exist over time.

Additionally, it is recommended that counselors return to the idea of US as a reason for seeking justice and fairness. Appropriate questions could include

- What role does justice have in your US?
- What is the difference between reacting to each other's pain with defensiveness and injury and with grace and justice?
- Why does grace need to come before justice?
- What do you expect to happen if justice doesn't arrive after grace is present?

The operant conditioning idea of shaping has been a useful metaphor at this juncture. Shaping is the manipulation of an organism by rewarding behavior that approximates the desired behavior. Applied to marriage and the formation of justice, spouses who demand all of their "justice" expectations be met will likely not experience any of justice's rewards. Being just is complicated. With the formation of any complicated skill in which legitimate self-interest must be met along with legitimate "other-interest," it will take a long time before justice is done well. In the meantime, frustration arises because performance does not meet expectations. The principle of shaping is to reward movement in the right or "just" direction. Therefore, partners/spouses should not wait until every aspect of a just response is accomplished. Rather, each should be searching for evidence of positive change and providing incentives for continued growth. Multiple small successes encourage more frequent successes.

Step 8: Empathy expression. "What all the definitions of empathy in psychotherapy have in common at a superordinate level is that they involve trying to sense, perceive, share or conceptualize how another person is experiencing the world" (Bohart & Greenberg, 1997, p. 419). Gottman's early research (1994) indicated that teaching constructing positive behaviors that enhance friendship was a more effective path than focusing on communication or empathy. Gottman did not disregard the role of empathy, but similar to others writing at the time, he affiliated it with a combination of many constructs that work together to establish positive affect. In relational repair the central goal was to decrease the manifestation of negative affect and behavior and increase positive affect and behavior (Gottman, 1994).

Empathy is the "I get it" declaration. It is the expression of understanding of each other's pain-defense pattern. "I get it" means that the relationship between a spouse's pain and a spouse's defense response is understood for what it is—an effort at pain management. With the expression of acceptance, defenses are unnecessary. I believe that empathy encourages the formation of new, more mature defenses. Therefore, discussions about the perceived need to act in established patterns and how to creatively develop alternative ways of acting are seen as outgrowths of empathy.

Step 9: Forgiveness communication. The theoretical and empirical basis for forgiveness as a treatment goal is extensive. Within the RCRM, forgiveness is seen as both an internal/individual and relational process. The internal aspects of forgiveness involve letting go of a wrong done, letting go of the right of retaliation, and freeing oneself from the entrapment of unforgiveness (Worthington, 2003). Most of the forgiveness research has concentrated on individual process, which focuses on a cognitive reorganization of injury. Benefits of forgiveness are established through identified physical health benefits, relational well-being and spiritual advancements (Toussaint & Webb, 2005).

There is also an abundance of studies on forgiveness as a relational construct (Fehr, Gelfand & Nag, 2010). Greenberg, Warwar and Malcolm (2010) present a discussion of outcome research using EFCT with a forgiveness protocol that reflects the core priorities of the RCRM model. They write:

> In this treatment, the process began with the injured partner expressing blame, complaint, or hurt and the offender being defensive about having

committed the injury, or minimizing its severity. In those couples who forgave, the injurer first shifted to a non-defensive position of acceptance for the responsibility of the injury, and the injured partner expressed a primary emotion related to the injury to which the offender responded empathically. (p. 39)

Ultimately, within the RCRM theory, forgiveness functions as the conduit to restore relational trust, and then to reinforce the couple's commitment to reinvest grace in the relationship. Forgiveness becomes the recharging source that allows the US to continue the ongoing confrontation and healing of pain.

The journey of forgiveness is both a personal and community trek. Conversations about the process of forgiveness can be initiated with questions such as

- What is the healing process employed within marriage after offense has occurred?
- Who occupies the role of forgiver and the one who needs to be forgiven within marriage?
- What happens when these roles are reversed?
- How was forgiveness modeled for you in your family of origin?
- Who has declared you forgiven, other than God?
- Who has come to rely on you to be there as they take risks of seeking forgiveness?

Forgiveness within the context is of marital restoration is a bi-directional process where both must forgive and be forgiven. The process of forgiveness includes an examination of the pain-defense cycle described earlier in the model with both parties articulating the pain, defense and injury experienced. The forgiveness process might address specific events occurring in the relationship, it might address prevailing attitudes or conditions but not be tied to any particular event or circumstance, or it may emanate from either partner's family of origin or previous life experience. Whatever the case, the purpose of the intervention is to articulate the connection between pain, defense and subsequent responses to the pain articulation that altered the process of the marital relationship. Second, after the pain-defense-injury cycle is defined, each is asked how they could alter their partner's need for defensiveness through the offering of some form of grace-gift. Third, the couple is asked to consider the boundaries needed in order to prevent injury from occurring in the same manner that it has occurred previously. Fourth, there is an active engagement concerning the understanding of current circumstances that propel each person toward the previous patterns, and an understanding of what prevents the recurrence of the patterns. Fifth, there can be an open declaration of release. I am careful to not make an apology the focus of a forgiveness intervention. Apologies can easily be substituted for the real work of "embodying forgiveness" (Jones, 1995). Jones's idea is that forgiveness is to be the defining characteristic of the life of the Christian. The prism that refracts the light of relational pain is a forgiveness lens. It is a way of being in relationship—as though each says to the other: "I know, see and understand your brokenness, and I participate in helping you stand straight as you participate in helping me stand as well." Forgiveness is the release of the rights to defend oneself and to retaliate against previous wrongs, and in its place is the commitment to heal and be healed.

Step 10: Trust formation. Trust, like empathy and forgiveness, is a construct that occupies a prominent position in psychology literature. In fact, trust is a "crossover variable" with a significant presence in sociology, economics, political science and many other fields as well (Dirks & Ferrin, 2002). Trust research has a profound importance in human existence.

To Mayer, Davis and Schoorman (1995), trust was the working together of the trustor's propensity to trust with the perceived trustworthiness of the trustee. "Propensity to trust" is seen as a personality variable originally affiliated with Rotter's (1971) classic work on interpersonal trust as a personality variable. Solomon and Flores (2001) found that trustworthiness is a complement to trust as a prerequisite. They hold that without the integrity and benevolence of trustworthiness, any indication of trust is viewed with suspicion.

Like forgiveness, trust formation involves two sets of tasks—developing both trustworthiness and a propensity to trust. Research findings indicate that trustworthiness consists of the ability, benevolence and integrity of the trustee. Therefore couples must have conversations about how to act carefully and consistently in a trustworthy manner with an intent to prioritize the other above one's self. In essence, the task of marriage is to build "trust in trust," that is, to make both trustworthiness and trusting secured endeavors within the marriage. Couples are coached in the process of trustworthiness and trusting. For example, Morgante (2012) uses trust-building activities to serve as physical metaphors that permit couple discussion within the therapy setting. These include a "trust lean," in which one partner leans into the other's arms and is physically supported by the other as a symbol of vulnerability. The symbolic exercise expresses central relational dynamics such as "if you don't hold me, I will fall," and "I carry a moral duty to support and maintain the safety and security of my spouse."

Valuable questions for discussion include

- Who tends to occupy the role of trustor (the leaper) and trustee (the catcher)?
- What happens when these roles are reversed?
- How was trust modeled for you in your family of origin?
- Who have you come to rely on to be there as you take risks of vulnerability?
- Who has come to rely on you to be there as they take risks of vulnerability?

Research in the RCRM process suggests that trust is equivalent to marital satisfaction. That is to say that trust is the sine qua non of relational success (Patrick et al., 2012). In their structural equation model, trust (along with marital satisfaction) was shown to be the culmination of the RCRM process, rather than a variable which contributed to satisfaction. Trust was the culmination of the restoration constructs of grace, justice, empathy and forgiveness.

Treatment implementation. In RCRM model, identification of the steps and processes of the conflict cycle—the pattern of pain-defense-injury—appears to be important. Couples come to counseling exasperated and hopeless. While their intention to love and support each other is high, their experience is that they are pulled into patterns that control them. Discovering that there is order, predictability and explanation to the pattern of conflict is often extremely valuable for them.

The intervention steps don't need to occur in a fixed order. Empathy need not come before forgiveness, or justice before empathy. Hargrave's (2000) "stations" are repetitive: they are conquered but continually revisited. The concepts are introduced linearly—that is grace is explained before justice, which is before empathy, which preceded forgiveness. However, it is not accurate to think that a couple "finishes" the empathy task in two weeks and then graduates to forgiveness. These themes are addressed repetitively, not progressively. They are revisited over and over.

CONCLUSION

The RCRM is a tool used to address relational conflict and to substitute destructive patterns with cyclical virtues. There is a growing body of empirical evidence for the model and the components within the model. A good marriage is like an elegant dance. Counselors coach, teach and guide couples toward sophistication, efficiency and beauty in their dance. Ugly dancing found in the pain-defense-injury cycle can be altered with insight, practice and instruction.

REFERENCES

Adolphs, R., Tranel, D., Damasio, H., & Damasio, A. (1995). Fear and the human amygdala. *The Journal of Neuroscience, 15*, 5879-91.

Bohart, A., & Greenberg, L. (Eds.). (1997). *Empathy reconsidered: New directions in theory research and practice.* Washington, DC: American Psychological Association.

Bokar, L., Sells, J., Giordano, G., & Tollerud, T. (2011). The validation of the marital conflict cycle. *The Family Journal, 19*, 7-14.

Boszermenyi-Nagy, I. (1987). *Foundations of contextual therapy: Collected papers.* New York: Brunner/Mazel.

Bowlby, J. (1969). *Attachment: Attachment and loss.* (Vol. 1). London: Hogarth Press.

Bradbury, T. N., Fincham, F. D., & Beach, S. R. H. (2000). Research on the nature and determinants of marital satisfaction: A decade in review. *Journal of Marriage and Family, 62*, 964-80.

Buber, M. (1970). *I and Thou.* New York: Charles Scribner's Sons.

Dirks, K. T., & Ferrin, D. L. (2002). Trust in leadership: Meta-analytic findings and implications for research and practice. *Journal of Applied Psychogy, 87*, 611-28.

Fehr, R., Gelfand, M. M., & Nag, M. (2010). The road to forgiveness: A meta-analytic synthesis of its situational and dispositional correlates. *Psychological Bulletin, 136,* 894-914.

Fowers, B. J. (2000). *Beyond the myth of marital happiness: How embracing the virtues of loyalty, generosity, justice, and courage can strengthen your relationship.* San Francisco: Jossey-Bass.

Gottman, J. M. (1994). *What predicts divorce?* Hillsdale, NJ: Lawrence Erlbaum Associates.

Greenberg, L. S., & Johnson, S. M. (2010). *Emotionally focused therapy for couples.* New York: Guilford Press.

Greenberg, L., Warwar, S., & Malcolm, W. (2010). Emotion-focused couples therapy and the facilitation of forgiveness. *Journal of Marriage and Family Therapy, 36,* 28-42.

Hargrave, T. D. (1994). *Families and forgiveness: Healing the wounds in the intergenerational family.* New York: Brunner/Mazel.

Hargrave, T. D. (2000). *The essential humility of marriage.* Phoenix, AZ: Zeig, Tucker & Theisen.

Hargrave, T. D., & Pfitzer, F. (2003). *The new contextual therapy: Guiding the power of give and take.* New York: Brunner-Routledge.

Heavey, C. L., Christensen, A., & Malamuth, N. M. (1995). The longitudinal impact of demand and withdrawal during marital conflict. *Journal of Consulting and Clinical Psychology, 63,* 797-801.

Johnson, S. M., Hunsley, J., Greenberg, L., & Schindler, D. (1999). Emotionally focused couples therapy: Status and challenges. *Journal of Clinical Psychology: Science and Practice, 6,* 67-79.

Johnson, S. M., Makinen, J. A., & Millikin, J. W. (2001). Attachment injuries in couple relationships: A new perspective on impasses in couples therapy. *Journal of Marital and Family Therapy, 27*(2), 145-55.

Jones, L. G. (1995). *Embodying forgiveness: A theological analysis.* Grand Rapids, MI: Eerdmans.

Leary, M. R., & Springer, C. A. (2001). Hurt feelings: The neglected emotion. In R. M. Kowalski (Ed.), *Behaving badly: Aversive behaviors in interpersonal relationships* (pp. 151-175). Washington, DC: American Psychological Association.

Leary, M. R., Springer, C. A., Negel, L., Ansell, E., & Evans, K. (1998). The causes, phenomenology, and consequences of hurt feelings. *Journal of Personality and Social Psychology, 74*(5), 1225-37.

Mayer, R. C., Davis, J. H., & Schoorman, F. D. (1995). An integrative model of organizational trust. *Academy of Management Review, 30,* 709-34.

McCarthy, C. (2012). Validating pain, defense and grace in the relational restoration model. Unpublished manuscript, Regent University, Virginia Beach, VA.

McCullough, M. E., Worthington, E. L., Jr., & Rachal, K. C. (1997). Interpersonal forgiving in close relationships. *Journal of Personality and Social Psychology, 73*, 321-26.

Morgante, C. (2012). Grace and trust in hope-focused couples therapy. Unpublished manuscript, Regent University, Virginia Beach, VA.

Ortberg, J. (1982). Accepting our acceptance: Some limitations to the Rogerian approach to the nature of grace. *Journal of Psychology and Christianity, 1*, 45-50.

Patrick, S., Beckenbach, J., Sells, J., Reardon, R. (2012). *Justice, grace, and forgiveness: Paths to relationship restoration.* Unpublished manuscript, Regent University, Virginia Beach, VA.

Pruyser, P. W. (1976). *The minister as diagnostician: Personal problems in pastoral perspective.* Philadelphia: Westminster Press.

Roberts, R. C. (2000). A Christian psychological view. In E. L. Johnson & S. L. Jones (Eds.), *Psychology and Christianity: Four views* (pp. 148-77). Downers Grove, IL: InterVarsity Press.

Rotter, J. (1971). Generalized expectancies for interpersonal trust. *American Psychologist, 26*, 443-52.

Sells, J. N., Beckenbach, J., & Patrick, S. (2009). Pain and defense versus grace and justice: The relational conflict and restoration model. *The Family Journal, 17*, 203-12.

Sells, J. N., Giordano, F. G., & King, L. (2002). A pilot study in marital therapy: Process and outcome. *The Family Journal, 10*, 156-66.

Sells, J. N., & Yarhouse, M. (2012). *Counseling couples in conflict.* Downers Grove, IL: InterVarsity Press.

Shi, L. (2003). The association between adult attachment styles and conflict resolution in romantic relationships. *The American Journal of Family Therapy, 31*, 143-57.

Soloman, R. C., & Flores, F. (2001). *Building trust in business, politics, relationships and life.* New York: Oxford University Press.

Toussaint, L., & Webb, J. R. (2005). Theoretical and empirical connections between forgiveness, mental health and well-being. In Everett L. Worthington Jr. (Ed.), *Handbook of forgiveness* (pp. 321-33). New York: Brunner-Routledge.

Vangelisti, A. L., & Crumley, L. P. (1998). Reactions to messages that hurt: The influence of relational contexts. *Communication Monographs, 65*, 173-96.

Worthington, E. L., Jr. (1999). *Hope-focused marriage counseling: A guide to brief therapy.* Downers Grove, IL: InterVarsity Press.

Worthington, E. L., Jr. (2001) *Five steps to forgiveness: The art and science of forgiving.* New York: Crown Publishers.

Worthington, E. L., Jr. (2003). *Forgiving and reconciling: Bridges to wholeness and hope.* Downers Grove, IL: InterVarsity Press.

Yarhouse, M., & Sells, J. (2008). *Family therapies: A comprehensive Christian appraisal.* Downers Grove, IL: InterVarsity Press.

12

Marital Couples and Forgiveness Intervention

Frederick A. DiBlasio

When couples come to therapy they usually bring with them not only current struggles, but a history of conflict through the years. Often the current conflict is a variation of an old and established interactional theme of past offenses that have reoccurred time and time again. Because the underlying theme is not fully addressed or the offenses thoroughly forgiven, couples tend to replay offensive patterns. For Christian couples, the lack of resolution and forgiveness with spouses also puts them in a spiritual dilemma. They feel that unforgiveness is a basic interference with their individual relationship with Christ.

The usual psychotherapeutic approach to this problem involves each partner espousing his or her perception and point of view, venting the hurt and pain they feel, and then moving forward with resolving the problem. Although at first glance this may seem a viable and biblically consistent treatment protocol, it actually does not directly address letting go of the resentment that has taken root (Heb 12:15). The answer for Christian couples is to move toward each other in Christlike love, forgiving each other and thereby reconciling the past and setting in place a plan to prevent the hurtful behavior in the future.

In two empirical studies of marital couples (DiBlasio & Benda, 2008), we found some beginning evidence that a decision-based therapeutic forgiveness session promoted forgiveness, increased marital satisfaction and decreased depression. These findings are consistent with those reported in the practice literature over the years (e.g., Cheong & DiBlasio, 2007; Di-

Blasio, 1998, 1999, 2000; Worthington & DiBlasio, 1990) and reported at national conferences such as American Association of Christian Counselors (AACC), Christian Association of Psychological Studies (CAPS) and the American Association of Marital and Family Therapy (AAMFT). This chapter will briefly summarize these studies, review scriptural support, describe each step of the forgiveness intervention using case material for illustration, and provide treatment implications and a four-year follow-up of the case. Unless otherwise noted, inferences, implications, case material and clinical observations are derived from the author's long-term practice experience of conducting forgiveness sessions. This chapter draws from sections (with expansion and modification and permission of the *Journal of Psychology and Christianity*) by DiBlasio (2010).

Empirical Support

Two empirical studies of marital couples (DiBlasio & Benda, 2008) found that a step-by-step forgiveness intervention promoted forgiveness, increased marital satisfaction and decreased depression. A primary advantage of these studies is that the therapeutic intervention was conducted by psychotherapists who met with each couple and processed the couple's offenses in a private session. The actual study of marital psychotherapy is rare in the forgiveness research (see Gordon, Baucom & Snyder, 2005; Greenberg, Warwar & Malcolm, 2008, 2009). In many other studies data are gathered from participants of a group intervention and seldom are the interventions interactive between spouses. Even more uncommon is the use of experienced Christian psychotherapists (see Worthington, Jennings & DiBlasio, 2010).

Study 1 was a randomized clinical trial with 44 couples ($N = 88$ participants) comparing a forgiveness treatment group (FT) ($n = 38$); an alternative treatment group (AT) ($n = 32$); and a no-treatment control group (NT) ($n = 18$). A pre- and posttest was completed by participants who rated forgiveness toward their spouse (Enright Forgiveness Inventory; Enright & the Human Study Group, 1991), marital satisfaction and depression/contentment (Hudson, 1997). Using groups that did not receive the forgiveness treatment helped to control for possible confounding variables such as improvements that could result from coming to a therapy session, or in the case of the NT, improvements due to the passage of time.

The findings for study 1 indicated that spouses who received the for-giveness intervention had the greatest positive gain in forgiveness, marital satisfaction and contentment. For example, mean score changes between pre-and post-tests for the FT on the Enright Forgiveness Inventory (EFI) were nearly four times greater than the NT and almost two times greater than the AT. However, repeated measure analyses demonstrated that statistical differences between the groups on the EFI were not significant. The authors point out that the sample size may not have been large enough for use with the EFI measurement. Statistical differences were found for the FT when compared to the NT on both marital satisfaction and contentment. The only statistical significant difference found for the AT over the NT was on the depression/contentment scale.

Study 2 involved devout Christian subjects (thirteen couples; $N = 26$) who were assigned to a Christian forgiveness treatment (CFT). This treatment was the same as the FT in study 1 except that prayer and discussion of forgiveness Scriptures were utilized. Whereas 53 percent of the participants from study 1 identified with Christian affiliations, the researchers in study 2 were interested in Christians who answered two questions in a way that reflected the belief that Jesus is the Messiah and that the participant's personal security of eternal salvation comes through Jesus' atoning death and resurrection. Although this is a popular way to define Christianity in the theologically conservative Christian community, this is the only empirical study that the author is aware of that uses acceptance of the gospel message for defining devout Christians. Devout Christians were not randomly assigned to study 1, but instead were selected to be studied separately. The word "devout" was used to describe subjects who affirm strong belief in the two items above, thereby avoiding the many value-laden terms given to Christians who believe in this particular interpretation of the gospel message.

Using *paired-sample t-tests* the effect of the forgiveness intervention from pretest to posttest was computed. As expected in the hypothesis, the group made significant mean changes on the three measures. In observational comparison, we find that the mean change at posttest of the study-2 group on the forgiveness measure was over twice the mean change of the study-1 FT, and over four times the mean change of the study-1 AT. Whereas the forgiveness intervention demonstrated efficacy in both studies 1 and 2, it is likely that the effect is even stronger with devout Christians. Caution must be employed because statistical comparisons between study 1 and study 2 are not possible. Furthermore, people in study 2 were selected for a treatment that was value congruent. However, it is interesting to note that the subjects from study 1 and 2 had similar pretest means on all measures used in the study and had no differences on demographic variables. Hopefully this study will provide a springboard for further scientific exploration.

Scriptural Overview

Scriptures used with the participants of study 2 were twenty-four verses that use the word *forgive* (or some variation of the term), as well as a handful of interpersonal examples of forgiveness, such as the parable of the prodigal son (Lk 15:11-32), which do not directly use a variation of the word *forgive.* The overwhelming and consistent theme of scriptural forgiveness is that we are to forgive as the Father has forgiven us (Col 3:13). Jesus taught that humans must forgive one another, and that God's forgiveness is associated with our forgiveness of others (Mt 6:12, 14-15; 18:21-22, 35; Mk 11:25; Lk 6:37; 11:4).

Since people can make a decision to forgive in a moment in time, such as at the bedside of a dying person, we therefore infer that God has created humans with the freewill ability to forgive immediately, despite possible countervailing negative emotions. This decision process is enhanced for Christians because they have the power of the indwelling Holy Spirit. Jesus said, "For if you forgive other people when they sin against you, your heavenly Father will also forgive you. But if you do not forgive others their sins, your Father will not forgive your sins" (Mt 6:14-15). Interestingly, these verses immediately follow the Lord's Prayer (Mt 6:9-13) and in context may be understood as Jesus giving special emphasis to interpersonal forgiveness. Scripture also teaches that (a) unforgiveness is sin (Rom 1:31; 2 Tim 3:3); (b) Christians have been forgiven a great debt (symbolic of forgiveness through Christ) and therefore we may not be unforgiving of others (Mt 18:23-35); (c) interpersonal forgiveness issues are to be resolved before continuing in prayer (Mk 11:25). Given that daily and unceasing prayer (1 Thess 5:17) is required of Christians by God, so too then one must continually take care of forgiveness issues (hence daily/immediate forgiveness). (d) Christians are to resolve offenses before bringing gifts to the altar (Mt 5:23-26); (e) love suffers long and keeps no record of wrongs (1 Cor 13:4); (f) Christians must forgive frequently (Mt 18:21-22) even if offended multiple times (Lk 17:3-4).

Whereas some have the viewpoint that couples should focus on love and relationship before they address their unforgiveness of each other, no Scriptures were found to show that this should be the case (for scriptural evidence see DiBlasio, 1999). Further, Scripture teaches that when it comes to the body of Christ, love, relationship and forgiveness go hand in hand (for scriptural evidence see Cheong & DiBlasio, 2007).

DESCRIPTION OF THE FORGIVENESS SESSION

The following section will outline the steps of a marital forgiveness session. Included in the description will be case material from Sharon and Frank, an African American couple from study 2. Because of the research procedure, initially they were told only that the intervention would be a long marital session and that they would be paid for their participation (DiBlasio & Benda, 2008). On arrival they were told about their selection for the Christian forgiveness intervention group.

This couple demonstrated typical results for Christian couples seen throughout the clinical practice of the author. In addition, the results of this couple were typical for study-2 couples. The forgiveness treatment couples over the years not only forgive each other, but increase intimacy, which produces more marital satisfaction and individual contentment.

Step 1: Discuss definitions of forgiveness. It is difficult for Christian couples to get a real understanding of God's love and forgiveness because they are deeply involved in the hurt and pain of their current situation. Intuitively, the human condition gravitates to self-protection, wanting to be understood, and most importantly wanting the pain to stop. These desires are understandable and are not wrong, unless of course they conflict with Christlike love and forgiveness. Forgiveness sounds desirable to Christians because it is central to their faith. Before taking people through a process of forgiveness, it helps to establish their objective thoughts about forgiveness and what forgiveness means to them. For example, the psychotherapist might inquire, "Since forgiveness is central to our faith, can we talk about forgiveness, not so much in the context of your marriage, but about what forgiveness means from an objective point of view?"

Often couples use phrases like *letting go* and *not holding the offense against someone*. Couples know that they cannot simply forget, but understand that they do not have to emphasize or dwell on the painful memory. They know that Jesus died for the forgiveness of sins and that love and forgiveness are central to the Christian life. After thorough discussion of clients' viewpoints, the psychotherapist discusses Scriptures on forgiveness and presents the definition of decision-based forgiveness. He or she asks the couple if they agree with the idea that the decision to forgive includes not only the cognitive letting go of resentment, bitterness and need for vengeance (Eph 4:31), but also includes the self-sacrificing acts of forgiveness and love, just as Christ has forgiven and loved them (Eph 4:32–5:2). The psychotherapist and couple discuss forgiveness as involving a willful decision to imitate and follow Christ, noting that a forgiveness decision does not have to be primarily driven by feelings. Christians find it insightful and freeing that they can choose to forgive despite hurt feelings.

Additional points to consider are: (a) forgiveness is an act of the will; (b) it is possible for people to have emotional pain, but determine to control vengeful thinking; (c) emotional pain and hurt will be addressed throughout the duration of therapy; (d) a forgiveness decision is a beginning, not an end, to therapy; (e) there are internal and interpersonal benefits of making a forgiveness decision; and (f) each person must make his or her own decision about forgiveness issues.

Frank and Sharon fully embraced the Scriptures used by the therapist and believed in the decision-based approach, which highlights a freewill choice to forgive at any time. Sharon added that prayer was needed and Frank said that a request for forgiveness needs to come with direct efforts to do better.

Step 2: Opportunity to seek forgiveness for self-decided wrongful actions. Spouses have an opportunity during the session to seek forgiveness for offenses they have committed. This is a time in which spouses can choose to confess their wrongdoing. Confessing to one another and taking responsibility for one's actions in resolving conflict has strong biblical support. Defensive posturing of each mate toward the other often hinders routine marital therapy. It is difficult to genuinely grasp one's own participation in the problem while simultaneously defending oneself from the accusations of another. The opposite is true in forgiveness sessions, because one releases control and expectations of the hurtful behavior and instead concentrates on self culpability. This leads to a deeper understanding of wrongdoing and encourages a repentant attitude. Although forgiveness is possible without the repentance of the offender (Educational Study Group, 1990), forgiveness is easier for the offended spouses if repentance occurs, because one's heart is more forgiving in situations in which the offenders are repentant and recognize their wrongdoing. Worthington (2006) has suggested that the difficulty of forgiving depends on the amount of injustice one believes still exists (i.e., the size of the injustice gap). If an offending partner is repentant, that is costly both personally and emotionally. Thus, the willingness for the partner to suffer on behalf of the relationship reduces the amount of injustice, making forgiveness easier. To the contrary, if a partner is unwilling to repent, that heaps injustice on injustice and also can lead to additional hurts—both of which increase the injustice gap.

Interestingly, spouses who choose their own offenses to confess will usually pick those offenses that their partners would have chosen for them. Spouses seem to own their offenses when the intervention is designed to give them the opportunity to do so. This is a welcome relief from routine therapy where spouses take turns revealing all the problems and sins of their mates, leaving psychotherapists feeling like referees. A psychotherapist could say, "We need to set a guideline to direct the session. Couples often bring many concerns about the hurtful behavior of the other, but seldom do they automatically concentrate on their own wrongdoing. If you decide to proceed in the session, are you willing to focus on your own contribution to problems when it is your turn to go through the steps and give up expectations of what your partner should be confessing? If your partner does not bring up the issue that is important to you, we can address that at a later session." If clients focus on what they hope to receive from the other, the forgiveness session can become egocentric and diminish the sacrifice being made by each. The gift of forgiveness has more worth when it is sought and granted without overt or implicit coercion or emotional demands. For example, if the wife focuses on how her husband should seek forgiveness for his neglect of her, however subtle, she adds pressure and expectations that reduce the power of the husband's request for forgiveness as a completely free act. And worse, she might inadvertently spark defensiveness in him.

The presentation of this step was well received by both Sharon and Frank. They strongly believed that each had to be accountable before God and should take ownership of their own offenses. They agreed to the guideline set that each would concentrate on self-culpability.

Step 3: *Introduction to treatment and decision to participate.* Given that the session has a task orientation, it is best to review the sequential stages so that couples can make an informed decision about whether to participate. It is the experience of the author that Christian couples are eager to proceed. If the couple agrees to the session, then one partner is chosen to go first. It is usually best to start with the spouse who has committed the more serious offense. Therefore it is helpful to get each spouse to decide on a few things for which they may want to seek forgiveness. It is helpful to look for common themes so that several items may be condensed into one major area. If the offenses are relatively equal, then perhaps the spouse who is best able to stay on target (in this case, Sharon) should go first in order to set a task-oriented example for the other partner.

The psychotherapist might say, "The structured forgiveness session does not resemble a typical marital therapy session. If you agree to proceed, Sharon will go through steps four through twelve in sequence, and then we will give Frank a turn. I will play an active role during the session, keeping the session on track and with your help deciding what information will be fruitful to pursue during the forgiveness session and what might be saved for a later time."

Step 4: *Statement of the offense.* The statement of the offense is an opportunity for the spouses to be very clear about the hurtful behavior. By verbally stating the offense, the spouse implicitly demonstrates awareness that the offense is wrong. The offense needs to be specifically stated in a way that shows culpability. Psychotherapists help clients to state solely their part in the dynamic. For example, consider the husband who states that he wants to seek forgiveness for verbally criticizing his wife in public for her erratic and volatile nature. By including his perception of his wife's role, it takes away from the culpability and increases defensiveness on the part of the wife. In these cases, it is wise to help spouses to reduce the statement to only include their part. After a clear offense is articulated, it is helpful for the psychotherapist to ask, "Was this offense wrong?" If offenders hedge, psychotherapists should point out the hesitation and suggest that an offense be chosen that the spouse believes is wrong. This elicits reconsideration by the offender who becomes more convinced that the offense was wrong and wants to proceed on that basis.

Sharon started by focusing on her problem as well as Frank's. With help she removed Frank's portion of the problem and stated that she wanted to seek forgiveness for planning social events without her husband's awareness. For example, instead of having a restful Sunday, a crowd of family members would show up at the door without Frank's prior knowledge. After Sharon completed steps four through twelve, Frank clearly stated that his offense was that he was a "couch potato" and was not social enough. In many cases, the original offenses comprise a host of other major issues that are revealed during the session.

Step 5: Offender provides explanation. Seldom are people in the genuinely receptive mode needed to understand the other person compassionately during conflicts. Without intervention, defensive posturing normally results because each person implicitly gravitates to self-protection and thereby misses the opportunity to connect at a deep and insightful level.

The psychotherapist begins by getting permission from the offended person to attempt to get a full explanation. By giving permission, offended persons are actively involved in a proactive situation in which defensive reactions are minimized as they join the psychotherapist in the goal of achieving understanding. The psychotherapist makes clear that most offenses in marriages have explanations, but that the explanations are sometimes lost because of the hurt and pain that is experienced. Therefore, an explanation should not be considered an *excuse*, but rather a search for information that will allow a thorough assessment of the offense.

Often an offense is not performed out of malice, but instead springs out of a combination of factors. In Sharon's case, her manipulation of her husband came in part because she had a need to socialize with others. Since her husband was less than accommodating to this desire, she intuitively drifted to inviting guests without consulting him. The psychotherapist wanted the wife to explore further to see whether the problem existed prior to meeting her husband. Sharon made painful connections to how she would organize and coordinate her family of origin. For example, although she was the youngest, at thirteen years old she was responsible for taking public transportation to visit her older brother weekly in jail on behalf of the family. Sharon began to understand how she had a lifelong pattern of over-functioning for others. Although having altruistic and self-sacrificing intentions, she understood that over-functioning can have the downside of manipulation and control. It became apparent to her that in giving and organizing to the degree that she did, she got to control what and how things are done in the marriage, which gave her power that she never understood until that moment. Hearing the loneliness and heartache of his wife's childhood brought Frank to a new understanding. Because the problem existed prior to their marriage, Frank felt less personally attacked by the manipulation. In fact, his resentment turned to empathy, as he began to comfort his crying wife.

After Sharon completed steps four through twelve, Frank brought up his self-described "anti-social nature." He confessed to being dull, emotionally unavailable and socially withdrawn. During the session, Frank realized that his isolation started when he returned from the Vietnam War. On his return he was spat on and called a baby killer by a protestor. His thoughts and dreams were filled with horrific memories of the death and destruction of war. His response was to withdraw and avoid people. Sharon gained a deep understanding of Frank's contrary social desires as she listened to his emotional account of his war experiences. This part of the session seemed to significantly increase Sharon's empathy toward her husband, which may have in part prepared her for the granting of forgiveness.

Step 6: Questions and answers about the offense. Most couples are not able to have a meaningful and objective discussion about an offense. Getting past the surface issues to the more substantive issues of the heart is critical but difficult. The hurt and pain associated with the offense usually results in a reduction of both intimacy and communication. When defensiveness and sarcasm are added to the dialogue, spouses rarely get enough objective information needed to answer their questions. Additionally, the many close-ended questions asked during marital conflict are often power maneuvers or are wittingly or unwittingly used to make a point rather than seek out objective information.

Whereas many questions would prove helpful, there are some questions that may be inappropriate and destructive. The psychotherapist attempts to screen the questions to avoid the unhelpful ones. On the other hand, sometimes the couple will avoid asking important questions or not ask enough questions. Because this type of loving and objective communication is not the norm for marriages in conflict, coaching is needed. The psychotherapist might say, "As strange as this may sound, seldom do couples get objective answers to their questions because of the defensive atmosphere around the offense. Often questions tend to be asked harshly and/or asked in a way to lead to a point. This is the time to get to the information in a spirit of love. Let's all work together to really understand this problem by asking questions."

If the proceeding steps of the forgiveness session have been successful, an atmosphere of objectivity and love will have been established. In some cases forgiveness in spirit has already occurred as partners listened to the explanation phase. It is easier to forgive when one has enough information about the offense to make an informed decision to let go and forgive. Accurate information is important in bringing clarity and thus avoiding more negative imagination or assumptions. Giving the answers and facts about the offense also provides the offender with a sense of cleansing. It is important for offenders to reveal the truth at this time even if the information will cause more hurt. Forgiveness built on partial truth leaves seeds of deception that will grow and cause spiritual harm for the transgressor and significant interpersonal harm to the spouse if the truth is revealed in the future. However, it is a judgment call as to the right amount of detail needed during the explanation. For example, Sharon revealed the truth that she manipulated her husband on a number of occasions, however, there is no significant advantage for Sharon to recall each time with specific details. A psychotherapist should help couples discern what questions and details are helpful and which may be counterproductive.

After Sharon provided an explanation of her actions, Frank was given a chance to ask his wife questions about the offense. He first asked whether the reason for not approaching him with social events was because she was afraid that he would say no. Although this was an obvious question, Frank needed to hear the answer to help him understand his wife's motivation. He then had a series of questions relating to two of her relatives who were inconsiderate and "disrespectful" whenever they would come to their house. When asked why invite them if they were disrespectful, Sharon explained that they were still family and she felt that she could not just exclude them and that she was at a loss as to what to do. This was the first moment that they understood that they were a team facing the same problem.

Step 7: *Offended person gives emotional reactions.* Intimacy includes the sharing of one's heart with another, even if the content shared is hurtful. Humans find connection as they share their hurts, pains and deep emotions. Empathy with offended persons concerning their perceived suffering is one way spouses can love like Christ.

Considerable care and time is spent focusing on the hurt feelings. In fact, clients may find it difficult to verbalize their feelings fully, and may at first show discomfort expressing themselves. Patient and gentle exploration is usually necessary. The psychotherapist promotes a spirit of non-defensiveness by stating, "Although it may be difficult for Frank to express his hurt for fear of causing you heartache, will you grant him permission to fully speak his heart to you about his hurt?" When spouses give permission, it seems to cause a shift from a self-protective to a receiving mode. Now the offended spouse becomes a team participant to help the partner.

Something special happened for Frank when asked to share his emotions about his wife's manipulation. He said, "I am a bit confused, do you want me to tell her how I felt about this before I came in here today, or how I feel about it now?" It was obvious that as Frank heard his wife's explanation, his emotions and thoughts were moved to love and forgiveness. He stated that he learned things that day about his wife that he has never heard before. He told her that previously he felt upset and angry over her selfishness and control. After the explanation, he saw the pain she was going through and his emotions shifted to empathy for her.

When Sharon expressed her emotions she mentioned a core disappointment in the marriage. After being raised by an alcoholic father and controlling mother, she wanted to have a different family life, and she was sad to find that in some ways things had not changed.

Step 8: Offender empathy and remorse for hurt. Normally in marital treatment, both people are hurting, making empathy for the other a difficult task. However, the session puts the couple in a new position of understanding and love in relation to each other, and by so doing creates unity. Unity helps promote empathy, which in turn also helps promote further unity. Having the offender thoughtfully reflect the hurt gives an acknowledgement that the spouse's suffering is understood. Therefore, the usual course of each person overly focused on his or her own hurt is avoided and is replaced by empathy. Injured partners respond more lovingly when they receive empathy (Worthington, 1998) and a sense of remorse from the spouse (Olson, Russell, Higgings-Kessler & Miller, 2002).

Some offenders find empathy difficult because they struggle with egocentric personality styles, or worse, personality disorders. Achieving empathy is possible, but requires therapeutic attention and reduced expectations as to the amount of empathy that will be demonstrated. Because empathy comes relatively easy to helping professionals, they must resist doing too much of the work. Instead, their strategy should be to coach couples toward empathetic expression. For example, a psychotherapist might say to the offending spouse: "When your wife said that she hurt so badly that she woke up crying in the night, what do you think that feels like?" Usually the more empathy that is demonstrated by the offender, the easier it is for the partner to forgive.

Frank and Sharon were moved to empathy for each other throughout the session. It was helpful to both to hear the remorse and empathy each had expressed for the other. This accentuated the Christlike love that was being demonstrated during the session.

Step 9: Offender develops plan to stop/prevent behavior. Sincerely seeking true forgiveness means that the offender plans to stop the offensive behavior and prevent it from happening in the future. Some offenses are tough to stop, as is sometimes the case with addictive behaviors, and require the offending spouse to take decisive steps to get help, such as contacting and following up with a rehabilitation center. Forgiveness of the offended spouse and repentance by the offender is facilitated when a process of corrective action is planned and a system of accountability is established. The plan needs to be specific and mostly created by the offender. Often people will be at a loss as to what to put into a plan, so the psychotherapist might first pray for the Holy Spirit to bring ideas to mind. To prompt the spouse the psychotherapist might then say, "Why not start with any commitments that you want to make and perhaps as you do so an action plan will come to mind?" A written record of each part of the plan is made that will later be kept at home in an accessible location.

Frank and Sharon understood that distinct changes needed to be made in their lives. Coming up with items for the plan became a team effort between husband, wife and psychotherapist. Sharon committed to the following plan: (a) check with Frank before arranging a social event; (b) ask a friend from church to be an accountability person and prayer partner (choosing a friend that both trust and getting permission from the spouse to share information is important); (c) discuss and write down specific details of events; (d) Sharon was to take the lead in coordinating with Frank about social events (a good fit given Sharon's spiritual gifts of hospitality and administration); (e) Sharon was to initiate a discussion of how to handle the two difficult family members; and (f) Frank committed to help her practice delegation (an area of strength for Frank). For example, instead of agreeing to host all family events, Frank suggested that she ask her siblings to take the lead on some.

Now Sharon's efforts no longer fit the concept of "manipulation" because in this session Frank agreed for her to provide the initiative. Sharon and Frank had a value that Frank was the leader of the family, and with the psychotherapist's help they learned that delegation is an important quality of leadership. By delegating the leadership of social events to his wife, Frank became an effective leader, a desire of both, by wisely utilizing Sharon's spiritual giftedness.

Frank requested that Sharon discuss reasons for desired social functions. Sharon readily agreed and further blessed her husband by giving the following reason why she wanted her husband with her: "He's my husband and I want him with me. I love him. He's handsome and I am proud to have him with me." The psychotherapist suggested that Sharon should tell him that each time, especially the handsome part.

Frank's plan included commitments to be open to social events and occasionally to take the initiative. It was clear that Frank had isolated himself and as a result had not fully utilized his spiritual gifts of administration and teaching. He agreed to focus more on his spiritual gifts and become more outward-focused in his service to the church and the community. Frank's new excitement for change was reflected in his enthusiasm about asking a certain man in his church, a veteran who lost his legs in the Vietnam War, to be his accountability person. Frank also agreed to get professional help for his depression, anxiety and unresolved issues from the war.

Step 10: Offended spouse shows empathy for offender's hurt. Marital problems usually involve significant hurts for the transgressor, as well as the offended spouse. The transgressor's behavior is in part explained by previous hurts in the relationship and/or hurts experienced in the past such as problems with parents (Stoop & Masteller, 1991). The preceding steps help to identify some of these issues and thereby prepare the heart of the offended spouse for true empathy and love. In addition, the transgressor must deal with the shame and guilt of having brought pain to the spouse. Sometimes offenders go into deep regret and self-loathing. This step promotes empathy that in turn encourages a sense of restored love. The humility that comes with realizing that the offended persons are human and have also made mistakes contributes to their ability to be empathetic toward offenders.

The psychotherapist might say to the offended spouse, "I realize that your wife's offense has brought significant hurt to you, but now we see that she is also hurting. Could you put into the words the feelings that she is experiencing?" Just as in step eight above, the psychotherapist helps and sometimes coaches the spouse to gain an empathic understanding.

Frank and Sharon freely and graciously found true empathy for each other. The session gave each a new and fresh perspective, as they felt the depth of hurt experienced by the other. Frank emotionally identified with the years of disappointment faced by Sharon with her own parents and siblings, her years of loneliness in the marriage with him, and now her regret for being manipulative. Sharon could empathize with her husband's trauma experienced in Vietnam and his return to a country that did not respect or honor him, and now his regret over the wasted years of not finding more intimacy with his wife, friends and family.

Step 11: Emphasis on choice and commitment to let go. The psychotherapist reminds the couple of the discussion in step one concerning the decision-based approach to forgiveness. If the offended spouse chooses to forgive, the commitment comes with a decision to purposely let go of the offense and not use it as a weapon in the future. This does not preclude discussing the offense or having residual hurtful emotions; in fact further working through the issue in later therapy is recommended. The intent is to "take captive every thought to make it obedient to Christ" (2 Cor 10:5) and not to bathe in future resentment and bitterness. Beginning in the session and followed through during therapy is discussion on how to handle possible future angry feelings and thoughts. The practice experience of the author is that the forgiveness session is effective in permanently eliminating the resentment and bitterness in many cases. Some serious offenses present a more difficult challenge in addressing the afterthoughts, but supportive and caring therapy through the aftermath helps the offended spouse to maintain the commitment (DiBlasio, 2000). If forgiveness is sought in the next step, the offended person makes a decision whether or not to forgive. Both Frank and Sharon freely accepted the challenge to keep the commitment to decision-based forgiveness as discussed and defined in the first step.

Step 12: Formal request for forgiveness. The biblical pattern for offenses is for the offender or the offended to initiate a face-to-face encounter to resolve the problem (Matt 5:23-24; 18:15) and to pursue peace (Rom 14:19; Heb 12:14; 1 Pet 3:11). To make the forgiveness clear, the spouses put into words the request and the granting of the request. The psychotherapist might say, "Now it is time, if Frank is willing, for him to ask formally for forgiveness in front of me as the witness. Sharon may then respond whether she will grant the forgiveness." Many couples will turn and face each other and hold hands. In a few cases, offending spouses will choose to drop to their knees. Although this is sometimes awkward for offended spouses, expressing remorse freely may help offenders in their own healing process. In one case, a woman jumped into her husband's lap as they spoke words of forgiveness tenderly to each other. Typically, after all is said and done, couples embrace with an emotional kiss and hug that signals a renewed intimacy. When getting reports back from clients over the years, the mental picture of this beautiful time seems indelibly etched in their minds. The formal request reinforces that a concrete forgiveness decision was made in front of a witness. The exact time is noted and couples are asked to record it in a special place (most Christians choose their Bibles).

Sharon turned toward her husband, took his hand, and immediately started to laugh. Her emotions were strong and the laughter was a part of the overwhelming joy she was experiencing. Although this was the moment of the formality of the forgiveness request, a forgiving spirit between the two had already occurred throughout the session. She then became very serious and said, "I love you and I care about you and the most important thing to us is our relationship—and making sure that we are on the same page always. And for the times I know I was manipulative and selfish, I want you to forgive me. Will you forgive me?" Frank replied that he did forgive her, and proceeded to admit his part in the problem. They sealed the seeking and granting of forgiveness with a kiss.

At Frank's turn, he talked about his "baggage" that he brought into the marriage and how during the session realized that he should not have kept his struggles with the Vietnam War from her. He also admitted that he was focused on himself, and did not choose to listen or be concerned enough for Sharon as he should have as a supportive husband. He could barely speak because of the tears, and his wife handed him back the handkerchief that he gave to her earlier. Frank stated, "That's one busy handkerchief today." He requested Sharon's forgiveness, who granted it freely and they again spontaneously kissed.

Step 13: Ceremonial act. Across cultures, ceremonial acts are often used when humans move from one stage to the next. For example, the wedding ceremony celebrates the move from single life to a new life of oneness with another. In the case of a ceremonial act of forgiveness, an outward act between spouses reinforces the time of forgiveness that they shared, and helps to cognitively, emotionally and spiritually solidify their decisions. The ceremonial act is a symbolic expression that the offense has been formally and permanently forgiven.

Frank and Sharon were asked, "How might you celebrate the forgiveness that has occurred here—something to symbolically represent the forgiveness, something ceremonial?" Frank quickly suggested that they write down their offenses and burn them, and then he said, "From the ashes will rise the new us." He remarked that he believed that the idea came to him from God. They decided that afterward they would pray on their knees and read relevant Scriptures. They planned to get a sitter for their daughter and continue the celebration with a special night out at their favorite restaurant.

TREATMENT IMPLEMENTATION

Any specifically Christian psychotherapeutic approach must be based in a biblical perspective and be understood within a theoretical framework and personal practice theory. Biblically, there is little disagreement among Christians that forgiveness is a major component of a Christian marriage. Likewise, widespread agreement also exists that issues of unforgiveness between marital partners must be addressed in a Christian psychotherapy. However, what is the therapeutic timing of suggesting a forgiveness session? What do you do in the psychotherapy after the forgiveness session? How do you conduct forgiveness sessions with difficult people? These questions are briefly addressed in this section.

Given the unforgiving servant parable taught by Jesus (Mt 18:23-35) and in other biblical passages (see scriptural support above), God's timing for a Christian to forgive an offender is immediate and urgent. One biblical position is that God provides Christian believers with the ability and the power of the Holy Spirit to do all that he asks us to do. Although this is true, God also gave each of us free will and therefore the timing decision must be left up to the couple. This process is consistent with the ethical value of self-determination within many helping professions. This raises a fundamental issue for Christian psychotherapists: Should the therapist discuss *right away* the possibility of the clients considering a forgiveness session at some point in the therapy or not? It is beyond the scope of this chapter to fully consider the ethical and spiritual pro and con treatment of this issue. However, the author decided that it is ethically and spiritually best to bring up in the first session during the contracting phase of therapy the possibility of spouses doing a forgiveness session (at a time of their choice). He has found that Christian couples overwhelmingly choose a forgiveness intervention at the beginning of psychotherapy (by their own freewill choice). Further, the author finds that the goodwill created in forgiveness sessions becomes an excellent springboard for the rest of the psychotherapy, and reduces the number of later marital therapy sessions needed.

Psychotherapy after the forgiveness session. The author believes that the forgiveness intervention puts the spouses in a proper position with Jesus at the center of their intimacy. The remaining therapy is supernaturally empowered by the Holy Spirit as the two spouses submit to God and became Christ focused. Interestingly, it has been my clinical experience that forgiveness tends to increase feelings of intimacy and compassion that are used in solving other problems and conflicts in the marriage.

After a forgiveness session, clinicians are advised to proceed as in any other type of psychotherapy, except perhaps to add the following. First, give praise to God as part of the prayer in every session for the forgiveness that occurred during the forgiveness session (obviously only with willing clients). Second, the Christian psychotherapist checks regularly to see how spouses are following through on their forgiveness commitments and plans. Finally, it is recommended that the psychotherapy stay focused on each spouse being responsible for improving his or her own thinking and actions.

Forgiveness sessions with difficult spouses. Sometimes people have personalities that make them difficult as marital partners. Given the closeness of marriage, difficult people are usually harder and more offensive toward their spouses. This happens partly because of the familiarity of a married relationship, as well as the perceived freedom to exercise less inhibition in expressing negative behaviors. Most difficult spouses believe that the home is a place to let their "hair down" and to freely express negative emotions and expectations. Ironically, many difficult spouses perceive themselves as victims, when in reality their behaviors are the most offensive. In addition, they have a hard time accepting the emotional stress that comes from the crucible of a close relationship.

Although a thorough analysis of how to intervene with difficult people (and personality disorders) is beyond the scope of this chapter, a few comments are noteworthy. First, difficult people tend to be more accountable when Christian psychotherapists use a "stroke-kick" approach. Insecurity tends to be a major problem of difficult spouses (although their presentation can appear just the opposite), so the clinician needs to build on strengths and compliment where possible before any constructive criticism is used. Second, whenever spouses begin to blame the other spouse during the session, ask that they focus only on their portion of the problem. Third, help the non-difficult spouse to design loving boundaries as part of the forgiveness plan if the partner were to become offensive again. For example, if the difficult spouse seeks forgiveness for verbal abuse, the plan should also address what the non-difficult spouse should do if the offending spouse becomes verbally abusive in the future. The plan should be something that the forgiving partner is able to control (such as lovingly leaving the room to pray). Usually in this case an additional backup plan is created in the event that the offending spouse decides to follow the forgiving spouse. Fourth, during the explanation phase, the clinician may emphasize that the difficult personality style existed prior to the marriage (and is usually rooted to childhood or adolescent years). This helps partners to see that the offensive behavior is not the fault of the offended spouse (although it is helpful to encourage that spouse to understand his or her unwitting systemic participation in the negative cycle).

CASE FOLLOW-UP

Four years after the single forgiveness session, Sharon and Frank were contacted to follow up on their marital relationship. The couple was convinced that the forgiveness that day was genuine, lasted over the years, and provided them a "life-changing" experience. Sharon said it was the beginning of challenging her previous assumptions about her husband and caused her to see him differently and appreciate him more fully. Frank stated that he learned that day that not only were his wife's feelings important, but that he was the "primary person to bring love and security to her life." Sharon now focuses more on how her husband feels, rather than how he should behave. Given the mutual sacrifice for the other, they reported that the marriage had become intimate and stronger. They shared that their deeper intimacy has been a positive influence on the security and family life of their now fourteen-year-old daughter. Whereas unforgiveness can linger and prevent conflict resolution in marriage (Fincham, Beach & Davila, 2004), practice experience suggests that forgiveness has the ability to escalate intimacy and help the couple resolve future problems.

Both partners reported getting an accountability person. (Sharon has continued to pray with her accountability partner for the past four years.) Frank came out of his shell, much like the person he was before the Vietnam

War, and started to enjoy social functions more, even to the point of initiating some events. Sharon found a new respect for Frank and found that it was not difficult to partner with him around social events. Their pastor noticed how well Frank and Sharon operated together and miraculously, without knowledge of their previous problem, asked them to become the "social coordinators" for a group of marital couples. Frank had social leadership skills that he never thought were possible, and Sharon rejoiced in having a ministry with her husband that utilized their spiritual gifts in a godly setting. This was a dream come true for Sharon. What was once a point of controversy and offense now has become a mutually satisfying ministry for the body of Christ.

CONCLUSION

The main emphasis of this chapter was to describe a decision-based psychotherapeutic technique designed to promote forgiveness in married couples. Furthermore, this chapter reviewed two empirical studies by the author that support this form of psychotherapy, discussed relevant practice implications reported by the author in the literature, and described a case study using an actual subject couple to bring to life the steps of the model. Given the success of the model clinically, as well as the limited quantitative research supporting its use, the author hopes that the above expansion of the steps will encourage further research and give practitioners more details about conducting forgiveness sessions with clients.

Whereas the model has shown effectiveness regardless of spiritual faith and religious intensity of beliefs, the focus here was on treating Christian couples who identify the gospel message (their salvation through belief in the sacrifice of Jesus) as central to their lives. These couples want marital therapy to be in line with Scripture and have it glorify God by drawing them closer to Jesus. This was the case with study-2 couples and is also true of many of the author's clients over the years.

The four-year follow-up provides additional support for the empirical findings. The couple reported that forgiveness, marital satisfaction and contentment significantly improved for them as a result of the intervention. The couple did not pursue additional individual and marital therapy as recommended at the forgiveness session. When asked about that in the four-year follow-up they reported that they saw no need for it because they forgave each other and found an exciting renewal in their relationship. The fact that the forgiveness intervention was their only professional therapy encounter gives further evidence that perhaps the lasting changes were initiated by forgiveness. However, in cases with actual couple therapy clients, it is beneficial to follow the forgiveness sessions with additional marital therapy.

For this couple, the offenses addressed during the session reflected deeper issues of control, betrayal, lack of emotional intimacy, depression, loneliness, isolation, insecurity, dysfunctional teamwork and problems in spiritual unity. It is theorized that these issues contributed to their unforgiveness, marital dissatisfaction, and depression. It seems that the methods employed during the forgiveness session addressed the underlying issues behind the offenses with a spiritual solution. A decision to love and forgive as Jesus demonstrated and taught reveals the beautiful redemptive work of God's Spirit of love in the souls of spouses. Such Christlike love and forgiveness satisfies God's divine purposes for marriage and brings about increased intimacy not only between husband and wife but also with Christ.

REFERENCES

Cheong, R., & DiBlasio, F. A. (2007). Christ-like love and forgiveness: A biblical foundation for counseling practice. *Journal of Psychology and Christianity, 26,* 14-25.

DiBlasio, F. A. (1998). The use of decision-based forgiveness intervention within intergenerational family therapy. *Journal of Family Therapy, 20,* 77-94.

DiBlasio, F. A. (1999). Scripture and forgiveness: Interventions with families and couples. *Marriage and Family: A Christian Journal, 3,* 257-67.

DiBlasio, F. A. (2000). Decision-based forgiveness treatment in cases of marital infidelity. *Psychotherapy, 37,* 149-58.

DiBlasio, F. A. (2010). Christ-like forgiveness in marital counseling: A clinical follow-up of two empirical studies. *Journal of Psychology and Christianity, 29,* 291-300.

DiBlasio, F. A., & Benda, B. B. (2008). Forgiveness intervention with married couples: Two empirical analyses. *Journal of Psychology and Christianity, 27,* 150-58.

Educational Study Group. (1990). Must a Christian require repentance before forgiving? *Journal of Psychology and Christianity, 9,* 16-19.

Enright, R. D., & The Human Development Study Group. (1991). The moral development of forgiveness. In W. Kurtines & J. Gewirtz (Eds.), *Moral behavior and development* (Vol. 1, pp. 123-52). Hillsdale, NJ: Erlbaum.

Fincham, F. D., Beach, S. R. H., & Davila, J. (2004). Forgiveness and conflict resolution in marriage. *Journal of Family Psychology, 18,* 72-81.

Gordon, K. C., Baucom, D. H., & Snyder, D. K. (2005). Forgiveness in couples: Divorce, affairs, and couple therapy. In E. L. Worthington Jr. (Ed.), *Handbook of forgiveness* (pp. 407-22). New York: Brunner-Routledge.

Greenberg, L. S., Warwar, S. H., & Malcolm, W. M. (2008). Differential effects of emotion-focused therapy and psychoeducation in facilitating forgiveness and letting go of emotional injuries. *Journal of Counseling Psychology, 55*(2), 185-96.

Greenberg, L. S., Warwar, S. H., & Malcolm, W. M. (2009). Emotion-focused therapy and the facilitation of forgiveness. *Journal of Marital and Family Therapy, 36*(1), 28-42.

Hudson, W. W. (1997). *The WALMYR assessment scale scoring manual.* Chicago, IL: Dorsey Press.

Kachadourian, L. K., Fincham, F., & Davila, J. (2005). Attitudinal ambivalence, rumination, and forgiveness of partner transgressions in marriage. *Personality and Social Psychology Bulletin, 31,* 334-42.

Olson, M. M., Russell, C. S., Higgings-Kessler, M., & Miller, R. B. (2002). Emotional processes following disclosure of an extramarital affair. *Journal of Marital and Family Therapy, 28,* 423-34.

Stoop, D. A., & Masteller, J. (1991). *Forgiving our parents, forgiving ourselves.* Ann Arbor, MI: Servant Publications.

Worthington, E. L., Jr. (1998). An empathy-humility-commitment model of forgiveness applied within family dyads. *Journal of Family Therapy, 20,* 59-76.

Worthington, E. L., Jr. (2006). *Forgiveness and reconciliation: Theory and application.* New York: Brunner-Routledge.

Worthington, E. L., Jr., & DiBlasio, F. A. (1990). Promoting mutual forgiveness within the fractured relationship. *Psychotherapy, 27,* 219-23.

Worthington, E. L., Jr., Jennings, D. J., II, & DiBlasio, F. A. (2010). Interventions to promote forgiveness in couple and family context: Conceptualization, review, and analysis. *Journal of Psychology and Theology, 38,* 231-45.

13

Christian-Accommodative Group Interventions to Promote Forgiveness for Transgressions

Julia E. M. Kidwell and Nathaniel G. Wade

Over the past twenty years, psychological research has increasingly focused on forgiveness as a possible response to interpersonal hurts. For many people, the roots of forgiveness lie in their religious teachings and traditions. This is particularly true for Christianity. Christianity has emphasized the importance of forgiveness for centuries and many would say that forgiveness is at the core of Christian theology (e.g., Rye et al., 2000). Understanding how these beliefs might be harnessed to help Christians forgive specific interpersonal transgressions in their lives might help clinicians to tailor treatments in the most effective way. In this chapter, we will review relevant research findings on Christian-accommodative group treatments used to reduce unforgiveness and promote forgiveness for interpersonal transgressions. Additionally, we will discuss clinical applications of forgiveness research for use in Christian psychotherapy settings.

DEFINITIONS OF FORGIVENESS AND UNFORGIVENESS

In order to understand forgiveness, it is necessary to determine what forgiveness and unforgiveness entail. Forgiveness is a popular concept, but it is understood in different ways. Confusion about the nature of forgiveness may cause individuals to become hesitant to consider forgiveness as a possible response to an offense (Kearns & Fincham, 2004; Macaskill, 2005). Many clinically-oriented researchers argue that forgiveness includes two significant elements: (1) reducing negative feelings and attitudes (or even behaviors), and (2) promoting positive emotions and attitudes toward an offender (Worthington & Wade, 1999). Reducing unforgiveness may include a decrease in feelings of anger, as well as a discontinuation of desires to seek revenge or retribution in response to an offense (Worthington & Wade, 1999). Also, when people reduce unforgiveness they may exhibit behavioral changes, such as ceasing to act aggressively toward an offender or discontinuing plans for revenge (McCullough & Worthington, 1999). Forgiveness also includes the increase in positive feelings and attitudes, which can consist of increasing wishes of overall well-being for an offender, increasing feelings of moral love, or even experiencing feelings of sympathy toward an offender. Therefore, forgiveness is ultimately a twofold process of decreasing negative emotions, thoughts and behaviors while also increasing positive emotions, thoughts and behaviors.

Additionally, it is important to emphasize what forgiveness is not. Forgiveness is not pardoning, overlooking or condoning an offense, nor is forgiveness excusing an offense or believing in any way that an offense was appropriate. Nor is forgiveness synonymous with reconciliation (Kearns & Fincham, 2004). It is possible to forgive an offender without choosing to reconcile (e. g., an individual may offer forgiveness to their offender without continuing an abusive relationship). Last, forgiveness is not forgetting. It is possible to remember an offense, but still extend forgiveness.

McCullough has actively focused the attention of researchers on the time-course of forgiving (McCullough, Fincham & Tsang, 2003). McCullough et al. (2003) observed that people begin with more or less unforgiveness, typically experience a decline in unforgiveness over time as a general trend, and may fluctuate from day to day due to mood or emotion triggers. McCullough et al. (2010) note that individuals typically decline in unforgiveness following a power curve (i.e., fast at first and approaching a lower level of residual unforgiveness as a steady state). Explorations of forgiveness within the psychological literature have grown in recent years (for a review, see Fehr, Gelfand & Nag, 2010), in part due to the increasing body of research demonstrating the psychological benefits of forgiveness. The promotion of forgiveness is associated with numerous psychological and physical health benefits. People who are able to extend forgiveness report positive emotional, behavioral and cognitive changes toward their offender.

Interestingly, researchers have also proposed that forgiveness may be related to physical health. Witvliet, Ludwig and Vander Laan (2001) examined differences in physiological reactions (including skin conductance, heart rate and blood pressure) of undergraduate participants as they engaged in forgiving or unforgiving imagery exercises. Witvliet and colleagues concluded that chronic emotions of anger and hostility (i.e., unforgiveness) when unresolved and prolonged can cause negative health reactions (increased blood pressure and possible greater susceptibility to various illnesses). Therefore, when not resolved, unforgiveness appears to be not only psychologically but physically damaging (for a review, see Worthington, Witvliet, Pietrini & Miller, 2007).

FORGIVENESS IN CHRISTIANITY

Christians have long considered forgiveness to be a core, foundational tenet of their belief system. Christian traditions place considerable emphasis on the importance of forgiving others for their transgressions (Marty, 1998; Rye et al., 2000; Worthington, Berry & Parrott, 2001). According to Christian beliefs, the significance of forgiveness originated with Christ's death for the salvation of the world. God the Father forgave all persons of their transgressions and provided them with salvation, regardless of any prior offenses, through the death of Jesus Christ. Consequently, Christians believe that because persons are forgiven by God, they are expected to forgive others (e.g., Mt 6:12, 14-15; Mk 11:25; Lk 23:34; see Beals, 1998; Rye et al., 2000). Beals (1998) explains the Christian justification for forgiveness by stating, "When we know we are forgiven by God for Christ's sake, we become moved to forgive others" (p. 123). Furthermore, "God's forgiving love in Christ remains freely offered to sinners and it seasons and sustains the lives of Christians. . . . We become forgiven to be forgiving" (p. 125). Christian Scriptures emphasize that to model Christ's forgiveness, humans must also attempt to extend forgiveness to their offenders (Rye et al., 2000). This type of interpersonal forgiveness is a cornerstone of Christian belief. Due to the considerable emphasis on forgiveness in Christianity, many Christians feel motivated to forgive in order to act in accordance with the teachings of Christ.

Researchers have also recognized the strong connection between Christianity and forgiveness. Worthington (1988) proposed a number of hypotheses about the experiences and behaviors of religiously committed persons in counseling settings, focusing primarily on how religious beliefs influence actions. In particular, Worthington stated that highly religious individuals evaluate and approach their environment (including their experiences in counseling and psychotherapy settings) according to their worldviews, which are determined by their religious beliefs. He proposes that values of highly religious individuals clearly determine their behaviors and responses to others. In subsequent research, Worthington et al. (1996) elaborated on Worthington's initial hypotheses by proposing that for the average person, religion may not be a part of their lives to the extent that it will influence their desire to forgive. However, for deeply religious persons, the desire to forgive according to their religious beliefs may be intensified (Worthington et al., 1996).

Forgiveness Models for Treatment of Unforgiveness

In recent decades, a variety of group interventions explicitly designed to promote forgiveness for past offenses has emerged within the literature (Wade, Worthington & Meyer, 2005). All of these interventions share a common goal of encouraging participants to reduce unforgiveness (defined broadly as reducing revenge, anger and avoidance) while also promoting forgiveness (defined as positive attitudes and emotions, such as wishes of well-being, toward an offender). Most of the interventions that have been examined empirically are provided to participants through a variety of components designed explicitly to educate participants about forgiveness and provide opportunities for resolving specific past hurts. Forgiveness interventions tend to vary in duration; however, the majority of them last an average of eight to nine hours and include anywhere from five to twenty distinct steps aimed directly at encouraging forgiveness (for a review, see Wade et al., 2005).

A number of secular forgiveness interventions have been developed. Two interventions have been most commonly used: (1) Enright's forgiveness model (Enright & the Human Development Group, 1991; Enright & Fitzgibbons, 2000) and (2) Worthington's (1998) REACH forgiveness model.

Enright's model has been demonstrated as effective in several studies (Al-Mabuk, Enright & Cardis, 1995; Hebl & Enright, 1993), as has Worthington's model (e.g., McCullough, Worthington & Rachal, 1997; Wade & Meyer, 2009). Available research that has directly compared secular and Christian-tailored psychoeducational group interventions has not found a statistical difference between secular and Christian-tailored approaches (see Worthington, Hook, Davis & McDaniel, 2011 for a meta-analysis). This is likely because Christians who go through a secular forgiveness group may apply their own Christian interpretation to these interventions. Thus, it is likely that one could effectively use any of the evidence-based treatments for Christians. However, only one psychoeducational program (a) has been tailored explicitly for Christians, (b) provides free leader and participant manuals (www.people.vcu.edu/~eworth), (c) provides a trade book describing the explicitly Christian approach (see Worthington, 2003, 2009), and (d) provides experimental evidence from independent labs of its efficacy with Christian participants. Although Enright's forgiveness model has also been a dominant forgiveness model in the field, this chapter will focus primarily on Worthington's REACH forgiveness model because it has been utilized more often with Christians and is one of the only models tested explicitly with Christians (see also DiBlasio & Benda, 2008 for its use with Christian couples; Hebl & Enright, 1993 with elderly people; Rye & Pargament, 2002 with college women rejected by romantic partners; Rye et al., 2005, with community divorced women). Therefore it is most directly applicable to forgiveness within the context of group treatments for Christians. Additionally, the REACH model has been utilized with a range of participants (including college students seeking to forgive a romantic hurt, persons who have recently divorced, and married couples wishing to overcome an interpersonal offense) and has been shown to effectively encourage forgiveness (e.g., Ripley & Worthington, 2002; Rye & Pargament, 2002; Rye et al., 2005).

Worthington's forgiveness intervention model includes five steps with each of the main components of the model represented in the acronym REACH (Worthington, 1998). In the first step of this model, clients recall (R) the hurt they have experienced. This step provides an opportunity for individuals to acknowledge the emotions they felt during and after the offense and to express them in a safe environment. Second, clients are encouraged to develop empathy (E) for their offender. In this step, clients attempt to see the offense from the offender's point of view and to understand why their offender may have committed the offense. For example, clients are asked to consider possible situational factors (perhaps a problematic family situation, intense stress and/or use of drugs or alcohol) that may have caused their offenders' actions. Third, clients discuss the option of offering a gift of forgiveness as an altruistic (A) response to the offender's actions. During this step individuals are encouraged to recall when they have received forgiveness from others and the gratitude they may have felt for receiving forgiveness (Worthington, 1998). Fourth, clients are encouraged to commit (C) to forgiving their offenders. For example, one might commit to forgive by telling a trusted individual (for example, a friend, counselor, spouse or pastor) of one's decision to forgive, or perhaps by writing a letter of forgiveness, which is normally not actually given to the offender. Fifth, clients hold (H) on to forgiveness through specific "relapse prevention" strategies, such as telling others about their decision to forgive and reminding themselves that they have chosen to forgive their offenders and move forward with their lives.

While this chapter will emphasize Worthington's model, it is important to note that other researchers have studied the effectiveness of forgiveness interventions with Christian participants. For example, DiBlasio and Benda (2008) examined the efficacy of a forgiveness intervention with Christian couples. After a three-hour intervention (consisting of thirteen individual steps), participants reported significant gains in forgiveness and marital satisfaction. Additionally, Hebl and Enright (1993) also utilized a forgiveness intervention with elderly females from a Christian community. Participants in the forgiveness intervention reported increased forgiveness, decreased anger and an increased ability to generalize forgiveness to others in their lives than participants in the control condition. As mentioned above, most forgiveness research to date has utilized forgiveness interventions that are predominantly secular in nature. There are few studies that examine religiously accommodative forgiveness interventions. Studies that have implemented religious-based forgiveness interventions for Christian participants allow for an important glimpse of factors that promote forgiveness in

Christian contexts. The following section will explore recent empirical studies examining the efficacy of group forgiveness interventions for Christian populations and will review specific factors that researchers suggest are instrumental to the promotion of forgiveness.

EMPIRICAL SUPPORT FOR GROUP TREATMENTS PROMOTING FORGIVENESS

Some of the first intervention studies examining the efficacy of a Christian-based group forgiveness intervention for the treatment of unforgiveness were conducted by Rye and colleagues (Rye & Pargament, 2002; Rye et al., 2005). Rye and Pargament (2002) examined the process of forgiveness for fifty-eight college-aged, Christian women who were seeking to overcome an interpersonal hurt by a romantic partner. Rye and Pargament randomly assigned women to either a secular forgiveness intervention condition (which did not incorporate religion) or a religious-based intervention condition (which included explicitly religious components). Both intervention conditions were loosely based on Worthington's model to REACH forgiveness (Worthington, 1998). However, the religiously based model incorporated additional religious elements (such as reading Scripture passages addressing anger and forgiveness, challenging participants to explore how unforgiveness had impacted their spiritual lives, exploring the theological basis of forgiveness and using strategies such as prayer to aid in forgiveness) and actively encouraged participants to utilize their faith commitments as much as possible while seeking to forgive.

After the intervention, participants completing the forgiveness intervention conditions (both secular and religious-based) reported significantly more forgiveness than the waitlist control condition. One interesting finding was that many participants, regardless of condition, reported using their own religious strategies in an effort to reach forgiveness. Even if the treatment condition did not explicitly utilize religious elements (as was the case for the secular condition), participants in *both* conditions reported using strategies such as praying for their offender and asking God for help forgiving. This finding suggests that for Christians, incorporating their religious beliefs into the forgiveness process is important, and may be instrumental in helping them to effectively reach forgiveness.

In a related study, Rye et al. (2005) compared a secular forgiveness intervention and a religiously based forgiveness intervention aimed at promoting forgiveness for 149 divorced participants seeking to forgive an ex-spouse for severe offenses, such as infidelity or abuse. Similar to their prior study, Rye et al. (2005) based both intervention conditions on Worthington's model to REACH forgiveness and incorporated religious elements into the religiously based condition. Rye et al. explain that participants in the religiously based condition were encouraged to "draw on their preexisting faith as a means of facilitating forgiveness," which was facilitated through discussions of Scripture passages about forgiveness, reading about biblical models of forgiveness, and encouraging participants to turn to religious methods (such as prayer) to help them forgive (p. 883). In accordance with their prior findings, Rye et al. (2005) again found that participants in both conditions reported greater increases in forgiveness than participants in the comparison control condition. The lack of significant difference in outcomes across conditions is likely due, as Rye and Pargament state, to "a combination of the content of the interventions (i.e., facilitating forgiveness) and the modality employed (i.e., group therapy)" (p. 436). An especially important finding of Rye et al.'s research is that, similar to their prior study, participants reported use of religious strategies (such as turning to God for assistance forgiving) regardless of condition assigned. The findings of Rye and Pargament (2002) and Rye et al. (2005) suggest that group forgiveness interventions appear to be highly effective for promoting forgiveness for Christian individuals. Additionally, religious persons seem to find value in interventions, such as the REACH forgiveness method, that have been modified to include relevant religious references and strategies (such as personal prayer or turning to God for help with forgiving). Although in these particular research studies those in the religious condition did not respond with greater forgiveness than those without the religious content, the self-reported reliance on religious and spiritual coping methods indicates that this is something that religious individuals value. The fact that this was not born out directly in these studies could be a result of low power (too few participants to detect a real effect), the overwhelming effectiveness of the programs, or the fact that both programs really were unique and yet equally effective (Rye & Pargament, 2002).

Besides research conducted by Rye and colleagues, additional studies have examined the use of forgiveness interventions with Christian populations. Lampton et al. (2005) compared the effects of a forgiveness intervention condition and a waitlist control condition using Christian college students. All students received a month of awareness raising about forgiveness, so the intervention was tested as an adjunct to the awareness raising. Similar to Rye's research, Lampton et al. utilized a forgiveness intervention based on Worthington's model to REACH forgiveness and supplemented this model with explicitly religious components (such as examining the biblical framework of forgiveness, reading scriptural references on forgiveness, reflecting on the Christian basis of forgiveness and exploring Jesus' model of forgiveness). At the completion of the study, participants in the REACH condition reported significantly greater reductions in revenge and avoidance than participants in the waitlist control condition. Of importance, Lampton et al. speculate that positive gains reported by participants in the treatment condition may be attributable to the congruency of the treatment interventions with Christian participants' own religious beliefs. In essence, Christian participants were likely able to make significant strides toward forgiveness by utilizing a forgiveness method that was in direct accord with their values.

In similar research on the role of religiously based interventions, Stratton et al. (2008) randomly assigned Christian college students to a forgiveness intervention condition (based on Worthington's model to REACH forgiveness and incorporating explicitly Christian elements), an alternative treatment essay-writing condition, a REACH-plus-essay-writing condition, or a waitlist control condition. Participants in the REACH condition completed a full forgiveness intervention. However, participants in the REACH-plus-essay condition completed the five REACH steps in addition to writing a one-thousand-word essay detailing their unique story of forgiveness (including a narrative of the experienced transgression, the decision to forgive, the experience of forgiving, and a specific discussion of the role religious beliefs played in the forgiveness process). Stratton and colleagues found that students in the workshop-plus-essay condition reported greater changes in forgiving their offenders than did the control condition.

Finally, Worthington et al. (2010) examined the efficacy of the REACH model when used with Christian participants in the Philippines. Worthington and his colleagues modified the REACH forgiveness model (by adding Christian and additional cultural elements) in an effort to examine the applicability of forgiveness interventions with an ethnically diverse Christian sample. Results indicated that, despite small sample sizes, participants did report increases in forgiveness and reductions in unforgiveness. Worthington and colleagues propose that their results appear to be a testament to the potential range of applications for the REACH model when applied to religious and/or culturally diverse populations.

We may conclude from this brief review of the Christian-accommodated REACH forgiveness model that it has been shown to be more effective than control conditions in five independent investigations, with most using randomized assignment to conditions. The studies have been conducted in Ohio (Rye's two studies), Arkansas (Lampton et al., 2005), Kentucky (Stratton et al., 2008) and the Philippines (Worthington et al., 2010). The studies have come from more than two completely independent labs. Thus the criteria have been met to designate the Christian-accommodated REACH forgiveness treatment as empirically supported (Chambless & Hollon, 1998). A fundamental assumption underlying the research conducted by Lampton et al. (2005), Stratton et al. (2008) and Worthington et al. (2010) is that religious persons will respond to interventions that are religious in nature and therefore in accord with their personal religious ideals and values. As stated above, Lampton and colleagues (2005) have suggested that the high level of congruency between participant religious values and the Christian-based treatment administered appears to be an essential aspect of treatment efficacy.

Worthington et al. (2011) recently conducted a meta-analysis of forty-six studies comparing religiously or spiritually accommodative treatments with secular treatments. These treatments included forgiveness treatments as well as treatments for psychological concerns (such as depression or anxiety). In line with research presented above, Worthington et al. propose that for religious clients, religiously and spiritually based interventions may have important benefits. For example, religious clients may feel most comfortable participating in religiously based treatments that coincide with their worldview, which in turn may decrease premature treatment termination. It is important to note that although Worthington et al. found that religious and spiritual treatments seem to have a greater impact on client measures of spiritual outcomes, no differences seem to exist between religious and secular treatments regarding psychological outcomes. Likewise, additional researchers have encouraged clinicians to attempt to provide clients seeking forgiveness with interventions that are highly relevant and applicable to their faith commitments (West, 2001). West (2001) has proposed that forgiveness interventions that are in accordance with an individual's faith commitment and draw on his or her religious values will be most efficacious. Research consistently indicates that group forgiveness interventions, particularly those that incorporate religiously based elements such as prayer or religious scriptures, are able to effectively encourage the reduction of unforgiveness and the promotion of forgiveness for Christian participants (Lampton et al., 2005; Rye & Pargament, 2002; Rye et al., 2005; Stratton et al., 2008). Ultimately, forgiveness interventions that draw on an individual's religious beliefs and utilize interventions specifically tailored to Christian participants appear to be highly effective at promoting forgiveness.

THERAPY DESCRIPTION

Worthington's model to REACH forgiveness has been well-researched and is highly applicable for use with Christians striving to forgive (Lampton et al., 2005; Rye & Pargament; 2002; Rye et al., 2005; Stratton et al., 2008). The five steps of the REACH forgiveness model are easy to follow, user-friendly, and can be adapted for use in both individual and group intervention settings. The following section will highlight specific techniques utilized at each step of the REACH model to promote forgiveness in group contexts. Free downloadable files containing detailed leader and participant manuals for (a) a six-hour Christian group, (b) a six-hour secular group and (c) twenty-hour groups can be downloaded free of charge at www.people.vcu .edu/~eworth. Permission is granted to use and adapt any materials as long as proper citation is given.

Recall the hurt. As mentioned above, the primary task of the first step of the REACH forgiveness model is to recall the experienced hurt. The most important goal of this step is to provide clients with a safe and supportive environment in which they can express painful emotions as they ultimately work toward healing and forgiveness. Various strategies are utilized at this step to help facilitate the recollection of difficult emotions. Often a guided-imagery exercise is used to gently direct clients through emotions associated with the transgression itself and their feelings toward the offender. One such example of a guided-imagery exercise involves instructing clients to imagine themselves back in the hurtful situation, interacting with the offender. This imagery can then be extended by having clients view themselves and their offenders from a third person perspective (e.g., to help contain overwhelming emotions and gain a more empathic perspective) and to connect the memory with images that engender more safety and relaxation for the client (e.g., a quiet wooded path).

Furthermore, the *recall* step of the model provides an opportunity for clients to share their offenses with others. Sharing one's experiences in a group setting gives individuals the chance to have his or her feelings validated and understood, which often facilitates healing. The experience of hearing others' offenses helps clients realize that other people have also coped with painful offenses, thereby solidifying feelings of universality. That is, people come to feel that they are not alone in feeling difficult emotions associated with an offense. Lastly, clear definitions of forgiveness (including what forgiveness is not) are typically provided. In addition to a definition of forgiveness, some clients find it helpful to explore Scriptures where Christ offers forgiveness (e.g., Mt 6:12, 14-15; Mt 19:21-25; Lk 15:11-32).

Cathleen was a thirty-four-year-old woman who experienced a physically abusive relationship with a past romantic partner. Although she ended this relationship and had no contact with her ex-partner, she would become angry whenever she thought of the relationship. Cathleen attended a forgiveness intervention group offered in her community. During the beginning of the group, Cathleen discussed her experience and reported that sharing her offense with others provided a sense of catharsis, universality (knowledge that others have experienced similar offenses) and validation. These benefits that she experienced from sharing her offense with others provided a foundation from which Cathleen could continue to work toward forgiveness and healing.

Empathize with the offender. Developing empathy for one's offender is a second key step of the REACH forgiveness model. Many researchers concur that empathy is a vital element of forgiveness and is often one of the first, and most important, steps in forgiving (McCullough, Worthington & Rachal, 1997). The REACH model clearly defines empathy as the ability to understand the offender and conceive of possible motives for the offense and also clarifies what empathy is not (i.e., sympathy, justification, freeing the offender from responsibility, etc.). Clients are encouraged to consider that the same event can often be explained from a number of various perspectives and are given the opportunity to consider what their offenders may have felt during the offense as well as possible reasons for the offenders' actions (even if those actions ultimately led to a very poor or hurtful outcome).

One strategy that the REACH forgiveness model employs to promote empathy is to encourage clients (in dyads) to take turns sharing their offense and listening to their partner brainstorm possible reasons why the offender may have committed the offense. In addition, clients are encouraged to explore the offense from God's point of view—that is, to consider how God may feel toward the offender and the specific motives behind the offender's actions that may be known to God. Some clients find it helpful to consider Christ as an example of empathy (specifically Christ's ability to empathize with people who scorned, ridiculed and ultimately crucified him). In addition, clients are encouraged to pray (both silently during time provided in the group and outside of the group) for their offenders as a strategy to further build empathy. Importantly, when people have trouble empathizing with their offenders, which sometimes occurs, they can seek to experience sympathy, compassion or love instead. The REACH forgiveness model is based on the theoretical premise that emotional forgiveness occurs through emotional replacement of unforgiving emotions with positive, other-oriented emotions. Empathy, sympathy, compassion and love are suitable emotions. Evidence supporting the emotional replacement hypothesis was summarized in Worthington (2006). Thus, the "E" step of the REACH forgiveness model could also be accurately named "emotional replacement."

Joseph, age fifty-five, grew up with an angry, emotionally abusive, and often volatile father. Joseph remembers his father was often not at home, did not attend his school and sports events, and frequently became angry with him (which included yelling and name-calling). Joseph felt angry, betrayed, and confused when he thought of his father's behavior. During Joseph's participation in a group forgiveness intervention, he wrote a letter addressed to himself from his father detailing his father's perspective and experiences. This helped Joseph to develop empathy for his father by considering possible reasons behind his father's angry moods and inconsistent presence in his life. Through this exercise, Joseph came to understand the role his father's drinking played in his behavior. Instead of viewing his father as a cruel man, Joseph was able to see his father as an alcoholic who struggled with a debilitating disease. Joseph also spent time in prayer, reflecting on how God views his father and God's understanding of his father's actions. By considering possible reasons behind his father's behavior and seeking a broader view of his father, Joseph was able to develop empathy and continue working toward forgiveness.

Altruistic gift of forgiveness. The third phase of the REACH forgiveness model involves encouraging clients to view forgiveness as an altruistic gift. A primary goal of this step is to allow clients to understand forgiveness as a nearly universal concept; that is, everyone will likely need either to give or receive forgiveness at some point in time. Clients are encouraged to recognize the humanity in each of us and the fallibility of human nature. To build an understanding of altruism, many clients find it helpful to brainstorm times they have committed an offense, asked for forgiveness and experienced a sense of gratitude and relief at being forgiven. Additionally, it is often beneficial to have clients share aloud with one another (either in dyads or as a group) the types of offenses they have committed, their intentions or motivations behind the offense and the resulting experience of forgiveness (if forgiveness was offered). This type of sharing reinforces that nearly everyone has committed an offense and been the giver or receiver of forgiveness. Lastly, similar to looking to Christ as a model of empathy, many clients find it helpful to examine Christ as a model of altruism. Specifically, Christ unselfishly gave forgiveness as a gift to others; likewise, some clients may find it helpful to draw on Christ's example of altruism for encouragement (Worthington et al., 2006).

Lucinda, age sixty-seven, joined a group forgiveness intervention in the hope of moving past her husband's infidelity. Approximately one year ago, Lucinda's husband confessed to a lengthy affair with a close friend of hers. Since then, Lucinda has felt devastated, betrayed and angry. She found herself dwelling on her husband's affair and the senselessness of his actions and ruminating on his many faults. Through the REACH model, Lucinda was encouraged to consider times when she too has committed offenses, made mistakes and acted in ways that have hurt those she loves. Lucinda prayerfully considered her own humanity, thereby allowing her also to see her husband through a more altruistic perspective. The altruism that she developed helped her to respond to her husband with more grace and mercy, despite the terrible pain that he had caused her. By considering an altruistic response, Lucinda was able to find meaning and purpose in her forgiveness that included not only helping herself past the hurt but offering an undeserved gift to her husband.

Commit to forgiveness. Fourth, the REACH forgiveness model invites clients to commit to offering forgiveness to their offenders. Once clients have completed the first three steps of the REACH forgiveness model, they often feel ready to commit to forgiveness through a variety of strategies. One technique commonly used during this step is to have clients write a letter of forgiveness to their offenders. This letter is typically not mailed, unless the client has a strong inclination to do so, and simply serves as a chance to express the decision to forgive tangibly. Some clients may feel it is helpful for them to further solidify their commitment to forgiveness by reading their letter aloud to the group. Alternately, if clients feel uncomfortable reading their letter aloud, they may appreciate the opportunity to process their experience of writing the letter by discussing portions that were difficult to write and their emotions associated with the letter-writing process. If clients struggle to write a letter to their offenders, they may sometimes find it helpful instead to write a letter to God detailing their desire to eventually offer forgiveness. Another effective strategy some clients find helpful at this stage is to write a list of experienced hurts (and/or a description of the offense) and to bury, burn or shred the paper as a symbol of releasing resentments and embracing forgiveness. Additional strategies, such as encouraging clients to tell others about their decision to forgive (either fellow group members or loved ones) can be a meaningful way to express forgiveness. Last, throughout the process of committing to forgiveness, many clients find it beneficial to turn to God for strength and to pray for themselves, their offenders and their desire to forgive.

Burton, age twenty-four, is a Christian male who experienced a significant betrayal when a friend borrowed a large sum of money and ultimately left town without repaying him or leaving any type of forwarding information. After completing a few sessions of a group forgiveness intervention, Burton began to feel more forgiving. Although still pursuing options to reclaim his money (e.g., legal action), Burton wrote a letter to God thanking God for assistance in the forgiveness process and detailing Burton's commitment to move forward in that process. Burton also discussed his decision to work toward forgiveness with his church pastor, thereby committing to forgiveness by telling another of his decision.

Hold on to forgiveness. The final step of the REACH forgiveness model emphasizes the importance of holding on to forgiveness for the long term. During this step, clients are encouraged to examine any perceived barriers that may be preventing them from reaching forgiveness (e.g., forgiveness seems too final) and to explore strategies to overcome these barriers. Clients are also reminded that forgiveness is a continual process and therefore that having some doubts about whether they have really forgiven is often a normal experience. In addition, clients are reminded that feelings of sadness or pain associated with a hurt do *not* mean they have not offered forgiveness; rather, these feelings can be a natural reaction to protect themselves from future offenses. It is certainly possible to feel the emotions associated with forgiveness, but also retain a sense of sadness or loss when thinking of an offense. Also, some clients find it helpful at this stage to meditate on Christ's positive reaction to the forgiveness they have offered their offenders as a way to reinforce the beneficial nature of forgiveness. Last, some groups choose to give clients a time to pray in a group setting (either aloud or silently) for their offenders and their ability to maintain forgiveness in the future.

Ann is a forty-five-year-old woman who experienced sexual harassment from a coworker. Although Ann's employer was able to intervene and the harassment ended when her coworker's job was terminated, Ann continued to feel a sense of betrayal, violation and anger toward this offender. After participating in a forgiveness intervention group, Ann feels she has nearly achieved forgiveness. In order to hold on to the forgiveness she has offered her offender, Ann spends time with her fellow group members debunking any final myths she holds about forgiveness and continuing to learn about the forgiveness process. Specifically, Ann realizes that although she feels she has reached a place of forgiveness, it is normal and expected to have days in which she experiences occasional anger toward her offender. Additionally, whenever Ann has times in which she finds it difficult to recall her choice to forgive, she reads her Bible to remind herself of the example of forgiveness Christ provides and her decision to forgive.

TREATMENT IMPLEMENTATION

Although researchers have documented the efficacy of forgiveness interventions, there are certainly elements of a process as transcendent as forgiveness that cannot simply be prescribed in specific, regimented steps. Ultimately, forgiveness models are guidelines and foundations for the promotion of forgiveness and are not meant to be rigid rules for every situation in which a person is seeking forgiveness. Forgiveness models serve as an outline of possible steps one can follow to achieve forgiveness, but they are by no means presumed to be the only way to forgive. Guidelines for using forgiveness-promoting strategies within Christian psychotherapy settings can provide some direction without overly constraining the process.

One of the foundational guidelines of the forgiveness process is the necessity for a clear and useful definition of forgiveness. Researchers have suggested that many individuals may be hesitant to forgive because they falsely believe forgiveness will be a form of pardoning or overlooking an offense (Luskin, 2002). Clinicians should consistently seek to educate individuals about what forgiveness does and does not entail. Walton (2005) has noted the importance of "clinical clarity," including a precise definition of forgiveness, when commencing clinical work with persons seeking forgiveness (p. 196). Common myths about what forgiveness includes (for example, the misconception that forgiveness excuses a behavior) should always be debunked.

Perhaps most importantly, clinicians should address the distinction between forgiveness and reconciliation. Researchers have indicated that people sometimes fear forgiveness will result in a forced reunion or unwanted reconciliation with an offender (Kearns & Fincham, 2004). In some situations, reconciliation is not recommended and is even contraindicated (Bass & Davis, 1994; Lamb, 2002), such as in cases of severe and persistent abuse. In instances such as these, clinicians need to emphasize the difference between forgiveness and reconciliation (specifically that forgiveness can exist with or without reconciliation).

A second important guideline to consider when working with people seeking forgiveness is to regard each individual as the expert regarding his or her own forgiveness. Because forgiveness models may not be comprehensive for every client, therapists may find that they wish to supplement forgiveness models with additional strategies or methods in order to reach forgiveness. Kidwell, Wade and Blaedel (2012) examined the process of forgiveness for ten religious individuals who worked to reduce unforgiveness associated with an interpersonal offense (many of which were severe in nature, such as physical and sexual abuse). Numerous participants reported adopting creative and unique strategies to allow them to reach forgiveness in a way that felt most comfortable for them. For example, one participant reported that a combination of religious prayer and reflection, coupled with physical and artistic activities including yoga and artwork, helped her reach forgiveness. Another participant described releasing balloons to represent her commitment to forgiveness and to symbolize that she was choosing to let go of the anger, bitterness and hurt she once held toward her offender. Clinicians should be aware of the importance of encouraging individuals to choose their own path to forgiveness.

On a similar note, clinicians working in Christian psychotherapy settings with religious clients should encourage individuals to explore specific religious methods they believe will help them forgive. Clinicians should supplement traditional forgiveness interventions with religious interventions (such as prayer, consultation with religious leaders, referencing Scriptures, meditation and considering biblical models of forgiveness). Because forgiveness is unique for each person and different factors will ultimately help different people forgive, clinicians should empower clients to explore elements (religious or secular in nature) they feel will enhance their forgiveness experience and have personal meaning for them.

Third, clinicians should remember that forgiveness is truly a progression and not an endpoint. The process of forgiveness, like any experience of growth or change, does not occur as an all-or-nothing experience. Instead, forgiveness is a process that can happen gradually over time. Even after one has forgiven an offender, it is possible to experience days in which anger toward an offender or rumination about an offense returns. Clinicians should provide realistic expectations about the nature of forgiveness (e.g., that feeling anger toward an offender one day does not necessarily mean one has not forgiven) and about the process and timing of forgiveness (specifically that forgiveness may take time to achieve).

An additional aspect of forgiveness that is important is the notion of time. Researchers have consistently demonstrated that timing and duration of treatment are key factors that contribute to one's ability to forgive (Wade, Worthington & Meyer, 2005). Ultimately, people forgive in their own time. Forgiveness is not something that can be hurried along but often only gently encouraged when and if one is ready to move toward forgiveness. Adequate time after an offense has transpired is necessary to give an individual the chance to process and experience emotions associated with the offense and to come to terms with the ordeal they have experienced. For forgiveness to be most successful, clinicians must remember that individuals typically forgive only after they have had time to reflect on an offense, and most importantly, to express and articulate painful or difficult emotions that arise from their experience.

CONCLUSION

This chapter has discussed the psychological benefits that accompany forgiveness and reviewed research investigating the efficacy of religious-based group treatments for the promotion of forgiveness. The REACH forgiveness model (Worthington, 1998, 2003) is a commonly used forgiveness model demonstrated to be highly effective for promoting forgiveness in both Christian and secular settings (Rye & Pargament, 2002; Rye et al., 2005; Ripley & Worthington, 2002) and is an effective treatment option for promoting forgiveness with Christian individuals (Lampton, 2005; Stratton et al., 2008; Worthington et al., 2010).

REFERENCES

Al-Mabuk, R. H., Enright, R. D., & Cardis, P. A. (1995). Forgiveness education with love-deprived late adolescents. *Journal of Moral Education, 24,* 427-44.

Bass, E., & Davis, L. (1994). *The courage to heal.* New York: Harper Perennial.

Beals, I. A. (1998). *A theology of forgiveness: Towards a paradigm of racial justice.* Bethesda, MD: Christian Universities Press.

Chambless, D. L., & Hollon, S. D. (1998). Defining empirically supported therapies. *Journal of Consulting and Clinical Psychology, 66,* 7-18.

DiBlasio, F. A., & Benda, B. B. (2008). Forgiveness intervention with married couples: Two empirical analyses. *Journal of Psychology and Christianity, 27,* 150-58.

Enright, R. D., & Fitzgibbons, R. P. (2000). *Helping clients forgive: An empirical guide for resolving anger and restoring hope.* Washington, DC: American Psychological Association.

Enright, R. D., & The Human Development Study Group. (1991). The moral development of forgiveness. In W. Kurtines & J. Gerwirtz (Eds.), *Handbook of moral behavior and development* (Vol. 1, pp. 123-52). Hillsdale, NJ: Erlbaum.

Fehr, R., Gelfand, M. J., & Nag, M. (2010). The road to forgiveness: A meta-analytic synthesis of its situational and dispositional correlates. *Psychology Bulletin, 136,* 894-914.

Hebl, J. H., & Enright, R. D. (1993). Forgiveness as a psychotherapeutic goal with elderly females. *Psychotherapy, 30,* 658-67.

Kearns, J. N., & Fincham, F. D. (2004). A prototype analysis of forgiveness. *Personality and Social Psychology Bulletin, 30,* 838-55.

Kidwell, J. E., Wade, N. G., & Blaedel, E. (2012). Understanding forgiveness in the lives of religious people: The role of sacred and secular elements. *Mental Health, Religion, and Culture, 15*(2), 121-40.

Lamb, S. (2002). Women, abuse and forgiveness: A special case. In S. Lamb & J. G. Murphy (Eds.), *Before forgiving: Cautionary views of forgiveness in psychotherapy* (pp. 155-71). New York: Oxford University Press.

Lampton, C., Oliver, G. J., Worthington, E. L., Jr., & Berry, J. W. (2005). Helping Christian college students become more forgiving: An intervention study to promote forgiveness as part of a program to shape Christian character. *Journal of Psychology and Theology, 33,* 278-90.

Luskin, F. (2002). *Forgive for good.* New York: HarperCollins.

Macaskill, A. (2005). Defining forgiveness: Christian clergy and general population perspectives. *Journal of Personality, 73,* 1237-65.

Marty, M. E. (1998). The ethos of Christian forgiveness. In E. L. Worthington Jr. (Ed.), *Dimensions of forgiveness: Psychological, research, and theological perspectives* (pp. 9-28). Philadelphia: Templeton Foundation Press.

McCullough, M. E., Fincham, F. D., & Tsang, J.-A. (2003). Forgiveness, forebearance, and time: The temporal unfolding of transgression-related interpersonal motivations. *Journal of Personality and Social Psychology, 84*(3), 540-57.

McCullough, M. E., Luna, L. R., Berry, J. W., Tabak, B. A., & Bono, G. (2010). On the form and function of forgiving: Modeling the time forgiveness relationship and testing the valuable relationships hypothesis. *Emotion, 10,* 358-76.

McCullough, M. E., & Worthington, E. L., Jr. (1999). Religion and the forgiving personality. *Journal of Personality, 67,* 1141-64.

McCullough, M. E., Worthington, E. L., Jr., & Rachal, K. C. (1997). Interpersonal forgiving in close relationships. *Journal of Personality and Social Psychology, 73,* 321-36.

Ripley, J. S., & Worthington, E. L., Jr. (2002). Hope-focused and forgiveness-based group interventions to promote marital enrichment. *Journal of Counseling and Development, 80,* 452-63.

Rye, M. S., & Pargament, K. I. (2002). Forgiveness and romantic relationships in college: Can it heal the wounded heart? *Journal of Clinical Psychology, 54,* 419-41.

Rye, M. S., Pargament, K. I., Ali, A. M., Beck, G. L., Dorff, E. N., Hallisey, C., Narayanan, V., & Williams, J. G. (2000). Religious perspectives on forgiveness. In M. E. McCullough, K. I. Pargament & C. E. Thorensen (Eds.), *Forgiveness: Theory, research, and practice* (pp. 17-40). New York: Guilford Press.

Rye, M. S., Pargament, K. I., Pan, W., Yingling, D. W., Shogren, K. A., Masako, I. (2005). Can group interventions facilitate forgiveness of an ex-spouse? A randomized clinical trial. *Journal of Consulting and Clinical Psychology, 5,* 880-92.

Stratton, S. P., Dean, J. B., Nonneman, A. J., Bode, R. A., & Worthington, E. L., Jr. (2008). Forgiveness interventions as spiritual development strategies: Comparing forgiveness workshop training, expressive writing about forgiveness, and retested controls. *Journal of Psychology and Christianity, 27,* 347-57.

Wade, N. G., & Meyer, J. E. (2009). Comparison of brief group interventions to promote forgiveness: A pilot outcome study. *International Journal of Group Psychotherapy, 59,* 119-220.

Wade, N.G., Worthington, E. L., Jr., & Meyer, J. E. (2005). But do they work? A meta-analysis of group interventions to promote forgiveness. In E. L. Worthington Jr. (Ed.), *Handbook of forgiveness* (pp. 423-40). New York: Brunner-Routledge.

Wade, N. G., Worthington, E. L., Jr., & Vogel, D. L. (2007). Effectiveness of religiously tailored interventions in Christian therapy. *Psychotherapy Research, 17,* 91-105.

Walton, E. (2005). Therapeutic forgiveness: Developing a model for empowering victims of sexual abuse. *Clinical Social Work Journal, 33,* 193-207.

West, W. (2001). Issues relating to the use of forgiveness in counseling and psychotherapy. *British Journal of Guidance and Counseling, 29,* 415-22.

Witvliet, C. V. O., Ludwig, T. E., & Vander Laan, K. L. (2001). Granting forgiveness for harboring grudges: Implications for emotion, physiology, and health. *Psychological Science, 12*, 117-23.

Worthington, E. L., Jr. (1988). Understanding the values of religious clients: A model and its application to counseling. *Journal of Counseling Psychology, 35*, 166-74.

Worthington, E. L., Jr. (1998). The pyramid model of forgiveness: Some interdisciplinary speculations about unforgiveness and the promotion of forgiveness. In E. L. Worthington Jr. (Ed.), *Dimensions of forgiveness: Psychological research and theoretical perspectives* (pp. 107-37). Philadelphia: Templeton Foundation Press.

Worthington, E. L., Jr. (2003). *Forgiving and reconciling.* Downers Grove, IL: InterVarsity Press.

Worthington, E. L., Jr. (2009). *A just forgiveness: Responsible healing without excusing injustice.* Downers Grove, IL: InterVarsity Press.

Worthington, E. L., Jr., Berry, J. W., & Parrott, L., III (2001). Unforgiveness, forgiveness, religion and health. In T. G. Plante & A. C. Sherman (Eds.), *Faith and health* (pp.108-38). New York: Guilford Press.

Worthington, E. L., Jr., Hook, J. N., Davis, D. E., & McDaniel, M. A. (2011). Religion and spirituality. *Journal of Clinical Psychology, 67*, 204-14.

Worthington, E. L, Jr., Hunter, J. L., Sharp, C. B., Hook, J. N., Van Tongeren, D. R., Davis, D. E., et al. (2010). A psychoeducational intervention to promote forgiveness in Christians in the Philippines. *Journal of Mental Health Counseling, 32*(1), 75-93.

Worthington, E. L., Jr., Kurusu, T. A., McCullough, M. E., & Sandage, S. (1996). Empirical research on religion and psychotherapeutic processes and outcomes: A 10-year review and research prospectus. *Psychological Bulletin, 119*, 448-87.

Worthington, E. L., Jr., Lerner, A. J., Sharp, C. B., & Sharp, J. (2006). Interpersonal forgiveness as an example of loving one's enemies. *Journal of Psychology and Theology, 34*, 32-42.

Worthington, E. L., Jr., & Wade, N. G. (1999). The social psychology of unforgiveness and forgiveness and implications for clinical practice. *Journal of Social and Clinical Psychology, 18*, 358-415.

Worthington, E. L., Jr., Witvliet, C. V. O., Pietrini, P., & Miller, A. J. (2007). Forgiveness, health, and well-being: A review of evidence for emotional versus decisional forgiveness, dispositional forgiveness and reduced unforgiveness. *Journal of Behavioral Medicine, 30*, 291-302.

Part Four

REFLECTING ON
EVIDENCE-BASED
TREATMENTS

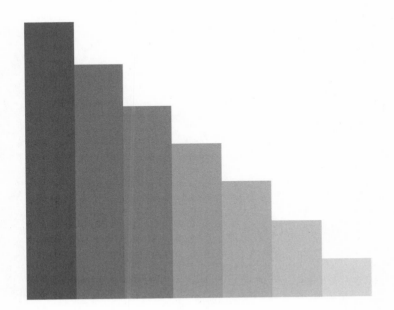

14

Promising Evidence-Based Treatments

Everett L. Worthington Jr., Joshua N. Hook,
Eric Johnson and Jamie D. Aten

At this point, you might be excited about your favorite approaches and have a general sense of the empirical support for many treatments that can be applied to Christian clients. But you might also want the bird's-eye view. What is the status of the field overall? What are some treatments that have not yet established a firm empirical base but might be worth developing further?

In this chapter, we review the psychotherapies and spiritual disciplines discussed in this book to identify promising evidence-based treatments and to compare the evidence base for each approach. Few of the approaches reviewed here currently meet the strict criteria for empirically supported treatments (i.e., independent verification of efficacy in two labs using randomized clinical trials), but many have an existing evidence base and show strong potential for becoming empirically supported (see table 14.1 at the end of this chapter). Some of the Christian treatments have direct research supporting their use. Perhaps the majority, however, rely on research relating to secular treatments; they have not yet accumulated direct research on the Christian-accommodative version of the treatment. Besides summarizing the existing research base for Christian treatments reviewed in this book, we provide recommendations for further developing and studying evidence-based Christian treatments.

REVIEWING THE EVIDENCE BASE

Relationship factors. The treatments covered in this section were divided into three groups. In the first, we examined the evidence base of general therapeutic relationship characteristics such as empathy, therapeutic alliance, expectancy, expertness and attractiveness of the psychotherapist. We conclude that a huge research base supports the clinical efficacy of such relationship characteristics in general, but investigators have done little research on relationship factors within Christian-accommodative treatments. Adapting a counseling relationship to match the client's religious or spiritual views is considered to be effective (Norcross, 2011), but little is known about other relationship factors beyond basic Christian beliefs and values. Second, we considered lay Christian counseling. Typically, for mild or moderate problems, there is no difference between lay- or professional-counselor outcomes. For severe problems, however, the professional counselor has the edge. Third, we found devotional meditation, which can be a psychotherapeutic method or simply a personal practice, to be a promising treatment. Unlike many therapeutic treatments, devotional meditation may be more effective with Christians when its content is specifically Christian (as opposed to nonsectarian).

Individual psychotherapies. Of the hundreds of approaches to individual psychotherapy, only a few have been accommodated to a Christian orientation. We examined (1) cognitive therapy and cognitive-behavioral therapy for depression, (2) psychodynamic process-experiential psychotherapy for adults, and (3) trauma-focused cognitive behavioral treatment for adolescents and children. We evaluated the evidence of CBT for depression in adults as meeting the criteria for empirically supported status. Christian CBT has not been shown to be superior to secular CBT for depression. Secular CBT has been applied to other problems with great success, but Christian-accommodated CBT has not been studied with problems other than depression. Secular psychodynamic therapies have likewise been tested thoroughly, as have secular process-experiential therapies. However, Christian-accommodative psychodynamic-process-experiential therapy is at present untested. Walker et al. reported on trauma-focused CBT for adolescents and children. They adduced substantial evidence supporting the secular version of the psychotherapy, but again, at present the scientific evidence base for Christian-accommodative CBT for adolescents and children is nonexistent and therefore must be considered untested as a Christian-accommodative approach.

There are many other approaches to individual psychotherapy that are currently untested in an explicitly Christian version. For example, none of the following approaches have existing research supporting Christian versions: (a) interpersonal approaches, (b) short-term psychodynamic psychotherapies, (c) relationally based attachment-focused approaches, (d) classic neo-psychoanalytic approaches (i.e., those originally formulated by Adler, Jung, Horney, Sullivan), or (e) social and ego psychological treatments (i.e., approaches by various ego psychologists such as transactional analysis or Gestalt therapy). Surely many Christian psychologists and counselors who were trained in those secular approaches have adapted the approaches to their Christian clientele locally. However, such Christian-accommodative approaches have not been subjected to systematic investigation by clinical researchers.

Another promising but still untested approach is a clearly articulated theory of psychotherapy by McMinn and Campbell (2008). Their integrated approach, which draws from interpersonal and cognitive therapies, is intuitively appealing and is thoroughly consistent with evangelical Christian theology. However, at this point, it too is untested. Furthermore, even though different elements are drawn from evidence-based theories, it has not been tested as a whole theoretical approach in the secular realm. Thus, we consider it an exciting approach, but lacking specific evidence supporting it as an integrated approach.

Couple and group treatments. Christian communities value couples, families and community-based groups. It is not surprising, then, that the largest collection of treatments with some evidence base is within this category. The Christian-PREP (CPREP) intervention to provide premarital counseling, couple enrichment and couple counseling is one of the best supported Christian-accommodative treatments. Yet most of its empirical support has come from the secular PREP approach. Barnes and Stanley argue that the secular approach is founded on Christian principles and that the Christian foundation for PREP is implicit rather than explicit. The secular version of PREP has been independently evaluated as empirically supported (Jakubowski et al., 2004). While CPREP has some research supporting its effectiveness—notably a large dissemination trial—it still is only considered to be promising as an explicitly Christian-accommodative approach.

Similarly, the hope-focused couples approach (HFCA; Worthington, 1989, 1999) was originally formulated and articulated as an explicitly Christian approach, but was first tested in a secular form (Worthington et al., 1997). It also gained independent evaluation as an empirically supported couple enrichment approach (Jakubowski et al., 2004). However, it remains untested as a Christian-accommodative approach.

The Parrotts' SYMBIS approach as a marital preparation treatment is popular and widely used in churches. One might say that it has a large base of users. However, it is considered an untested approach from the standpoint of empirical evidence.

Sells's relational conflict and restoration model (RCRM) is a combination of emotionally focused couple therapy (EFCT) and contextual family therapy (CFT). EFCT is well supported empirically; CFT is less supported. The combined approach has only been tested in one small outcome study. The secular version, therefore, is at best considered to be promising. At present the Christian version is untested.

DiBlasio's decision-based forgiveness approach for couples involves meeting with a couple prior to couples counseling to deal specifically with forgiveness issues. He has found that helping couples decide to forgive each other makes couples counseling smoother. However, the empirical basis for the approach rests on a single study, even though several publications have emerged from the study. DiBlasio's approach is also therefore considered promising.

As with individual psychotherapies, the number of couple psychotherapy treatments that have been developed is astounding. Surely many Christian practitioners have accommodated treatments like integrative behavioral couple therapy, cognitive-behavioral couple therapy, emotion-focused couple therapy, or treatments based on family systems theory to Christians in their local practices. Yet these approaches have not been investigated to provide a scientific evidence base for their efficacy. For example, Sharon May has often presented a Christian-accommodative emotionally focused couple therapy at meetings of the American Association of Christian Counselors. Likewise, Linda Mintle has presented a Christian-focused version of

Gottman's (1999) empirically based marriage clinic. Yet, these Christian-accommodative versions, undoubtedly used by some who have attended the AACC workshops, have not been empirically evaluated.

Likewise, other approaches to promoting forgiveness in couples have research support in the secular arena. For example, Greenberg's approach to promoting forgiveness (based on EFCT) has multiple studies supporting its efficacy and effectiveness (e.g., Greenberg, Warwar & Malcolm, 2008). Gordon, Baucom and Snyder (2004) have a secular approach that combines CBT for couples and psychodynamic couple therapy to treat couples who are trying to recover from an affair. A secular version of Worthington's REACH model has been tested in multiple studies with couples. Again, no studies have tested an explicitly Christian version of these approaches.

In the area of group interventions, Kidwell and Wade investigated the group treatment to promote forgiveness in ad hoc groups. Three types of groups have been studied: (a) psychotherapy groups, (b) psychoeducational groups and (c) process groups. Most of the existing research has been secular. Enright's process model (Enright & Fitzgibbons, 2000) has been found to be empirically supported as a treatment in both psychotherapy groups and psychoeducational groups. Worthington's (2006) REACH forgiveness model is empirically supported as a psychoeducational intervention. Wade's group process model (Kidwell et al., 2012) is considered promising because it has been tested in only one lab. However, only the REACH forgiveness model has been Christian-accommodated. It has been shown to be effective in three different labs.

Summary. The status of evidence-based Christian-accommodative treatments is in its infancy. Many treatments rely on an evidence base from secular research rather than on direct RCT tests of the Christian-accommodative approach. Many create amalgams from approaches that have research-supported components (e.g., psychodynamic and process-experiential model; SYMBIS; marriage conflict and restoration model; McMinn and Campbell integrative approach). Yet the integrated whole has generally not yet been empirically tested. This limitation is important because the integrated whole is not necessarily greater than the sum of its parts. In fact, many times, two approaches can be combined and the integrated whole might not function as well as either part did individually. Research is necessary on amalgamated approaches to determine whether the amalgam actually works.

As with most research reviews, we conclude our study of the existing approaches with a common refrain: *More research is necessary.* In the remainder of this chapter, we provide direction for extending and developing research on some of these promising approaches to Christian counseling and psychotherapy.

EXTENDING RESEARCH ON TREATMENTS

In this section, we provide some ideas for extending the research on the Christian treatments covered in this book. First, we encourage researchers to increase the sophistication of the research questions they ask, specifically focusing on the hypothesized mechanisms of change for various treatments. Second, we address some exciting areas for future research within Christian CBT, Christian relational therapy, Christian couple therapy and Christian interventions to promote forgiveness.

Increase sophistication. Our first recommendation for moving forward in developing and studying evidence-based Christian treatments is to extend the research on approaches that were reviewed in this book. Recall from chapter 1 that two kinds of evidence are needed to support each psychotherapy: efficacy and effectiveness. We also need research supporting the theory of change suggested by the approach to show that the interventions are working for the reasons the theorists say they are working (David & Montgomery, 2011).

The general field of psychotherapy research, active for over sixty-five years, has itself provided much efficacy research in the form of case studies, single-case design studies using multiple measures, and randomized clinical trials. Yet the general field of psychotherapy research has just begun to conduct serious effectiveness research, and only a few large-scale dissemination trials are underway (McHugh & Barlow, 2010). The status of theory-of-change research is much less developed. Thus, even for the approaches that have several research studies supporting their effectiveness, there is a need for more knowledge. We might argue that the Christian psychoeducational treatment for unforgiveness is among the most well-documented to be effective (see table 14.1). It has many research studies investigating the secular approach, as well as studies investigating the explicitly Christian-accommodative approach. However, there is little research examining the theories of change for Christian treatments for unforgiveness.

For example, Worthington (who developed the REACH forgiveness model) suggests that forgiveness occurs because participants make a decision to forgive and also experience emotional forgiveness through the replacement of unforgiving emotions toward the offender (e.g., resentment, bitterness, hostility, hatred, anger and fear) with positive other-oriented emotions (e.g., empathy, sympathy, compassion and love) for the offender. However, even though Worthington (2006) has adduced evidence that emotional forgiveness might involve the replacement of unforgiving emotions by other-oriented positive emotions, there is still little evidence that emotional replacement is the mechanism that is occurring *during* the REACH psychoeducational interventions to promote forgiveness. To demonstrate that the interventions are working due to the mechanism of change of emotional replacement, the nature of outcome research would need to change. Researchers would need to measure change intensively over time, rather than simply measuring unforgiveness at pre-treatment, post-treatment and follow-up (which are necessary to demonstrate efficacy). By following the progress of the clients during the intervention using multiple baselines that track positive and negative emotions (as well as other indices not related to the proposed change mechanisms), researchers might demonstrate that changes in forgiveness are indeed related to the hypothesized mechanism of change (emotional replacement).

Some recommendations for turning treatments with weak evidence into well-established empirically supported treatments. Simply providing RCT efficacy research has often daunted Christian investigators. If we add the additional layer of complexity in investigating the theory of change, they may be inclined to wonder how good research can ever be done. How can we turn promising treatments with a sometimes weak evidence base into those with solid theoretical and research foundations?

Such research must be conducted by a team rather than as an individual thesis or dissertation project or an independent outcome research project by a faculty member. The work of excellent clinical research is too complex for a single investigator. Ideally there should be separate treatment, assessment and statistical analysis teams. In addition, theological and philosophical experts might consult to help formulate and refine the theoretical foundations of the model. These teams might also work together to turn out publications based on the work produced by the team.

Model formulation team. Long before any investigation begins, a theory should be formulated. Issues to address include examination of the (a) worldview assumptions of the secular model, (b) philosophical issues relevant to the study, such as philosophy of science and epistemology, philosophical anthropology, ethics (including the model's maturity ideals), Christian philosophy of religion, (c) theological resources relevant to the interventions (e.g., God's involvement, creation concepts, effects of fallenness, benefits of redemption), and (d) relevant theory and research from outside the Christian community. These considerations should ideally result in a paper that outlines the theoretical framework of the study.

Assessment team. Assessment alone is labor intensive when meeting current standards of high-level outcome research. Assessment must occur at multiple times and each time must involve multiple self-report and other types of measures (other report, physiological, behavioral). Careful consideration should be given to outcome measures, including those that reflect Christian assumptions.

Treatment team. Treatment is also rigorous and requires a team of people to attend to the details. Treatment needs to be done by several psychotherapists of different genders, amounts of experience, and skill levels. People must be randomly assigned to treatments. Manuals must be explicit about what is necessary and what is desirable but not necessary. Areas where clinical judgment is needed should be anticipated. Manuals should tell exactly how a Christian-accommodative approach is changed from the secular to accommodate to Christians. Counselors must rigorously adhere to the manuals. Systematic deviations from the protocol, if they occur across psychotherapists, need to be coded and analyzed to determine whether treatment protocols need adjustment to make them psychotherapist-friendly.

Statistical team. Statistical analysis is becoming increasingly sophisticated. Multilevel modeling can examine the effects of nested variables within other nested variables. But this is far beyond what the average graduate student or professor can do. In fact, having separate data analysis teams—who receive groups of numbers with the identity of the treatment groups masked—can have the added advantage of protecting against data snooping and opportunistic analysis of data to support a researcher's predetermined theoretical preference.

Christian-accommodative cognitive and cognitive-behavioral therapy. We have frequently noted the clinical value of Christian cognitive-behavioral models. The following are some extensions into new areas in CBT. Because of content richness of Christian psychotherapy and counseling, we might expect Christian cognitive therapy to spend significantly more time promoting the understanding of core beliefs that may have special therapeutic value for Christians both in session and as homework.

Other distinctive Christian topics amenable to cognitive therapy include (a) promoting the differentiation of counselee's self-representations between created, fallen and redemptive selves (Johnson, 2007); (b) crucifixion of the old self and world (Gal 2:20; 6:14); and (c) a focus on eternal life in heaven, where the suffering of believers will be forever alleviated and for which they will be perfectly compensated (2 Cor 4:18), and where there will be a perfect judgment against all the evil and abuse suffered.

Christian-accommodative relational therapy. Psychodynamic and relational therapists have highlighted limitations in the psychotherapy-efficacy research to date, noting that it tends to favor relatively brief, manualized treatments in order to promote experimental control, which compromises long-term efficacy. They argue further that substantial, long-term improvement for psychological disorders usually requires longer-term therapy (Levy & Ablon, 2010). There is a small but substantial literature of Christian-accommodative relational therapy, and despite the difficulty in studying the inner workings of relationships, the efficacy of this approach deserves investigation (Hoffman, 2011).

Christian marriage therapy. Cohabitation is on the rise, even among Christians. From a Christian point of view, this is lamentable. However, it is also a reality. No one has worked out a Christian-consistent approach to treating couples who live together and often choose to have children together without marrying. According to the *Time* magazine Pew Survey of 2011, this trend is steadily gaining traction, especially among the non-college educated. So, either Christian couple therapists must turn the couples away (driving them to secular couple therapists); moralize, admonish and coerce marriage (often driving the couples away from Christianity as well as from Christian counsel); or articulate a Christian consistent approach that allows couple therapists to help couples stay engaged in counseling and in their relationships and perhaps move toward marriage. Such an approach is not available at present but is sorely needed.

Christian forgiveness. Treatments exist to help Christians forgive. However, at present they are "blunt instruments," that do not consider some of the specific aspects of Christian forgiveness that need to be addressed. For example, one especially troublesome problem is pastors who fail morally. Each year, perhaps hundreds of thousands of Christians are profoundly affected because a trusted pastor or church leader betrays the trust of the congregation by blatantly sinning. Violations of standards that Christians regard as sacred are particularly difficult to forgive. A similarly pertinent forgiveness issue for Christians is in-group transgressions. These transgressions range from a person who maliciously gossips and sows seeds of dissension to a fellow member of a congregation who slights or offends another member. In-group transgressions are particularly hurtful. We need to work out ways to heal individuals and divided congregations. In addition, splits and differences seem to be increasingly hurtful between denominational bodies (e.g., worldwide Anglican fellowship) and congregations within those fellowships, leading to disputes over resources claimed by both the denomination and the congregation.

Also, special attention needs to be paid to relationships with out-groups. Some Christians make hurtful public statements about people in other religions (i.e., Islam, Buddhism, Judaism, Hinduism), Christian-like sects (i.e., Mormons, Jehovah's Witnesses), people who do not accept Christianity or people who profess Christianity but do not practice. Some make hostile combative statements (often over-generalizations) that favor Israel, or blame or disparage Palestinians, Arab nations, or nations with other religions embraced by the majority of citizens. We live in an increasingly interconnected and interdependent world. We must develop better, more collaborative relationships with those who are not followers of Jesus.

EMPIRICAL INVESTIGATIONS IN RELATIVELY UNEXPLORED REGIONS

Specific disorders. Much of the secular outcome research has focused on examining specific treatments for specific types of disorders. As we have seen, a few studies have examined the impact of Christian CBT with specific psychological problems (see Jennings et al. and Walker et al. in this volume). Obviously, much more work needs to be done examining the efficacy of Christian treatments with various kinds of disorders (an observation first made years ago in Worthington, Kurusu, McCullough & Sandage, 1996).

One controversial area that deserves more empirical attention is treatment for same-sex attraction. Contrary to the position of modern psychiatry and psychotherapy, some Christians continue to believe that same-sex attraction is sinful and a psychological abnormality. Other Christians, however, do not consider homosexuality to be a psychological disorder. Some Christian psychotherapists have developed models of psychotherapy for those who consider same-sex attraction to be incongruent with their Christian faith and wish to attempt to modify their orientation (Hamilton & Henry, 2009; Yarhouse & Burkett, 2003). For example, a quasi-experimental study of the impact of weekly support group involvement on ninety-eight Christian believers over six to seven years found that a slight majority felt the treatment was a success, and a reduction in same-sex attraction was found in 23% of the clients (Jones & Yarhouse, 2011).The success found with support-group involvement alone for such an intractable disposition would seem to warrant research on Christian psychotherapy and counseling for same-sex attraction. However, on the other hand, reviews by the American Psychological Association have concluded that the empirical evidence favors not attempting to change orientation. In the spirit of listening to psychological research—that is, the evidence base of treatments—which we have championed in this book, we suggest that neither side has a conclusive case at this point. If clients seek psychotherapy aimed at changing same-sex attraction, this should not be withheld, and we should not categorically eliminate providing new empirical evidence on this topic. Furthermore, advocates of reorientation therapy should realize that the empirical base is not firm and rates of change are far below those usual with Axis I disorders (i.e., more acute problems) and comparable to serious Axis II disorders (i.e., chronic personality changes).

Pastoral care. Pastors are not trained in psychotherapy, and they typically receive little training in counseling (though some may receive a fair amount of training in pastoral care). Nonetheless they are called on to counsel people on a regular basis—a reality that highlights the value of research on pastoral counseling. Unfortunately, very little research has been done in this area. There are likely many reasons for this lack of research. Few pastors and pastoral theologians are trained in empirical methods, and historically, those who are trained have tended to favor qualitative methods (O'Connor, Koning, Meakes, McLarnon-Sinclair, Davis & Loy, 2001). On the other hand, many conservative pastors have tended to favor biblical counseling (Tripp, 2002), an approach which historically has been uninterested in documenting its effectiveness and in some cases has even been antagonistic toward research efforts (Adams, 2011). However, pastoral counselors, who are typically clergy with seminary training and at least a master's degree in counseling or psychotherapy, do have substantial training and therefore seem uniquely equipped to contribute to advancing evidence-based practice research in this area.

Collaboration between pastoral care and Christian mental health professionals. Another area that deserves further investigation is the collaboration between Christian ministers and churches and professional Christian psychotherapists and counselors. In premodern cultures, most psychological care was administered by religious leaders. Even in contemporary cultures, it would be ideal for the Christian community to develop a continuum of care beginning with ministers in local churches who then refer to professional counselors for problems outside their expertise and to licensed psychologists and psychiatrists for the most serious problems. Research on such a collaborative agenda has begun relatively recently (see McMinn & Dominquez, 2005), so much work remains in this area.

Christian spiritual direction and spiritual formation. Spiritual direction is a form of Christian soul care that has been around for centuries. Many have argued for an integration of Christian psychotherapy and spiritual direction when desired by counselees (Benner, 2005). Coe and Hall (2010) have recently described a complex model that combines spiritual direction and relational psychotherapy that could be researched. Moreover, Garzon (see chapter 4) recommended the use of three kinds of devotional meditation, all of which can be categorized as forms of spiritual direction.

Spiritual direction usually relies on various spiritual disciplines to promote psychospiritual well-being. Such disciplines include (a) Scripture memorization, (b) prayer, (c) meditation, (d) silence and solitude, (e) fasting, (f) bibliotherapy, (g) self-examination and confession and (h) involvement in social action, as well as (i) teaching about spiritual direction concepts and inner activities such as purgation, contrition, mortification, detachment, recollection, contemplation, union and spiritual betrothal (Tan, 2003). In spite of its use over the centuries, there has been no systematic investigation of the psychospiritual benefits of most Christian spiritual direction or spiritual disciplines. In addition, different forms of spiritual direction have developed over the centuries (Moon & Benner, 2004), and eventually study of the respective therapeutic value of these traditions would be desirable.

Models of lay counseling. Tan (see chapter 3) reviews a number of promising approaches to Christian lay counseling that currently do not meet the criteria for evidence-supported practice. However, research has suggested they have strong potential. Tan also reported on one model of lay counseling that has some empirical support. Here we consider lay models of helping that have been written about and are being widely used in the Christian community, but have not yet been studied. Because of their enormous popularity among lay Christians and the fact that they have arisen outside of the Christian psychotherapeutic and counseling communities, we might consider them to be "grass-roots" lay-counseling movements. There are basically two streams in the literature that deserve empirical attention: Christian truth models and healing prayer models.

Christian truth models. One stream focuses particularly on the application of Christian truth to individual problems. Some lay counselors emphasize the need to make a commitment to the truth and against "lies." These models share some features in common with cognitive-behavioral approaches. Among some of the most popular and well-developed are nouthetic counseling, biblical counseling, "seven steps to freedom," and spirituotherapy (for a partial review, see Garzon, Tan, E. Worthington & R. Worthington, 2009). Nouthetic and biblical counseling have been favored by many pastors. In addition, a few similar models designed for laypeople have been further developed by Christian professionals in the field.

Healing prayer models. Another stream has focused more on emotions and (often) on painful memories (for a partial review, see Garzon, Tan, E. Worthington & R. Worthington, 2009). Many approaches in this stream are associated with the practice of healing prayer, including the Sanfords' healing prayer, Seamands's healing of emotions, Leanne Payne's pastoral care ministry model, theophostic prayer ministry, and biblical healing and deliverance (see Garzon et al., 2009).

Summary. In spite of the wide use of these models in the Christian community and much anecdotal evidence of their value, little research has been done on them. This is in part due to the fact that few of them were developed by psychologists and others familiar with empirical research, and most of the works associated with them have been written for lay audiences. However, they are notable for the degree of distinctive Christian content that characterizes them. This no doubt is due in part to the fact that they were developed by those who were not especially socialized by the contemporary field of psychology. However, this is also their weakness. In order for these models to be researched empirically, some of their proponents must carefully formulate their respective models and develop well-designed treatment manuals, perhaps with the help of those in the field of psychology. The widespread use of these models in the church and the richness of their Christian orientation suggests there is a need for developing these approaches into formal Christian counseling models that can be tested.

CONCLUSION

In the present chapter, we have looked at the current status of the promising evidence-based treatments that have been described and reviewed in this book. From a bird's-eye view, we conclude that the empirical basis for the treatment of clients using evidence-based treatments is relatively weak. However, there is some research supporting many Christian-accommodative approaches. Furthermore, there is research that suggests that the secular approaches on which many of the Christian-accommodative approaches are built are well-established.

We also described some Christian-accommodative approaches that need additional research to provide an empirical basis for their use. Some are heavily used in the Christian community and many are well-justified in terms of scriptural support. Yet they simply have not attracted investigators who have been able to study the approaches with sufficient rigor to bring the scientific reports to publication. We encourage clinical researchers to continue to investigate and bring more empirical support to established approaches, as well as to research new approaches in order to provide a larger evidence base for Christian treatments.

REFERENCES

Adams, J. E. (1972). *Competent to counsel.* Philadelphia: Presbyterian and Reformed Publishing Company.

Adams, J. (2011). What empirical evidence do you have that nouthetic counseling is superior to other forms of counseling. Retrieved from www.nouthetic.org /nouthetic-counseling/adams-answers/77-what-empirical-evidence-do -you-have-that-nouthetic-counseling-is-superior-to-other-forms-of-counseling .html.

Benner, D. G. (2005). Intensive soul care: Integrating psychotherapy and spiritual direction. In L. Sperry & E. P. Shafranske (Eds.), *Spiritually oriented psychotherapy* (pp. 287-306). Washington, DC: American Psychological Association.

Coe, J. H., & Hall, T. W. (2010). *Psychology in the Spirit: Contours of a transformational psychology.* Downers Grove, IL: InterVarsity Press.

David, D., & Montgomery, G. H. (2011). The scientific status of psychotherapies: A new evaluative framework for evidence-based psychosocial interventions. *Clinical Psychology: Science and Practice, 18*(2), 89-104.

Enright, R. D., & Fitzgibbons, R. P. (2000). *Helping clients forgive: An empirical guide for resolving anger and restoring hope.* Washington, DC: American Psychological Association.

Freedman, S. R., & Enright, R. D. (1996). Forgiveness as an intervention with incest survivors. *Journal of Consulting and Clinical Psychology, 64,* 983-92.

Garzon, F., Tan, S.-Y., Worthington, E. L., Jr., & Worthington, R. K. (2009). Lay counseling approaches and the integration of psychology and Christianity. *Journal of Psychology and Christianity, 28*(2), 113-20.

Gordon, K. C., Baucom, D. H., & Snyder, D. K. (2004). An integrative intervention for promoting recovery from extramarital affairs. *Journal of Marital and Family Therapy, 30,* 213-31.

Gottman, J. M. (1999). *The marriage clinic: A scientifically based marital therapy.* New York: W. W. Norton.

Greenberg, L. J., Warwar, S. H., & Malcolm, W. M. (2008). Differential effects of emotion-focused therapy and psychoeducation in facilitating forgiveness and letting go of emotional injuries. *Journal of Counseling Psychology, 55,* 185-96.

Hamilton, J. H., & Henry, P. J. (2009). *Handbook of therapy for unwanted homosexual attractions: A guide to treatment.* Maitland, FL: Xulon Press.

Hoffman, M. T. (2011). *Toward mutual recognition: Relational psychoanalysis and the Christian narrative.* New York: Routledge.

Hoyt, W. T., Wade, N. G., & Worthington, E. L., Jr. (2012). *Group promotion of forgiveness: A meta-analysis.* Unpublished manuscript, University of Wisconsin–Madison.

Jakubowski, S. F., Milne, E. P., Brunner, H., & Miller, R. B. (2004). A review of empirically supported marital enrichment programs. *Family Relations, 53,* 528-36.

Johnson, E. L. (2007). *Foundations for soul care: A Christian psychology proposal.* Downers Grove, IL: InterVarsity Press.

Jones, S., & Yarhouse, M. (2011). A longitudinal study of attempted religiously mediated sexual orientation change. *Journal of Sex & Marital Therapy, 37,* 404-27.

Kidwell, J. E., Wade, N. G., & Blaedel, E. (2012). Understanding forgiveness in the lives of religious people: The role of sacred and secular elements. *Mental Health, Religion, and Culture, 15*(2), 121-40.

Levy, R. A., & Ablon, J. S. (Eds.). (2010). *Handbook of evidence-based psychodynamic psychotherapy: Bridging the gap between science and practice.* New York: Humana.

McHugh, R. K., & Barlow, D. H. (2010). The dissemination and implementation of evidence-based psychological treatments: A review of current efforts. *American Psychologist, 65*(2), 73-84.

McMinn, M. R., & Campbell, C. D. (2008). *Integrative psychotherapy: Toward a comprehensive Christian approach.* Downers Grove, IL: InterVarsity Press.

McMinn, M. R., & Dominquez, A. W. (Eds.). (2005). *Psychology and the church.* New York: Nova Science Publishers.

Moon, G. W., & Benner, D. G. (2004). *Spiritual direction and the care of souls: A guide to Christian approaches and practices.* Downers Grove, IL: InterVarsity.

Norcross, J. C. (Ed.). (2011). *Psychotherapy relationships that work: Evidence-based responsiveness* (2nd ed.). New York: Oxford University Press.

O'Connor, T. S., Koning, F., Meakes, E., McLarnon-Sinclair, K., Davis, K., & Loy, V. (2001). Quantity and rigor of qualitative research in four pastoral counseling journals. *Journal of Pastoral Care, 55* (3), 271-80.

Shidlo, A., & Schroeder, M. (2002). Changing sexual orientation: A consumers' report. *Professional Psychology: Research and Practice, 33,* 249-59.

Tan, S.-Y. (2003). Integrating spiritual direction into psychotherapy: Ethical issues and guidelines. *Journal of Psychology and Theology, 31*(1), 14-23.

Pew Research Center (2010). The decline of marriage and rise of new families. www .pewsocialtrends.org/2010/11/18/the-decline-of-marriage-and-rise-of-new-families.

Tripp, P. D. (2002). *Instruments in the redeemer's hands.* Phillipsburg, NJ: Presbyterian & Reformed Publishing.

Wade, N. G., Worthington, E. L., Jr., & Vogel, D. L. (2007). Effectiveness of religiously tailored interventions in Christian therapy. *Psychotherapy Research, 17,* 91-105.

Worthington, E. L., Jr. (1989). *Marriage counseling: A Christian approach to counseling couples.* Downers Grove, IL: InterVarsity Press.

Worthington, E. L., Jr. (1999). *Hope-focused marriage counseling.* Downers Grove, IL: InterVarsity Press.

Worthington, E. L., Jr. (2006). *Forgiveness and reconciliation: Theory and application.* New York: Brunner-Routledge.

Worthington, E. L., Jr., Hight, T. L., Ripley, J. S., Perrone, K. M., Kurusu, T. A., & Jones, D. R. (1997). Strategic hope-focused relationship-enrichment counseling with individual couples. *Journal of Counseling Psychology, 44,* 381-89.

Worthington, E. L., Jr., Hook, J. N., Davis, D. E., & McDaniel, M. E. (2011). Religion and spirituality. *Journal of Clinical Psychology: In Session, 67*(2), 204-14.

Worthington, E. L., Jr., Kurusu, T. A., McCullough, M. E., & Sandage, S. J. (1996). Empirical research on religion and psychotherapeutic processes and outcomes: A 10-year review and research prospectus. *Psychological Bulletin, 199,* 448-87.

Yarhouse, M. A., & Burkett, L. A. (2003). *Sexual identity: A guide to living in the time between the times.* Lanham, MD: University Press of America.

Table 14.1. Bird's-Eye View

Chapter	Authors	Evidence for Theory of Change	Evidence for Secular Version	Evidence for Explicitly Christian or Christian-Accommodative Version
2 Relationship and Therapist Factors	Stegman, Kelly & Harwood	Lots of evidence for why some of the relationship factors produce change but not so much for others. Relationships can be quite complex. For example, one just has to think about psychodynamic, emotionally focused, cognitive, interpersonal, and behavioral psychotherapists to see that, while relationship factors are important, what precisely goes into a therapeutic relationship can vary dramatically and yet still be equally effective at stimulating or facilitating change.	Evidence that relationship factors produce change is strong; recent meta-analyses in Norcross (2011) document many relationship factors that are important. **Therapeutic alliance, expectancy and empathy are well documented, as are qualities like expertness and attractiveness of the psychotherapist.** Matching of client and therapist on some variables can be important or not so much. Religious matching matters.	Norcross, Worthington, Hook, Davis and McDaniel investigate religious/spiritual (R/S) accommodation. R/S accommodative treatments tend to produce change that is not much different from secular treatments. However, R/S accommodative treatments tend to be preferred by clients and to produce superior spiritual well-being relative to secular treatments. The amount of research that compares the two head-on, however, is weak at this point. In general, nonspecific relationship factors have been rarely studied in explicitly Christian psychotherapy except for matching clients, treatments, and psychotherapists on religious factors. **R/S matching was considered an empirically supported relationship factor at the highest degree of evidence by Norcross (2011).**
3 Lay Counseling	Tan	In many ways, lay counseling is not as much a treatment modality as it is a therapist factor, which is comparable to relationship factors (in chapter 2). Lay counseling suggests a theory of change that similarities between counselor and client might produce more responsiveness by the client, better working alliance, better receptivity to counselor suggestion.	Lay and paraprofessional counseling has been thoroughly investigated. **Typically, secular treatments that compare lay, paraprofessional and professional counselors find that they are comparable when the problems are mild or moderate.** However, professional counselors typically get better outcomes on severe problems and when following a treatment manual.	Christian lay counseling has been tested quite a number of times. It has been shown to be effective when comparing pre- to post-treatment (with no control group). It is better than untreated controls. Lay Christian counseling has been tested in a variety of labs and has been found to be effective relative to controls. **Lay Christian counseling is considered to be an empirically supported relationship factor.**

Table 14.1. Bird's-Eye View (Continued)

Chapter	Authors	Evidence for Theory of Change	Evidence for Secular Version	Evidence for Explicitly Christian or Christian-Accommodative Version
4 Devotional Meditation	Garzon	There is no theory of change put forth to account for why spiritual meditation should produce less anxiety, better mood and better pain control. One might assume that spiritual mediation might attune people to God and bring peace, but this has not been tested. The theory of change needs to be carefully articulated and tested.	Wachholtz and Pargament (2005, 2008) conducted two studies (84 and 83 participants, respectively) that compared spiritual meditation with secular meditation and relaxation. **In general, research on secular meditation has found it to be efficacious.**	Carlson et al. (1988) studied CDM compared to a no treatment group using a total of 36 participants. Wachholtz and Pargament (2005, 2008) conducted two other studies (84 and 83 participants, respectively) involving scriptural meditation. Neither was done on a clinically troubled population. The two methods are related in that they both use meditation, and yet they are clearly more different than similar. The spiritual meditation was superior in reporting less anxiety and better mood in both studies and also increased pain control in the latter study, so the finding that spiritual meditation is superior is encouraging. However, the research comes from a single lab. **Spiritual meditation is considered, at this point, promising for non-clinical application.** On the strong side, this method has more research supporting its use in a religiously tailored treatment than with secular people—a rarity in this book.
5 Cognitive Therapy for Depression	Jennings, Hook, Davis & Worthington	Change is produced by changing cognition, which produces changes in emotion and behavior. Substantial experimental evidence that this can occur; however, changes in environment, emotion and behavior also produce change in cognition. Kahneman (2011) also shows that cognition is not as rational as cognitive therapies make it seem, so the theory of change is oversimplified.	**The evidence base for CBT is huge and uncontested.** Cognitive therapy produces change in many clients. The approach requires establishing a collaborative set, teaching the cognitive paradigm, and using recognized methods and techniques of cognitive therapy—not merely dealing haphazardly or even systematically with thoughts and behaviors (which it can be argued that all approaches do).	Of the treatments covered in this book, this approach is the best researched, especially for treating depression. Generally, accommodating the treatment explicitly to Christians has not improved it markedly over secular CBT treatment. **Cognitive or cognitive-behavioral therapy is considered to be an empirically supported treatment for depression, and promising for other targets of treatment.**

Table 14.1. Bird's-Eye View (Continued)

Chapter	Authors	Evidence for Theory of Change	Evidence for Secular Version	Evidence for Explicitly Christian or Christian-Accommodative Version
6 Trauma-Focused Cognitive-Behavioral Therapy for Children and Adolescents	Walker, Quagliani, Wilkinson & Frederick	Change is produced by changing cognition, which produces changes in emotion and behavior. There is substantial experimental evidence that this can occur; however, changes in environment, emotion and behavior also produce change in cognition. It is unclear, however, whether the same research that supports a CBT model for adults applies when the clients are children and adolescents.	TF-CBT has been investigated in secular form by several treatment studies. **TF-CBT is arguably the most empirically supported treatment method** for children and teens who have been victims of childhood physical and sexual abuse. Online training is available and it is well disseminated.	The Christian-accommodative approach to TF-CBT follows the components of the secular method, but it adapts each to particular issues with Christian children and adolescents. There is substantial empirical support for most of the elements that make up the secular model, but there is no research that investigates how or whether the Christian accommodation helps, hurts or does not affect the effectiveness of the secular model. **Overall, the Christian-accommodative version is best evaluated as untested.**
7 Psychodynamic and Process-Experiential Psychotherapies	Edwards & Davis	Both process-experiential and psychodynamic therapies have long histories of secular research supporting theories of change. Psychodynamic theory describes change as occurring as a result of a variety of mechanisms, depending on the theory. These mechanisms can range from re-parenting, getting insight and exerting ego control over basic impulses, and reworking of the attachment relationship. Edwards and Davis suggest three processes: accessing and allowing emotional experience, relational processing and making sense of emotional experience, and transformation and restructuring of emotional experience. These are hypothesized to take place in three therapeutic phases. Little research supports the sequencing, but substantial research supports the three processes.	Both process-experiential and psychodynamic therapies have long histories of secular research on treatment programs. Many psychodynamic treatments—long-term and short-term are considered evidence-based though, as Edwards and Davis observe, only two are considered to have evidence supporting **probably effective status** and none justifying empirically supported status. **Process-experiential treatments, while not having the same degree of support as psychodynamic treatments, are nonetheless well supported and several have empirically supported status.**	There are no randomized controlled trials examining the efficacy of Christian-accommodative psychodynamic treatments. Two studies have supported the efficacy but neither one employed control treatments. However, there is a strong secular base of studies and generalization at least draws on strong evidence. Similarly, no studies[a] have tested Christian-accommodative process-experiential treatment. **The combination of the two, put forth by Edwards and Davis, is strong conceptually and logically, and it is rooted in personal psychotherapy experience of many practitioners, but at this time it must be considered untested empirically.**

Table 14.1. Bird's-Eye View (Continued)

Chapter	Authors	Evidence for Theory of Change	Evidence for Secular Version	Evidence for Explicitly Christian or Christian-Accommodative Version
8 The SYMBIS Model	Parrott & Parrott	At the root of the SYMBIS theory for marital preparation, enrichment and therapy is Bowen's family systems theory of differentiation of self. People learn to identify unconscious roles and rules that govern their couple patterns. In addition, there is a developmental assumption that unconscious forces act on couples differently as they tackle different life tasks. If each partner can uncover and learn to exert ego control over those patterns, the couple interactions should be better. Whereas there is a huge wealth of experience that supports these Bowenian assumptions, experimental evidence in support is not voluminous, though it is not absent either.	SYMBIS draws eclectically from many approaches with an overall integrating theory of Bowen family systems. Many of the secular methods have substantial support empirically. The Parrotts have conscientiously tried to use empirically justified components in their treatment throughout. It has been used widely in the secular arena. The Parrotts worked with the state of Oklahoma one year, and promulgated the use throughout the state. Thus, **the SYMBIS model has been widely used but has not in itself been tested in the secular arena.**	Jakubowski et al. (2004) evaluated the SYMBIS model as promising. However, only one study supports it, and that study is not a randomized clinical trial. Despite the widespread employment of the SYMBIS method, the evidence base is not systematic or documented. The wide usage warrants the attention of investigators. **From an experimental point of view, SYMBIS would have to be deemed untested as a whole.**
9 Christian PREP	Barnes & Stanley	Commitment is a key variable producing change in couples' communications, intimacy and conflict patterns. Also, willingness to sacrifice is vital to good marriage. Stanley has created and accumulated much evidence of this theory of change. The approach also draws heavily on integrative behavioral and cognitive methods, which have a good research base as a theory of change. Barnes and Stanley provide a thorough set of supports from Scripture for the principles of the CPREP approach.	Secular PREP was evaluated as one of four empirically supported couple enrichment approaches. It has been used nationwide and tested empirically in numerous research labs in numerous studies. **PREP has perhaps the strongest empirical base and is empirically supported as enrichment.**	Among the relationship enrichment approaches, only CPREP has evidence as an explicitly Christian accommodative treatment. Its approach has been supported in a large dissemination trial, but the research with Christians is from one lab. Barnes and Stanley argue that, in many ways, CPREP and PREP are at root fundamentally Christian. However, **from the empirical studies, we conclude that CPREP must be considered promising.**

Table 14.1. Bird's-Eye View (Continued)

Chapter	Authors	Evidence for Theory of Change	Evidence for Secular Version	Evidence for Explicitly Christian or Christian-Accommodative Version
10 Hope-Focused Couples Approach	Ripley, Maclin, Hook & Worthington	The theory of change has three elements: (1) to promote hope, (2) to teach a strategy of faith, work and love and (3) to use methods that make change "sensible," which the authors define as using methods that rely on structural or behavioral manipulations as well as talk—not just discussion alone. They evaluate the evidence as partially supporting the theory of change and urge additional research on the uninvestigated aspects of the theory of change.	**The secular version of the HFCA has been evaluated as an empirically supported approach to couple enrichment.** The secular version of the HFCA for couple therapy is supported in one study. Thus, **the HFCA is considered to be promising as a secular therapy.**	The efficacy of the Christian version of the HFCA relies in large part to extensions from the secular version. Explicitly Christian versions of both couple therapy and enrichment have been developed, with training materials, a book, DVDs, and other training resources. The explicitly Christian version for couple therapy has been found in completed and ongoing research to be comparable to the secular approach. The dissemination of the approach is beginning to be established (Hook & Worthington, 2009). **Overall, the evidence supports the HFCA as promising as an explicitly Christian approach to couple therapy, but it is untested in the Christian setting as a couple enrichment approach. It has broad usage with evidence supporting secular and Christian versions and the theory of change.**

Table 14.1. Bird's-Eye View (Continued)

Chapter	Authors	Evidence for Theory of Change	Evidence for Secular Version	Evidence for Explicitly Christian or Christian-Accommodative Version
11 Marital Conflict and Restoration Model	Sells	The theory of change rests on principles from the emotionally focused couple therapy (EFCT) and contextual family therapy (CFT) approaches. EFCT theory holds that individuals conduct life and form relationships through internal models of relationship in which the world is seen through a variation of safe and trustworthy images, and dangerous and uncertain images. These attachment models, when threatened, elicit a protective response to defend the self and the relationship. EFCT advocates creating trust that can repair the damaged attachments. CFT is about perceived injustices in sacrifice and love. CFT seeks to restore balanced family processes to form the foundation to build trust. Change occurs when fair exchanges of regard and respect are re-established. The evidence related to attachments is good, but less is related to CFT. A couple of research studies have investigated the particular combination advocated by the Marital Conflict and Restoration Model.	One research project (called a pilot study) studied the marital conflict and restoration model (MCRM) with 12 couples. **Evidence is available on secular EFCT,** and to the extent that MCRM shares that approach, the evidence is generalizable. **Fewer empirical controlled trials support CFT.** There is considerable usage by secular therapists of the CFT, and the clinical experience lends some generalizability to the method. **There is also support for each of the ten components of the MCRM.** The difficulty in evaluating the degree of research supporting the MCRM is the degree to which the evidence supporting each approach (EFCT and CFT) and each component is additive when incorporated in the MCRM. **Without explicit outcome research except for a small pilot study, it is impossible to classify the method as more than promising (at best).**	There are no studies that investigate the MCRM approach with Christian accommodation used with Christian couples. **The Christian-accommodative method is at best promising and is more accurately described as untested.**

Table 14.1. Bird's-Eye View (Continued)

Chapter	Authors	Evidence for Theory of Change	Evidence for Secular Version	Evidence for Explicitly Christian or Christian-Accommodative Version
12 Forgiveness in Couples	DiBlasio	In general, the theory of change in treatment of couple problems by forgiveness is not well specified. DiBlasio implies that making an explicit decision to forgive will generalize change; this is untested. Greenberg's theory implies that forgiveness helps people repair attachment bonds. Gordon, Baucom and Snyder suggest that change comes about because people make cognitive changes and also gain deeper psychodynamic insights in the latter stages of treatment. There is a huge data base relating cognition to change and also psychodynamic insights to change. Worthington claims that forgiveness helps repair the emotional bond in couples, which results in a stronger relationship. There is a lot of support across basic relationship and couple therapy research supporting this theory of change.	Several secular forgiveness approaches have tried to promote forgiveness in secular couples. Among those are **DiBlasio's** two studies (but one data collection effort), **Greenberg's** emotionally focused empty-chair intervention to promote forgiveness (two separate studies but from the same lab), and **Gordon, Baucom and Snyder's** treatment for infidelity (several separate studies, but all from the labs of the originators). These are considered promising approaches. **Worthington's REACH or FREE model has been investigated in several studies from at least two independent labs. Only Worthington's approach is empirically supported, but it deals with couple enrichment rather than couple therapy.**	DiBlasio reports in detail on his decision-based couples approach, which has compared Christian and secular responses. While DiBlasio has reported several studies, all of the research comes from his lab. Only DiBlasio's approach to promoting forgiveness in couples has any evidence base. **DiBlasio's decision-based forgiveness with Christian couples is considered a promising approach.**
13 Group Interventions for Forgiveness	Kidwell & Wade	Group nonspecific factors are thought to provide part of the impetus for change in the group promotion of forgiveness. In process groups, those factors tend to be magnified. In psychoeducational groups, factors are not as salient, but content of producing emotional transformation within a relational context are thought to produce change. Secular research provides a rich background supporting both nonspecific and psychoeducational factors, but these have not been investigated in Christian-accommodative groups.	**Secular forgiveness groups have been shown to be effective in about 50 or more randomized clinical trials.** The most frequently effective with **psychotherapy problems are Enright's.** In psychoeducation, **Worthington's** has been most researched, although Enright's has been frequently tested as well. Other treatments, such as Luskin's, Rye's, and others are less often researched. In sum, **Enright's process forgiveness therapy and process model for psychoeducation and Worthington's REACH forgiveness psychoeducational groups are empirically supported with strong evidence.**	Only Worthington's REACH forgiveness and Rye's approach (which has been drawn from the REACH model) have been explicitly tested with Christians. **Worthington's REACH forgiveness approach is considered empirically supported**, with multiple research studies from four independent labs. **The group process model has been tested in only one lab and is considered to be promising.**

15

Conducting Clinical Outcome Studies in Christian Counseling and Psychotherapy

Joshua N. Hook, Everett L. Worthington Jr.,
Jamie D. Aten and Eric Johnson

The chapters in the present volume have described practices in Christian psychotherapy that are supported by evidence. Although historically there has been relatively little rigorous research evaluating religious psychotherapies (Johnson, 1993), this appears to be changing as the number of outcome studies has increased over the past ten years (see Hook et al., 2010; Post & Wade, 2009; Smith, Bartz & Richards, 2007; Worthington, Hook, Davis & McDaniel, 2011, for recent reviews and meta-analyses). As Christian psychologists who value both practice and research, we are encouraged by this development.

The purpose of the present chapter is to provide guidelines for researchers and clinicians who would like to add to the growing body of literature on evidence-based practices in Christian psychotherapy by conducting clinical outcome research. The information in this chapter is based on the guidelines presented by the division 12 task forces on (a) psychological intervention guidelines (APA Task Force on Psychological Intervention Guidelines, 1995) and (b) promotion and dissemination of psychological procedures (Task Force on Promotion and Dissemination of Psychological Procedures, 1995; see Chambless & Hollon, 1998 for a summary of these guidelines). We also provide information about issues specific to conducting research on Christian psychotherapy. We provide guidelines for best practices in several areas, including research design, participants, outcome assessment, treatment implementation and data analysis. We conclude by offering a logical progression for conducting research on a Christian psychotherapy. Throughout this chapter, we also acknowledge some challenges that may present for Christians interested in conducting clinical outcome studies and provide some suggestions for addressing these challenges.

Our hope is that even more clinicians will team up with clinical researchers to create better documented evidence-based treatments and more Christian treatments that are firmly grounded in clinical research evidence. We believe that the future of practice will be to some extent dependent on showing our clients and other observers (such as third-party payers and the gatekeepers of our profession) that Christian treatments are efficacious (in controlled trials) and effective when they are taken into the actual clinic.

RESEARCH DESIGN

Understanding treatment efficacy and effectiveness. Some have argued that psychotherapists should only use psychotherapy techniques or models that have "proven" clinical value according to high quality experimental studies. Others have expressed concern that evidence-based practices are not relevant to the "real" world. In this section we try to get at the heart of both of these arguments—and show that both camps make valid points. Both approaches are needed if we are going to advance the best of what science and practice have to offer.

As a result of these concerns, when evaluating the base of evidence for a treatment, researchers now distinguish between its efficacy and its effectiveness. Put simply, *efficacy* refers to the extent to which a treatment is shown to work under highly controlled research conditions (particularly those involving randomly assigning clients to treatment conditions) in which it is reasonable to conclude that the treatment did in fact cause a desired outcome (e.g., decreased depression). *Effectiveness* refers to the extent to which a treatment is shown to work in actual clinical practice (Chambless & Hollon, 1998). This distinction is important in showing that treatments really work. Research studies that stress efficacy tend to be higher in internal validity but lower in external validity. That is, the researchers have documented what occurred within the particular clinical study, but the results do not as easily generalize to other clinical contexts. On the other hand, research studies that stress effectiveness tend to be higher in external validity but lower in internal validity. That is, they reflect more closely what is actually done in clinical practice, but the results are somewhat more questionable because of limitations in the research design.

When first establishing empirical support for a specific treatment, the focus is generally on efficacy research conducted in a highly controlled manner. Those strict controls permit more confidence that a treatment—and not merely the personality of the clinician or client, the particular relationship, or local practices—is really causing the effect on clients. Effectiveness research is viewed as vitally important, but it is usually conducted after a psychotherapy has been shown to be efficacious. When conducting efficacy research, randomized controlled trials are the gold standard (Atkins, 2009). In that type of study, participants are randomly assigned either to (a) the treatment of interest, or (b) one or more comparison conditions. The comparison condition could be a waitlist control condition or an alternate treatment, and the alternate treatment might be more or less similar to the treatment of interest. In treatments examining a type of Christian psychotherapy, some alternative treatments are similar in virtually every way except for the Christian content. Others are treatments that are thought to be efficacious but might not be similar to the treatment of interest. An example of an efficacy study is one of the earlier studies on Christian psychotherapy where depressed college students were randomly assigned to one of three conditions: (a) Christian cognitive-behavioral therapy, (b) secular cognitive-behavioral therapy, or (c) waitlist control (Pecheur & Edwards, 1984).

Importance of replication. In psychotherapy outcome research, replication of findings by independent investigators is very important for a number of reasons (Chambless & Hollon, 1998). Statistical fluctuations occur and one study might make a treatment look efficacious when the efficacy was due merely to chance. But replication is also important because, even in the most carefully controlled studies, some of the active ingredients producing client change might not be exactly what the study's authors thought to be the case. If another independent lab attempts to do the same study and arrives at a different outcome, local variations might be at work—for example, the type of training that the originators of a treatment provided the psychotherapists who did the treatment in the first study. In such cases, unique features of a particular study may influence the results, rather than the actual treatment itself. To be deemed *efficacious*, a treatment must either (a) outperform a control condition or (b) be equivalent to a treatment already established in efficacy in at least two research studies by at least two independent research teams. If only one study supports a treatment's efficacy, or if multiple studies from only one research group support a treatment's efficacy, the treatment is deemed *possibly efficacious*. If a treatment outperforms an alternate treatment or placebo in at least two research studies by at least two independent research teams, the treatment is deemed *efficacious and specific*. The same criteria of replication apply to designations of specificity.

There is a limitation to the designations of efficacy and specificity. The designations of *efficacious, possibly efficacious*, or even *efficacious and specific* do not tell how strong (or influential) a treatment is. Rather they tell how confident we may be that the treatment can produce therapeutic effects that are not due to chance. Imagine a very strong treatment that thus far researchers have only studied with a single clinical trial. That treatment (which is designated possibly efficacious) might be much stronger than an efficacious treatment that has been studied and found efficacious in two independent labs. The designation speaks to the confidence we have that a treatment can produce some therapeutic effect but does not tell how large the effect is or whether its effects are larger or smaller than some other treatment.

Evaluating effect of religious elements. One interesting aspect of outcome research on Christian psychotherapies involves evaluating whether the religious aspects of the psychotherapy had any specific effects on outcome. Did the change detected actually come from the religious aspects of the intervention, or was the change caused by another factor? The most rigorous evaluations of Christian psychotherapies compare a Christian treatment with an alternate treatment in which the two treatments are absolutely similar except for the religious components. This is called a *dis-*

mantling design because the Christian component is being dismantled from the rest of the treatment (Worthington et al., 2011).

For example, Rye and Pargament (2002) compared two group forgiveness interventions, one that incorporated Christianity and one that did not. The two forgiveness interventions utilized the same theoretical orientation and duration of treatment, but differed on whether or not religious components were included. On the other hand, Carlson, Bacaseta and Simanton (1988) compared levels of anxiety between participants who were involved in a Christian devotional meditation intervention and participants who were involved in a progressive relaxation intervention. The progressive relaxation intervention was a bona fide alternate treatment, but it differed from the Christian treatment in theoretical orientation. If differences appear between these two treatments, it is difficult to determine whether (a) the Christian components caused these differences or (b) other differences between the two treatments caused the differences. This is why the dismantling design provides the most confidence that the Christian aspects of treatment are making a difference.

Statistical power and sample size considerations. Many psychotherapy outcome research studies suffer from low statistical power. This is a technical term that quantifies the likelihood of actually finding an effect when it exists. Chambless and Hollon (1998) note that to discover a medium-sized difference between two treatment groups with 80% power, a researcher must have at least fifty participants per condition. In contrast, in a recent review of religious and spiritual psychotherapies, the median sample size per condition in studies of Christian psychotherapies was thirteen (Hook et al., 2010). The effect of including a Christian framework would have to be *huge* to show a statistical effect. Not surprisingly, in most studies examining psychological symptom reduction, participants in Christian treatments did not statistically differ from the secular treatments; however, participants in the Christian treatments did show more gains in spiritual health outcomes (Worthington et al., 2011).

Low sample sizes are less problematic when one treatment clearly outperforms another, but they do raise concerns when claims of efficacy are made on the basis of equivalent results. For example, Johnson and Ridley (1992) compared Christian and secular versions of rational emotive therapy for depression, and reported no differences between conditions. However, with only five participants per condition, it is difficult to determine whether the equivalent findings stemmed from actual equivalence of treatments or a lack of statistical power to detect differences between conditions. To prevent problems such as this, Chambless and Hollon recommended that a study must have a sample size of twenty-five to thirty participants per condition to determine efficacy based on equivalent results.

Quasi-experimental designs. Although we agree that randomized clinical trials are the gold standard in psychotherapy outcome research, we note that these studies are often difficult and expensive to conduct and are not feasible for every type of researcher and clinician. We believe that there are other types of research designs that are helpful in developing the base of evidence for Christian psychotherapies. Quasi-experimental designs involve research that in some way falls short of a true experiment. Because of this, such designs often suffer from one or more problems with internal validity. Three common types of quasi-experimental designs in outcome research on Christian psychotherapies are single-case experiments, the two-group comparative design, and the single-group pretest-posttest design.

Single-case experiments. Single-case experiments involve administering a treatment to a single participant and measuring its effects repeatedly over time (Barlow, Nock & Hersen, 2008). Before administering the treatment, the researcher must establish a baseline measure of the outcome, preferably at a minimum of three time points. Two common single-case experimental designs are ABAB design and multiple baseline designs. In the ABAB design, the baseline is established (A), improvement occurs with treatment (B), reversal or leveling occurs when treatment is removed (A), and improvement again occurs when treatment is readministered (B). In the multiple baseline design, at least three behaviors are identified that are independent of one another, and the researcher must show that a specific behavior improves when it is the target of treatment (while the other behaviors remain unchanged).

Imagine that the clinical researcher identified depression, anxiety and impulsiveness (as measured by standard instruments) as the three behaviors on the basis of three goals selected by the client. In the first phase of treatment, the psychotherapist conducts cognitive-behavioral treatment

(CBT), targeting the client's depression. By the end of that phase, depression has mostly lifted, but no changes may be detected in either anxiety or impulsiveness. In the second phase, the CBT targets anxiety, resulting in lower anxiety levels but no changes in depression or impulsiveness. Single-case experiments are a type of research design that may be especially useful for clinicians who desire to contribute to the body of evidence on Christian psychotherapies. Such research could also be done by three to ten psychotherapists--in-training within a university counseling service, community clinic, or even in a group practice. Chambless and Hollon (1998) suggested that a treatment should be considered *efficacious* only if it is shown to be beneficial for at least three participants from at least two research groups.

Two-group comparative design. The two-group comparative design involves comparing two treatments, but this type of design falls short of a randomized clinical trial because it does not randomize participants to condition. For example, Hawkins, Tan and Turk (1999) compared Christian and secular versions of cognitive behavioral therapy for inpatient depressed Christians. However, because this study did not randomly assign participants to condition, it is impossible to rule out the possibility that other factors, such as selection bias, may have influenced outcomes. For example, perhaps more religious participants chose to take the Christian version, and this religiousness (rather than the treatment itself) caused differential outcomes. In such cases, the study does not meet the gold standard of a randomized clinical trial.

Single-group pretest-posttest design. Similarly, studies sometimes use a single-group pretest-posttest design. They measure clients at the beginning and end of psychotherapy but do not have a control group to which they have randomly assigned people. The clinician might find that participants improve, but it is difficult to differentiate the effect of the treatment from other factors that might have occurred between the pretest and the posttest. For example, there might be placebo effects, or there might have been the occurrence of some external effect such as a stock market crash or the end of a harsh winter. In addition, something statistical might have happened, such as the tendency for extreme scores to balance out by regression to the mean. Thus, people who are very depressed might just have become less depressed over time regardless of the treatment. Without a control group, we simply cannot be sure what caused people to get better.

Despite their limitations, we believe that quasi-experimental designs do have some merit. First, quasi-experimental designs can provide important preliminary information that a treatment has some positive effects, which might be important to establish before conducting a time-consuming and often expensive and labor-intensive randomized clinical trial. Second, quasi-experimental designs can provide important information on effectiveness after the efficacy of a treatment has been established. It is often very difficult to conduct highly controlled, random-assignment efficacy research in real-world settings. Quasi-experiments, therefore, can be very useful.

Thus, when considering research design, we suggest a hierarchy of designs (see figure 15.1). These research designs differ in level of experimental control from most rigorous at the top (e.g., randomized clinical trial using a dismantling design) to least rigorous at the bottom (quasi-experimental one-group pretest-posttest design). We encourage researchers and clinicians to use the most rigorous design that is feasible given their setting and resources.

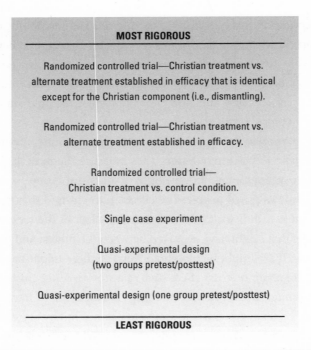

MOST RIGOROUS

Randomized controlled trial—Christian treatment vs. alternate treatment established in efficacy that is identical except for the Christian component (i.e., dismantling).

Randomized controlled trial—Christian treatment vs. alternate treatment established in efficacy.

Randomized controlled trial— Christian treatment vs. control condition.

Single case experiment

Quasi-experimental design (two groups pretest/posttest)

Quasi-experimental design (one group pretest/posttest)

LEAST RIGOROUS

Figure 15.1. Hierarchy of research designs

PARTICIPANTS

Incorporating Christian content into clinical research is only part of the equation. We also need to give serious thought to the selection of the target population and the study participants. It is important to define clearly the population for which the treatment was designed and tested (Chambless & Hollon, 1998). In other words, researchers often are interested in determining the extent to which a treatment is effective in treating a specific type of person and problem. We would encourage researchers to define their participants along two domains: problem characteristics and religious or spiritual characteristics.

Problem characteristics. First, participants are often identified in relation to a specific type of problem. A study that evaluated a Christian treatment for depression, for example, would recruit participants who are actually struggling with depression. This may be determined in several ways. First, participants could meet criteria for a specific problem using a diagnostic system such as the *Diagnostic and Statistical Manual of Mental Disorders* (DSM-IVR; American Psychiatric Association, 2000). Second, participants could meet criteria as defined by a cutoff score on a reliable and valid instrument. For example, to participate in their study, Johnson, DeVries, Ridley, Pettorini and Peterson (1994) required that participants have a score of at least 15 on the Beck Depression Inventory (Beck, Ward, Mendelson, Mock & Erbaugh, 1961), which indicates moderate depression. In addition, we must consider that people who are recruited into a treatment study are often different from people who actually seek treatment, even though they might score similarly on a standard instrument assessing symptomology. The actual clients might be more motivated to change or might be at a different stage of readiness for treatment. The actual clients might also be more receptive to psychotherapy or less resistant to it given that they have actively sought treatment. Obviously, the best participant selection is to have people in the study who have sought psychotherapy rather than those who merely have clinically significant scores on assessment instruments.

Religious or spiritual characteristics. Second, participants can be distinguished according to their religious or spiritual beliefs. Some outcome studies evaluating a Christian psychotherapy have simply required that participants "identify with" Christianity. We believe that using religious identification to describe a person's religious or spiritual beliefs is necessary but not sufficient. It might be that some define *Christian* rather broadly (e.g., "I'm from the USA, therefore I'm a Christian"), and some rather narrowly (e.g., "I am a fundamentalist, born-again, Southern Baptist," or "I'm a post-Vatican II theologically moderate Roman Catholic"). Using only religious identification may be problematic for other reasons as well, because participants who self-identify as Christians may differ in their level of religious commitment.

Indeed, persons with high levels of religious commitment are more likely to view the world through a religious lens than those with low levels (Worthington, 1988). Highly committed Christian individuals, for example, might especially benefit from a Christian version of psychotherapy. Some studies have used a religiosity scale to provide a minimum cutoff score for inclusion into the study (e.g., Propst, 1980). We think that this is probably an adequate strategy to help ensure that participants are at least moderately committed to their religious beliefs and values. However, perhaps a better strategy is to measure religious commitment and use this variable as a moderator to evaluate whether participants at different levels of religious commitment respond better or worse to Christian versions of a treatment (see Razali, Aminah & Khan, 2002, for an example of this type of data analysis strategy).

OUTCOME ASSESSMENT

Instrument selection. The selection of instruments is an important issue when conducting outcome studies of Christian psychotherapy. Obviously, the main outcome instruments should measure the complaint (or area of growth) that the psychotherapy is purported to help (or promote). Outcome instruments should have evidence supporting their reliability and validity, preferably in the specific population of study. Furthermore, if possible, studies should also include measures that assess (a) general functioning and quality of life, (b) Christian spirituality and religiosity, and perhaps (c) distinctly Christian constructs such as awareness of sin (Watson, Morris, Loy & Hamrick, 2007) and grace (Sisemore, Arbuckle, Killian, Mortellaro, Swanson, Fisher & McGinnis, 2010). As we mentioned earlier, a recent review of the literature on religious and spiritual psychotherapies found that (a) participants in religious and nonreligious treatments showed equivalent reductions in psychological symptoms (e.g., less depression) and (b) participants in religious treatments had more improvements on spiritual outcomes (e.g., spiritual well-being; Worthington et al., 2011). For example, in their study of Christian and non-Christian forgiveness interventions, Rye and Pargament (2002) not only measured forgiveness as the primary outcome measure, but also spiritual well-being and other measures of mental health such as depression, anxiety and hope.

Follow-up data. Assessing the long-term effects of psychotherapy as evaluated by follow-up data is highly desirable (Chambless & Hollon, 1998); however, such data are difficult to obtain. Besides the obvious practical difficulties of collecting data from multiple participants over a long period of time, follow-up assessments have their own unique problems. Participants might feel finished with psychotherapy and not want to complete any other questionnaires. They are often free to pursue additional treatment, which confuses the outcome because the researcher is not sure whether the additional treatment or the original one might be responsible for the results. Even with these difficulties and concerns, it is important to do our best to assess the effects of treatment after treatment is over. Thus, we encourage researchers to collect follow-up data when feasible, but also to be aware of and discuss the limitations of these data. For example, in one of the most rigorous early studies of Christian cognitive-behavioral therapy for depression, Propst, Ostrom, Watkins, Dean and Mashburn (1992) assessed participants both before and after treatment, and then again at three-month and two-year follow-ups.

Clinical significance. One additional issue that is often unaddressed in psychotherapy outcome studies is *clinical significance*, which refers to whether changes that occur in psychotherapy are meaningful in practice (Jacobson, Roberts, Berns & McGlinchey, 1999; Jacobson & Traux, 1991). It is possible that an effect could be statistically significant (i.e., it is unlikely that this effect occurred by chance) but be so small that it is of little practical value to clinicians in their everyday practice. Researchers have used several methods to assess clinical significance. Many researchers compare outcomes against a particular standard. For example, Propst (1980) evaluated the percentage of participants who still fell within the depressed range of the BDI at posttest. Other researchers have developed specific criteria to evaluate clinically significant change (Jacobson et al., 1999).

TREATMENT IMPLEMENTATION

Treatment potency. One way to improve the power of a study is by intensifying or increasing the potency of the treatment—for example, increasing a dosage of medication in medical research. One presumably could increase the potency in Christian psychotherapy research by exposing those in the experimental conditions to psychotherapies that are especially saturated with the therapeutic resources of the Christian tradition. In chapter 16, we summarize some of those resources.

Treatment manual development. Researchers are encouraged to develop treatment manuals when conducting an outcome study of a Christian psychotherapy. The main purpose of a treatment manual is to provide a description of the treatment and guidelines for its implementation (Carroll & Nuro, 2002). Manuals allow researchers to replicate a particular treatment (Chambless & Hollon, 1998), and also help researchers to ensure that the treatment is administered consistently by different psychotherapists (Luborsky & DeRubeis, 1984; Miller & Binder, 2002). Manuals may include information such as a description and rationale of the treatment, conception of the disorder treated, treatment goals, comparison/contrast with other treatments, description of interventions, session content, format of delivery, troubleshooting, nonspecific or common aspects of treatment, psychotherapist selection, training, supervision, clinical care standards and diversity issues (Carroll & Nuro, 2002).

At the same time, we acknowledge that the use of treatment manuals is not without controversy (Chambless & Ollendick, 2001). What most see as their strengths (their consistency, uniformity), others may consider weaknesses (rigidity, inflexibility). Treatment manuals may be easier to use with psychotherapies that are more cognitive or educational, time-limited, problem-oriented and use relatively straightforward strategies. They may be more difficult to use with psychotherapies that are more psychodynamic, long-term, charismatic and work with more intractable problems such as personality disorders. This may make treatment manuals less useful in the study of certain Christian psychotherapies that especially rely on the Holy Spirit and individual spiritual gifts. Nevertheless, treatment manuals greatly enhance the validity of clinical research, so we recommend their use when feasible.

One example of the use of manuals for a study of Christian psychotherapy was Propst (1988), who developed a manual that described her approach for Christian cognitive-behavioral therapy for depression. As we mentioned earlier, having a treatment manual is important, especially when two different studies purport to follow exactly the same treatment manual but get different results. Sometimes differences not included in the treatment manual are actually responsible for the treatment gains. Having a thorough treatment manual and ensuring that it is followed can uncover active therapeutic ingredients that the creator of the treatment manual might not have realized were helping.

Therapist monitoring. Related to the importance of manuals is the need for psychotherapists to be monitored to ensure that the treatment was delivered adequately (Chambless & Hollon, 1998). Ideally, the monitoring of psychotherapists would include the assessment of both adherence and competence. *Adherence* refers to the extent to which psychotherapists used interventions and clinical approaches prescribed by the treatment manual and avoided interventions and clinical approaches proscribed by the treatment manual (Waltz, Addis, Koerner & Jacobson, 1993). *Competence,* on the other hand, refers to the psychotherapist's level of skill in delivering the treatment. Measures of adherence and competence are important because they serve as a manipulation check for the treatment being evaluated. Among Christian psychotherapy outcome studies, measures of adherence and competence have been rare.

One example of measuring adherence was Johnson et al. (1994), who examined the videotape recordings of each session and used a checklist to determine whether the psychotherapist used several interventions that were required in each session. Over all sessions, 92% of the required interventions were used in the Christian condition and 96% of the required interventions were used in the secular condition, indicating a high level of adherence to the treatment protocol. Overall, monitoring a manualized treatment helps us to be more confident that the Christian psychotherapy was actually implemented in the study.

Investigator allegiance. A final consideration when addressing treatment implementation is investigator allegiance, which refers to the way a researcher's preference for a particular psychotherapy may cause that psychotherapy to fare better when compared to alternate psychotherapies (Luborsky et al., 1999). This may be especially pertinent in outcome studies that involve religion, which is an issue that may arouse strong feelings. Such differences in researcher allegiance do not imply bias. Rather, unconscious factors such as enthusiasm, sense of confidence, and even expertness (i.e., people usually do a better job at delivering treatments they have known and used than unfamiliar treatments) can affect outcomes. Thus, whether intentional or not, researchers may end up "tipping" off participants or creating expectations that participants may feel implicit pressure to help confirm.

It is probably impossible to eliminate all investigator allegiance, and we agree with others who have suggested that perhaps the best solution is for investigator allegiances to be balanced (Chambless & Hollon, 1998). In other words, each treatment should utilize experts in that particular modality to oversee psychotherapists who are committed to that particular approach. For example, in their study comparing Christian and secular cognitive-behavioral therapy for depression (Hawkins et al., 1999), the Christian treatments were conducted by pastors and Christian psychotherapists who ascribed to Christian beliefs and values, and the secular treatments were conducted by psychotherapists who either (a) did not ascribe to Christian beliefs or (b) did not desire to incorporate Christian beliefs into psychotherapy. Another example of balancing investigator allegiances occurred with Project MATCH (Project Match Research Group, 1997), which evaluated three treatments for alcoholism (cognitive-behavioral coping skills therapy, motivational-enhancement therapy, twelve-step facilitation), each given by psychotherapists trained and committed to that particular approach.

DATA ANALYSIS

Chambless and Hollon (1998) noted several common mistakes made when analyzing data from psychotherapy outcome studies. Some of the most common errors they found were

- As previously noted, many psychotherapy outcome studies suffer from low statistical power. We cannot make efficacy claims based on equivalent findings if sample sizes are low. We recommend that researchers use samples of at least twenty-five to thirty people per condition.

- Researchers often conduct many statistical tests on several outcome measures, find one that supports their hypothesis (amidst several that do not), and claim that one treatment is superior to another. In analyzing their data this way, researchers are in danger of committing a type I error (i.e., concluding that a difference exists when in fact it does not), because a small percentage of tests are likely to be significant simply due to chance. We recommend that researchers decide beforehand which outcome measures and comparisons they will run, and keep the number of comparisons reasonable. If multiple tests are conducted, the majority of the tests must favor one treatment if that treatment is to be concluded superior.

- Instead of comparing the conditions directly, researchers may (a) report the pretest-posttest comparisons separately for each condition and (b) report that one condition improved significantly and the other did not. This strategy is questionable because one condition may have just attained significance (e.g., $p = .04$) whereas the other condition may have just missed significance (e.g., $p = .06$), when in reality there is little or no difference between conditions. When analyzing comparative psychotherapy outcome studies, we recommend that researchers analyze the between-group comparisons directly.

- The conditions may have different retention rates, which may be ignored by the researcher, and thus bias results. For example, a treatment may have high success rates for the participants who actually complete the treatment. However, if only 50% of the participants complete the treatment, analyzing only the treatment completers will give a biased view of the efficacy of that treatment. Intention-to-treat analyses (Pagoto et al., 2009) include all randomized participants in analyses (irrespective of whether or not they complete the study). To use this analysis, researchers can (a) attempt to get a final data point from participants who do not complete the study or (b) carry the last data point forward to the end of the study. Intention-to-treat analyses should be used in cases in which differential dropout is present.

EFFECTIVENESS

Most of the guidelines in the present chapter have focused on evaluating the efficacy of a psychotherapy treatment. However, some researchers have criticized efficacy research and argued that conducting outcome studies under highly controlled research conditions does not adequately capture the realities of treatment in the real world (e.g., Seligman, 1995). Three issues pertinent to effectiveness research are generalizability, treatment feasibility and cost-effectiveness (Chambless & Hollon, 1998).

Generalizability. Whether psychological treatments are useful across different populations, psychotherapists and settings is referred to as generalizability. Outcome studies of Christian psychotherapy are unique in that they are generally focused on Christian participants. The issue of generalizability in this case pertains to the usefulness of the treatment being investigated to the population of all Christians, or at least those with the problem being treated (e.g., depression). In addition, other questions of generalizability across populations are relevant. For example, to what extent does a treatment work for clients from different types of Christian sects or denominations? To what extent does a treatment work for Christian clients from different racial or ethnic groups? To what extent does a treatment work for Christian clients with more complex psychopathology? Questions such as these remain largely unanswered.

Regarding the type of psychotherapist, most psychotherapists in outcome studies of Christian psychotherapy have either been Christian psychotherapists, pastoral counselors or psychotherapists-in-training. One interesting study had both Christian and non-Christian psychotherapists deliver Christian-accommodative treatment (Propst et al., 1992). This study found that non-Christian psychotherapists were just as effective in delivering treatment as Christian psychotherapists, supporting the notion that nonreligious psychotherapists might be able to incorporate religion into psychotherapy effectively without being religious themselves. It is important to determine whether treatments work in real-world settings, because these clinical settings may differ from the research setting in important ways (e.g., limited number of sessions, assignment to psychotherapist randomly rather than personal choice). Thus, effectiveness studies that evaluate psychotherapy in more realistic settings are important adjuncts to the highly controlled randomized clinical trial (e.g., Hawkins et al., 1999; Hook, Worthington, Davis & Atkins, 2012; Wade, Worthington & Vogel, 2007).

Treatment feasibility. How easily the treatment is accepted by clients and able to be disseminated to psychotherapists is defined as treatment feasibility. If clients refuse to participate in a treatment, it is unlikely that psychotherapy will have much lasting value. Some studies have incorporated a program evaluation component in which participants indicate how satisfied they are with different aspects of the program (e.g., Rye & Pargament, 2002).

Cost-effectiveness. The cost-effectiveness of a treatment refers to an evaluation of the costs and benefits of a treatment, both in the short run and over the entire life of the patient (Miller & Magruder, 1999). For example, though a treatment may have significant evidence supporting its adoption, is the typical client able to successfully adopt the practices it promotes and maintain them afterward? That is, how practical is the intervention? Is the financial, social or other cost worth the improvement? Or does the improvement perhaps come at the expense of well-being in other areas of one's life? There has been almost no research evaluating the cost-effectiveness of Christian psychotherapies.

SYSTEMATIC OUTCOME RESEARCH

We now offer a logical progression for researchers and clinicians to work toward establishing empirical support for a Christian psychotherapy. This material is based on the guidelines presented by Johnson (1993) for programmatic psychotherapy outcome research.

Step 1: Describe the psychotherapy. The first step in establishing a base of evidence for a treatment is to establish what exactly constitutes the treatment. At this stage, researchers should also begin to establish a treatment manual (Carroll & Nuro, 2002). Along with the development of a treatment manual, case studies with specific clients are often helpful to illustrate the details of a treatment approach.

Step 2: Evaluate efficacy. The second step in establishing a base of evidence for a treatment is to evaluate whether the psychotherapy works. Researchers should begin with small (but adequately powered) pilot studies to assess whether there is any positive benefit from treatment. Single group pretest-posttest designs are appropriate at this stage, as are single case experiments. If these projects yield encouraging results, a randomized controlled trial comparing the Christian psychotherapy to a control group would be a logical next step.

Step 3: Evaluate specificity. The third step in establishing a base of evidence for a treatment is to evaluate whether the psychotherapy works better than an alternate treatment. This provides evidence of specificity and controls for nonspecific factors found in all types of psychotherapy (e.g., supportive relationship, plan for recovery). If a treatment is shown to outperform another established treatment, researchers are better able to argue that this treatment should be the treatment of choice when treating a particular type of client. In evaluations of Christian psychotherapies, a popular design is comparing a Christian treatment with a similar secular treatment. The most rigorous of designs involves a randomized clinical trial using a dismantling design, in which the modalities, strategies and duration of psychotherapy is identical in the Christian and non-Christian condition.

Step 4: Determine variables that interact with treatment. The fourth step in establishing a base of evidence for a treatment is to determine whether there are client or psychotherapist variables that interact with treatment. For example, one hypothesis that has rarely been tested empirically is that religious psychotherapies might work especially well with clients who have high levels of religious commitment (Worthington et al., 2011). A study could measure variables such as religious commitment and evaluate whether such variables interact with treatment to produce better (or worse) outcomes.

Step 5: Assess effectiveness. The fifth step in establishing a base of evidence for a treatment is to assess how well the treatment works in clinically relevant settings. For example, how well does the treatment generalize to different client populations, psychotherapists and settings? How accepting are clients of the treatment and how easily is the treatment disseminated to psychotherapists? To what extent is the treatment cost-effective? At this stage of research, randomized clinical trials are still the gold standard, but they are often difficult to conduct practically. Other types of research designs (e.g., single case experiments, quasi-experimental designs) may be more plausible.

OVERCOMING CHALLENGES TO CONDUCTING
CLINICAL OUTCOME STUDIES

As we have shown, conducting clinical outcome research can be difficult, costly and time-consuming. We also recognize that to do this type of research well requires certain areas of expertise, access to clients and infrastructure. This recognition comes not just from our own experience, but also from the challenges others have shared with us. We have heard colleagues say: "You can't conduct clinical outcome research unless you are at a big research university"; "It's almost impossible to conduct such research at a Christian college or practice, because there just aren't the resources"; or "I'm just not a stats kind of person." While these are all valid points, we believe that with some creativity almost all of those challenges can be overcome by focusing not on what is *missing* but on what is *present*. In the following paragraph, we offer a few suggestions for helping readers, no matter their situation, to contribute to Christian evidence-based practices.

Cooperation. Researchers and clinicians often have different issues when conducting psychotherapy outcome research. Researchers often have the time available and knowledge for designing and running experiments, but often lack the ability to recruit clinical populations. Clinicians, on the other hand, often have access to clinical populations, but may lack the time and knowledge for designing and running a study. One way to increase the quantity and quality of Christian psychotherapy outcome research is to promote cooperation between Christian researchers and clinicians. If you are a clinician who practices a Christian psychotherapy, perhaps you might recruit a researcher to develop a method for evaluating the outcomes of your clients. If you are a researcher who is interested in evaluating a Christian psychotherapy, perhaps you might recruit clinicians who are also interested in that approach and invite them to partner with you on a research project.

CONCLUSION

In the present chapter, we have tried to offer guidelines for researchers and clinicians to follow when conducting clinical outcome research on Christian psychotherapies. It is not enough to think and hope that what we do is effective. In order to provide ethically sound treatment for clients, we must work together to determine empirically that what we do actually works. We hope that you will contribute to this process.

REFERENCES

American Psychiatric Association. (2000). *Diagnostic and statistical manual of mental disorders* (4th ed.).Washington, DC: American Psychiatric Association.

American Psychological Association Task Force on Psychological Intervention Guidelines. (1995). *Template for developing guidelines: Interventions for mental disorders and psychological aspects of physical disorders.* Washington, DC: American Psychological Association.

Atkins, D. C. (2009). Clinical trials methodology: Randomization, intend-to-treat, and random-effects regression. *Depression and Anxiety, 26,* 697-700.

Barlow, D. H., Nock, M. K., & Hersen, M. (2008). *Single case experimental designs: Strategies for studying behavior change* (3rd ed.). Boston, MA: Allyn & Bacon.

Beck, A. T., Ward, C. H., Mendelson, M., Mock, J., & Erbaugh, J. (1961). An inventory for measuring depression. *Archives of General Psychiatry, 4,* 561-71.

Carlson, C. R., Bacaseta, P. E., & Simanton, D. A. (1988). A controlled evaluation of devotional meditation and progressive relaxation. *Journal of Psychology and Theology, 16,* 362-68.

Carroll, K. M., & Nuro, K. F. (2002). One size cannot fit all: A stage model for psychotherapy manual development. *Clinical Psychology: Science and Practice, 9,* 396-406.

Chambless, D. L., & Hollon, S. D. (1998). Defining empirically supported therapies. *Journal of Consulting and Clinical Psychology, 66,* 7-18.

Chambless, D. L., & Ollendick, T. H. (2001). Empirically supported psychological interventions: Controversies and evidence. *Annual Review of Psychology, 52,* 685-716.

Hawkins, R. S., Tan, S., & Turk, A. A. (1999). Secular versus Christian inpatient cognitive-behavioral therapy programs: Impact on depression and spiritual well-being. *Journal of Psychology and Theology, 27,* 309-18.

Hook, J. N., Worthington, E. L., Jr., Davis, D. E., & Atkins, D. C. (2012). *Religion and couple therapy: Description and preliminary outcome data.* Unpublished manuscript, Denton, TX.

Hook, J. N., Worthington, E. L., Jr., Davis, D. E., Jennings, D. J., II., Gartner, A. L., & Hook, J. P. (2010). Empirically supported religious and spiritual therapies. *Journal of Clinical Psychology, 66,* 46-72.

Jacobson, N. S., Roberts, L. J., Berns, S. B., & McGlinchey, J. B. (1999). Methods for defining and determining the clinical significance of treatment effects: Description, application and alternatives. *Journal of Consulting and Clinical Psychology, 67,* 300-307.

Jacobson, N. S., & Traux, P. (1991). Clinical significance: A statistical approach to defining meaningful change in psychotherapy research. *Journal of Consulting and Clinical Psychology, 59,* 12-19.

Johnson, W. B. (1993). Outcome research and religious psychotherapies: Where are we and where are we going? *Journal of Psychology and Theology, 21,* 297-308.

Johnson, W. B., DeVries, R., Ridley, C. R., Pettorini, D., & Peterson, D. R. (1994). The comparative efficacy of Christian and secular rational-emotive therapy with Christian clients. *Journal of Psychology and Theology, 22,* 130-40.

Johnson, W. B., & Ridley, C. R. (1992). Brief Christian and non-Christian rational-emotive therapy with depressed Christian clients: An exploratory study. *Counseling and Values, 36,* 220-29.

Luborsky, L., & DeRubeis, R. J. (1984). The use of psychotherapy treatment manuals: A small revolution in psychotherapy research style. *Clinical Psychology Review, 4,* 5-15.

Luborsky, L., Diguer, L., Seligman, D. A., Rosenthal, R., Krause, E. D., Johnson, S., Halperin, G., Bishop, M., Berman, J. S., & Schweizer, E. (1999). The researcher's own therapy allegiances: A "wild card" in comparisons of treatment efficacy. *Clinical Psychology: Science and Practice, 6,* 95-106.

Miller, N. E., & Magruder, K. M. (Eds.). (1999). *Cost-effectiveness of psychotherapy: A guide for practitioners, researchers, and policymakers.* New York: Oxford University Press.

Miller, S. J., & Binder, J. L. (2002). The effects of manual-based training on treatment fidelity and outcome: A review of the literature on adult individual psychotherapy. *Psychotherapy: Theory, Research, Practice, Training, 39,* 184-98.

Pagoto, S. L., Kozak, A. T., John, P., Bodenlos, J. S., Hedeker, D., Spring, B., & Schneider, K. L. (2009). Intention-to-treat analyses in behavioral medicine randomized clinical trials. *International Journal of Behavioral Medicine, 16,* 316-22.

Pecheur, D. R., & Edwards, K. J. (1984). A comparison of secular and religious versions of cognitive therapy with depressed Christian college students. *Journal of Psychology and Theology, 12,* 45-54.

Post, B. C., & Wade, N. G. (2009). Religion and spirituality in psychotherapy: A practice-friendly review of research. *Journal of Clinical Psychology, 65,* 131-46.

Project Match Research Group. (1997). Matching alcoholism treatments to client heterogeneity: Project MATCH posttreatment drinking outcomes. *Journal of Studies on Alcohol, 58,* 7-29.

Propst, L. R. (1980). The comparative efficacy of religious and nonreligious imagery for the treatment of mild depression in religious individuals. *Cognitive Therapy and Research, 4,* 167-78.

Propst, L. R. (1988). *Psychotherapy in a religious framework: Spirituality in the emotional healing process.* New York: Human Sciences Press.

Propst, L. R., Ostrom, R., Watkins, P., Dean, T., & Mashburn, D. (1992). Comparative efficacy of religious and nonreligious cognitive-behavioral therapy for the treatment of clinical depression in religious individuals. *Journal of Consulting and Clinical Psychology, 60,* 94-103.

Razali, S. M., Aminah, K., & Khan, U. A. (2002). Religious-cultural psychotherapy in the management of anxiety patients. *Transcultural Psychiatry, 39,* 130-36.

Rye, M. S., & Pargament, K. I. (2002). Forgiveness and romantic relationships in college: Can it heal the wounded heart? *Journal of Clinical Psychology, 58,* 419-41.

Seligman, M. E. P. (1995). The effectiveness of psychotherapy: The Consumer Reports study. *American Psychologist, 50,* 965-74.

Sisemore, T. A., Arbuckle, M., Killian, M., Mortellaro, E., Swanson, M., Fisher, R., & McGinnis, J. (2010). Grace and Christian psychology—part 1: Preliminary measurement, relationships, and implications for practice. *Edification, 4*(2), 57-63.

Smith, T. B., Bartz, J., & Richards, P. S. (2007). Outcomes of religious and spiritual adaptations to psychotherapy: A meta-analytic review. *Psychotherapy Research, 17,* 643-55.

Task Force on Promotion and Dissemination of Psychological Procedures. (1995). Training in and dissemination of empirically-validated psychological treatments: Report and recommendations. *Clinical Psychologist, 48,* 3-23.

Wade, N. G., Worthington, E. L., Jr., & Vogel, D. L. (2007). Effectiveness of religiously tailored interventions in Christian therapy. *Psychotherapy Research, 17,* 91-105.

Waltz, J., Addis, M. E., Koerner, K., & Jacobson, N. S. (1993). Testing the integrity of a psychotherapy protocol: Assessment of adherence and competence. *Journal of Consulting and Clinical Psychology, 61,* 620-30.

Watson, P. J., Morris, R. J., Loy, T., Hamrick, M. B. (2007). Beliefs about sin: Adaptive implications in relationships with religious orientation, self-esteem, and measures of the narcissistic, depressed, and anxious self. *Edification, 1*(1), 57-67.

Worthington, E. L., Jr. (1988). Understanding the values of religious clients: A model and its application to counseling. *Journal of Counseling Psychology, 35,* 166-74.

Worthington, E. L., Jr., Hook, J. N., Davis, D. E., & McDaniel, M. E. (2011). Religion and spirituality. *Journal of Clinical Psychology: In Session, 67,* 204-14.

Evidence-Based Practice in Light of the Christian Tradition(s)

Reflections and Future Directions

Eric L. Johnson, Everett L. Worthington Jr.,
Joshua N. Hook and Jamie D. Aten

In this book, we have considered a wide range of research on Christian psychotherapy and counseling. We are particularly impressed with the varieties of approaches from which Christian psychotherapists can draw. We express our indebtedness and gratitude for that work. Science and psychotherapy are communal activities that rely on previous work to make progress. In this chapter, we express dreams that originate out of the previous work of many (including some not represented in this book).

In the same way that we have sought to present you with a variety of perspectives on psychotherapy and counseling, we also realize that not everyone in the Christian community will see things similarly in terms of the relation between theology and psychology. There are different worldviews, different approaches to psychological science and different ideas about how to help people. There are different interpretations of the past, the state of the present and the future. So we consider it a strength of the present book that it doesn't have a "party line." We believe that Christians are relational and Christianity at its root is based on relationship, with the uniqueness of individuals embedded within a framework of different relationships with God and local communities. It is through dialogue and humility that people negotiate those relationships.

Even as editors we reflect several different perspectives on psychological practice and psychological and clinical science, including the future of evidence-based Christian counseling and psychotherapy! Though we share a common faith and core Christian beliefs, we differ on some of the less central issues. Even as we wrote this final chapter, we found ourselves in dialogue with one another. We sincerely hope that you will be enriched by the discussions that we have included here.

GOOD TIMES, GREAT OPPORTUNITIES

The twentieth century was difficult for Christians in psychology. From its origins in the late 1800s, modern psychology assumed a positivistic epistemology and a naturalistic worldview, commitments which automatically ruled out reference to the supernatural. In the clinical realm, leading figures such as Freud and Rogers repudiated "dogmatic" religious faith, and for decades religion was widely considered to be associated with psychopathology (e.g., schizophrenia; see Rokeach, 1964). To complicate matters further, many evangelical Christians, especially in the first half of the century, became skeptical of the academic enterprise and scholarship, since American and European universities seemed to be leading Western culture's turn away from the God of Christianity (Noll, 1995; Smith, 2003). As a result, for much of the century, Christians in psychology rarely mentioned religion in their work, while the majority of Christians paid psychology little heed.

The situation is considerably different today. In the space of a decade, positive psychology almost single-handedly legitimated the empirical investigation of ethical topics (such as virtues), which had long been considered inappropriate for psychological science. For the last half-century, researchers have slowly compiled an impressive body of literature documenting the physiological and psychological benefits associated with intrinsic religious belief. Religion and spirituality are now recognized as positive factors in clinical work, and therapists-in-training are being encouraged to explore and work with these dimensions.

In addition, a growing postmodern sensibility along with research in crosscultural psychology have mandated respect for cultural (and subcultural) diversity, including diversity of religious belief (Richards & Bergin,

2000). Of special significance is the recent advocacy for *theistic* psychology (Slife & Reber, 2009) and psychotherapy (Richards & Bergin, 2005), which assume a necessary role for God in human life and healing. Indeed our field has come a long way since the days of Freud. It is a great time to be a Christian in psychology, psychotherapy and counseling. What opportunities for research on Christian psychotherapy and counseling are afforded to us in the early twenty-first century?

WORLDVIEW COMMUNITIES AND PSYCHOTHERAPY AND COUNSELING RESEARCH

It is well known that research on psychotherapy and counseling over the past thirty years has found what are termed common factors—variables correlated with positive outcomes that transcend the particular psychotherapy orientation—such as therapist alliance, affect experience and in vivo practice (Lambert, 2003), which raises questions about how distinctive the various psychotherapy models actually are. Some analysts have suggested that almost all this research has assumed a positivistic epistemology and naturalistic worldview and has focused on therapies with the same assumptions (see Slife, Reber & Richardson, 2005). As a result, the question of the impact of different worldview beliefs on psychological and psychotherapy research has been relatively unexplored (though see Slife & Reber, 2009; Watson, 2011).

Research on species (Christianity) as well as genus (religion and spirituality). So while Christians have much to be thankful for today, the fact remains that most of the research and discussion in these areas has still maintained the "universal perspective" of modernism and has largely left worldview issues unaddressed. The majority of discourse is conducted at the general conceptual level of "religion" and "spirituality" (see, e.g., Miller, 1999; Plante, 2009; Richards & Bergin, 2005; Sperry & Shafranske, 2005)— that is, the *etic* perspective—in contrast to the local and particular conceptual level of specific religions, spiritualities and life-philosophies (such as Christianity, Hinduism, humanism and naturalism) and within their communities—that is, the *emic* perspective (Triandis, 2007).

While science is often advanced by a generalization of findings across groups, there is also much scientific value in examining phenomena in greater detail within groups, in order to make specific distinctions that are lost in generalizations. Sometimes this has been recognized within the field of psychotherapy. An excellent emic approach to religion, for example, can be seen in the *Handbook of Religious Diversity and Psychotherapy* (Richards & Bergins, 1999) that attempts to introduce readers to a wide range of religious ideologies and associated treatment recommendations. This kind of book reflects the shift that has occurred in psychotherapy research since the 1960s to move beyond the grand psychotherapy theories that "explain everything," and to seek which treatments work for whom under which conditions. Overall, the field appears to be at an interesting crossroads. While the assumptions of naturalism still markedly constrain what is considered legitimate scientifically, at the same time there is a renewed interest in matters of faith. Still, claims beyond the empirical, especially theological claims and interpretations, may be met with hesitancy.

These issues become even more complex in the investigation of psychotherapy and counseling. These practices often have an unarticulated end—a "healthy human being"—as well as assumptions regarding human nature, ethics, maturity ideals, definitions of psychopathology and methods of psychological healing, which are all shaped by values, ethics, worldviews and notions of the "good" that vary considerably across cultures (Cushman, 1995; Taylor, 1989). The growing realization of such worldview differences will make it increasingly necessary in the future to be mindful of the different assumptions of various worldview communities and to be explicit about one's own worldview orientation in one's research. A simple way to reframe the options for Christians in the field is to reconsider the audience (or addressees) of one's research and publications and recognize that these audiences may vary depending on one's communicative purposes. Christians may desire to communicate primarily with mainstream psychotherapists and counselors, but they may also write to the Christian community of psychotherapists and counselors or directly to the church.

RESEARCH ON CHRISTIAN-ACCOMMODATIVE PSYCHOTHERAPY AND COUNSELING

As we have noted elsewhere, much of the best research to date in this area has investigated *religion-accommodative* therapies (McCullough, 1999), which result from bringing religious elements into an existing secular psychotherapy model (e.g., cognitive-behavioral therapy). This book is focused on *Christian*-accommodative therapies, which incorporate specifically Christian elements into existing secular models of psychotherapy. The value of research on such Christian-accommodative approaches is twofold: (1) it has demonstrated that Christian psychotherapy and counseling is at least as effective as secular psychotherapy; and (2) it has done so by utilizing the basic framework of some already empirically validated secular models, and therefore has built bridges to other schools of psychotherapy practice within mainstream psychology. In addition to the approaches that have been explored in this book, research presumably could be done on other Christian psychotherapies that accommodate current secular psychotherapies. Some of the most promising for future accommodation include narrative therapy, motivational interviewing, multimodal therapy, the transtheoretical model, emotion-focused therapy, and many elements of acceptance and commitment therapy and dialectical behavior therapy.

However, the accommodative approach also has some weaknesses. When Christians begin with already extant models and accommodate to them, there will be great diversity in *how* they accommodate. Thus far, there has been little unanimity and commonality across studies regarding the precise Christian contributions to the therapies under investigation. On one extreme, Propst (1988) offers perhaps the widest range of distinctly and well-described Christian strategies in her Christian-accommodative cognitive-behavioral therapy. However, such richness has generally proven to be the exception rather than the rule. As a result, we currently have relatively little understanding of what specifically Christian factor(s), if any, contribute to the positive therapeutic outcomes in the research—or how much accommodation is necessary or desirable. In future studies, we would ask that researchers think carefully about what specifically Christian strategies and techniques they will introduce and then carefully describe them. Perhaps the time is right for some significant collaborative discussions among the interested parties where such complex issues can be explored. Together we might aim to forge greater community-wide consonance and a clearer understanding of what and how to accommodate, as well as how to increase the concentration of distinctly Christian influence.

Second, what are the limitations when members of one worldview community—in our case the Christian community—accommodate a psychotherapy model that originated out of a different worldview community that holds different basic assumptions about human beings and perhaps even about the basis of reality? Also, the question of which aspects of a model may be fruitfully accommodated has not yet been settled. Typically elements, explanations, rationales, and methods or counseling techniques of secular models are adapted for Christian clients, leaving the secular model largely intact while drawing from Christian teachings or rituals. Yet unanswered questions abound. How much accommodation *should* occur, and what is legitimate to accommodate? Furthermore, how much must theories and strategies be changed in order to be deemed "accommodated"? For example, some currently popular psychotherapy strategies, like mindfulness, promote obviously useful self-regulation skills but were derived directly from Buddhism and are missing some core Christian features (such as union with Christ and communion with God). Worldview beliefs are even more complicated to address, because they constitute the "deep grammar" of a psychotherapy system, influencing it pervasively, but usually operating as unstated assumptions (Johnson & Sandage, 1999). This can make it difficult at times to tease out the worldview beliefs from relatively unproblematic, "surface features" of the system. However, some have argued that accommodating the implicit secular and naturalistic worldview beliefs of certain modern psychotherapy models into Christian psychotherapy practice could be inherently self-destructive, operating as syncretistic solvent on the belief system of Christians and undermining their faith (see MacIntyre, 1990, for an exploration of these kinds of issues in the area of moral philosophy). Therefore Christian researchers and practitioners ought to exercise great care in determining what exactly is accommodated. The complexity of these questions extends far beyond the reaches of this chapter or book, but it would seem desirable for Christians in the field to understand better the relevant issues and increasingly take them into account in future research. It is clear that Christian psychotherapists and counselors may differ on how these questions are answered. We hope that by raising these questions we provoke people to think, talk and write about them so that positions will be clarified to facilitate better decision making by practitioners in the field.

Questions raised by measurement. Empirical investigation, of course, is only as good as the instrument used to collect the data. Questionnaires are very often used in psychotherapy research as measures of efficacy and effectiveness, including that of the religion- and Christian-accommodative approaches. However, such questionnaires may themselves be more or less reflective of assumptions that are foreign to some Christian worldviews (e.g., measures of psychological well-being). Consequently, the reports of future research studies could also include some assessment of Christian worldview beliefs associated with the secular psychotherapy model being accommodated (as seen in Jones & Butman, 2011; Tan, 2011). Furthermore, if worldview bias is suspected in an instrument, perhaps measurement of and statistical correction for its effects could be conducted, as Watson et al. (1987, 1988, 1995) have done with a number of contemporary psychological concepts and questionnaires, using his ideological surround model. In addition, as suggested in chapter 14, Christian philosophers and theologians could be used as consultants in future studies (similar to how statisticians are consulted) to help with conceptual clarification and to offer critical analysis regarding the possible biases of contemporary clinical theories, practices and measures of psychological phenomena.

RESEARCH ON CHRISTIAN-DERIVED PSYCHOTHERAPY
AND COUNSELING

In addition to the accommodative approach, a second approach to the investigation of Christian psychotherapy and counseling that could be attempted in the future engages in the strategy of "retrieval." Encouraged by anecdotal and limited empirical evidence of a number of Christian lay counseling models that place significant emphasis on the use of Scripture, and the roles of Christ and the Holy Spirit (addressed in chapter 14), these Christian lay counseling approaches aim to *begin* with the Christian intellectual and soul-care tradition. One may start by using the Bible, and at a second level of authority, Christian theological and philosophical writings and the literature of Christian soul care over the centuries. Such an approach seeks to draw out Christianity's own distinctive psychotherapy-relevant resources and then, analogous to the development of many kinds of models of psychotherapy and counseling that have arisen over the last one hundred years, develop to complex psychotherapy models to test that are especially saturated with Christian sensibilities. So in contrast to the accommodative approaches, which begin with an already existing model of secular psychotherapy and accommodating Christian elements to that model, this approach seeks to derive new models of psychotherapy from Christianity's root or core essence. This can also be called "maximal integration" or "Christian psychology" (Johnson, 2011).

If valid, this strategy could benefit future research in another way. We mentioned in the previous chapter that the power of a study can be improved by intensifying or increasing the potency of the treatment. Presumably, the efficacy and effectiveness of Christian psychotherapy would be enhanced the more saturated the treatment is with psychotherapy-relevant Christian content and practice. What are some of the psychotherapy-relevant themes and resources of Christianity that most well-informed Christians would agree on? We do not have the space to discuss them in detail, but the following is a plausible summary. (For further exploration, see Charry, 1997; Oden, 1987–1992; Webster, Tanner & Torrance, 2007.)

1. God's centrality in human life. Christianity and Christian psychotherapy and counseling differ most considerably from the worldview of modernism (and modernist psychotherapy and counseling) by the assumption that the Creator God is supposed to be the object of worship, ultimate authority and supreme love of human persons (Mt 22:37). This entails the belief that human beings are fundamentally relational beings and cannot be understood properly apart from their relation with God and by derivation their relationship with one another. Modern psychology by contrast has tended to view humans as though they can be grasped properly as individuals and treats them as though they are their own ethical and spiritual center (Cushman, 1995; Vitz, 1994; consider, for example, the influence of Rogers, 1961).

Admittedly, not all secular psychological approaches would agree with this rendering. Indeed, many modern psychologists advocate a relational approach to human beings, including many social psychologists, community psychologists, and relationally oriented psychologists and psychotherapists. Others (e.g., modern psychologists of religion and spirituality) would argue that psychology can study the human experience of God objectively without taking a stance regarding whether God exists. We also recognize that the assumption of Christian beliefs such as the existence of a Creator God and the relational nature of humans cannot be proven to be true to those who do not share those beliefs. But assuming these beliefs does allow Christian psychologists and psychotherapists to construct a biblically consistent narrative and operate within that framework.

2. A three-personed God. Christianity is distinguished from other forms of theism by its belief that the Creator God is triune: one being in three persons—Father, Son and Holy Spirit (Mt 28:19). Could this doctrine have clinical implications? A handful of studies have examined the therapeutic benefits of Christian meditation in general (see chapter 4), but there has been no documentation of what constitutes or how to cultivate a *personal relationship* with God—or what its therapeutic impact is—much less on the psychological benefits of a deep and intimate relationship with the three-personed God.

3. Human creation and human fallenness. Historic Christianity assumes that although humans were created good by God, they are now alienated from their Creator and therefore under his judgment and unable to do what is ultimately good for them (Rom 3:10-23). Within some theological systems (notably Reformed Protestant Christianity), this universal form of psychopathology is believed to be the ultimate source of the personal, social and societal evils that humans experience. Some assert that the Fall has led to specific kinds of psychopathology, such as depression. While many moderns might consider the concept of sin to be an impediment to psychotherapy, it can be argued conversely that it can encourage Christians to be honest about and take responsibility for their hurtful actions, which can lead, in turn, to a transparency and humility valuable in psychotherapy. Watson et al. (2007), for example, have developed sin-belief scales and have found that positive mental health outcomes are related to the recognition of one's sinfulness. However, the therapeutic value of Christian teaching on universal human sinfulness, as well as healthy Christian responses to sin such as contrition, repentance and mortification, has not yet been much investigated.

4. The role of the moral law in human life. Christianity also places a far higher value on ethical norms and discourse in human life than has been typical in modern psychology and modernist psychotherapy and counseling. Traditionally, modern psychology has treated morality as a function of socialization, whereas Christianity views it as an imperfect reflection of God's character and law "written on their hearts" (Rom 2:12-15), and therefore as both transcendent and integral to human life. This more intense ethical tone provides Christians with guidance for living, but this intensity also undoubtedly adds to the distress of Christians to the extent that they are aware of falling short of that ideal. The point here is that ethical norms and discourse will likely play a greater role in Christian psychotherapy and counseling than they typically have done in modernist psychotherapy and counseling (perhaps with the exception of models such as reality therapy [Glasser, 1965] and existential therapy). Some preliminary Christian research has been done on legalism (Bassett et al., 2012).

   5. Jesus Christ and redemption: God's psychotherapeutic intervention. Since its founding Christianity has understood Jesus Christ to be God's primary means of healing (Gk *therapeuo*) the human soul (Gk *psyche*). Christians believe that Jesus is both the ideal human and the Son of God and that through his life, death and resurrection, God established a radical positive change in humanity's relationship with God. Those who believe and surrender their lives to Christ gain a new status and identity before God. Christians believe that through union with Christ they receive from God many salutary benefits that can contribute to a divinely empowered form of personal and relational healing and growth to the extent that they are deeply appropriated by faith. Of special importance is a believer's personal relationship with Christ, the Father and the Holy Spirit. The practice of Christian psychotherapy and counseling is most distinguished from modern practice and other kinds of religious psychotherapy by its reliance on Christ-centered resources.

   The trajectory of this redemptive therapeutic orientation fundamentally turns the attention of believers from themselves to Christ, granting reconciliation with the Creator God by the Creator God (Col 1:20), forgiveness for sin and ultimate resolution of its accompanying shame and guilt (1 Jn 1:9), adoption into God's family (Gal 4:5-6), the indwelling of the Holy Spirit (Rom 8:9), and the creation of a new self (Eph 4:22-24). It thereby creates conditions in which counselees can explore and modify their internal dynamics without the threat of ultimate condemnation and its shame and guilt. Shame in particular has been found to be correlated with many forms of psychopathology (Tangney & Dearing, 2002), so the resolution of shame in the work of Christ would seem to be of momentous import for Christian psychotherapy and counseling. "Some type of objective transcendent perspective or vantage point from which to evaluate [the healing] process will always be necessary. Jesus the Christ, the model of fulfilled humanity, and the 'One for others' is such a vantage point for the Christian" (Propst, 1988, p. 192).

The therapeutic maturity goal of Christianity could simply be called conformity to Christ and described as living in worship and love of God, loving others, living in radical dependence on and gratitude to God for his blessings of creation and redemption, maintaining humble and joyful self-awareness, and acting as virtuous agents in the world.

6. The church. God has instituted the church to be the social location where transformation in Christ is especially realized in relationship with other humans. Persons gifted in facilitating these changes will therefore be especially needed (e.g., Christian ministers, psychotherapists and counselors). In addition, potent Christian psychotherapy and counseling may need to include involvement with the local church.

7. The problem of suffering. Christianity, along with a growing number of modern therapy approaches (e.g., mindfulness), seeks to help people face and come to terms with suffering, particularly when it is in the past or unavoidable in the present. Suffering in childhood and adulthood is a contributing factor to much psychological distress, and Christianity has much to say about suffering. Research on religious coping strategies has found that believers in God are benefitted psychologically by surrendering their problems to God and working with God collaboratively to resolve problems (Pargament, 1997). Specifically, Christian psychotherapy can promote the revaluation of the significance of suffering in light of God's loving, providential purposes as described in New Testament and Christian teaching.

Three considerations might provide additional resources for a specifically *Christian* coping style. First, the recognition that God has personally experienced suffering in Jesus Christ, especially on the cross, presumably creates a special sense of connection with God. Second, this connection may be strengthened by the realization that the personal suffering of Christians shares mystically in Christ's suffering (Rom 8:17; Col 1:24; Phil 3:10), enabling Christians to associate their own suffering with their God and his infinite capacities. Finally, Christians can appropriate divine significance for their suffering as they identify with Christ's resurrection by which he overcame suffering and death.

8. The Future. Christians believe that Jesus Christ is now alive in heaven, that this world will someday come to judgment, and that because they are in Christ they will receive an undeserved and unimaginable blessedness for eternity. This highly positive view of their future likely has beneficial psychological outcomes that enable Christians to cope with past and present suffering. This is significantly more optimistic than the tragic future dictated by naturalism.

What is needed for development of Christian-derived models of psychotherapy? The development of models of psychotherapy derived from biblical and Christian therapeutic sensibilities will necessitate the inclusion of Christian theologians and philosophers in the early formulation stage of the research. Moreover, saturation with the Christian tradition is an ideal, so in principle the potency of a given model can always be increased. Nevertheless, resources such as those outlined above seem to make it possible to work toward the construction of highly Christian-saturated models of psychotherapy. Such models will require researchers and counselors involved in the research to become well informed about Christian therapeutic teachings, and it will probably be best if they have personally experienced their therapeutic benefits (Coe & Hall, 2010). Indeed, it seems likely that the development of highly potent Christian models will require the active involvement of Christian theologians, philosophers and spiritual directors on the research teams.

In light of the research on common factors in psychotherapy, Christian-derived psychotherapy and counseling models would, of course, be expected to share many features of modernist psychotherapy and counseling. In addition, Christian-derived psychotherapy and counseling would likely include both psychoeducational and cognitive strategies that communicate the therapeutically relevant truths of Christianity, as well as psychodynamic and affective/experiential strategies (such as the devotional meditation discussed in chapter 4) that promote what Kierkegaard (1990) called "inward deepening" of the faith (p. 24) and lead to more substantial psychological and relational improvement. Examples of distinctly Christ-centered psychotherapy strategies can be found in the lay counseling and spiritual direction material mentioned in chapter 14, as well as in Johnson (2007), Propst (1988), Tan (2011), and elsewhere. However, much work needs to be done to develop comprehensive Christian-derived psychotherapy and counseling resources, including theoretical expositions, treatment manuals and training programs.

As Stegman, Kelly and Harwood (chapter 2) noted, religious counseling will be of most interest to those who expect religious and spiritual issues to be central to psychotherapy with explicit spiritual interventions (p. 30). When doing Christian-derived psychotherapy and counseling research, therefore, counselee religious and worldview beliefs and commitments will undoubtedly have to be taken into account (Pargament & Krumrei, 2009).

ASSESSING THE STATE OF CONTEMPORARY CHRISTIAN PSYCHOTHERAPY AND COUNSELING

As is widely acknowledged, there is a good deal of confusion and little agreement in the field today regarding what exactly constitutes Christian psychotherapy and counseling. One way to address this issue would be to conduct a large-scale study of a wide variety of therapists who publicly identify themselves as Christian working with a variety of clinical conditions around the United States (and eventually in other cultures). For a start, see Wade, Worthington and Vogel (2007), who surveyed 51 Christian psychotherapists and 220 of their clients to seek to determine what was actually happening in Christian psychotherapy. Audio and video digital recordings of multiple sessions with clients at different stages of psychotherapy could be analyzed to document exactly what is occurring under the banner of Christian psychotherapy and counseling. Codes could be developed that would assess such variables as the therapist's skill level, clinical sophistication, quality of relationship, and distinctive Christian content and practice manifested in session and assigned in homework.

Some valuable outcomes of such a large-scale exploration of Christian psychotherapy and counseling could be: (1) development of objective criteria to establish what counts as Christian psychotherapy and counseling; (2) formation of standards for evaluating claims of Christian psychotherapy and counseling; (3) determination of high-potency Christian psychotherapy and counseling; and (4) development of meaningful codes of conduct that warrant the label of Christian psychotherapy and counseling; (5) all of which would lead to better training of Christian psychotherapists and counselors. As we suggested in chapter 15, with any experimental intervention, the potency of the intervention increases its measurable impact, so criteria regarding Christian treatment potency would be helpful to enable Christian therapists to attain the highest quality of Christian psychotherapy and counseling. Such criteria would also aid consumers and insurance companies in their ability to make informed decisions regarding the selection of Christian therapists.

Christian psychotherapy and counseling and the therapeutic use of the Bible. It is widely recognized in the field that Scripture is important to most forms of religious or spiritually oriented psychotherapy, and reading and meditating on the Christian Scriptures has been one of the most important means of promoting well-being among Christians over the centuries. However, little research has been done on the different ways that Scripture can be used therapeutically and the effects of each type of use. Among the most common is the reading of a passage that relates to the topic at hand in session. Researchers also have not studied the assignment of daily Scripture reading or meditation as homework between sessions. Other homework assignments include memorization and writing down verses to carry around (either to combat temptation or to remind oneself of God's presence or care).

One of the greatest challenges with the use of Scripture in psychotherapy is the tendency many contemporary Christians have to read Scripture intellectually and factually—from the standpoint of a student—rather than, for example, as a lover receiving a love letter from one's beloved (see Kierkegaard, 1990). Christians historically have valued objective knowledge of God, but not in a way that is divorced from subjective appropriation. One might describe the Christian goal here as the internalization of the objective realities that Scripture records (Johnson, 2007). This aim is especially important in a therapeutic reading of Scripture. Future research on

Christian counseling and psychotherapy could examine and contrast methods of Scripture appropriation that vary according to their "depth of processing"—for example, Bible study, spiritual reading *(lectio divina)*, meditation, contemplation, journaling, relating a passage to real-life situations, the use of the imagination (e.g., envisioning oneself in a biblical story), lamenting (as in the Psalms), and the implementation of scriptural virtues through imaginative rehearsal, role-playing and in-vivo practice (see Garzon, chapter 4).

Christian psychotherapy and counseling based on different Christian traditions. While we have used the term tradition to refer to Christianity, the fact is that many orthodox versions of Christianity have developed over the centuries, and research could be done on their respective therapeutic benefits. So far, distinctive models of psychotherapy have been discussed by Catholic (Dilsaver, 2009; Tyrrell, 1975) and Eastern Orthodox (Chrysostomos, 2007; Muse, 2004) Christians. Wesleyan therapists have explored the relevance of their theology to Christian psychotherapy and counseling (see Strawn, 2004). Healing prayer has tended to be especially practiced by Pentecostals and charismatics; however, a formal Pentecostal/charismatic model of psychotherapy has not been developed yet. Johnson's (2007) framework for psychotherapy could be considered broadly Reformed in orientation, but we are not aware of any models of psychotherapy derived explicitly from the Lutheran or Anglican traditions. To our knowledge, no empirical investigations of differential approaches to psychotherapy based on respective Christian traditions have yet been conducted.

The Catholic tradition has distinguished among three kinds of prayer by their depth of processing: mental (prayer to God with just the mind), affective (prayer that engages one's emotions) and contemplative (prayer that is singularly focused on God) (Tanquerey, 1930). Research on the respective therapeutic benefits of each type would likely be valuable for Christian psychotherapy and counseling. The Catholic and Orthodox traditions have also identified three major stages of spiritual development: the *purgative* (characterized by a gradual overcoming of sinful and other hindrances to one's relationship with God), *illuminative* (typified by a growing awareness and experience of God) and *unitive* (focused on the experience of union with God, usually attained only by the most spiritually advanced) (Mc-

Gonigle, 1993). Groeschel (1993) has argued that this model has significant clinical implications. Perhaps Christian psychotherapy and counseling can foster movement from the purgative to the illuminative stages. If so, it would be beneficial to document this.

Christian psychotherapy and counseling as a "trialogue" with the Trinity. In chapter 7, research on Christian-accommodative psychodynamic treatments were discussed, and one of the benefits noted was a change in participants' god image ("i.e., the mental/neural representations that underlie a person's embodied, emotional relationship with God") (see Edwards & Davis, chapter 7, p. 127). As noted above, research could also be done on the therapeutic impact of one's personal relationship with the triune God himself. In such a scheme God would constitute a third active partner in the therapeutic relationship, making Christian psychotherapy and counseling more of a therapeutic *trialogue* than a dialogue. This, of course, assumes that the triune God is a real being and not *merely* a god image. Valuable theory and research has been done on the profound relation between one's relationship with God (and one's god image) and one's relationship with others, especially in one's family of origin (Hall et al., 2009; Moriarity & Hoffman, 2007). Presumably Christian relational psychotherapy could be enhanced by appropriate reference to the persons of the triune God (Father, Son and Holy Spirit) and assigning counselee homework utilizing the spiritual disciplines (specifically prayer and meditation) aimed at the promotion of positive experiences with God. Learning how to receive the love of one's perfect, heavenly Father, to pray dialogically with Jesus mindful of all that he has done on one's behalf, and to relish and depend on the presence of the indwelling Spirit would all seem to offer significant transformational relational experiences and promote changes in one's god image. These strategies also might contribute to top-down changes in one's experience of oneself and other humans, complementing the human-relational changes that occur in session with the psychotherapist. Research has documented that changes can occur in one's attachment status through secular relational psychotherapy, which is called *earned secure attachment* (Hesse, 2008). Perhaps this too could be facilitated by cultivating one's attachment with the triune God (Granqvist & Kirkpatrick, 2008).

This leads to the controversial topic of prayer within psychotherapy. Few

Christians would argue against prayer outside sessions. Some have suggested, however, that within-session prayer should be used cautiously in psychotherapy and professional counseling because of various problems associated with its misuse or because of client-presenting issues (McMinn, 1995). On the other hand, as long as the psychotherapist handles it carefully, within-session prayer could be considered a marker of models of psychotherapy in which God is understood by the counselor and counselee to be an actual and central participant in the healing process.

Difficulties concerning one's relationship with God. At the same time, investigation of Christian psychotherapy and counseling is needed in light of the many kinds of problems that attend one's relationship with God, including legalism, spiritual abuse and the distorted god images of counselees (Moriarity & Hoffman, 2007). With regard to the last of these, growing up with parents who resembled God poorly and going to churches which portrayed God inaccurately usually results in some distortions to one's felt experience of God (one's god image), regardless of one's theology. As suggested by Edwards and Davis (chapter 7), this can be an important therapeutic issue, especially for models of psychotherapy and counseling in which God is understood to be an active participant. Helping counselees to distinguish their god image from scriptural teaching about God (god concept) can create an openness to engage in the process of undermining its distortions and replace it by receiving more accurate portrayals in meditative prayer with Scripture (as well as through the therapeutic relationship). Also deserving of investigation is the impact of various spiritual struggles, such as anger at God, personal sin, attacks from the spiritual realm and the challenges of one's religious community (Exline & Rose, 2005).

Neuropsychology and Christian psychotherapy and counseling. It is widely acknowledged today that successful psychotherapy and counseling promotes changes in the brain (Cozolino, 2010). Consequently, research on Christian psychotherapy and counseling will eventually need to employ brain scanning technology and physiological measures of symptoms associated with psychopathology. Of special importance in this area is research on the neurological effects of distinctly Christian meditation (e.g., focus on the use of discourse). Hundreds of studies have been done on the psychological benefits of meditation. However, the vast majority of these studies have only examined the effects of either secular meditation (e.g., relaxation therapy) or Eastern forms of meditation (associated with the Buddhist and Hindu religious traditions). Christian meditation is distinguished from those forms by prayer to the triune God, and for most Christians, the use of Scripture and Christian content (including concepts and symbols). Far more documentation of the benefits of these ancient Christian practices is desirable.

Conclusion

There is enough work to keep Christian psychotherapy and counseling practitioners, theorists and researchers busy for decades. The standards for the practice of psychotherapy and counseling today and increasing pressures from insurance companies and state and federal governments are demanding empirical documentation. Multiple studies and research programs from a wide variety of Christian and therapeutic standpoints are needed if the Christian community as a whole is to develop an array of efficacious and effective models of professional care in accordance with its own worldview and self-understanding that will also be respected within contemporary psychology.

In this book, we have tried to provide a variety of evidence-based Christian practices that you, as undergraduate or graduate student, professor, practitioner on the front lines, pastoral counselor, or researcher can use to improve your helping of people who have psychological problems. Inevitably, as we argued from chapter 1, practice will need to be affected by research. We hope you have found the book informative and enriching in a practical way. If you are a researcher, we hope you will pursue collecting new evidence about existing and new modes of Christian psychotherapy and counseling. If you are a practitioner, we hope you will look for opportunities to collaborate with researchers and that you will continue to grow in your own appropriation of the tremendous therapeutic resources available in the Christian faith.

References

Bassett, R. L., Bonnett, M., Cobstill, S., Gardner, E., Harrman, G., Tiddick, D., & Zherka, N. (March 2012). Assessing legalism and grace: Being a law man or God's man (Galatians 2:19). Poster session presented at the meeting of the

Christian Association for Psychological Studies, Washington, DC.

Charry, E. T. (1997). *By the renewing of your minds: The pastoral function of Christian doctrine*. New York: Oxford University Press.

Chrysostomos, Archbishop. (2007). *A guide to orthodox psychotherapy: The science, theology, and spiritual practice behind it and its clinical application*. Lanham, MD: University Press of America.

Coe, J. H., & Hall, T. W. (2010). *Psychology in the Spirit: Contours of a transformational psychology*. Downers Grove, IL: InterVarsity Press.

Cozolino, L. J. (2010). *The neuroscience of psychotherapy: Building and rebuilding the human brain* (2nd ed.). New York: W. W. Norton.

Cushman, P. (1995). *Constructing the self, constructing America: A cultural history of psychotherapy*. Reading, MA: Addison-Wesley.

David, D., & Montgomery, G. H. (2011). The scientific status of psychotherapies: A new evaluative framework for evidence-based psychosocial interventions. *Clinical Psychology: Science and Practice, 18*(2), 89-104.

De Caussade, J.-P. (1986). *The joy of full surrender*. Brewster, MA: Paraclete Press. (Original work published 1861).

Dilsaver, G. C. (2009). *Imago Dei psychotherapy: A Catholic conceptualization*. Ave Maria, FL: Ave Maria Press.

Elliott, M. (2008). *Feel: The power of listening to your heart*. Carol Stream, IL: Tyndale House.

Exline, J. J., & Rose, E. (2005). Religious and spiritual struggles. In R. F. Paloutzian and C. L. Park (Eds.), *Handbook of the psychology of religion* (pp. 315-30). New York: Guilford Press.

Fonagy, P., Gergely, G., Jurist, E., & Target, M. (2002). *Affect regulation, mentalization, and the development of the self*. New York: Other Press.

Foucault, M. (1988). Technologies of the self. In L. H. Martin, H. Gutman & P. H. Hutton (Eds.), *Technologies of the self: A seminar with Michel Foucault* (pp. 16-49). Amherst, MA: University of Massachusetts Press.

Glasser, W. (1965). *Reality therapy*. New York: Harper & Row.

Goetz, S., & Taliaferro, C. (2008). *Naturalism*. Grand Rapids: Eerdmans.

Granqvist, P., & Kirkpatrick, L. A. (2008). Attachment and religious representations and behavior. In J. Cassidy & P. R. Shaver (Eds.), *Handbook of attachment* (2nd ed., pp. 906-933). New York: Guilford.

Groeschel, B. (1993). *Spiritual passages: The psychology of spiritual development*. New York: Crossroad.

Hall, T. W., Fujikawa, A., Halcrow, S. R., Hill, P. C., & Delaney, H. (2009). Attachment to God and implicit spirituality: Clarifying correspondence and compensation models. *Journal of Psychology and Theology, 37,* 227-42.

Hesse, E. (2008). The adult attachment interview: Protocol, method of analysis, and empirical studies. In J. Casidy & P. R. Shaver (Eds.), *Handbook of attachment: Theory, research, and clinical applications* (2nd ed., pp. 552-98). New York: Guilford Press.

Johnson, E. L. (2007). *Foundations for soul care: A Christian psychology proposal.* Downers Grove, IL: InterVarsity Press.

Johnson, E. L. (2011). Three faces of integration. *Journal of Psychology and Christianity, 30*(4), 339-55.

Johnson, E. L. (2012). Let's talk: Embeddedness, majority-minority relations, principled pluralism, and the importance of dialogue. *Journal of Psychology and Theology, 40*(1), 26-31.

Johnson, E. L., & Sandage, S. J. (1999). A postmodern reconstruction of psychotherapy: Orienteering, religion, and the healing of the soul. *Psychotherapy, 36,* 1-13.

Johnson, E. L., & Watson, P. J. (in press). Worldview communities and the science of psychology. *Research in the Social Scientific Study of Religion.*

Jones, S. L., & Butman, R. E. (2011). *Modern psychotherapies: A comprehensive Christian appraisal.* Downers Grove, IL: InterVarsity Press.

Kierkegaard, S. (1990). *For self-examination/Judge for yourself!* (H. V. Hong & E. H. Hong, Trans.). Princeton, NJ: Princeton University Press.

Lambert, M. J. (Ed.). (2003). *Bergin and Garfield's handbook on psychotherapy and behavior change* (5th ed.). New York: Wiley & Sons.

Lazarus, A. A. (1989). *The practice of multimodal therapy.* Baltimore, MD: The Johns Hopkins University Press.

MacIntyre, A. (1990). *Three rival versions of moral inquiry: Encyclopedia, genealogy, and tradition.* South Bend, IN: University of Notre Dame Press.

McCullough, M. E. (1999). Research on religion-accommodative counseling: Review and meta-analysis. *Journal of Counseling Psychology, 46*(1), 92-98.

McGonigle, T. D. (1993). Three ways. In M. Downey (Ed.), *The new dictionary of Catholic spirituality* (pp. 963-65). Collegeville, MN: Liturgical Press.

McMinn, M. R. (1995). *Psychology, theology, and spirituality in Christian counseling.* Wheaton, IL: Tyndale House.

Miller, W. R. (Ed.). (1999). *Integrating spirituality into treatment: Resources for practitioners.* Washington, DC: American Psychological Association.

Moriarity, G. L., & Hoffman, L. (2007). *God image handbook for spiritual counseling and psychotherapy: Research, theory, and practice.* Binghamton, NY: Haworth.

Muse, S. (Ed.). (2004). *Raising Lazarus: Integral healing in Orthodox Christianity.* Brookline, MA: Holy Cross Orthodox Press.

Noll, M. A. (1995). *The scandal of the evangelical mind.* Grand Rapids: Eerdmans.

Oden, T. C. (1987–1992). *Systematic theology.* New York: HarperCollins.

Pargament, K. I. (1997). *The psychology of religion and coping: Theory, research, practice.* New York: Guilford Press.

Pargament, K. I., & Krumrei, E. J. (2009). Clinical assessment of clients' spirituality. In J. D. Aten & M. M. Leach, *Spirituality and the therapeutic process: A comprehensive resource from intake to termination* (pp. 93-120). Washington, DC: American Psychological Association.

Plante, T. G. (2009). *Spiritual practices in psychotherapy: Thirteen tools for enhancing psychological health.* Washington, DC: American Psychological Association.

Plantinga, A. (2011). *Where the conflict really lies: Science, religion, & naturalism.* New York: Oxford University Press.

Propst, L. R. (1988). *Psychotherapy in a religious framework: Spirituality in the emotional healing process.* New York: Human Sciences Press.

Richards, P. S., & Bergin, A. E. (Eds.). (2000). *Handbook of psychotherapy and religious diversity.* Washington, DC: American Psychological Association.

Richards, P. S., & Bergin, A. E. (2005). *A spiritual strategy for counseling and psychotherapy* (2nd ed.).Washington, DC: American Psychological Association.

Rizzuto, A. M. (1979). *The birth of the living God.* Chicago: University of Chicago Press.

Rogers, C. (1961). *On becoming a person.* Boston: Houghton Mifflin.

Rokeach, M. (1964). *The three Christs of Ypsilanti.* New York: Alfred A. Knopf.

Slife, B. D., & Reber, J. S. (2009). Is there a pervasive bias against theism in psychology? *Journal of Theoretical and Philosophical Psychology, 29*(2), 63-79.

Slife, B. D., Reber, J. S., & Richardson, F. C. (Eds.). (2005). *Critical thinking about psychology: Hidden assumptions and plausible alternatives.* Washington, DC: American Psychological Association.

Smith, C. (2003). Introduction: Rethinking the secularization of American public life. In C. Smith (Ed.), *The secular revolution: Power, interests, and conflict in the secularization of American public life* (pp. 1-96). Berkeley: University of California Press.

Spero, M. H. (1992). *Religious objects as psychological structures: A critical integration of obuect relations theory, psychotherapy, and Judaism.* Chicago: University of Chicago Press.

Sperry, L., & Shafranske, E. P. (Eds.). (2005). *Spiritually oriented psychotherapy.*

Washington, DC: American Psychological Association.

Strawn, B. D. (Ed.). (2004). Special issue: Psychology and Wesleyan theology. *Journal of Psychology & Christianity, 23.*

Tan, S.-Y. (2011). *Counseling and psychotherapy: A Christian perspective.* Grand Rapids, MI: Baker Academic.

Tangney, J. P., & Dearing, R. L. (2002). *Shame and guilt.* New York: Guilford Press.

Tanquerey, A. (1930). *The spiritual life: A treatise on ascetical and mystical theology.* Tournai, Belgium: Society of St. John the Evangelist, Desclee & Co.

Taylor, C. (1989). *The sources of the self: The making of the modern identity.* Cambridge, MA: Harvard University Press.

Triandis, H. C. (2007). Culture and psychology: A history of the study of their relationship. In S. Kitayama & D. Cohen (Eds.), *Handbook of cultural psychology* (pp. 59-76). New York: Guilford Press.

Tyrrell, B. (1975). *Christotherapy.* New York: Seabury Press.

Vitz, P. C. (1994). *Psychology as religion: The cult of self-worship* (2nd ed.). Grand Rapids, MI: Eerdmans.

Von Hildebrand, D. (2001). *Transformation in Christ: On the Christian attitude.* San Francisco: Ignatius.

Wade, N. G., Worthington, E. L., Jr., & Vogel, D. L. (2007). Effectiveness of religiously tailored interventions in Christian therapy. *Psychotherapy Research, 17,* 91-105.

Watson, P. J. (2011). Whose psychology? Which rationality? Christian psychology within an ideological surround after postmodernism. *Journal of Psychology & Christianity, 30*(4), 307-16.

Watson, P. J., Hood, R. W., Jr., & Morris, R. J. (1988). Existential confrontation and religiosity. *Counseling and Values, 33,* 47-54.

Watson, P. J., Milliron, J. T., Morris, R. J., & Hood, R. W., Jr. (1995). Religion and the self as text: Toward a Christian translation of self-actualization. *Journal of Psychology and Theology, 23,* 180-89.

Watson, P. J., Morris, R. J., & Hood, R. W., Jr. (1987). Antireligious humanistic values, guilt, and self esteem. *Journal for the Scientific Study of Religion, 26,* 535-46.

Watson, P. J., Morris, R. J., Loy, T., Hamrick, M. B., & Grizzle, S. (2007). Beliefs about sin: Adaptive implications in relationships with religious orientation, self-esteem, and measures of the narcissistic, depressed and anxious self. *Edification 1*(1), 57-65.

Webster, J., Tanner, K., & Torrance, I. (Eds.). (2007). *The Oxford handbook of systematic theology.* Oxford: Oxford University Press.

List of Contributors

Jamie D. Aten (PhD in Counseling Psychology, Indiana State University) is founder and codirector of the Humanitarian Disaster Institute and Dr. Arthur P. Rech and Mrs. Jean May Rech Associate Professor of Psychology at Wheaton College (Wheaton, Illinois). Dr. Aten's interests include the psychology of religion and disasters, disaster spiritual and emotional care, and faith-based relief and development.

C. Gary Barnes, ThM, PhD, is a professor at Dallas Theological Seminary. He is a licensed clinical psychologist in Texas, a certified sex therapist and an ordained minister. He specializes in sexuality, marriage and family, with research, training and therapy.

Don E. Davis, PhD, is assistant professor of counseling and psychological services at Georgia State University. His major research interests are humility, forgiveness, positive psychology, and religion and spirituality.

Edward B. Davis, PsyD, is assistant professor of psychology at Wheaton College. His major research interests are god representations, religion and spirituality, psychological assessment and interpersonal neurobiology.

Frederick A. DiBlasio, PhD, is professor of social work at the University of Maryland School of Social Work, and is a licensed clinical social worker in Maryland. His major research and practice areas are forgiveness, clinical intervention with devout Christian clients and clients with personality disorders, and he is the author of the decision-based forgiveness intervention model for individuals, couples and families.

Keith J. Edwards, PhD, is professor of psychology in the Rosemead School of Psychology at Biola University. He also is a licensed clinical psychologist in California. His major research interests are marital and individual therapy using emotionally focused, attachment-based, experiential approaches. He also conducts research on relationships integrating emotion theory, attachment theory and spirituality.

Dana Frederickson, MA, LMFT, LPC, is a licensed marriage and family therapist and licensed professional counselor working in private practice at Generations Counseling Services, LLC, in the greater Atlanta, Georgia, area. She specializes in Christian psychotherapy with children, families and adults.

Dr. Fernando Garzon is a professor at Liberty University in the Center for Counseling and Family Services, and a licensed clinical psychologist. Dr. Garzon's research interests focus on spiritual interventions in psychotherapy, lay Christian counseling approaches (such as Freedom in Christ and Theophostic Ministry), integration pedagogy and multicultural issues. His clinical experience encompasses outpatient practice, managed care, hospital, pastoral care and church settings.

T. Mark Harwood, PhD, is former director of clinical training and core faculty in Wheaton College's doctoral program in clinical psychology. He served five years as managing associate editor of the *Journal of Clinical Psychology* and serves on the board of that and several other scientific journals. Dr. Harwood is currently in private practice in St. Charles, Illinois, and has published widely on psychotherapy outcome research.

Joshua N. Hook, PhD, is assistant professor of psychology at the University of North Texas, and a licensed clinical psychologist in Texas. His research interests include humility, forgiveness, and religion and spirituality.

David J. Jennings II, PhD, is assistant professor of psychology at Regent University. His major areas of research fall within the field of positive psychology, including inspiration, forgiveness, and religion and spirituality.

Eric L. Johnson, PhD, is Lawrence and Charlotte Hoover Professor of Pastoral Care at The Southern Baptist Theological Seminary. He edited *Psychology and Christianity: Five Views* and wrote *Foundations for Soul Care: A Christian Psychology Proposal,* and he is the director of the Society for Christian Psychology.

Sarah L. Kelly, MA, is a doctoral student in the clinical psychology program at Wheaton College, Wheaton, Illinois. She will complete her predoctoral internship at the Denver Health Medical Center.

Julia Kidwell, PhD, is a licensed psychologist in clinical practice in Minneapolis, Minnesota. She is also an adjunct professor at the University of St. Thomas. Her research and clinical interests include forgiveness, trauma recovery, resiliency and the integration of spirituality and psychotherapy.

Vickey L. Maclin, PsyD, teaches at Regent University. Her major research interests are religion and spirituality, community psychology, multicultural psychology and marriage and family.

Drs. Les and Leslie Parrott are a husband-and-wife team who not only share the same name but also a passion for helping others build healthy relationships. The Parrotts are #1 *New York Times*–bestselling authors, and their books, including the Gold Medallion winner *Saving Your Marriage Before It Starts,* have sold over two million copies in more than two dozen languages. The Parrotts are founders of the Center for Relationship Development on the campus of Seattle Pacific University, where Les is a psychologist and Leslie is a marriage and family therapist. Their Marriage Mentoring Academy has trained and certified more than 250,000 couples (www.MarriageMentoring.com). Learn more at LesandLeslie.com.

Heather Lewis Quagliana, PhD, is executive director of the Play Therapy Center and assistant professor in the psychology department at Lee University. Her research interests focus on play therapy, childhood trauma, and spirituality and child psychotherapy.

Jennifer S. Ripley, PhD, is professor of psychology and director of clinical training at Regent University. She is a licensed clinical psychologist in Virginia. Her major areas of research and practice are in the hope-focused couple approach.

James N. Sells, PhD, is professor of counselor education and supervision at Regent University, and is licensed in Virginia as a clinical psychologist. He serves as department chair for the PhD program in counselor education and supervision at Regent, and as assistant dean for academics. His major interest areas are marital and family therapy, supervision/professional identity formation, international applications of counseling, and forgiveness and reconciliation.

Scott M. Stanley, PhD, is a research professor and codirector of the Center for Marital and Family Studies at the University of Denver. He has published widely with research interests including commitment, communication, conflict, confidence, risk factors for divorce, the prevention of marital distress, couple development and the Prevention and Relationship Enhancement Program (PREP).

R. Scott Stegman, MA, is a doctoral student at Wheaton College, Wheaton, Illinois. He is currently pursuing a PsyD in clinical psychology and an MA in systematic theology.

Siang-Yang Tan, PhD, is professor of psychology at Fuller Theological Seminary, and senior pastor of First Evangelical Church Glendale. He is a licensed psychologist and fellow of the American Psychological Association. He has published numerous books, including *Counseling and Psychotherapy: A Christian Perspective, Full Service, Coping with Depression* (with John Ortberg), *Rest, Disciplines of the Holy Spirit* (with Douglas Gregg), and *Lay Counseling.*

Nathaniel G. Wade, PhD, is associate professor of psychology at Iowa State University and a licensed psychologist. His major research interests are forgiveness, religion and spirituality, and stigma, all in the context of counseling and psychotherapy.

Donald F. Walker, PhD, is director of the Child Trauma Institute and assistant professor in the PsyD program at Regent University. His research interests focus on helping children to resolve spiritual issues related to childhood abuse, and spiritual interventions in child and adolescent psychotherapy.

Morgan Wilkinson, PhD, is assistant professor in the counseling department at Geneva College. Her research interests include research related to social justice issues such as abuse prevention and the problem of human trafficking, career counseling and work-life balance issues.

Everett L. Worthington Jr., PhD, is professor of psychology at Virginia Commonwealth University and a licensed clinical psychologist in Virginia. His major research interests are forgiveness and positive psychology, religion and spirituality, and the hope-focused couples approach. See www.EvWorthington-forgiveness.com.

Subject Index

CAPS
INTERNATIONAL

An Association for Christian Psychologists,
Therapists, Counselors and Academicians

CAPS is a vibrant Christian organization with a rich tradition. Founded in 1956 by a small group of Christian mental health professionals, chaplains and pastors, CAPS has grown to more than 2,100 members in the U.S., Canada and more than 25 other countries.

CAPS encourages in-depth consideration of therapeutic, research, theoretical and theological issues. The association is a forum for creative new ideas. In fact, their publications and conferences are the birthplace for many of the formative concepts in our field today.

CAPS members represent a variety of denominations, professional groups and theoretical orientations; yet all are united in their commitment to Christ and to professional excellence.

CAPS is a non-profit, member-supported organization. It is led by a fully functioning board of directors, and the membership has a voice in the direction of CAPS.

CAPS is more than a professional association. It is a fellowship, and in addition to national and international activities, the organization strongly encourages regional, local and area activities which provide networking and fellowship opportunities as well as professional enrichment.

To learn more about CAPS, visit www.caps.net.

The joint publishing venture between IVP Academic and CAPS aims to promote the understanding of the relationship between Christianity and the behavioral sciences at both the clinical/counseling and the theoretical/research levels. These books will be of particular value for students and practitioners, teachers and researchers.

For more information about CAPS Books, visit InterVarsity Press's website at www.ivpress.com/cgi-ivpress/book.pl/code=2801.